The Fall of Cromwell's Republic and the Return of the King

The Fall of Cromwell's Republic and the Return of the King

From Commonwealth to Stuart Monarchy, 1657–1670

Timothy Venning

First published in Great Britain in 2023 by
Pen & Sword History
An imprint of
Pen & Sword Books Ltd
Yorkshire – Philadelphia

Copyright © Timothy Venning 2023

ISBN 978 1 52678 939 6

The right of Timothy Venning to be identified as Author of this work has been asserted by him in accordance with the Copyright, Designs and Patents Act 1988.

A CIP catalogue record for this book is available from the British Library.

All rights reserved. No part of this book may be reproduced or transmitted in any form or by any means, electronic or mechanical including photocopying, recording or by any information storage and retrieval system, without permission from the Publisher in writing.

Typeset by Mac Style
Printed in the UK by CPI Group (UK) Ltd, Croydon, CR0 4YY.

Pen & Sword Books Limited incorporates the imprints of Atlas, Archaeology, Aviation, Discovery, Family History, Fiction, History, Maritime, Military, Military Classics, Politics, Select, Transport, True Crime, Air World, Frontline Publishing, Leo Cooper, Remember When, Seaforth Publishing, The Praetorian Press, Wharncliffe Local History, Wharncliffe Transport, Wharncliffe True Crime and White Owl.

For a complete list of Pen & Sword titles please contact

PEN & SWORD BOOKS LIMITED
47 Church Street, Barnsley, South Yorkshire, S70 2AS, England
E-mail: enquiries@pen-and-sword.co.uk
Website: www.pen-and-sword.co.uk

Or

PEN AND SWORD BOOKS
1950 Lawrence Rd, Havertown, PA 19083, USA
E-mail: Uspen-and-sword@casematepublishers.com
Website: www.penandswordbooks.com

Contents

List of Main Dramatis Personae — vi
Restoration: The Return of the King — xliii
Prologue — xlvii

Section One: The Finale and Fall of the Protectorate — 1

Chapter 1   A Monarchy Without a King. Stability Thwarted or Cromwell Loses his Nerve? The Offer of the Crown, 1657 — 3

Chapter 2   1658–9: The Collapse of Richard Cromwell's Protectorate. Inevitably Doomed – Or Is This Only Hindsight? — 42

Section Two: The Return of the King: October 1659 to the Early 1660s — 89

Chapter 3   From Military/ Parliamentary Rule to Stuart Monarchy: Events to the Recall of Charles II — 91

Chapter 4   The Restoration, 1660: a missed opportunity for moderation? If so, who was to blame? — 136

Chapter 5   The 'Cavalier Parliament': the Royalist and Anglican backlash gathers strength. Inevitable? — 179

Conclusion — 236
Notes — 239
Bibliography — 253
Index — 261

List of Main Dramatis Personae

Alured, Matthew (1615–94): hardline New Model Army republican commander, born near Hull in Yorkshire, who was serving as second in command in Colonel Gell's regiment in Scotland in 1650 when his senior was cashiered and he succeeded him. An able if obscure officer whose competence in Scots campaigns led to him becoming commander in the western region there, he was then appointed to an Irish command but was ruined by his political dabbling. Known for his integrity but stubbornness, he refused to accept the semi-monarchic Protectorate's right to control and dismiss Parliament as contravening the 'free Parliaments' promised to the army's democratically elected representatives in 1648. He was elected as an MP in 1654 and signed the 'Petition of Three Colonels' which denied Cromwell's right to veto MPs and measures, drawn up by the Leveller John Wildman. He was then kept out of the Commons, cashiered, and given a year in prison for this as alleged subversion, and continued to protest about the illegality of this; after Cromwell died he was allowed back with the restored Rump Parliament and given a regiment in 1659 but lacked importance; Monck purged him from the army in spring 1660. The end of army power in 1660 neutralised him. He was also uncle to the stepmother of the poet Andrew Marvell, through whom glimpses of his career emerge.

Anne 'of Austria' (in fact Spain) (1601–66). Queen-Mother of France; widow of King Louis XIII and regent for her son Louis XIV 1643 to 1652. Daughter of King Philip IV of Spain; married 1615. In her youth seen as an agent of hardline 'devot' Catholic and Habsburg influence at the French court, and as involved in factional intrigue there; most famous now as a character in Alexandre Dumas' *Three Musketeers* books, which uses the rumours of her affair with the English Duke of Buckingham in 1625; as regent, she had to negotiate the civil wars of the 'Fronde' in 1648–52, mainly with those great nobles who sought to oust her effective co-regent and rumoured lover or husband, the Italian cleric Cardinal Jules Mazarin/Giulio Mazarini.

Annesley, Arthur, earl of Anglesey (1614–86): moderate Irish Presbyterian gentry leader, and in 1659–60 a key figure in arranging the Restoration in Dublin. Sidelined there by the hardline Anglicans. Later a minister in London, as a key figure in keeping moderate Presbyterians aligned to an increasingly hostile Anglican regime, but failed to get his Presbyterian cleric allies to join and dilute the new official Church. This and his moral character and lack of social congeniality in a raucous court probably cost him serious influence with Charles II, and in the mid-late 1660s his role and standing diminished.

Baxter, Richard (1615–91): influential West Midlands Presbyterian leader, theologian and writer. Born in Shropshire, from a poor family; a clever and dedicated Christian thinker who was broadly Presbyterian (but not Calvinist) in his outlook and critical of but not irrevocably alienated from the bishop-led Anglican church. Missing out on the usual elite clerical education at Oxford, he became a local schoolmaster in Bridgnorth and in 1641 was elected by a parish in Kidderminster as its clergyman as the authoritarian Anglican church regime collapsed and served until expulsion by the royalists in 1661. A major source for the regional Presbyterian outlook on events and a learned and individualistic theologian, he was a man of moral integrity who viewed the extremes of the radical Independents and the extreme monarchist Anglicans with equal concern. Opposed to both sides in 1642 and deploring the war where he tried to avoid taking sides, he eventually accepted a New Model army chaplaincy (Whalley's regiment) in 1645–7. He preached to, but was critical of, Cromwell, and opposed military rule after 1649/53 but promoted the idea of a comprehensive and tolerant new Church order. He was a key figure in the failed attempt to get moderate Presbyterians into the Church in 1660–1 and was then pushed out into the political wilderness as a Dissenter and sporadically imprisoned by the local Anglican gentry.

Bennet, Henry, earl of Arlington (1618?–85): royalist adviser and diplomat in exile to 1660, and a former officer who proudly wore a plaster over his battle-damaged nose at Charles II's court. He had managed Charles' relations with vital allies like Spain in exile, and had no qualms about being practical in aligning with Catholic nations where necessary; his rivalry with the more cautious Hyde carried on after 1660 and he outmanoeuvured him. He became the senior minister running foreign policy (Secretary of State for the South 1663–74), and one of the so-called 'Cabal' running the country in 1667–72; he was seen as the leading figure in the anti-French, Protestant Triple Alliance set up in 1668 but accommodated himself to his master's wish to align with France and attack the Dutch in 1670–2. Regarded as a master of backstairs intrigue and versatile diplomacy, and pragmatic in putting Britain's interests first – and deserting allies where useful.

Berkenhead, Sir John (1614?–79): senior royalist journalist and 'spin-doctor', 1640s to 1660s. A Fellow of All Souls, Oxford in 1641–8, including during the royalist occupation of the city, he enthusiastically wrote for the pioneering royalist newsletter *Mercurius Aulicus* from 1643 and was its main satirist and slanderer of the Parliamentarians. Marginalised in the 1650s as a royalist but linked to their underground networks, he re-emerged as a journalist at the Restoration and was made the national licensor of publications, i.e. the man in charge of what was allowed to be printed and the regime's controller of the official narrative of events. He was also put in charge of their new official newsletter, *Mercurius Politicus*, with Henry Muddiman but appears to have given less time to personally writing government spin than in the 1640s, acting more behind the scenes as an organiser. He served in Parliament for Wilton from 1661 and was Master of Requests, a lucrative legal administrative office, in 1664–79.

Birch, Colonel John (1615–91); senior republican Parliamentarian officer and MP, 1650s, critic of Cromwell. Presbyterian beliefs; from Ardwick, Manchester (family owned manor) and officer at Bristol until its fall to Rupert in 1643, thence in London and in General Waller's Hampshire army. Badly wounded at siege of Arundel; entered Commons 1646 for Leominster, where he bought estates (some church land, confiscated 1660). He played a leading role in the restive Cromwellian Parliament of 1653–4 as head of the public accounts committee, investigating the regime's funds and using the 'power of the purse' to try to insist that the Protector and Council acted as agents not masters of parliament and followed its wishes. His group of opposition MPs, many regional Presbyterians from the 1640s parliamentarian gentry, were also critical of Cromwell's planned Church as too inclusive of radical sects. The clash led to Parliament's dismissal in 1655, and Birch was sidelined from office by Cromwell as a troublemaker and banned from taking his seat again; in 1661 he rejoined Parliament for Penryn, Cornwall, thence in 1679–81 and 1689–91 Whig MP for Weobley, Herefordshire, his main estate. Supported 'Exclusion', and ditto Glorious Revolution

Booth, Sir George, Lord Delamere (1622–84): heir to the Booth baronetcy of Dunham Massey, Cheshire, and leading Parliamentarian in that county in 1640s. Sympathetic to Presbyterianism and backed restricted monarchy as MP for Cheshire 1645–8, but purged by Colonel Pride in Dec 1648. Also MP for county in Nominated Parliament 1653 and in Cromwell's Parliaments. Presbyterian underground leader vs army rule in later 1650s, alarmed at sects; led unsuccessful 1659 Cheshire revolt in link-up with royalists but defeated and was captured fleeing. Re-emerged as moderate Presbyterian-allied county gentry leader in helping Restoration and in Convention Parliament and their delegation to offer Charles II the crown. Given £10,000 grant for 1659–60 services plus peerage, but alienated from Restoration regime in mid-late 1660s over religious intolerance.

Bordeaux, Antoine de Neufville, Sieur de: French ambassador to England, 1652–60. Senior adviser to Cardinal Mazarin, and skilfully helped persuade the suspicious Cromwell not to attack France as an ex-ally of Charles II but agree peace 1655 and alliance 1657. His diplomatic reports are major source for undercurrents in and gossip about English politics in 1650s.

Boyle, Roger, lord Broghill (1628) and earl of Orrery (1660), (1621–79): leading pro-Cromwell 'settler' gentry leader in Munster, Ireland, 1650s, later Royal adviser. Third son of the earl of Cork, from leading Munster Protestant settler dynasty, and brother of the scientist Robert Boyle; married into Howard family. Educated at Trinity College Dublin and Gray's Inn, London; travelled abroad in 1630s, then fought for the king against the Scots rebels and in the Irish Rebellion after 1641 under the marquis of Ormonde. Later joined up with the Parliamentarian regime in Dublin, probably over fears of Catholic influence on Irish royalists, and after regicide was caught by the Commonwealth heading for France to contact Charles II and was 'turned' by Cromwell in person. He then aided the Cromwellian conquest of Ireland, was instrumental in winning Munster, and assisted General Ireton; he was also close to Cromwell personally and urged him towards civilianizing his regime, e.g. as lord president of council in Scotland in 1656; also supposed to be involved in plan to reconcile Cromwell to a Stuart restoration. Crucial in winning Ireland for Charles II peacefully in 1660 and was made one of lords justices and Lord President of Munster, but was later sidelined, probably as not biddable enough by central authority.

Bridgeman, Sir Orlando (1606?–74): influential Royalist lawyer post-1660 and later Lord Keeper of the Great Seal, 1667–72. Acquired reputation as a hardline devotee of untrammelled royal power in the 1660–1 regicide trials as he denounced the idea that a king could be constrained by his subjects, and expatiated on the wickedness of killing the divinely-appointed sovereign. He came across as the ideologist of ultra Royalism, but more charitably was seeking to 'shut down the debate' on allowing resistance to the King to preserve order after the horrors of civil war .

Butler, James, Marquis of Ormonde (1610–88): senior Protestant Royalist aristocratic leader in Ireland, formerly Charles I's supreme commander there. Hereditary head of the wealthy landed Butler dynasty that had dominated Munster since the late twelfth-century and descendant of many generations of leading Anglo-Irish officials in the Dublin regime, his family's Protestantism and support for English colonial schemes pre-1642 aligned him to the 'new' English colonial magnates but he was able to work with the 'old' Catholic Anglo-Irish too. He was a staunch royalist and one of their major funders in the 1642–52 civil wars, serving as Charles I's military supremo there and as royalist Lord Lieutenant in 1643–51 (superseded in Dublin in 1646 by Parliamentary nominees). He then went into exile with Charles II but returned in 1660, and was LL again in 1662–9 and 1677–85; he was the Stuart regime's main supporter in Ireland but was pushed aside by James II in 1685 as not 'on message' about reincorporating Catholics into the elite.

Campbell, Archibald, marquis of Argyll (1607–1661): hardline Calvinist strongman of the 1637–51 Presbyterian regime in Scotland. Head of the Campbell clan of Argyll; a staunch Calvinist opponent of Charles I's episcopal Church reforms in Scotland and behind the scenes co-leader of the Covenanter revolt in 1637–40, then provided clan manpower to its armies; the chief organizer and enforcer of regime, and foe of the more moderate earl of Montrose who he had sidelined in 1641 for alleged plots. He dominated the 1640s Presbyterian regime but had his lands pillaged by Montrose's royalists, and Montrose famously defeated him in person at Inverlochy in 1645; after royalist defeat he was unable to prevent the moderate 'Engagers' invading England to try to save Charles I's throne in 1648, but took power back after their defeat. Masterminded Charles II's nominal leadership of the regime in 1650–1, had the defeated Montrose executed, and crowned Charles king at Scone; nicknamed 'King Campbell'. Sidelined by Cromwell and Monck in the 1650s; re-emerged in 1660 but lost out to royalists and was abandoned to execution by Charles II for his earlier killings.

Catherine of Braganza, Queen (1638–1705): Charles II's Portuguese Catholic wife. Daughter of King John IV, and lynch-pin of the Anglo-Portuguese treaty of 1662 that gave her, Tangier and Bombay, to Charles II. The subject of fears of Catholic influence in England, unable to give the king children, and required to accept the king's mistress Barbara Villiers as her lady-in-waiting, the devout and sheltered queen was humiliated repeatedly by her husband but put up with it with grace and dignity and he came to respect her, refusing to divorce her to acquire a legitimate child. After his death she lived at Somerset House, London until her return home to lead the regency for her nephew.

Charles I, King of England, Scotland and Ireland from March 1625 (1600–49): executed 30 January 1649 and built up as royalist 'martyr'. Controversy has always raged over his responsbility for the Civil War; was he a man of integrity and good intentions hit by bad luck and pushed around by forces beyond his control, or an arrogant, clumsy and unlucky schemer who did not understand how to rule his three disparate kingdoms skilfully? His shyness, lack of imagination, insistence on deference by his subjects, and untrustworthiness probably undermined his cause throughout, and after 1646 he showed a fatal unwillingness to compromise with those who had defeated him or ability to stop planning his revenge on them.

Charles II, King of England, Scotland and Ireland 25 May 1660–6 Febuary 1685 (1630–85); claimed to be *de iure* since father's execution. His bravery and versatility in his attempts to regain his father's crowns in 1649–51 are undoubted, but his ruthless willingness to come to terms with his father's worst foes and his abandonment of the late king's most brilliant general Montrose in 1650 have caused controversy ever since. He managed his time in exile with fortitude and skill and successfully steered his way through the chaos of the collapsing republic in 1659–60 back to the throne, but his attempts at political and religious reconciliation were thwarted – more by Parliament than at his own wishes. The easy-going and jovial libertine of legend, a skilful and often lazy politician, was hugely popular and stayed on the throne for nearly twenty-five years, so he succeeded in avoiding 'having to go on his travels again' – reckoned as his main aim. But the equally clever, charismatic and debauched grandson of France's 'evergreen gallant' King Henri IV drifted into an unpopular French alliance in the 1670s, probably in search of stability, and was seen as a conduit of Popish influence – arguably sparking off the Popish Plot crisis. After defeating this he stabilised the monarchy on an autocratic basis, but once he was dead his less skilful brother James II wrecked this.

Clifford, Thomas, lord Clifford of Chudleigh (1630?–1673); royalist adviser and Catholic, later treasurer of the royal household 1668–72 and Lord Treasurer in the 'Cabal' ministry in 1672–3. Gentry family from Ugbrooke, South Devon; related via mother to locally prominent Chudleighs and one of the younger Devon royalists backing Charles II. Educated at Exeter College Oxford; MP for Totnes 1660 ff. Seen by his foes as a hardline proponent of autocracy and Catholic influence but probably more pragmatic; also crucial in formulating 1660s foreign policy as ally of Bennet but more favourable to Catholic autocracies on Continent so feared by Protestant anti-French faction; supposedly major backer of abandoning the Dutch for a French alliance in 1660. Largely backstairs operator; a loyal servant of the king but politically not as influential as his more senior colleagues or as rumoured. He was also a depressive, and after his forced retirement in 1673 due to his inability as a Catholic to comply with the Test Act was presumed to have committed suicide.

Cooper, Sir Anthony Ashley, earl of Shaftesbury (1621–83): Dorset gentry, from Wimborne St Giles. Former royalist turned Parliamentarian (1644); played a minor role in Civil War and emerged as a principled pragmatist in the Commons and the republican councils of state in 1650–3. He rallied to the moderates favouring a stable civilian regime against the proponents of religious and military radicalism and so backed Cromwell's coup in April 1653 and the Protectorate in December. A Cromwellian councillor to 1654, thence joined the republican opposition after objecting to Cromwell reining in the Commons' power. He joined the moderate supporters of a restored Rump Parliament in 1659–60, opposing the Cromwellian generals, and accepted Restoration as the best guarantee of stability. A moderate royalist and minister 1660s, as chancellor of the exchequer 1667–70 then treasurer (acting) 1670–2 and Lord Chancellor 1672–3. One of the 'Cabal' but opposed to alliance with autocratic and Catholic France so he was 'left out of the loop' about the secret 1670 alliance with France; his discovery of this and his unease at Catholic influence on the king drove him to leave government. He ended up as Charles II's sternest critic and founder of the Whig party in the late 1670s, leading their bold attempt to coerce him into denying his Catholic brother James the succession in the 1679–81 'Exclusion Crisis'. By manipulating the 'Popish Plot' panic and winning the successive parliamentary elections he forced Charles to readmit him to the Council and adopt some of his policies, but was outmanoevured in the royalist reaction in 1681 and forced to flee the country to escape arrest. Alleged to be involved in later plots to kill or remove Charles, he died in exile in Holland. Denounced as the power-mad schemer 'Achitophel' (referencing King David's treacherous courtier in the Old Testament) by the playwright Dryden, he was hated and feared by royalist hardliners. Plausibly, his principles were fairly constant for forty years but politics changed around him.

Cromwell, Henry (1618–74): second surviving son of Oliver Cromwell, viceroy in Ireland 1657–9. More vigorous and politically capable than his retiring brother Richard but younger so was not considered as an heir; was disliked as having no army links or republican credibility and pushed aside by his radical officers in 1659. Lived in retirement after 1660 and was largely left alone by the royalists, as he had made no major enemies, had no riches to be pillaged, and was careful to keep out of politics.

Cromwell, Oliver (1599–1658): originally an obscure backbench MP from the Huntingdonshire gentry as of 1642, distantly related to Henry VII's minister Thomas Cromwell. His family had distinguished connections but he was the son of a younger son with little prospects or money and was a farmer in the 1630s, going through some sort of religious crisis and turning against the Anglican church; he was supposed to have considered emigrating to Massachusetts in search of a more godly government. Of little importance as a principled but junior MP in the Long Parliament except as cousin and ally to the opposition's most effective legal expert Oliver St John, he emerged as a vigorous raiser and leader of his own regiment for Parliament in 1642 and then an active and skilled if self-taught cavalry officer. He served with distinction and increasing prominence in the cavalry of the 'Eastern Association' in 1643–4 and was one of the few commanders to keep his nerve when faced by, and then outmanoeuvre and out-fight, the Royalist cavalry. Commander of their cavalry at Marston Moor in 1644, he made a name among the principled 'godly' Parliamentarian officers from the emerging plethora of radical independent sects by insisting that the post-war settlement must grant all such sects religious toleration, not just replace an officious state Anglican church with a Presbyterian one, and clashed with senior officers – nobles – who he regarded as not keen enough on fighting to win. The champion of meritocracy, military effectiveness, and determination to secure a just settlement for the troops and the 'godly' rather than peace at any price, he was the most effective commander of and deputy to Fairfax in the New Model Army in 1645–50. He only emerged as a leading commander in his own right in 1645–6, but then eclipsed Fairfax and in 1647–8 led the military and (as an MP) parliamentary opposition to a pro-Presbyterian settlement. He helped to mastermind the defeat of the moderate Presbyterians who sought to neutralise the army and patch up a settlement on easy terms with Charles I in 1647, then with Fairfax led the defeat of the royalist revolt and Scots invasion in 1648. The mastermind of the execution of the king and defeat of the army's democratic dissidents in 1649. Commander of the NMA and Lord General 1650–8, in which capacity he defeated the Scots and Charles II; expelled Parliament and served as virtual dictator 1653; Lord Protector 1653–8.

Cromwell, Richard (1626–1712): eldest surviving son of Oliver, Lord Protector 1658–9. A modest country gentleman by inclination and not interested in politics or war, he lived on his wife's estate at Hursley, Hants until his role as Oliver's eldest son made him the chosen heir to the increasingly monarchic Protectorate in 1657 and he joined the Council. He did his best for reconciliation and stability in 1658–9 and was not as hopeless as he has been portrayed, but 'Tumbledown Dick' lacked army backing and religious radicals feared him as close to the Presbyterians and the royalists targeted him as a usurper. Refusing to be the front-man for his father's generals, he was deposed by them and lived in retirement into 1660, was considered as a compromise unity candidate for rival factions then but was overtaken by the better-backed Charles II, and left England to avoid harassment after Restoration by vengeful royalist litigants. Eventually returned, quietly and under an assumed name; mostly lived in Hertfordshire, with relatives until died aged eighty-five.

Desborough, Colonel John (1608–80): Oliver Cromwell's republican brother-in-law, and senior New Model Army commander. A minor officer in the army in 1640s but noted for bravery, especially in 1645 campaign, he was an anti-monarchist backing Oliver Cromwell, in 1648–9; chosen for Cromwell's council as a trusted relative, and later a major-general in 1655 and opposed the Commons, shutting them down 1656–7; emerged as one of the hardline republican generals opposing the civilianization and monarchic trend of the Protectorate in 1657 and helped to talk Cromwell out of taking the throne. A competent administrator and commander, he then tried to 'manage' his nephew Richard as Protector and on being rebuffed helped to overthrow him in 1659. A leading figure in the military regime of 1659–60, but overshadowed by the younger Lambert; he gave up power reluctantly after Monck's invasion in 1660 and kept out of trouble at the Restoration, but was banned from office and occasionally harassed.

Digby, George, 2nd earl of Bristol (1612–77): veteran royalist courtier, diplomat and intriguer, a man of great talents but also flawed judgement who made many enemies. Son of first earl, the ambassador to Spain, and born in Madrid; Catholic and royalist but sporadically took anti-Catholic stance in English politics. MP for Dorset in both Parliaments 1640; backed impeachment of autocratic minister Strafford and reform in early 1641 but then reverted to royalist stance and earned fury of Pym's group so elevated to Lords by king to protect him. Allied to hardliners and involved in plan to arrest the Five Members 1642, and had to flee to Holland; royalist adviser and backed queen's 'line of' inviting foreign Catholic aid, Secretary of State 1643–6, and unsuccessful commander in north England 1645–6. Known for impractical and quixotic schemes, and disliked by Hyde/Clarendon. Major figure in exiled court 1646–60, but also served in French army until Cromwell made Mazarin expel him 1655; after Restoration foe of his old rival Clarendon and failed to get him sacked in 1663 in clumsy intrigue; marginalised by king 1663–7 but returned to prominence after helping his enemy's ruin 1667, though still suspected over Catholic links.

Downing, Sir George (1624/5–1684): notoriously slippery but effective diplomat and adviser to both Cromwell and Charles II. The son of East Anglian 'Puritan' barrister Emmanuel Downing and the sister of John Winthrop, founding governor of Massachussets, he followed his father to North America in 1638 as the family settled at Salem. One of the first year's graduates at Harvard university, he then served as a chaplain on board (slaving) ships in the West Indies and returned to England late in the civil war as chaplain to Colonel John Okey's regiment in the New Model Army. He served with distinction as Scoutmaster-General, i.e. chief of intelligence, to the English army in Scotland and fought at Dunbar and Worcester, then moved into English government as brother-in-law to Cromwell's young aristocratic ally Charles Howard (later earl of Carlisle). His connections and blunt, ruthless promotion of English and Protestant interests made Cromwell appoint him as envoy to (Catholic) France to protest at their ally Savoy's massacre of the Vaudois Protestants in 1655, then to Savoy in 1656 and to England's Dutch commercial rivals in 1657–60. He countered royalist exiles and Dutch threats to English commerce successfully, then swiftly turned royalist in 1660 and offered his services to Charles II who kept him on. His most notorious act was his illegal rendition, i.e. kidnapping, of his ex-employer Okey and two other top regicides in Holland to be returned to England for execution, ever since seen as indicating his faithlessness. As MP and an expert on Dutch evasion of the Navigation Acts he helped to have a new, tougher Act drawn up in 1660, and advised the king on the need to snatch the colony of New Amsterdam (now New York) from the Dutch in the next war in 1664–5. His Restoration diplomatic services in Holland were supplemented by effective work and reform at the treasury as a commissioner, but he is best known for his land-speculation purchase and building on Whitehall Palace property of 'Downing Street'.

Fairfax, Sir Thomas, lord Fairfax (1612–71): owner of estate at Denton in Yorkshire and peer with Scottish title so eligible for election as English MP. Principled opponent of Catholic expansionism and royal power; served as mercenary in Dutch service against Spain in the 1630s, under his future father-in-law Sir Horatio Vere. One of the small number of men with military experience and competence in Charles I's war against the Scots Covenanters in 1639–40, but was uneasy at the drift to civil war and tried to present a petition to the king to stop mobilization in 1642; he was ignored and was second-in-command to his father Ferdinando Fairfax in the Yorkshire parliamentary army in 1642–4. Highly competent and popular general, the 'Rider on the White Horse' or 'Black Tom' helped to stem the royalist tide in the region, save Hull, and win at Marston Moor in 1644; then made supreme commander and Lord General of the New Model Army 1645–50. He staged highly effective and well-run campaigns and kept his men's loyalty, in contrast to his predecessors, and won the vital battle of Naseby and at many sieges – and was less vindictive to royalists/Catholics than his deputy Cromwell except at Colchester in 1648. The man who won the war as much as Cromwell; but eclipsed politically and religiously in the army in 1647–8 was less attuned to his men's beliefs and priorities than Cromwell. Won the second civil war in 1648 and defeated the Leveller rising, with moderation, in 1649; retired in 1650 sooner than fight the Scots. Returned to help Restoration 1660, and treated with honour by Charles II. Moderate Presbyterian leader of Parliamentarian Yorkshire gentry and also a noted devotional Christian writer; patron of Marvell.

Fiennes, Nathaniel (1608? – 69); second son of senior Parliamentarian peer Lord Saye and Sele. Educated at Winchester and New College Oxford; travelled abroad in 1630s to Switzerland and said to have thus acquired dislike of Anglican (or any centralised) church; supporter of Independents and toleration. MP for Banbury 1640–8; served in Parliamentarian army 1642–3, at first clash of war at Powick Bridge; under a cloud after his surrender of Bristol (his governorship) to Rupert 1643 and called a coward by army militants; sentenced to death by tribunal but reprieved, left country, and returned after war as army ally and on their committee of safety 1648. Purged by Colonel Pride as he tried to save monarchy, but friend of Cromwell and senior councillor 1653–8, also Commissioner of Great Seal 1655–9; backed Cromwellian monarchy plan 1657 and purged by generals 1659. Exonerated at Restoration but lived in retirement and hostile to regime's religious policy; father by second marriage of travel-writer Celia Fiennes (b 1662).

Finch, Sir Heneage (1620–82), lord Finch (1661) and earl of Nottingham (1681). Son of the 1626 Speaker of Commons of same name, from Sussex/Kent gentry dynasty in royal service. Educated at Winchester and Christ Church Oxford; successful municipal lawyer in London 1650s, living at Kensington (later built 'Nottingham House', basis of Palace). MP for Canterbury 1660 and Oxford 1661–78; hardline and trusted royalist lawyer who played leading role in 1660–1 prosecution of regicides as Solicitor-General (1660–70). Later Attorney-General (1670–3) and Lord Keeper/Lord Chancellor (1673–82); a capable and hard-working regime lawyer who showed scepticism over the more lurid allegations of the 'Popish Plot' and was loyal to royal priorities.

Fleetwood, General Charles (1619? – 1692): Oliver Cromwell's son-in-law, succeeding General Ireton as husband to Bridget Cromwell in 1652. Son of minor royal official, Sir Miles Fleetwood of Aldwinkle, Northants; joined Parliamentarian army and fought at Newbury 1643 and Naseby 1645, and strong Independent religious beliefs; later a Baptist. Rose to prominence as senior New Model Army officer, as lieutenant-general of horse in Scotland 1650 and later in Ireland; Cromwell's Lord Lieutenant of Ireland 1652–5, and also senior councillor 1653–9. Led the ruthless evictions of Catholic Irish to 'Hell or Connacht' and did his best to Protestantise the kingdom, also ensured dominance of radical officers in Irish army so they backed his London army takeover in 1659. Encouraged Cromwell to aggressive Protestant foreign policy; the leader of the republican Junto of officers that deposed Richard Cromwell in 1659. Proved not up to tasks of keeping them united or formulating political programme, dithered, and was left helpless and shocked by the regime's collapse as Monck invaded; excluded from power by Restoration and spent remaining years aiding local Nonconformists near Islington home.

Fox, George (1624–91): Quaker leader, much feared as alleged extremist sectary by royalist gentry. Son of a Leicestershire weaver, and self-taught; worked as a shoemaker and occasionally as shepherd, and made much of his humble roots, association with the ordinary people, and humility in contrast to the prevailing social ethos. One of the numerous seekers after God and true religion that sprang up under the impetus of civil war, and avoided the latter as a pacifist in his wanderings after 1643; his individualistic view of religion cohered by 1647 as opposed to any state church or religious coercion, worship in 'steeple-houses' (churches), or authority by the clergy (or to some degree the Bible), and he believed anyone (of either sex) with the 'Holy Spirit' in them could preach and teach. This and the rapid spread of his following caused conservatives, e.g. the local gentry on his provincial tours, to regard him as a dangerous social revolutionary and anarchist, and he suffered persecution and imprisonment for illegal preaching, subversion, causing disturbances etc from both the republicans in 1650s and royalists after 1660. Had a strong following in northern England, to local gentry's alarm, and married his Furness JP ally Thomas Fell of Smarthmoor Hall's widow, Margaret, another major Quaker leader. Particularly feared in late 1650s and 1660s, and so influenced conservative swing in politics and religion 1658–64. Later also preached and won converts in North America, and was temporarily courted by James II in 1685–8 as opponent of Anglican dominance.

Gauden, John (1605–62): moderate Presbyterian cleric, a leader who attempted their inclusion within the Anglican church in 1660–1. The son of an Essex vicar, he was related via his mother to the Russells of

Chippenham, Cambridgeshire, who were connected to the Cromwells. One of the more 'godly' wing in East Anglia of the 1630s Anglican Church, sympathetic to Presbyterian-style reform, he was protege and chaplain to the reformist leader and royal critic, the Earl of Warwick. Rural dean of Bocking, Essex from 1641, he supported Parliament but was severely critical of regicide and made a protest about it to Fairfax; he later claimed to have been a secret royalist in the late 1640s and author of the *Eikon Basilike* ('Image of the King'), a seminal royalist work presenting Charles I's own musings c. 1647–8 on his piety and Christian mission. Others, including Hyde/Clarendon, claimed that it was entirely Charles' work and written earlier, but Gauden may have co-written it. If he was indeed a 'royal Presbyterian', this stood him in good stead in 1660, but he stayed out of trouble in the republican 1650s and retained his parish. He was promoted to the minor see of Exeter in 1660 and Worcester in 1662 as a key figure in trying to admit the Presbyterians to the Church, but was said to have been disappointed not to get richer Winchester; he soon died.

Goffe, Colonel William (1605?–c. 1679): New Model Army figure, and personal friend of Oliver Cromwell. Son of the expelled 'Puritan' rector of Bramber, Sussex, and shared father's antipathy to episcopal High Church rule; apprentice to London salter and imprisoned for anti-episcopal petition 1641. Captain in Colonel Harley (Herefordshire) Parliamentary regiment, but rose to prominence in NMA and crucial Cromwellian connection as son-in-law to Cromwell's cousin Colonel Whalley (he was in Whalley's regiment). An outspoken 'godly' idealist in 1647–9, vocalising the reformist misson of the army Independents and attacking the king, e.g. at Putney Debates; led calls for royal prosecution and moral government 1647–8, and an unashamed regicide. Served with distinction at Dunbar and Worcester; a moralist and centralising major-general for Oliver Cromwell 1655–7, then took over Lambert's regiment when he resigned; spoken of as confidante and possible successor to Cromwell. Backed Richard Cromwell 1659 and sidelined by republicans; fled to North America as regicide with Whalley 1660, and his last years in hiding are shrouded in mystery but he seems to have been protected by local sympathisers, e.g. Increase Mather and governor Leverett. The central figure in Massachusetts 'Angel of Hadley' (1675/6?) incident/ legend, as bearded army veteran who led town to fight off Native American attack.

Grenville, Sir John, earl of Bath (1661) (1628–1701): senior Cornish royalist gentry leader and 1660s courtier. Son of the civil war royalist hero Sir Bevil Grenville (killed 1643 at Lansdown) of Stowe, Cornwall, and head of his branch of the large Grenville dynasty; gentleman of bedchamber and adviser to Charles II as nominal commander in south-west England 1645–6, then key supporter in exile; appointed by him as governor of Scilly Isles 1648. After their fall to Parliament, arrested but allowed to reside quietly at Stowe and kept out of trouble 1650s; surreptitiously funded king and used his relationship to cousin General Monck, whose clergyman brother was his employee, in 1659–60 to help Restoration 1660. Key royal supporter in and after 1660, and peerage, Groom of Stole (key court role of access to king), and grants including £2,000 p.a.; supported monarchy to autumn 1688 then as governor of Plymouth defected to invading William III.

Grimston, Sir Harbottle, 2nd Bt (1603–85): moderate Parliamentarian, MP for Colchester 1640–8 and 1659–60, 1661–81, and for Essex, 1656; from gentry family of Manningtree, Essex, and one of pro-Presbyterian 'godly' Essex opponents of Laudian church. Supported Parliament but not very active, and in 1648 a leader of the moderate Commons delegation to negotiate with Charles I at Newport to try to save monarchy; excluded by Pride's Purge. Inactive but principled opposition to military rule in 1650s, and forbidden to take seat in Commons 1656 as distrusted; important role in restored Rump 1659–60 and Speaker of 'Convention' Parliament 1660. Key background role in Restoration in bringing his allies to back Charles II; Master of Rolls 1662–1685.

Harrington, James (1611–77): idealistic but isolated late 1650s republican theorist. From minor Northants gentry, related to Haringtons of Exton; educated at Trinity College Oxford but apparently left Lincolns Inn early out of animus to lawyers' profession; travelled widely on Continent in 1630s including Dutch military service, Switzerland, Venice and Rome and probably acquired interest in workings of republican constitutions there, especially Venice. Had unclear role in 1640s, variously said to have aided both king and Parliament, and ended up as trusted by Parliament 1647 to help commission getting Charles I to move to Holdenby/ Holmby House; groom of bedchamber to king on Isle of Wight 1648, and possible personal sympathy to him as said to have been sacked by Parliament for refusal to spy on him. Lived in retirement in 1650s, and published controversial theoretical study of an idealised constitution, *The Commonwealth of Oceana*, in 1656 – favoured benevolent and moral dictator (Cromwell??) and rotated elected senate to share power among landed elite. His work was initially banned as dangerous, allegedly reprieved due to his patron Elizabeth Claypole (daughter of Oliver Cromwell); it acquired vogue among reformers at London club in 1659 as possible solution to domestic turmoil but lacked support. Harrington was then sidelined, and in trouble 1661 as possible subversive; then fell into obscurity as health and mental state declined.

Harrison, General Thomas (1616–60): son of mayor of Newcastle-under-Lyme, and attorney at Clifford's Inn, Fleet Street, London, by outbreak of war; signed up for earl of Essex's Parliamentary lifeguard. Later in earl of Manchester's East Anglian army and New Model Army as colonel; involved with his notably radical regiment in democratic and pro-sect agitation 1647, and by this point one of the leaders of the millenarian Fifth Monarchists; critic of monarchy, feared by king by late 1647, and hardline republican and radical sectary; distinguished in second civil war 1648, and commanded the king's guard when escorted him to London for trial with Charles reportedly fearing murder by him; general 1650, served at Worcester, but split from Cromwell over the closure of the 'Nominated Parliament' in 1653 where he led the frustrated religious zealots; 1650s leader of the millenarian 'Fifth Monarchist' radical grouping. Surrendered to new regime 1660 but swiftly tried and hung, drawn and quartered as first regicide to be made example of.

Henrietta Maria, Queen of England (1609–69); French Catholic, daughter of Henri IV and Marie de Medici; wife of Charles I 1625, and mother of Charles II and James II. Sidelined as teen bride by husband's domineering friend the duke of Buckingham and feared by public as catholicising agent, but marriage prospered once duke was dead; star of court masques and generous patron, especially to co-religionists; alarmed

'Long Parliament' threatened impeachment 1641–2 and she stiffened husband's will to resist; left England to pawn jewels for arms 1642, returned 1643–4, and then back to France, rallying European aid for royalists and seen as leader of hardliners by enemies; tried to influence Charles II into catholic alliances 1650s and opposed his 1650–1 link-up with Scots Covenanters; England again 1660, but mostly lived in France thereafter.

Henriette Anne ('Minette'), duchess of Orleans (1644–70); younger daughter of HM, born in Exeter during civil war; married off to Louis XIV's bisexual younger brother Philippe (d 1701) by her mother, and acted as Charles II's unofficial representative at French court; urged strong French alliance to stabilise English regime, but shrewd, loyal to brother's interests, and far from the 'French agent' which many have called her; the secret alliance treaty of Dover 1670 was largely her doing, and she died suddenly (probably peritonitis, poison rumoured) shortly afterwards.

Haselrig/Heselrige, Sir Arthur, 2nd Bt (1601–61); veteran 1640s Parliamentarian MP and army commander. Son of 1st baronet, of Noseley Hall, Leics; hardline critic of Strafford and Archbishop Laud in the 'Long Parliament' as MP for Leics (1640–53), and one of the 'Five Members' targeted for arrest by Charles I January 1642. He raised his own regiment, nicknamed the 'Lobsters' from red coats, and fought at Edgehill and (leading role) Lansdown; nearly killed or captured and regiment decimated at Roundway Down 1643. Ally of Cromwell and army in late 1640s, and supported regicide but did not participate; republican and pro-Presbyterian in 1650s, MP for Leicester 1653–9; stood apart from Cromwell 1653–8 as regarded dissolution of Rump illegal. Leading civilian republican in 1659, and struggled for power with Lambert and army who he tried to rein in; after Lambert closed Rump, led mutiny at Portsmouth and assisted Monck's takeover; leading civilian republican 1660, opposed Restoration but left behind by events' momentum, and imprisoned in Tower until death as dangerous.

Holmes, Sir Robert (1622?–92): originally son of minor English (Lancs) planter in County Cork, Ireland; junior officer under Prince Maurice in

West Country campaign 1643, including Roundway Down; left England 1646 to join French service, then dashing royalist naval captain in Prince Rupert's privateering squadron in Mediterranean and West Indies early 1650s; after 1660 senior Royal Naval commander, especially under Duke of York (James II) in West Africa 1663–4 where his attacks on Dutch helped to precipitate war; commander in Dutch War 1665–7 including success against merchant naval convoys, and again in 1672–4; best known as governor of Isle of Wight in later years, building large house at Yarmouth (commanded castle) and waylaying statue of Louis XIV to remodel it for his own one; archetypal bluff 'tarpaulin' self-made naval officer.

Hyde, Sir Edward, earl of Clarendon (1607–74): son of minor Wiltshire gentry, and originally critic of royal policies and reformist in Long Parliament; alarmed at slide to war and threat to Church and defected to king; politically moderate royalist adviser to Charles I in 1640s and senior Royalist minister in exile 1649–60 (secretary of state); advised Charles II towards moderate policies and reaching out to disenchanted Cromwellian/ Presbyterian moderates, and against catholic alliances and rash revolts so disliked by hardline militant Royalists and Queen; helped to coax the Monck regime and moderate allies into Restoration 1660, but his promises of accommodation for moderate sects and no political reprisals failed for which he was unfairly blamed; Lord Chancellor and chief minister to Charles II 1660–7, and was blamed for harsh Anglican 'Clarendon Code' and exclusion of Dissenters from Church but was really forced into it by militant MPs. Critic of and disliked by the more morally lax younger royalist courtiers and officers ever since the 1640s; blamed for mistakes of regime in general e.g. sale of Dunkirk and Dutch War defeats and sacrificed by king to enemies in impeachment 1667; retired in disgrace to France.

Hyde, Anne, duchess of York (1637–71); Hyde's daughter, wife of James, Duke of York from 1660; he was accused of pandering her to the duke to secure role as grandfather to future sovereign as Charles II's wife barren. Later Anne became Catholic, and was accused of influencing husband that way too. Mother of queens Mary II and Anne; shrewd and underrated.

Ingoldsby, Colonel Richard (1618–85): cousin to Oliver Cromwell, younger son of Sir Richard Ingoldsby of Lethenborough, Bucks; captain in John Hampden's Buckinghamshire Parliamentary regiment 1642–3, and trusted New Model Army officer who Fairfax asked to relieve Taunton 1645 and garrison captured Royalist capital Oxford 1646–7. Backed the Army vs Presbyterians and Cromwell's 'grandees' against his own Leveller mutineer soldiers 1647–9; a regicide in 1649, though ingeniously claimed 1660 that Cromwell forced him to sign death-warrant. MP Wendover 1647–53, Council of State 1652–3; senior adviser to Cromwell but no official role. Backed Richard Cromwell 1659 and purged by Lambert and Fleetwood; assisted Monck 1659–60; pardoned by Charles II after rounding up the most dangerous republican commander Lambert in 1660, and untouched in retirement despite Cromwellian connection; MP Aylesbury 1660 and 1661–85.

James II, King of England (Duke of York to 1685) (1633–1701): younger brother of Charles II. Loyal to brother throughout, and famously escaped from custody in London to France in 1648 dressed as girl; served with distinction in French and Spanish armies in exile in 1650s, and capable officer but politically naive and inflexible. Lord Admiral 1660–73, reformed navy helped by Pepys and others; also prominent in advancing mercantile/colonial interests, e.g. Royal Africa Company (including slavery) and North America ('New York' named after his title); capable commander in Dutch Wars, but his Catholicism presented problem as he was brother's heir and he had to resign naval office 1673; refused to abandon his faith for political safety, and faced 'Exclusion' from succession in 1679–81 unsuccessful campaign by Shaftesbury and Whigs; governed Scotland capably but harshly, and repeated inflexible autocratic authoritarian approach and blunders in alienating people as king 1685–8. Advanced religious toleration for sects as well as Catholics, but his zealous promotion of the latter and failure to accomodate alarmed Anglican elite led to their invitation to son-in-law William of Orange to invade; had to flee, lost Ireland too in 1690–1, and in exile until death as French pensioner trying to use Louis XIV to regain thrones.

Jermyn, Sir Henry, earl of St Albans (1660) (1605–84); second son of head of a branch of extensive Suffolk dynasty; MP for Bodmin

1625–6, Liverpool 1628–9, Corfe Castle 1640, Bury St Edmunds 1640–3 (deprived); friend and adviser to Henrietta Maria from 1630s to 1660s, alleged to be her lover; political meddler, 'bon vivant' courtier, and hardline Royalist intriguer during civil war, allegedly mixed up in assorted failed plots vs Parliament from 1641 onwards; in exile 1646–60, mostly in Paris as adviser to queen, and urged hardline alliance of exiles to Catholic powers so distrusted by Hyde; returned home in triumph 1660, and minor political role but successful property speculator, owner of much of St James', London (built Jermyn Street); foe of Hyde/Clarendon since the 1640s and helped to ruin him 1667; lord chamberlain 1671–4.

Johnston of Warriston, Archibald (1611–63): hardline Presbyterian Scots figure, son of Edinburgh merchant and educated at University of Glasgow; lawyer to 1637, thence co-leader of the Covenanter organizers and co-author of the Covenant; clerk to their 'Tables' (executive committee representing different social orders). Devout and uncompromising on full and godly Presbyterian church regime, possibly scarred by early death of godly first wife; criticised Charles I openly as unreliable, and also keen for England to join his Church model as commissioner to their Westminster Assembly 1643–6; leading Covenanter on Scots/Parliamentary 'Committee of Both Kingdoms' 1644–8 and ally of Argyll. Opposed 'Engagement' to try to rescue Charles in 1648; hardline confidante of Argyll regime 1648–50 and allegedly interfered in General Leslie's plans for battle of Dunbar 1650 so helping his defeat; Clerk Register 1649–50; opposed alliance with Charles II, and in 1657–8 reconciled to Oliver Cromwell; represented Covenanters on Lambert's junto's Committee of Safety 1659–60, fled abroad at Restoration and extradited from France for execution.

Jones, Colonel Philip (1618–74): Glamorgan gentry figure, self-made as son of farmer near Swansea; minor role in civil war and Parliamentarian governor of Swansea 1647; adviser and senior minister to Oliver and Richard Cromwell 1653–9, and Steward of the Protectoral Household. An administrator rather than politician or soldier, and especially involved with matters of trade under Cromwell; pursued by allegations of using his office and contacts to build up estates by sharp practice (owner of

Fonmon Castle near Barry) and had many local foes. Seen as one of the civilian strongmen behind Oliver and Richard, backing Cromwellian monarchy 1657–9, and excluded from power by New Model Army coup 1659; after Restoration retired to private life and harassed legally by foes over his earlier deals.

Juxon, William (1582–1663); from Chichester, educated Merchant Taylors School and St John's College Oxford; vicar of St Giles' Oxford 1609 and Somerton, Somerset 1615, president of St John's 1621–33 as protégé of his friend and fellow High Anglican Laud; dean of Worcester 1627, bishop of Hereford 1633 then of London 1633–46. Chosen by Laud for the latter, crucial see with dissident Puritan congregations, to impose Laudian reform and discipline; also clerk of closet to King from 1632 and treasurer 1636–41. Laud's effective deputy, but not prosecuted 1640s as less authoritarian and fewer enemies; kept out of politics and with Charles I on scaffold 1649; retirement in Cotswolds 1650s. Chosen as archbishop of Canterbury 1660–3 as most senior and renowned Laudian by the royalist hardliners; the distinguished but elderly Anglican figurehead after 1660, with Gilbert Sheldon as stronger deputy.

Lambert, General John (1619–84); close colleague and ally of Oliver Cromwell from the late 1640s. From minor gentry family at Kirkby Malham near Skipton, Yorkshire; captain of parliamentary horse under Fairfax's father Ferdinando in Yorkshire 1642 and colonel 1643, with distinguished service at Hull, Nantwich, and Marston Moor; second-in-command to General Poyntz in Yorkshire 1645–6, then given New Model Army regiment. Emerged into army politics 1647–8 to help the New Model Army soldiery in cause of religious toleration and political reform, then took major role in suppressing 1648 second civil war risings in north-east; helped Cromwell win battle of Preston, then led siege of royalist Pontefract. Cromwell's deputy in Scottish 1650–1 campaigns, led victory at Inverkeithing, and major role at Worcester. Lambert was the leading moderate in 1653 Nominated Parliament who steered the Cromwellians to its blockage of radicals and then its replacement by the Protectorate, and was the main author of the December 1653 constitution, the Instrument of Government. Cromwell's deputy and leading Councillor in 1653–7, then resigned in protest at monarchic leanings of the regime in 1657 and was possibly manoeuvred out by the civilians as too republican; re-emerged as republican military leader in 1659, shut down Rump, and fought Monck for power. The effective leader of the military junto with Fleetwood; tried to stop the Restoration by force after escaping from the Tower but was rounded up. Supposedly pardoned 1660, but kept in custody as too dangerous to free and prosecuted on dubious grounds for treason 1662; the king feared his potential, as he was kept isolated on Guernsey in 1662–7 then moved to island in Plymouth Sound; still imprisoned when died, reputedly mentally fragile.

Lawson, Admiral John (c. 1615 – 1665): Parliamentarian merchant navy captain from Scarborough, in their navy from 1642 and important in supplying Hull during 1643 siege. Commander of *Centurion* under Blake 1650–2, aided pursuit of Prince Rupert's privateer squadron to West Indies and taking French and Portuguese prizes; commanded ship *Fairfax* in First Dutch War 1652–4. Vice-admiral of the Red squadron 1652 ff; crucial role in battle of the Gabbard 1653 and deputy to admiral Edward Montague 1656. Suspected by Cromwell over Leveller sympathies (helped leader Wildman to Parliamentary seat in Scarborough) and support for seamen's petition, and dismissed for alleged subversion against Protectorate after delay due to his popularity among his men; accused over Fifth Monarchist plot 1657. Reinstated by Rump 1659, as deputy to Montague, and aided latter to use navy for defeat of the army and then the Restoration in 1660 – probably crucial in unexpected Leveller/royalist linkup. He was then given naval squadron in Mediterranean 1662–4, centred on new British base at Tangier, and coerced Barbary pirates; mortally wounded in battle of Lowestoft vs Dutch 1665.

Lenthall, William (1591–1662): from Henley-on-Thames, minor town family; later owner of Burford Priory, Oxfordshire. Educated St Albans Hall Oxford (did not graduate) and Lincolns Inn; senior bencher at Lincolns Inn and recorder of Woodstock 1621, Gloucester 1638; MP for Woodstock 1624, 1640–53, 1659–60 and Oxfordshire 1654 and 1656. Respected lawyer; Speaker of Parliament 1640–53, 1654–5, 1659–60. Most famous as the presiding officer of the Long Parliament who backed the opposition against the king, especially attempt on the 'Five Members' 1642, and gave them extra legality by staying in London against royal orders; backed Independent MPs and New Model Army against Presbyterian bloc's coercion 1647, fleeing London to join army, and so was trusted by latter to stay on after Pride's Purge. Technically head of state after regicide, and presided over Commons until OC's coup 1653 and again over OC's first Parliament 1654–5 and Rump in 1659–60; earned prestige and trust but was accused of bending with the political wind, not standing up to army in 1648 or 1653–5, and being a short-sighted placeman lacking initiative. Not prosecuted after Restoration despite Prynne's attempts, and allowed to retire.

Lisle, John (1609/10–64) Radical republican lawyer from Isle of Wight gentry, second son of Sir John Lisle of Wootton. Educated Magdalen Hall, Oxford and Middle Temple; respected and reformist lawyer, married to famous 'Judge Jeffreys victim' Frances, nee Beconshaw, of Moyle Court, Hampshire (ex 1685). MP for Winchester 1640–53 and leading Parliamentarian county commissioner; hostile to King throughout, and Commissioner of the Great Seal to Parliament from 1644 and Rump/Cromwell from 1649. Regicide judge, and advised the trial on legal matters so hated by Royalists; reputation for sharp practice and enjoying the fruits of office. Served but wary of Cromwell, was retained by the Rump 1659, and opponent of Restoration 1659–60. He fled to Switzerland and was subsequently assassinated by royalists in a public 'hit' in Lausanne; dislike of him was shared by his relatives.

Louis XIV (1638–1715), King of France since the age of five in 1643; chief ally to Cromwell from 1655 under Mazarin's guidance, and then to his cousin Charles II except in 1665–7 when backed Dutch. Talented, showy and arrogant devotee of royal autocracy (*L'etat c'est moi*) and Catholic intolerance, feared by English Protestants as their arch-foe and determined to extend French frontiers; married to Spanish princess/heiresss Maria Theresa, and notorious for extravagant court, Versailles palace-building, centralised government, and military aggression. Tried to turn Charles II into his dependent ally through offering subsidies and military aid, and later gave refuge and help to exiled James II; plunged Europe into repeated wars.

Ludlow, General Edmund (1617?–1692). Son of squire of Maiden Bradley, Wiltshire; educuated Oxford and Inner Temple. Parliamentarian soldier; a junior officer in commander-in-chief Essex's regiment 1642, then captain in local Wiltshire regiment of Sir Edward Hungerford and unsuccessful defender of Wardour castle 1643–4. After capture there headed to London and major under future republican Sir Arthur Haselrig; Sheriff for Wiltshire 1645 and MP from 1646. Idealistic republican officer in New Model Army, religiously Baptist and aligned to freedom for sects and to republican Henry Marten; helped army in Pride's Purge, regicide ally of Cromwell, then in Ireland under Cromwell 1649 and deputy to next commander General Ireton; his de facto successor 1651–2 and led repression. Opposed to the Protectorate 1653 as not democratic and betrayed ideals of 1649, and was sacked from post in Ireland, but not detained on return to England as promised OC to be acquiscent. Returned to politics 1659 and leading member of junto, trying to reconcile generals and Rump but not satisfying either; surrendered to royalist regime 1660 but not promised security so fled to Switzerland. In exile to 1689 as a foe of the Restoration, based at Vevey, and wrote revealing memoirs of the era – but the published version (1698–9) was heavily edited and now seen as unreliable. Returned under William III but quickly deported as a republican threat.

Maitland, John, lord/earl and (1672) **duke of Lauderdale** (1616–82): son of 1st earl, Lothian gentry; senior moderate Scots Calvinist peer and a 1640s anti-royalist Covenanter, commissioner from the latter in England 1643–6 and in abortive Uxbridge negotiations with king 1645 to try to obtain a Presbyterian church in both realms. As commissioner with Scots army in England after end of war 1646–7, tried to help king to reach accomodation with his masters and then switched to royalist side vs New Model Army to sign secret treaty with king (Carisbrooke) whereby Scots invaded England. 'Engager' ally of king and Hamilton to try to enforce Presbyterian church on England and defeat New Model Army in 1648 civil war; eclipsed by Cromwellian invasion 1650, but then aided Argyll to install Charles II as puppet king; captured in invasion of England at Worcester, interned 1651–60 as irreconcilable, and aided moderate Scots Presbyterian support for Restoration. Ended up as senior 1660s-70s royal minister, failing to get moderate Presbyterians to accept bishops in new

Scots church then deserting them for royalists; effectively ruled Scotland from 1667–80 as secretary of state, aided by hostess second wife Elizabeth Murray, countess of Dysart, of Ham House Surrey.

Mary, Princess of Orange (1631–60): the elder of Charles II's two surviving sisters, married off by Charles I to the Dutch 'Stadtholder' William II (d 1650) in attempt to get aid at start of civil war. Aided family as much as Dutch mercantile oligarchy would allow, but sidelined politically 1650 when husband died and posthumous son excluded from political role. Mother of the later Stadtholder and British king William III; assisted brother's return from exile at Restoration 1660 but died in epidemic shortly afterwards.

Mazarin, Cardinal Jules (Giulio Mazarini) (d 1661): Italian Papal official, who came to France to assist chief minister Cardinal Richelieu 1630 after mediating in Franco-Spanish war at siege of Casale. Chief minister of France from Louis XIII's death in 1643 to to his death in 1661, effectively co-regent; reputed lover of Queen-Mother/regent Anne, and his unpopularity with nobles led to the 'Fronde' rebellions in 1648–52 in attempt to drive him out; then steered France into alliance with Cromwell 1655–7 but kept on good terms with Charles II from 1659/60 .

Middleton, John, 1st earl of Middleton (1656) (1608–74): son of minor Kincardineshire gentry, volunteer in French army 1630s. Talented but hard-drinking professional soldier; second in command to Montrose in Covenanter campaigns 1639–40, then major in Scots army aiding English Parliament 1643–5; deputy to Leslie at Montrose's defeat at Philiphaugh 1645, but backed Engagers 1648 and captured fighting for Charles I at Preston; aided Charles II in 1650–1 and disliked by hardline Presbyterians, morals suspect; captured at Worcester 1651, escaped from Tower of London, and in 1654 led Charles II's supporters in unsuccessful Royalist rebellion in Scotland, exile 1654–60. Then leading Royalist military figure in Scotland; chief minister in Scotland as commissioner to their Parliament, commander-in-chief and ditto of Edinburgh castle 1660–3. Backed episcopal solution to Church controversy successfully, but politically outmanoeuvred and disgraced due to Maitland 1663;

aided king vs Dutch as governor of Rochester 1667, then commanded at Tangier 1667–74 where died after drunken fall.

Milton, John (1608–74). Son of minor legal writer from London; educated at Christ's College, Cambridge (MA 1632) and friend/contemporary of American theologian Roger Williams whose opposition to state church oppression he shared. Brilliant and learned Cambridge intellectual star in early 1630s, famous for masque 'Comus' performed at Ludlow Castle 1634 and pastoral epic 'Lycidas'; broke with mainstream academic elite and studied privately but with some well-connected patrons. Early Continental Catholic cultural enthusiasms and toured France and Italy late 1630s, acquiring Latin and Greek influences, but emerged as devout and 'godly' backer of Parliament after 1640. Famous subsequently as poet and author of *Paradise Lost* and *Paradise Regained*, turning the classical epic genre to Old Testament legend and justifying the ways of God to Man, but in the 1640s-50s a major pro-republican intellectual figure. Articulate and energetic pamphleteer who was main spokesman for New Model Army and Commonwealth regimes in justifying radicalism towards Commons majority and royalty; 'Latin Secretary' (wrote and translated diplomatic letters and manifestoes) to Cromwell 1653–8. Opposed Presbyterian intolerance towards sects, especially in 1640s debate over future nature of state church when he defended freedom of press and religion from the authoritarian likes of Prynne, and later the Restoration in 1660; driven into hiding and then retirement in Buckinghamshire by royalist hostility and wrote his major epics in seclusion.

Monck, General George, later duke of Albemarle (1660) (1608–70). Self-made north Devon farmer turned royalist officer (Ireland early 1640s), turned Parliamentarian officer and part-time admiral (1644–60) after he was captured by Parliament. Highly capable and soon seen as now loyal to Parliament, and probably also motivated by fear of Catholics after 1641 Irish massacres of deserting Royalists. He was entrusted by Cromwell with conquest then rule of Scotland in 1652–8, and turned his hand to sea command too; was stern but fair in controlling Scotland and set up network of military bases and roads in Highlands. He was reluctantly accepting of the military coup in 1659 against Richard, probably to keep his disunited army together, but turned against the Lambert-led junto once he was sure of his military support after purging unreliable men; led his army to overthrow the junto regime in London January 1660, unobtrusively purged the New Model Army of radicals, and held an uneasy coalition of moderates and anti-military radicals together in the name of Parliamentary rule. He then organised the Restoration as the instability of the new regime aided moderates to link up with royalists in the interest of stability – but did he lead or follow majority opinion? Subsequently senior royalist minister (lord treasurer 1667–70) and courtier, and kept the military loyal to King as commander-in-chief 1660–70. The crucial enabler of Restoration and expert both at winning allies and at purging threats, but his political and religious positions were flexible and remain ambiguous.

Montague, Edward, 2nd earl of Manchester (1602–71): son of 1st earl, senior Carolean minister. 'Godly' patron of clergy in East Anglia, critic of Laud and his church model in Lords 1640–2; leader of the moderate Presbyterian English peers in the 1640s-50s; Parliamentarian general as commander of Eastern Association 1642–5, but cautious commander and also hostile to sectaries in his ranks. Co-commander at Marston Moor victory 1644, but refused to lead his troops out of area to aid exposed Parliamentarians in south-west and timid in Second Newbury campaign which led to row with exasperated Cromwell who his faction tried to impeach. Also clashed with insubordinate democrat officer, Leveller leader John Lilburne. Retired reluctantly 1645 under Self-Denying Ordinance amidst accusations of insufficient determination; in favour of a restricted monarchy and state Presbyterian church in Lords as leader of House 1646–8, but neutered by New Model Army coups; foe of religious toleration for the sects and hence of his ex-deputy commander, Oliver Cromwell, through to 1658; re-emerged as moderate Presbyterian leader in the House of Lords 1660 and helped Restoration, and acquired court offices (chamberlain 1660–71) but little power.

Mountague/Montague, Edward, earl of Sandwich and admiral (1625–72): Manchester's cousin. Junior member of the large Fenland Montague dynasty; former Parliamentarian colonel, and chosen as councillor to Oliver Cromwell in 1653–8, probably via brother-in-law Pickering (qv); admiral 1656–9, especially coercing Portugal 1656, keeping an eye on Dutch threat to Sweden 1657, and forcing Sweden to terms with Denmark 1659; led the Navy to back Monck 1659–60 and Restoration 1660, and escorted king to England. Acquired an earldom and power at court; cousin and patron to the diarist Samuel Pepys; senior admiral in Dutch Wars 1665–7 and 1672, killed in action as flagship blew up off Lowestoft.

Mordaunt, John, viscount Mordaunt (1659) (1628–75): younger son of 1st earl of Peterborough, a senior royalist who co-led revolt 1648, and also nephew to former lord admiral, Howard of Effingham (earl of Nottingham). Swashbuckling, bold but rash co-leader of royalist plotters 1650s, but at odds with their main 'Sealed Knot' organization; helped Ormonde to arrange futile rising early 1658 to link up with Charles II in Brussels and Spanish aid, but plan collapsed; tried for treason but (just) acquitted; second plot in 1659, and helped to bring his followers into the Monck regime and organise the Restoration early 1660 after failed attempt to take over direction from Monck. Royalist courtier 1660s, as governor of Windsor castle, keeper of Windsor great park and lord lieutenant of Surrey, but damaged by rape allegations 1668; thence politically marginalised .

Morice, William (1602–76): Devonian, son of minor Exeter diocesan official but later acquired useful connection via mother's remarriage into Prideaux family; JP from 1640, Parliamentarian and Presbyterian, commissioner for sequestered estates late 1640s and sheriff of Devon 1651–2 so seen as reliable by Rump. MP for Devon 1648 (excluded by Pride's Purge) and 1654, 1656; MP for Newport, Cornwall 1659 and (Convention) 1660 via buying nearby Werrington estate. A moderate Presbyterian protégé and distant relative of General Monck, so made governor of Plymouth by him 1660; chosen by Monck's recommendation as Secretary of State 1660–8, but not close to either king or courtiers and less important than colleague Bennet; reliable bureaucrat rather than policymaker, removed 1668 as too close to disgraced Clarendon; Dissenter patron and theological enthusiast in retirement; anti-Catholic throughout.

List of Main Dramatis Personae   xxxv

Nicholas, Sir Edward (1593–1669): minor Wiltshire family, educated Salisbury grammar, Winchester, and Queen's College Oxford; clerk to Lord Zouche as Lord Warden of Cinque Ports in 1620s, then ditto to successor, Buckingham; also MP for Winchelsea 1621 and 1624, Dover 1628–9; transferred to royal service as secretary to Admiralty 1625, also clerk to privy council 1625–41; secretary of state to king 1641–6 and to exiled Charles II 1654–60. Loyal royalist man of business, and king's organiser for Uxbridge negotiations 1645 and surrender of Oxford and Scots army negotiations 1646; retired to Continent and helped Charles II, but constrained by poverty and hostility of Queen's pro-Catholic faction; as senior royalist organiser and Secretary of State in exile, made secretary of State (for south) 1660–2 but with waning influence; sacked 1662 in favour of Bennet and retired to Surrey estate, West Horsley Place.

Okey, Colonel John (1606–62): from fairly wealthy London civic family, but working in brewery when joined earl of Essex's Parliamentary army 1642 as quartermaster; archetypal self-made officer risen by talent, and later major under Haselrig and from 1645 New Model Army colonel of dragoons; his cavalry played crucial role at Naseby and other clashes of 1645 campaign. 'Godly' officer and determined republican, backing the Independents vs Presbyterians in 1646–9 but himself Congregationalist supporter and became Baptist; possible backer of John Bunyan, and eager for triumph of 'godly' strivers who had won the war. Unrepentant regicide 1649, and built up landed estates in Bedfordshire (county MP 1659) but dubious about Protectorate as anti-democratic and cashiered 1654 for supporting 'Petition of Three Colonels'. Targeted for royalist revenge 1660 and fled abroad to Holland; kidnapped and rendered back to GB by ambassador Downing, his former regimental chaplain, for execution.

Philip IV: king of Spain 1621–65 (1605–65), brother of Queen-Mother Anne of France, and host and patron to exiled Charles II in 1656–60 after Cromwell attacked Spanish Caribbean and this broke up Anglo-Spanish talks. Formerly putative ally of England in failed marital alliance plan of 1623, but regarded with hostility by English public and most of elite as Catholic hardliner and co-occupier of Charles I's sister's Palatinate lands in Thirty Years' War. Competed with France to be Charles' ally in 1630s (Spanish-French war 1635–59), and as Charles leaned towards France in

1640s he set up link to Parliament via ambassador Cardenas. Difficult relationship with British government after 1660, as he had failed to aid king and was foe of their Portuguese allies and of his daughter's (1659) husband Louis XIV; Louis coveted his Netherlands dominions.

Pickering, Colonel Sir Gilbert (1611–68): senior adviser and councillor to Oliver Cromwell. Eldest son of squire of Titchmarsh, Northamptonshire, and uncle of playwright John Dryden; married into prominent local Montague dynasty and so was patron of future admiral/councillor, cousin Edward Montague (earl of Sandwich). MP for Northants 1640–53; anti-Laudian in religion and said to have changed religious loyalties across various radical sects; ally of Cromwell from c. 1648, regicide judge and senior figure in Rump and its councils of state, more known for reliability than initiative; moderate backer of Cromwell in Nominated Parliament 1653, then his court chamberlain as Protector and on his council; an assiduous man of business and a practical supporter of alliance with France and of trade initiatives; also one of Cromwellian monarchy backers 1657 and leading role at Cromwell's funeral 1658; purged by army 1659. A determined foe of Quakers as anarchistic. Protected from prosecution at Restoration by Montague, but had occasional legal tussles with vengeful local royalists; could be ruthless but generally respected as honest.

Prynne, William (1600–69): from Swainswick, Bath; educated at Oriel College, Oxford and Lincoln's Inn but 'struck off' on royal orders after his first trial. A determined, incautious, and intolerant radical critic of the Anglican church and Stuart monarchy, starting with anti-Arminian pamphlets in late 1620s, and of pro-Presbyterian views; also violently against assorted decadent habits like men's long hair and all signs of Catholic cultural influence; well-known for his enthusiasm for vigorous legal authoritarianism. He famously had his ears cropped (twice) for insulting libels; his vitriolic abuse extended to the theatre and to the Catholic queen for appearing on stage like a whore in *Histiomastix* (1632) He was deported to Jersey to get him out of the way, and was pardoned and recalled as a hero by Parliament in 1640; MP for Newport (Launceston, Cornwall) 1648. 'Marginal Prynne' was a vitriolic anti-Laudian backer of church reform and removing bishops and all Popery in 1640s, but opposed clergy rather than 'godly' laymen running church; he led the prosecution of and death-sentence for his old enemy Laud 1645. He backed a Presbyterian State church in the religio-political struggle with army in 1645–9 and was excluded and marginalised by Pride's Purge, opposing regicide and the new republic and arrested for agitation 1650. Backing a Presbyterian church in 1650s, he ended up facilitating royalists' and Anglican church's return in 1660 as less dangerous than rule by army and extreme sects, hating Quakers more than the king; he hoped for Presbyterian comprehension in a wide church but was disappointed of that too. Kept at arms' length by the Monck leadership as too inflammatory. He made up for his earlier anti-Stuart abuse and saved himself from royalist investigation by joining in abusive attacks on the arrested regicides 1660–1, and called for a harsh purge of the republicans and sects. Notorious for his intemperate pamphleteering and ability to make enemies, he ended up as keeper of the royal records in the Tower; he was throughout a principled but vitriolic loner.

Rich, Robert, earl of Warwick (1587–1658): veteran Presbyterian critic of Charles I in the 1630s, leader of Protestant colonial Caribbean 'Providence Island Company' project vs Spain, and urged French alliance on unimpressed king; backed 'godly' Covenanter cause in Scotland as allied to resisatnce to Laud in England, and threatened peers' mutiny vs king in wartime 1639–40 so regarded as treasonous; the 'eminence grise' of the Parliamentarian revolt against Charles in 1640–2, patron of Pym, and endeavoured to neuter monarchy; Parliamentarian Lord Admiral 1641–48, and major service in Channel e.g. relieving Lyme Regis 1644; part of navy mutinied for king 1648, and lost influence as Lords pushed aside by militant Independent MPs and NMA; sidelined thereafter; re-emerged in mid-1650s as ageing ally of Oliver Cromwell after a family marital alliance.

Robartes, John, 2nd Lord (1606–85): son of baronet/peer, rising Cornish family which acquired Lanhydrock House; son-in-law to and sympathiser of Parliamentarian leader Warwick; senior Cornish moderate Parliamentarian leader/Presbyterian, army officer 1642–5, especially in Essex's south-west strategy 1644; retired by Self-Denying Ordinance, avoided 1650s service, but re-emerged as Presbyterian monarchist ally of royalists in 1660; thence courtier and 1661–73 Lord Privy Seal, 1669–70

Lord Lieutenant of Ireland; criticised for poor administrative ability, e.g. by Pepys, sacked, but returned 1679–84 as lord president of council to combat Whigs.

Rupert, Prince, duke of Cumberland (1619–82): nephew to Charles I, dashing officer younger son of Charles I's sister Elizabeth Stuart, briefly Queen of Bohemia and nicknamed 'the Winter Queen'; trained in Thirty Years' War in anti-Habsburg armies, and from 1642 cavalry commander to king; led charge at Edgehill but criticised for heading off field to loot and leaving infantry exposed; similar complaints throughout war, and also of looting/brutality in sack of Parliamentary towns e.g. Birmingham and Leicester; known as 'Prince Robber'; capable strategist and led impressive northern campaign to rescue York 1644 but then lost at Marston Moor; led cavalry at Naseby 1645, then prudently surrendered Bristol to overwhelming New Model Army attack and was sacked by angry king; undermined by intrigue and allegations of defeatism (or facing reality?) 1644–6; cousin, senior adviser, and naval commander to Charles II, especially Mediterranean, Africa and West Indies 1649–51; sidelined to 1660, but then senior courtier, governor of Windsor Castle, colonial backer, and amateur scientist.

Scot, Thomas (c. 1616–1660): minor Buckinghamshire lawyer, and secretary to parliamentary county committee; MP Aylesbury 1646–53 and 1656–8, Wendover 1654–5 and 1659; leading critic of monarchy and organiser of regicide 1648–9, so targeted by royalists; republican regime's chief of intelligence and senior political/diplomatic adviser in 1659–60, rival to Thurloe; purged by Monck and executed by royalists 1660.

Sheldon, Gilbert (1598–1677); minor Staffordshire family, educated at Trinity College Oxford; fellow and (1636) warden of All Souls, Oxford; bishop of London 1660–3; archbishop of Canterbury 1663–77. Staunch Anglican disciplinarian, junior ally to Laud late 1630s, and chaplain to lord keeper Coventry from 1622, thence clerk of closet to king; in attendance on Charles in Oxford and in prison 1642–8, and close aide; helped to organise and keep up morale of excluded Anglican clergy in 1650s and emerged to help them regain property and full control of church at Restoration. Leader of the hardline Anglicans after the Restoration and probable chief organiser of the relatively intolerant Restoration religious settlement; assisted by and encouraged younger royalist Anglicans in Commons to force Clarendon Code penal measures on Clarendon.

St John, Oliver (1598?–1673): son of minor gentry of Cyshoe, Bedfordshire, but related to lords St John of Lydiard Tregoz; cousin and adviser to Cromwell, educated at Queen's College Cambridge and Lincoln's Inn; lawyer to reformist and anti-Laudian 4th earl of Bedford 1630s, and worked for opposition's Providence Island Company colonial venture which brought connection to future leader Pym; rose to prominence as defence counsel to John Hampden in the Ship Money case vs royal prerogative taxes 1637–8; leading reformist MP (Totnes 1640–53) in Commons 1640–2, led legal dismantling of royal powers, led move to abolish bishops, and as solicitor-general led prosecution of Strafford whose execution he encouraged; senior Parliamentarian civilian war-organiser in 1640s with ally Vane; helped to organise link to Scots Covenanters 1643 to win war, but also Commons leader of the pro-sectary Independents against threat of intolerant Presbyterian state church until 1648, probably sponsored Oliver Cromwell's rise in politics as their link to army; backed New Model Army in 1646–8 vs Presbyterians, but tried to secure a neutered monarchy and opposed and refused to take part in regicide; Chief Justice of Common Pleas 1648–60, and ambassador to Dutch 1651 to try to negotiate union of Protestant states; offered Cromwell some backstairs advice, and back on Rump committees 1659–60; successfully defended his 1640s conduct at Restoration, was judged harmless, and was left alone by royalists but in 1662 retired to Continent.

Sydenham, Colonel William (1615–61): son of minor Dorset gentry, capable Parliamentary officer in 1640s and 1644–5 governor of Weymouth; actions included taking of Wareham and Abbotsbury, then retaking of Weymouth; MP for Melcombe Regis (N part of Weymouth) 1645–53; social conservative, in favour of retaining Lords 1649 and state church 1653, but had religious scruples over taking oaths; council of state 1653 and moderate in Nominated Parliament, prominent in dissolution to thwart radicals; councillor to OC 1653–8, as ally of Lambert and Fleetwood, and as MP for Dorset 1654–5, 1656–8 opposed persecution of Quakers and stood up for traditional liberties; moderate in Lambert's regime 1659, on committee of safety and helped his alliance with civilian republicans; sacked and had regiment seized by restored Rump 1660, excluded from office at Restoration.

Thurloe, John (1616–68): self-made Cromwellian bureaucrat, son of Essex vicar. Lincoln's Inn lawyer, and secretary to parliamentary delegation at Uxbridge talks 1645 and to Cromwell's cousin Oliver St John, including on Dutch alliance mission 1651. Probably recommended by St John to cousin Cromwell; secretary of state 1652–9 and 1659–60; chief of intelligence (1653ff), spymaster, postmaster-general (1655 ff), effectively 'foreign secretary', and administrative lynchpin of the Protectorate in 1653–9; believed by his army critics to be the real strongman behind Richard Cromwell's regime; sidelined by New Model Army 1659 but re-emerged 1660 to assist Monck. Investigated for treason 1660 but pardoned, allegedly due to blackmailing Royalists over knowledge over who of them had earlier offered to help Cromwell in return for cash; lived in retirement and wrote advice for Hyde/Clarendon; his papers (hidden in his attic, found 1740s) are major source for 1650s.

Vane, Sir Henry the Younger (1613–62); son of the elder Sir Henry Vane, secretary of state to Charles I; Essex gentry. Educated at Westminster, where knew Thomas Scot (qv), and Magdalen Hall, Oxford; travelled widely on Continent, e.g. Switzerland, and as diplomat father's aide; strong anti-Laudian beliefs, and migrated to Massachusetts where he was colony's governor 1636–7; backed toleration for dissidents, e.g. Roger Williams and Anne Hutchinson, and defeated by Presbyterian centralisers led by Winthrops but on good personal terms with them; naval treasurer 1639–40 as father's protege, but turned against king; MP for Hull and Parliamentarian activist 1640–53, and critical of any power for any clergy; in 1641 used his father's papers to help bring about fall of hated minister Strafford. Leading organiser of his side's war effort and committee-man, opposed to compromises that helped royal powers or any disciplinarian state church; principled leader of the Independents in the Commons against the intolerant Presbyterian threat to sects in the 1640s, and as such had overtures from king; co-leader of the 'Committee of Both Kingdoms' 1645–8 but had doubts over religious coerciveness of Covenanter allies. Worked with Oliver Cromwell, and leading critic

List of Main Dramatis Personae xli

of Charles I as untrustworthy with early consideration of deposing him; backed New Model Army in 1647–9 after failed attempts to lure the king into pro-Independent deal, and reluctantly accepted regicide. One of the main figures of the Rump and Commonwealth in 1649–53 and Cromwell's main civilian ally, also chief organiser of Dutch War 1652–3, but believed in civilian supremacy over army; broke with Cromwell over his 'illegal' coup in 1653 and left politics, temporarily exiled to Isle of Wight 1656 over writings critical of Protectorate, and kept out of Commons; as a republican idealist and administrator important again in 1659–60 but resisted monarchy; left isolated at the Restoration and refused to flee; destroyed as a feared rival by Charles II, with dodgy legal proceedings and execution.

Villiers, George (1628–87), second duke of Buckingham (1628): son and heir of Charles I's murdered minister, the first duke; boyhood friend and senior courtier to Charles II, and leading aide in exile 1650s but maverick who returned home early to marry into General Fairfax's family; behind-the-scenes Royalist plotter and after 1660 trusted courtier and friend to king but limited political influence; foe of Clarendon and helped to ruin him 1667; one of the 'Cabal' 1667–72, but the influence his intrigues had on events exaggerated.

Whalley, Colonel Edward (1607?–c. 1675): cousin and aide to Oliver Cromwell, from minor Northamptonshire family; father was sheriff of county, but Whalley was woollen draper and farmer in 1630s and apparently fled debts to Scotland 1639; cornet of horse in Nathaniel Fiennes' brother's regiment 1642 (possibly due to Cromwell's friendship with Fiennes' father) and at Edgehill; later major in cavalry regiment, commended by him for service at Gainsborough battle 1643; Marston Moor 1644, then New Model Army officer and regimental commander under Cromwell at Naseby; moderate republican, friend of Cromwell and regicide 1649; at Dunbar 1650, and major-general in Midlands 1655–7; fled to North America as regicide 1660 with son-in-law Goffe, lived in Massachusetts and died in hiding from royalist hunters.

Whitelocke, Bulstrode (1605–75): Bucks gentry lawyer, educated Oxford and Middle Temple, bencher of latter; MP for Great Marlow

1640–53; helped prosecution of Strafford and other opposition bills to diminish royal powers 1641; senior moderate Parliamentarian in 1640s, on Buckinghamshire county committee, and ally of Holles in attempting Parliamentary approaches to King 1643–5; in abortive 1645 Uxbridge conference; backed NMA against Presbyterians in 1646–8; leading figure for moderation in Rump and advised his friend OC on form of government in favour of monarchy but did not get suggestion of under-age Prince Henry as new king accepted; chosen by OC as ambassador to Sweden 1653–4, and also trade and European diplomatic adviser to OC 1653–8, commissioner of great seal and treasury 1655–9; advised Richard Cromwell 1658–9, and kept on by republicans on committee of safety; opposed Monck, but favoured Restoration and not prosecuted but had to bribe vindictive Royalist enemies and was harassed and blackmailed, e.g. by Clarendon; his autobiographical writings are major source for 1650s history .

Wolseley, Sir Charles (1630–1714): young Staffordshire gentry in 1650s; a moderate Cromwellian who as MP helped to bring down the faction-ridden Nominated Parliament in 1653 and became councillor and behind-the-scenes adviser to Oliver Comrwell; marginalised in 1659 but survived to write in favour of constitutional government and religious toleration into the 1680s.

Wriothesley, Thomas, 4th earl of Southampton (1607–67); son of 3rd earl, ex-patron of Shakespeare, and owner of Titchfield Abbey (Charles I fled there in 1647) and Beaulieu estate; senior royalist courtier, formerly a moderate Parliamentarian in 1640s who tried to aid king/Parliament reconciliation 1646–8 and was involved in abortive peace settlement plans; Lord Treasurer 1660–7, competent but politically minor.

Restoration: The Return of the King

Introduction

The final outcome of the 'Wars of Three Kingdoms' (as the English Civil War of 1642–6 and its linked conflicts in Scotland and Ireland are now more often called) was unexpected to most participants and observers. The unprecedented victory of the Parliamentarian forces in England against the established order and a supposedly secure monarchy was the first time that a rebel grouping had triumphed against the English (and since 1603 now Anglo-Scots) monarchy on behalf of a politico-religious coalition rather than a pretender to the crown from within the elite, barring the temporary and soon reversed revolt of Simon de Montfort's reformist barons and clerics in 1264–5. This was aimed at a permanent reversal of the balance of power in state and church alike, with the monarchy – perceived by the Parliamentarians as untrustworthy, incompetent and dominated by sinister 'Papist' Catholic and autocratic forces – intended as of 1646 to be constrained by constitutional bonds into being a figurehead for a reformed regime. As Charles I complained, he was to be reduced to a puppet like the Doge of Venice, forced to rubber-stamp decisions by a hostile oligarchy and not allowed to choose his own ministers or the state's policies, the nature of the religious establishment and laws included. The various factions within the victorious New Model Army, civilian MPs (either in favour of a 'purified' and tightly-controlled Presbyterian state church or greater laxity for the many and mushrooming new Protestant sects), and 'reformist' pressure-groups such as the Levellers set out their rival solutions to the problem of 'What next?' for state and church in England in 1646–8. But a solution was delayed – and Parliament's Presbyterian Covenanter allies who ruled Scotland had possession of the fugitive king and were demanding a Presbyterian solution to England's religious problems too, plus a large payoff for their army. In Ireland, the hard-pressed pro-Scots Presbyterians in Ulster, the pro-Parliament regime in Dublin, and the Anglican and Catholic royalists in parts of south-central Ireland were all threatened by a triumphant and autonomist Catholic rebel regime based at Kilkenny – representing the majority of the population and prepared to do a deal with the king if he accepted their demands for virtual autonomy.

As a result a complex and unstable situation of intrigue, would-be deals, and multiple betrayals delayed any solution to the problems of the three kingdoms in 1646–8, and Charles – negotiating with all sides and offering mutually contradictory pledges to each – ultimately threw away the chance of an agreement with the militarily strongest and most coherent faction, the 'godly' ultra-Protestant leadership of the New Model Army under Sir Thomas Fairfax and his deputy Oliver Cromwell, for the desperate plan of a joint Scots invasion of England plus a royalist revolt there. Both failed miserably and the king, his reputation fatally damaged and regarded as the 'man of blood' who had inflicted a second civil war and more suffering on his hard-hit people, ended on the execution-block at Whitehall Palace on 30 January 1649 as a supposed traitor to his people. The Presbyterian majority of MPs, having attempted a last-minute deal with the king that saved both monarchy and a Presbyterian state church from the army radicals and their 'heretic' ultra-Protestant sects, had to be purged from Parliament by the military to achieve the Commons' legal backing for the effective coup. The monarchy and House of Lords were abolished, and from then on a purged House of Commons – known derisively as the Rump – governed in conjunction with the army and a military-civilian Council of State, with the new republic carefully not called this but known as the 'Commonwealth' to stress its traditional role as representing the said body, a term used for the people of England. Most of the new regime's non-army leadership had either backed the coup and regicide or reluctantly come to accept and serve the government as the de facto incumbent in the interests of political stability, but were reluctant revolutionaries (as compared to the leadership of the regicidal French and Russian revolutions) and were social if not religious conservatives – and they were deeply suspicious of rule by the military, the 'swordsmen'.

With Fairfax opposing a war with the Covenanter Scots – who were mostly opposed to regicide and duly invited the late king's son Charles II to rule their country provided that he acted as their docile figurehead – he resigned command and the more ruthless Cromwell, the deeply religious East Anglian self-made officer who had been the war's most effective general and had led the way in killing Charles I, took over command. Firstly the Irish Catholics and then the Scots were militarily crushed by the brutally effective New Model Army, and the plans of the 'rebel' regimes in both countries for autonomy (probably under a nominal Stuart monarch) from a centralising Parliamentarian government in London were ended; a first 'union' of the three states now took place as determined by armed force under the army leadership. But the tensions between soldiers and civilians in the new English regime and the lack of any long-term constitutional settlement made the faction-ridden Commonweath less successful at securing internal long-term stability than it had been in crushing royalists, Scots, and Irish and seeing off these opponents' former allies. The paradox of military success and political failure was to haunt and ultimately bring down the new republic, and many politically moderate legalists (and Presbyterian enemies of the sects and their vociferous army patrons) among the triumphant Parliamentarian coalition of 1642–6 would not take part in any regime that accepted the 'illegal' military coup of December 1648. This basic split was worsened when Cromwell, still head of the powerful army, whose garrisons across the country ate up taxes, meddled with local civilian authority, and inflamed provincial opinion among MPs' electors, lost patience with the dilatory Rump. Apparently fearing that it was intending to delay or fix a general election to preserve the privileges of its current membership, he evicted the Commons at gunpoint on 20 April 1653 – and earned the enmity of another large section of Commonwealth supporters as an illegal military dictator. From then on the question of how stability was to be restored long-term – and the accompanying one for civilians of reining in the expensive and disruptive army – became even more toxic, and Cromwell's own short-term solution of a reformist nominated Parliament of the 'godly', his own supporters as selected by him and his allies, was an equal failure. The so-called 'Barebones Parliament' (named by royalist pamphleteers after an emblematic fanatical and 'low-born' religious MP, London's 'Praise-God' Barbon) split up between moderates and radicals and ended in deadlock, with Cromwell and his associates – now dominated by the constitutional enthusiast General John Lambert – arranging the resignation of its authority to Cromwell on 10 December

1653. Collegiate rule by MPs having failed and the new British state seeming to be sunk in irreconcilable factional antagonism, the attractions of an appropriately 'godly' strongman beckoned as the way of securing stability, controlling the Army, and warding off a Royalist revanche. But the events of the next six-and-a-half years were to show that the new Protectorate was not secure, or at best was secure for only Cromwell's lifetime – and religious and political radicals who he had betrayed as well as Royalists – would be happy to assassinate him. The following study will seek to investigate what measures were taken or planned to achieve the elusive target of stability, how and why they failed, and how inevitable or not was the ultimate result of a Stuart restoration.

Prologue

December. 1653. The Protectorate: Britain's first written constitution. A monarchy in effect, but without a king.

Cromwell's shutting down the Commons at gunpoint in April 1653 left the army in unashamed control of England without an elected 'figleaf' and many civilian MPs out of politics. He assumed full power in his role as Lord General of the army and replaced the Commonwealth's executive, the Commons-nominated Council of State, with one nominated by the Army. He and his advisers then gave way to pressure from moralist Protestant sectaries (including military officers such as the millenarian General Thomas Harrison who believed in the immanent Second Coming of Jesus Christ) to avoid an immediate election but set up a new legislative body composed of their own nominees, 'godly' men who would supposedly put the needs of the 'Chosen People' (as zealots now saw the new union of England, Scotland and Ireland in 'Great Britain') first. So for the only time a form of theocracy was created in the British Isles with its rulers chosen for their religious and other virtues, as desired by Protestant radicals from the multitude of sects that had sprung up in the 1640s. These men – proponents of religious toleration (for Protestants not 'satanic' and 'Popish' Catholics) for the English Church instead of the previous rigidly disciplinarian Anglican regime or the equally exclusive Presbyterian one desired by many MPs – had seen the cause of Parliament as that of God and the cause of the King as that of the Antichrist in Rome, the Pope. They had rallied to and dominated the New Model Army and had then confronted and purged Parliament of Presbyterians in 1647–8 and forced the trial and execution of Charles I, the 'Man of Blood'. A monarchy was unacceptable to them as God had seemingly withdrawn His Favour from it by allowing the 'Divine Right' Stuarts to be overthrown, and some believed that in any case 'King Jesus' would soon be arriving as the recent chaos had been prophesied in the Bible and must be a sign of the 'Last Times'.

In summer 1653 a Nominated Parliament was set up, a mixture of politically and religiously moderate future Cromwellians and radical sectaries, some of them (but fewer than royalist critics alleged) fanatical millenarians such as the Fifth Monarchists who believed that the destruction of the Stuart regime and its Papist backers marked the arrival of the 'Last Times' before the 'Second Coming' of Jesus Christ. The Fourth Monarchy of Rome was being destroyed and the next, fifth monarchy would be that of Christ, which it was their duty to hasten – and the 'godly' Nominated Parliament was part of this work. In fact it contained many members of the usual political elite, among them county gentry and London lawyers and merchants, though only loyal supporters of the Commonwealth and men who were prepared to excuse the coup of 20 April 1653 were chosen and most were selected as reportedly devout non-Anglican Protestants who favoured religious toleration for the sects. Its lack of coherence and internal disputes turned into political deadlock over the questions of legal and church reform, and on 10 December 1653 it too was dissolved. But this was less dramatic or illegal than the way that Cromwell had marched into the Commons with a troop of soldiers in April to sack the Rump. This time a substantial faction of the more moderate MPs, led by the Speaker (the veteran Prebyterian theologian Francis Rous, 1640s Parliamentary leader John Pym's half-brother) marched from the Commons to Council of State to Cromwell's lodgings in Whitehall Palace to resign their authority to him, so it was not a coup.

Notably, most of the leadership of this group were also members of the government's executive wing, the Council of State, and were to keep their seats in the new Council chosen shortly by Cromwell and his allies, and did not share the millenarian religious enthusiasm of the Parliament's more religiously radical members; they can thus be categorised as a Cromwellian faction within the Parliament. The figure who had made the opening and most important speech in favour of dissolving Parliament shortly before was indeed a very young and inexperienced MP, the Staffordshire landowner Sir Charles Wolseley (aged twenty-three), who was shortly to emerge as a personal favourite and trusted supporter of Cromwell on the new Council. He was not even a former soldier or long-serving politician in the 1640s Parliamentary cause, and served as a symbol of a new generation emerging into politics who looked to a just but not radically religious (or republican) regime that would deliver stability – though he was backed up by senior New Model Army veterans like Cromwell's brother-in-law General John Desborough. Wolseley would be arguing in favour of a politically moderate monarchical regime delivering religious toleration as late as the 1689 Glorious Revolution, and his allies on this occasion also included the future founder of the Whig party and minister, then opponent of Charles II, Anthony Ashley Cooper (later earl of Shaftesbury), a moderate reformist Cromwellian who had fought for both the king and later Parliament in the Civil War. Many of those more radical MPs who had been pressing for further reform (e.g. of the cumbersome English legal procedures and of the hotly contentious payment of tithes to a state church) had not been consulted, were opposed to the sudden dissolution of Parliament, and denounced it as a deliberate attempt to halt reform. This was particularly true of the group of zealots known as the 'Fifth Monarchy Men', led by Cromwell's army colleague General Thomas Harrison, who believed that the overthrow of firstly the sinful and 'Popish' Stuarts and then of the corrupt and unholy Rump presaged the way to establishing the 'Rule of the Saints' – which the Nominated Parliament was designed to further. The Fourth Monarchy of the Catholic church in Rome (as continuing the Roman Empire) would soon be superseded by the Second Coming of Jesus Christ (to be assisted by them as the 'Elect'). To these religious enthusiasts the selection of MPs for this assembly by the army and local Protestant religious congregations by nomination on merit, not by election, was part of its intended role to provide 'godly rule' by the morally upright, and its frustration was a defeat for the holy cause – a defeat arranged by their ungodly enemies. This could turn worrying if their supporters in the army, a disparate group of religious enthusiasts not all amenable to strict military hierarchy, chose to challenge the action – and more secular and democratic political reformers such as the Leveller movement still had supporters in the army too despite a purge in 1649. The removal of a second Parliament in eight months thus seemed to illustrate and add to the endemic instability of the British political scene since the end of the Civil War in 1646 – a problem that Cromwell was continuingly attempting to resolve by increasing authoritarianism but which would continue on some level until the legitimate Stuart dynasty was restored.

1 The Fall of Cromwell's Republic and the Return of the King

The power vacuum of December 1653 left Cromwell, the 'Lord General' of the New Model Army who had summoned Parliament, and the Council of State which he and the Army had set up that spring, as the sole effective authority. Both were strictly speaking illegal, Cromwell having evicted the remnants of the legitimate Long Parliament at gunpoint on 20 April 1653 – an act for which assorted civilian MPs in the latter never forgave him. This in itself put a block on him being able to use such senior fellow-republicans as Sir Henry Vane and Sir Arthur Haselrig, fellow-veteran radicals of the 1640s, in any government of his thereafter and so reduced the options open to him. The loss of Vane, a leader of the pro-toleration 'Independent' faction in Parliament against the threat of a disciplinarian Presbyterian state church in the mid-1640s and a skilled administrator of the navy in the current Dutch War, was specially damaging. Cromwell had not helped his cause by abusing Vane, a long-term previous ally, in person as he dismissed the Commons on 20 April 1653 – although it is probable that he was under a misapprehension about the MPs trying to prolong their sitting and delay an election to protect their positions. Religious radicals' hopes and religious and political moderates' fears of what the Nominated Parliament with its bloc of 'godly' millenarians would do had proved exaggerated, although it has always had a bad press as a den of idealistic incompetents and at the time its plethora of lowly-born personnel from outside the normal social elite did not help. The moderate leadership in this institution (including future Cromwellian stalwarts Francis Rous, its Speaker, and young Sir Charles Wolseley) had kept a grip on procedure, preventing some controversial reforms and thwarting the sectaries, and finally handed power back to Cromwell sending a signed document of resignation to him on 12 December. The group who did this (a majority of MPs, perhaps two-thirds of them, but not all) were led by future Cromwellians – and former royalist officer Anthony Ashley Cooper, later the radical Whig leader in the late 1670s.[1] Almost all would end up on the Protectorate's new Council of State, and Cooper (later earl of Shaftesbury) and diarist Samuel Pepys' cousin and patron Edward Mountague (later earl of Sandwich and naval commander-in-chief to his death in action in 1672) would go on to serve Charles II. This represented the final exclusion from power of assorted sects who had hoped the Parliament would open the way to the rule of the 'godly', led by the Fifth Monarchists under General Harrison. The latter was the man who had collected Charles I from Hurst Castle on the Solent on behalf of the military leadership and taken him to London for his trial and execution, with the late king fearing that his arch-foe intended to murder him en route – and at his trial for regicide in 1660 he would boast that the officers had put the king to death by an open legal process as a tyrant.

Setting up a 'godly' House of Commons of MPs chosen by the army leadership and friendly clergymen had proved a disaster, although lurid (mainly royalist) stories about it being a hotbed of low-born religious fanatics seem to have been exaggerated and a solid body of future Cromwellians sat in it. More to the point, it had ended up deadlocked concerning reform, e.g. of payment of tithes to the church, despite a few solid achievements (eg instituting civil marriages and requiring the law to be interpreted in English not Latin in court).[2] Now the circle of military and civilian advisers around Cromwell sought to restore stability with a mixed constitution that balanced executive and legislature. There would be no king, but there would be a long-term 'Single Person' as Head of State – Cromwell, who would guarantee the army's role in and loyalty to the new regime. The idea of having a single person as lynchpin of the new regime for stability, a government with 'something of the monarchical in it', had already been discussed by Cromwell and his senior allies around 1652 according to the memoirs of the conservative lawyer Bustrode Whitelocke. The new constitution, the 'Instrument of Government', was presented to an assembly of army officers in the Council Chamber at Whitehall by Lambert on 13 December, as recalled later by radical republican General Edmund Ludlow. Lambert, a political moderate but a firm Protestant sectary (i.e. opponent of a state church, Anglican or Presbyterian), had been the dashing young second-in-command to Cromwell in the 1648–51 campaigns, assisting in his victories at Preston, Dunbar, and Worcester, and was apparently the main author of the constitution. Indeed, he had been planning it before the recent Parliament was dismissed. Unlike Cromwell, a master of vague and grandiloquent rhetoric and not that strong on detail, he was a master of organization and was to take the pragmatic attitude in forthcoming foreign policy of ignoring the temptation to attack and loot the rich and Papist Spanish empire. (Cromwell ignored him.) According to royalist gossip in 1653 he was the 'coming man', and as he was twenty years younger than

Cromwell he should outlive – and even succeed? – him. He did not allow any amendments to the constitution to be discussed. He also had the document of abdication by the majority of the Nominated Parliament, evidently given to him by Cromwell – and the new arrangements were read out as a 'given' not a draft.³ He had arrived in London from his regional command on 19 November, so the discussions had probably begun seriously then; and so had rumours about a change in constitution, some of them that Cromwell would be made king.⁴ Possibly that idea, which would add to stability as following legal precedent, was 'leaked' to see the reaction and dropped as it was too controversial. According to what Cromwell told his first Parliament a couple of months later, he had not been privy to their discussions but had been warned that if a new and stable constitution could not be created, 'blood and confusion' would follow.⁵ Cromwell was to claim in 1657 that seven of the constitution's framers had brought him the original Instrument of Government 'with the name of King in it' but he had firmly refused to take the crown⁶ – Lambert would presumably have been one of the seven and logically their leader. Also, the contemporary collections of State Papers include a collection of the warrants and other legal orders made by Charles I which was apparently brought together for consultation by some figures in government – suggesting that the practicalities of how Cromwell could govern as king were being discussed.⁷ One of the more radical officers recalled in a pamphlet of autumn 1655 that at this time the officers had been called to Whitehall and kept waiting while their seniors were engaged in some sort of argument. At the end of this Lambert had come out and told them to go home as they were not now needed – had he been trying to persuade Cromwell to take the crown, and had Cromwell agreed were the officers to have been told this?⁸ The revised Instrument however did not have the royal title, merely the powers of a regulated chief executive at the head of a Council and a Parliament similar to the pre-1649 plans for a reformed monarchy by the army 'Grandees' that Charles I had evaded in their autumn 1647 discussions at Hampton Court Palace. Cromwell then consulted the officers informally at his Cockpit lodgings on the west side of Whitehall (on the site of modern Downing Street), and on the 16th he was escorted by a mixed military, legal, and City dignitaries' procession to Westminster Hall for his inauguration.

The result of the ceremony was supposed to have been a surprise to many who attended it, though this may be hearsay or republican/royalist propaganda. Once he had signed his assent to an oath of office promising to obey the laws he seated himself on a chair of state. This took place in the Court of Chancery, one of the law-courts based in the Hall; the Commissioners and senior judges stood closest to him, with the Council and senior army officers to his right and the Lord Mayor and leading aldermen to his left. Lambert presented him with a new sword to replace his current one, and buckled it on for him; it symbolised the replacement of his 'military' power with 'civil' one, though he continued his military office as Lord General and Lambert had no formal position or legal powers to act thus. The Lord Mayor then presented Cromwell with the City's sword of state and cap of maintenance, and received them back. The participants then journeyed by coach to Whitehall for a banquet.[9]

The possible models for the ceremony were the legal assumptions of power by two Yorkist sovereigns when their predecessors had been alive – Edward IV in March 1461 and Richard III 1483 in June. Both had also taken power by a civil ceremony and sat in the king's seat in the Court of King's Bench in Westminster Hall, but there had been no oath-taking.[10] (The insertion of oaths probably reflected the new regime's need to have a legal fallback to prosecute any participant who subsequently undermined the new Protector.) Richard had also been Lord Protector beforehand, by the term of his late brother Edward IV's will; the term was that of a regent with the full legal powers of a sovereign, acting during a minority, as with Richard in April-June 1483 for Edward V and the Duke of Somerset for Edward VI in 1547–9. The question of whether a Protector had the power to over-ride his Council in a regency government was more contentious, and it appears that early drafts of the new constitution and a rumour which reached French ambassador Bordeaux spoke of Cromwell as Lord Governor, not Protector. As far as Parliaments went, the 1641 Triennial Act was upheld in that Parliament was to meet every three years – and, crucially, if the Protector did not summon it measures were put in place to do so. (The more radical calls for a biennial Parliament in 1647–8 were ignored.) There were to be 400 MPs, with some redistribution of seats (reducing the amount of 'rotten' borough seats from about four-fifths in 1640 to a third), as proposed in the 'Heads of the Proposals' in 1647 but with less extensive revision than that had wanted. The first Union

Parliament also encompassed thirty Scottish and thirty Irish MPs. The franchise was set at property valued at £200 in land or moveable goods; thus the perceived problems over the franchise limits for freeholders were removed. Royalists and all others charged with disaffection to the post-1642 government were to be banned from voting for three Parliaments (nine years) unless they had given signal signs of assisting the government in the past five years, and Catholics and 1641 Irish rebels were banned permanently. This was designed to save the government from being swamped or undermined by hostile MPs elected by a groundswell of county royalism – a realistic prospect given the way the king's party had made the most of a national mood of discontent with arbitrary rule in 1648 and one which became a reality in the Cavalier Parliament of 1661. The events of 1661, when a militantly Royalist Parliament overturned its predecessor's moderate measures, indeed show the political wisdom of such a ban – at least at this stage of the new regime. Banning all rebels included those English Presbyterians who had joined up with the royalists in 1648, and the Scottish 'Engagers' and Kirk Presbyterian 'Covenanters' who had backed the royalists in 1648 and 1650–1.

The armed forces were to be set at 20,000 foot and 10,000 cavalry – about half the size of the present body, implying either that the constitution's framers feared that keeping the current size of army was unpalatable to the public or that they hoped to reduce it once the Royalist/Scots and overseas threats were reduced. The size of the navy was not specified; in any case the latter was at present occupied by the current commercial war with the Dutch mercantile oligarchy and peace was still uncertain with the Dutch – or with France, which was suspected of backing Charles II's invasion and was where he had taken refuge (his mother Henrietta Maria was the under-age King Louis XIV's aunt). As far as the issue of state religion, the stumbling-block of the Nominated Parliament, went, freedom of worship for all except Catholics and followers of prelacy (i.e. Anglicans) was to be allowed but private Anglican services were not banned by law (unlike the Catholic mass) so were not likely to be interfered with. This freedom of worship was subject to the caveats of causing public disorder or licentiousness, both of which were liable to interpretation by the local magistracy but could target the more extreme sectaries; large gatherings of peaceful worshippers or inflammatory or lewd preaching could be prosecuted by JPs or invaded by soldiers if they saw fit to interpret the law in that fashion. The formal proclamation of Cromwell as Protector was made on Monday 18 December in the City – and that at Temple Bar by a military herald was disrupted by a scornful onlooker who responded to being struck for heckling by pulling him off his horse.[11] Nobody intervened.

The only open challenge came, predictably, from the outraged Fifth Monarchists – though not yet from General Harrison. Radical preachers Abraham Feake and Vavasour Powell abused Cromwell's alleged usurpation with reference to Old Testament prophecy at the Sunday service at Christ Church, Newgate (Feake's parish) on 18 December, implying that he was the beast with the 'little horn' mentioned in the Book of Daniel who would make war on the 'Saints'. He was called 'the most dissemblingest perjured villain in the world', a line of attack showing disappointment and fury at his treachery to their cause. He was supposed to be the low-born usurper in Daniel, Chapter XI, who would come to power peaceably by flattery and not take the royal title. Next day at the regular Blackfriars prayer-meeting Powell asked the congregation to pray for guidance whether they would rather have Jesus Christ or Cromwell to reign over them.[12] (The implication was to give any rebellion Biblical sanction, and it thus amounted to incitement to commit treason.) Both were briefly imprisoned and told to cease offending, and the meetings were banned; Powell later escaped to Wales to preach sedition more safely but late in January Feake and his ally John Simpson were imprisoned at Windsor Castle for more offences. Their Army patron Harrison was summoned before the Council on 21 December, asked if he was prepared to serve the new regime, and on his refusal deprived of his commission.[13] An equally dangerous opponent of the new government from a diametrically opposed, secular standpoint was John Lilburne, still in custody in the Tower since August. In a blatant legal manoeuvre to put him beyond the writ of the law and either trial or release, he was removed to Jersey by executive order of the Council in March 1654 and locked up in Mount Orgeuil Castle. Unlike when he was in London's prisons, the distance from his cell to his supporters should mean that it was difficult for him to communicate with them – or to publish new treatises asking awkward questions about the legality of the Protectorate. Nor was Jersey subject to English law, so he could not appeal for his release on the basis of habeas corpus; an imprisoned seditious pamphleteer from 1653,

Captain Streeter, had been freed on 11 February 1654 on a similar appeal on the grounds that the Parliament which had charged him was no longer sitting. Jersey now became a Cromwellian Guantanamo Bay.

The new constitution installed a stronger executive with Cromwell as a constitutional monarch, using the venerable title of the nation's interim guardian – Protector during a royal minority – for his new office. The name was probably a compromise forced on Lambert's group due to Cromwell's refusal to become king, and suggests someone with a knowledge of legal precedent choosing a past office with semi-monarchical powers. A main argument for monarchy had been – and was to be again in 1656–7 – that people could be sure that they were safe from legal challenges if they carried out actions in the name of a legal authority; a 'Protector' was a historical office unlike a 'Lord General' or a 'Nominated Parliament'. It was a return to relative normality and orderliness after the chaotic experiments and weak central government of 1649–53. But returning to the normal procedures of election for the new Commons in late summer 1654 brought back social and religious conservatives determined to reassert the Commons' power, including Presbyterians still brooding over the army's veto on their own desired politico-religious settlement in 1647–8. The safeguard against this was that the Council could veto the public's choice of MPs, as they did extensively in 1656 – a safeguard against a hostile Parliament found nowadays only in Iran.

Hopes of 'healing and settling' were expressed by Cromwell in his usual rambling inaugural speeches to MPs – undoubtably genuine but naïve about the MPs' priorities. But the latter were determined to assert their superiority over his office, not least to repay him for the April 1653 coup; the unelected swordsmen in the army should not dominate the legislature. For men like veteran 1640s Presbyterian leader Sir Arthur Haselrig, purged by the army in 1648 and deeply hostile to Cromwell for dissolving the previous legal Parliament by force, the assembly of a proper Commons later in 1654 was an opportunity to claw back the influence of elected MPs, and make the swordsmen concede the supremacy of the elected assembly. Thus when the first Protectorate Parliament met, Haselrig's main concern was to establish the supremacy of the legislature over the executive and thus call the details (or ultimately the entire structure?) of the Instrument of Government into question. In seeking to gain moderate Prebyterian MPs' support he shamelessly abandoned his usually more tolerant attitude to the sects by proposing a structured national state church and a ban on the sects on 5 September,[14] and the government had to concede a detailed discussion on the Instrument to stop the Commons proceeding with this. The House then voted to have a detailed examination of the Instrument by a full 'Committee of the Whole House', and sought new wording for the constitution to establish power in the lands of themselves alone.[15] The Protector was thus to be the servant not the master of the House, and legal expert Matthew Hale proposed that it be written into the constitution that the House should be able to alter the Single Person's powers as it thought fit.[16] Others spoke of the Councillors being liable to re-election every three years, or of the Commons not the Protector controlling the army. Cromwell failed to convince many MPs in his subsequent appeal in one of his rambling and evasive addresses on 12 September, in which he alleged that his new constitution had been backed by the army across the three nations and they should accept him as the necessary bastion against anarchy, not quibble over minor details. However, his proposal for an oath of 'Recognition' by MPs, accepting that the government should be in the hands of a 'Single Person' and the Commons was accepted by the vast majority of MPs and smoked out the republican minority.[17] Haselrig and his ally John Bradshaw, former President of the regicide court in January 1649, could not accept it and left Westminster. With the moderates in the ascendant Parliament proceeded to debate their degree of control over the executive, and agreed that they would need to approve all new Councillors of State after appointment but rejected a more restrictive proposal to draw up the list of nominees from whom the Protector would select Councillors.[18] Lambert's attempt to have the Protectorate made hereditary was rejected; it would be elective and thus preserve civilian, legislative control.[19] A final attempt was to be made to set up a Cromwellian monarchy by ex-royalist MP Augustine Garland in December, backed by councillor Cooper and Cromwell's second son Henry Cromwell, but it was abandoned without a vote – a sign of lack of support.[20] But MPs' determination to assert their control over the Army, either by becoming their legal master or by disbanding the standing army altogether and reviving the national miltia, was a more serious threat. In addition to that, republican discontent rumbled on in the army and in October the 'Three Colonels' (radicals Saunders, Okey and Alured) set up a petition for a free Parliament (and no Protector) that led to them being cashiered by Cromwell.[21] The dissident colonels were also linked to MP Colonel John Birch, whose Commons committee on the proposed revenue for the Protectoral government struck a major blow to it by proposing a lower than expected Parliamentary financial grant (£1,210,000) on 5 January 1654. This would require the disbandment of some 27,000 soldiers (about half the army) and the current non-Channel fleet, plus reducing the remaining soldiers' pay, and was unacceptable to Cromwell – and they wanted to be able to decide on religious toleration themselves.[22] Cromwell duly dissolved Parliament without any settlement of the constitutional questions on 22 January 1655.

The republicans who were not admitted to or left Parliament and the moderates who stayed to argue after October 1654 had inherited the antagonism of the Presbyterian civilian MPs in 1647–8 to being told what to do by the 'illegal' and intimidatory army, and after the April 1653 coup were determined to assert the legal authority of the civilian legislature over the army-appointed chief executive. However, they showed similar short-sightedness to the junto of Cromwell's senior officers, led by Charles Fleetwood (his Baptist son-in-law), John Desborough (his brother-in-law), and Lambert, in summer 1659 so it was not merely a case of personal hostility to Cromwell for his military coup. The battles of 1647–8 were fought out again by civilian MPs obsessed by their past defeats and determined to reassert the dominance of civil over military authority. The hostility between Protector and MPs was inevitable but was not sufficient to challenge the functioning of the constitution, and in practice the regime was more autocratic than it was supposed to be according to the 'Instrument' where the Council functioned as the executive/legislature in the intervals between Parliamentary sessions. It was a hopeful sign that the judiciary rallied to the new regime despite the technical illegitimacy of its creation, and that Matthew Hale – head of the eponymous commission to reform the law in 1653 – agreed to serve as a senior judge in January provided that he did not have to try political cases. The potentially hostile Commissioners ruling Ireland (nominees of the Rump, in 1650, not Cromwell), men like Colonel John Jones, who mostly also had noted religious zealotry, accepted the new regime and swore the necessary oath to it, with the exception of the secular republican Edmund Ludlow. Taking no chances, Cromwell sent his second but most politically able son, Henry, to Dublin to keep an eye on them and the mainly 'Baptist' so potentially ideologically unsympathetic military officers serving the commander-in-chief, his son-in-law Fleetwood. Ludlow was potentially dangerous as a noted war hero of the 1640s with appeal to the English army plus principled objections to the notion of a regime appointed by the military, of which he openly informed Henry Cromwell; he pointed out the problem that the Protectorate might behave like a moderate civilian government but really relied on armed force. When he returned to England in autumn 1654 he was immediately arrested on suspicion of conspiracy but managed to talk his way out of prolonged detention in a meeting with Cromwell. It is one of the 'what ifs' of the narrow-based Protectorate that he, like Sir Henry Vane, was as hostile to Harrison and the 'Saints' as any Cromwellian pragmatist but refused to take part in the new government.

Section One

The Finale and Fall of the Protectorate

Chapter One

A Monarchy Without a King. Stability Thwarted or Cromwell Loses his Nerve? The Offer of the Crown, 1657

(i) A 'moderate' civilian Cromwellian plan for future stability for decades to come? The run-up to the offers.

Leading pro-regime figures revived the idea of Cromwell as king in 1656–7 as an answer to the problems of constitutional deadlock and a force for stability after the closure of Cromwell's first Parliament (which had been seeking to constrain the executive by vetoing its finances and personnel) and the failure of the Protector's next drastic expedient – military rule by provincial 'Major-Generals'. The first of these experiments had foundered on the obsession of a body of MPs with reasserting the supremacy of the legislature, i.e. themselves, and thus of the elected representatives of the people over the Protector and his Council – not least by controlling the membership of the Council and the financing of the army. Their demands to cut the size of the army – which was risky at a time of continued threats of royalist revolt and invasion – and to control the local militia reflected a continuing struggle by MPs to curb an untrustworthy executive authority that had begun under Charles I in 1640–2, but had been given added impetus by the army evicting part of the Commons in December 1648 ('Pride's Purge') and the remainder of it in April 1653. But Cromwell did not trust the Commons enough to be prepared to submit to its authority, not least given Presbyterian MPs' past attempts to curb religious toleration, and ended up dismissing the obstreperous Parliament just as Charles had done in 1629.

He then resorted to a form of martial law in the aftermath of the royalist 'Penruddock Rebellion' of March 1655, dividing the country up among regional military commands headed by a network of senior Army officers, the Major-Generals. The low social origins, religious fanaticism, and administrative excesses committed by the latter have been exaggerated, as they included the politically moderate creator of the semi-monarchical constitution of December 1653, John Lambert, and the aristocratic Charles Howard (later Earl of Carlisle) as well as self-made lower-class religious zealots such as James Berry, Hezekiah Haynes, and John Barkstead. It is argued by Christopher Durston that the notion of their appointment as a sudden, drastic, alien, and aggressively militaristic and 'godly' layer of government has been overstated, and the newness of their role and the extent of resentment at it by bullied local gentry JPs has also come under question – there had been politically active military garrisons across the country intruding in local governance since 1646. But they undeniably affronted some provincial elites by their high-handed interference in local affairs (especially religion) and in most cases had few local connections and not much tact. They were a political blunder of the first order when it came to securing compliant MPs from the regions in 1656–7, however useful they were in terms of security, efficiency and 'getting things done'. The county gentry who had seen their usual roles usurped by these London-nominated military governors, men nicknamed the 'bashaws' after Turkish military governors by the Royalists, would now have to elect MPs for the next Parliament and so could not be expected to be sympathetic to the government that had imposed these men on them. As in his forcible dissolution of the elected Commons in April 1653, Cromwell had taken the line favoured by his most arbitrary and politically naïve followers, mostly in the army, not that of civilian Councillors, and stated that he acted partly out of religious reasons – the 1655 rebellion seemed to indicate a degree of divine disapproval for his regime so was this for their lack of godly zeal and reforms of immorality? But he had the excuse of needing reliable military men in control of the provinces to deal with widespread royalist conspiracy after the spring 1655 'Penruddock rebellion'. The military experiment thus had advantages for his formidably efficient security chief, head of intelligence and Council secretary John Thurloe – the man who would in 1658–9 back a civilian regime against the Cromwellian generals. Lambert, creator of the semi-monarchical 'Instrument of Government' with its chief executive acting as a constitutional monarch, was also involved with the Major-Generals despite his political conservatism and clearly put security above widening the regime's support. But the plan was only a 'stop-gap', and in autumn

1656 Cromwell was moving back towards ruling with Parliament though his position as an 'illegal' and arbitrary military dictator (as seen by his many enemies and played up by royalist propaganda) had been cemented rather than allayed by his recent actions.[1]

The new Parliament of September 1656 had to deal with the same problems of long-term instability as the old one, though it had fewer critics of the Protectorate within its ranks than the 1654–5 legislature due to the exclusion of so many MPs. Indeed, the recent experience of direct military rule by interfering and often religiously zealous or shamelessly authoritarian Major-Generals had put the country in a ferment during the elections. Those new MPs who were allowed to take their seats excluded those who were suspected of wishing to overthrow the executive arm of the government, but they were still affected by their own and their electors' adverse experience of military rule. The very notion of subjecting the provinces to close supervision and direction from London was offensive to the county gentry who made up the bedrock of MPs, and the best safeguard against such an experiment being repeated was to make the regime more traditional and politically secure. The key to this would be to revive hereditary rule, the ultimate guarantee of legitimate – and permanent – government and security from future chaos. This however posed a dilemma – was it to be a hereditary Protectorate, continuing the existing regime under its current non-royal chief executive, or a restoration of the monarchy per se but with the 'sinful' Stuarts excluded? The latter would arguably prevent fears of revenge by the royalists once their candidate Charles II was back on the throne and so secure the present elite free from reprisal, and also reassure those (mainly 'godly' army men) who felt that the Stuarts had been defeated in war and deprived of power thanks to their sins and any move to restore them would cause God's wrath. This was arguably Cromwell's own view. But had God decided against monarchy as well as the Stuarts by allowing the regicide and abolition of the monarchy to go ahead, had the Parliamentarians won by defeating monarchy as an institution as well as the Stuarts as its current holders, and so was monarchy to be avoided as sinful? Recent research has indicated a divergence between those Cromwellians who preferred a hereditary chief magistracy without the name of 'King' – including some of the senior 'godly' generals around Cromwell – and those, mainly civilians, who had no objection to the rank of king as such.[2] The idea that the plan to restore a monarchy grew out of initial Commons moves for a hereditary, non-monarchic chief magistracy in autumn 1656 was first suggested by Sir Charles Firth in 1909, but has recently been investigated in detail. John Morrill argues that the silence of various leading Cromwellians in autumn 1656 and early 1657 about restoring kingship (as opposed to creating a hereditary Protectorship) indicates how contentious the first of these options was, and probably the opposition of the great generals around Cromwell such as Desborough to it. Jonathan Fitzgibbons has investigated the moves towards firstly hereditary chief magistracy and then monarchy in the Commons in 1656–7 in detail, and argues that Cromwell was deeply uneasy about monarchy (under that specific name) throughout, partly from belief that God had showed His disfavour towards it in 1649 and partly out of a need to bring his senior officers with him to support and back up any long-term settlement.[3] Certain notedly radical senior officers, such as Major-General John Berry, were openly antagonistic to monarchy and argued this point with its backers.[4] Notably, when a delegation of MPs first raised the issue of any hereditary ruler (under whatever name) as a guarantor of long-term stability with Cromwell on 27 November 1656 he was unenthusiastic and ordered them not to go on with it, according to what Venetian ambassador Giavarina heard.[5] The move to debate the notion of a hereditary ruler also followed a successful Bill (26 September) by Cromwell's young confidante Sir Charles Wolseley to make it explicitly treason to try to overthrow or kill the Protector, extending the normal legal rights of a king to him – but it is unclear if this was a deliberate preliminary to the 'monarchy' plan or an attempt to put the Protectorhip on the same legal plane as the monarchy so there would be no need for the latter. And was Cromwell or his spymaster and diplomatic expert John Thurloe lurking behind Wolseley's move, anxious to 'test the waters' and see the reaction of MPs or the generals to it? It appears from a complaint by Colonel Fitzjames, reported by this Parliament's diarist Thomas Burton at this point, that he and other influential radical officers both opposed a hereditary role for the Protectorship and blamed MPs for this plan.[6]

The Commons' success in depriving the contentious major-generals of funding, via the Militia Bill, then revived their confidence to ignore military pressure in January 1657 – after the reminder of Cromwell's mortality and the lack of a successor in the Miles Sindercombe assassination plot. The first motion to this end was tabled in the Commons by John Ashe MP, directly after a vote of thanks for Cromwell's preservation from assassination – as if taking advantage of MPs' anxieties over how near they had been to leaderless chaos. It has been suggested that either Cromwell or Thurloe (or both) played up the danger of this plot and of an invasion by Charles II to scare MPs and generals in to backing a hereditary Protectorate or the idea of 'King Oliver'. Conversely the enthusiasm of generals like Desborough for continuing with the major-generals may have been due to a desire to persuade Cromwell that this tier of 'police state' government could secure long-term stability without any need to appease pro-monarchic county gentry and lawyers in Parliament – and if so the Militia Bill's defeat scuppered this by cutting off the funds needed for it. Patrick Little thinks that Thurloe was behind this.[7]

There was certainly renewed determination for hereditary rule from conservative pro-government figures like senior lawyer Bulstrode Whitelocke; this moderate civilian lawyer had also been consulted about an abortive idea to make the late king's youngest son Prince Henry the new king.[8] In July 1656, before Parliament met, he told Swedish ambassador Count Bonde that he favoured it and Bonde expected the new Parliament to offer Cromwell the crown.[9] Lambert told Bonde in August that most of the nobility now desired this outcome (but did not reveal his own opinion), and in September the pro-regime poet Edmund Waller hailed the fleet's success in ransacking the Spanish 'Plate Fleet' with the significant lines:

> Let the rich ore forthwith be melted down,
> And the state fixed by making him a crown;
> With ermine clad, and purple, let him hold
> A royal sceptre, made of Spanish gold.[10]

As a nominally Parliamentarian MP but in favour of saving the monarchy's powers and halting a ruinous civil war, Waller had risked his life (or played the traitor to his cause, as hardliners would see it) in a 'Peace Party' plot named after him in early 1644. He was accused of time-serving by both sides in the 1640s, and this embarrassing call for Cromwell to become king was to be excised from post-1660 editions of his works – but it indicated which way he thought the wind was blowing.

There was also a legal argument why royalists should back the move, as French ambassador Antoine de Bordeaux recognised; if a monarchy was restored it would make it easier to later replace the House of Cromwell by that of Stuart.[11] Another argument was put forward by the moderate Irish Cromwellian peer Lord Broghill, head of a ruthlessly assertive family of Anglo-Irish 'new men' and president of the ruling council in Munster (and brother of the future scientist Robert Boyle). An Act of 1495 created by 'usurper' Henry VII, who had seized power by killing the reigning king like Cromwell had done, had established a legal defence for those who had served his overthrown predecessor Richard III, by legalizing actions carried out under a crowned king even if this man was removed.[12] This had then protected Richard's servants from prosecution by his successor – so as this act was still in force it could protect a 'King' Oliver and his officials from abuses of power during the Civil Wars, or even regicide, by a restored Stuart monarchy. This could sway some Cromwellian moderates to back a monarchy, to protect their future positions. The implication for political reality as seen by 'moderate' royalists in 1657 would also be for an elected King – with Cromwell's death leading to Charles II being elected to succeed him. (Did this argument also appeal to certain anti-military Councillors as a way of preserving stability in future decades, or were they not looking so far ahead?) The task of outfacing the 'Commonwealthsmen' republicans would fall on the Cromwellian monarchists, making the pro-Stuart faction's task easier; their desired form of regime would be put in place and only the person in charge would need to be altered. That had been done before, several times in the struggles between York and Lancaster in the period 1460–85; and indeed there had been rumours in 1641–4 that moderate Parliamentarian nobles from the 'Bedford group' and later moderate Royalists had considered deposing Charles I for his nephew the Elector Palatine's benefit. The main survivor of this group still connected to Cromwell in 1657 was the Earl of Warwick, Parliamentary admiral in 1642–8 and head of the so-called Junto of Calvinist peers who had sought to turn Charles I into a powerless constitutional monarch in 1640–2; his grandson married into Cromwell's family. It would thus seem logical – though unproven – that cautious civilian Councillors were looking to protect their position from potential treason charges as 'agents of the regicide dictator' should

Charles II eventually return to power after Cromwell's death; they could claim legal immunity as serving a legally legitimate king.

Open royalists, as identifiable by their conduct in 1642–8, were banned from standing for Parliament in 1656 as in 1654, but this did not exclude those of passive sympathies for a monarchy – or those Presbyterians who had fought against the king in 1642–6 and not risen on his behalf in 1648. There were also younger scions of old royalist families, men who were likely to be embittered against the army by the imposition of the 'Decimation Tax' on their families in 1655. As in the provincial backlash in the monarchy's favour in 1647–8, unwelcome experience of fiscally and administratively oppressive central government in 1655–6 led to a rise in sympathy for the old order. The many cries at the hustings in 1656 against 'swordsmen and decimators' could be marshalled in favour of the election of politically conservative MPs, and in Parliament be used in favour of conservative revision of the constitution. The votes in favour of a Second House (to curb the power of the Commons) as well as a monarchy and a formal 'confession of faith' for all clergy in 1657 illustrate this conservative mood. This could now be harnessed by Cromwellian conservatives to agitate for a monarchy – which Whitelocke had been backing in 1652 – as well as to diminish the influence of the army and its political and religious radicals. The question arises of a hidden group of Councillors (and other senior figures) lurking behind the successive Parliamentary proposals for Cromwell's enthronement and aiming to marginalise Lambert's generals that way. Such secret direction of seemingly spontaneous MPs' campaigns was nothing new, as seen by the opposition' peers activities in 1625–8 (against the unpopular chief minister, the Duke of Buckingham) or 1640–1 (against Charles I's ministers Laud and Strafford). Indeed, the idea of Councillors using tame MPs to urge a policy on an undecided monarch and/or undermine Court rivals had been seen back in Tudor times, over the 'spontaenous' requests for Elizabeth I to name an heir in 1563 and 1566. Were Lambert and the republican generals the latest victims of this form of pressure in what was rapidly reverting to Court politics? Who was organizing it – Thurloe? But in private when he had no need to lie, in a letter to General Monck in Scotland on 24 February 1657, Thurloe denied that he or Cromwell was secretly behind the proposals in Parliament to make Cromwell king.[13]

(ii) 1657: the first attempt to make Cromwell a king. But was Parliament manipulated into agreement by a convenient 'Royalist assassination plot' scare?

Rumours that Parliament would make Cromwell king were afloat among the Royalist community in Paris in December 1656, and reached the chief minister and effective but unpopular 'regent', Cardinal Mazarin (really an Italian, Giulio Mazarini). The marginalised but still well-connected Sir Henry Vane, now abroad in The Hague, commented when he heard the rumours in February that he had always believed that this Parliament intended to make Cromwell king.[14] For the moment Parliament had other priorities, namely seeking to ensure that the government never again dared impose arbitrary rule on the localities. The regime also had a priority of raising finance, with Cromwell having been so short of money in summer 1656 that he had warned Swedish ambassador Count Bonde that England might have to make peace with Spain if the terms were satisfactory. (This might also have been intended as an excuse for England not funding any Anglo-Swedish war in Europe.) The 1656 anti-Spanish campaign had been restricted to a probe of the Mediterranean by Blake's fleet, which lacked bases for supply or re-fitting ships until Portugal was bullied into signing a satisfactory treaty. It was also authorised to explore the possibility of taking Gibraltar as a permanent English naval base to reduce dependence on local allies – a full forty-eight years before this was carried out in another Anglo-Spanish war in 1703.

Charles II was now a Spanish pensioner in Bruges as of summer 1656, having been forced to leave his mother's homeland France (his initial refuge and feared as a potential invader by Cromwell and Thurloe) in the Anglo-French peace-treaty of November 1655. He and his small court had access to Flemish ports and ships for an invasion and shaky networks of plotting supporters in England, most notably the famous 'Sealed Knot'. But he was kept short of money due to Spanish poverty, and Spain did not have any large fleets available to land him in England; Cromwell's fleets in the Mediterranean and Caribbean and privateers in the latter were busy disrupting Spanish trade and trying to take their 'Plate Fleet' (bringing silver to Europe) so these had to be fended off. He was reckoned to have received only two months' funds in his first nine as Spain's guest – and the local Papal Nuncio refused to help him unless he became a Catholic. His mother Henrietta Maria, with her usual political crassness regarding reality in England, was wasting the king's time and damaging his Protestant reputation by trying to persuade her third son, Prince Henry, to convert to Catholicism – a potential propaganda coup for the Protector. Charles' hosts, the military governor of the Netherlands (Don Juan Jose of Habsburg) and his general the Marquis of Caracena, could or would not act quickly and concentrated on the practicalities of defending the French frontier – where Charles' presence served to incite Irish troops in French service to defect to him and Spain. The latter helped Cromwell, by worsening France's military position and thus encouraging the reluctant Mazarin to sign up to Cromwell's demands that any offensive alliance include the handover of Dunkirk and French payment for any English troops serving on the Continent. (This agreement was significantly delayed throughout 1656 until March 1657.) Charles' Irish recruits gave him a better army, but endangered his attractiveness for Protestant dissidents in England (royalist or Leveller). Multiple agent Colonel Bamfylde (who had once smuggled Prince James out of London disguised as a girl for Charles I), now working undercover for Thurloe in Paris, gloated that:

> ten thousand Irish and Papists will contribute much to the preservation of Protestantism in England and the liberties and freedom of the nation.[15]

Bamfylde indeed urged Cromwell to sign a temporary peace with Spain, which had greater interest in events in Germany than in fighting England, to give him a breathing-space.

Despite their slowness in moves towards engaging in European land-warfare in 1656 neither England nor Spain sent out feelers for peace; instead Spain threw away a chance to end its French war by demanding harsh terms of a French envoy, deputy foreign minister Hugues de Lionne. The cost of the war, Court and clerical 'devot' intrigues, and the unpopularity of fighting fellow-Catholics all induced chief minister Cardinal Mazatin to seek terms from Spain not England. Whether the devious Mazatin was sincere in wanting a Franco-Spanish peace or just placating his critics in Paris – and scaring Cromwell into ameliorating his terms for alliance – is another matter. Luckily Philip IV of Spain demanded the return of all French conquests, abandonment of the rebels in Catalonia, and the pardon of the exiled rebel Prince of Conde, chief semi-royal detractor of Mazarin, by Paris. The latter was unacceptable to Conde's arch-foe Mazarin, always at risk of aristocratic intrigues as a low-born Italian 'arriviste', and the talks collapsed; Mazarin had to accept Cromwell's terms and pay for an English expedition to Flanders in April 1657. England was to have Dunkirk and the adjacent fortress of Mardyke, but to hold nearby Gravelines as a surety for these terms being carried out if Gravelines was taken first. If Ostend and other coastal towns were taken they would go to England too so Charles II could not use shipping there – but how was near-bankrupt Cromwell to pay for their garrisons?

The regime had achieved a useful financial and propaganda windfall when Captain Stayner intercepted the Spanish 'Plate Fleet' as it brought the year's output of the South American mines to Europe in autumn 1656, enabling Britain to operate its forces abroad and drive Philip IV and Charles II onto the defensive. He took or sank five ships on 9 September, with an estimated 2,600,000 'pieces of eight' being seized (with 7–8,000 bars of silver) and 1,000,000 more sunk in the wrecked ships. This provided both funds (the captured bullion was melted down for a new coinage) and a bonus for nostalgic Elizabethan-style propaganda about the glories of a Spanish war, with the poet Edmund Waller used to spin the success in a poem harking back to the triumphs of Drake. By implication, Cromwell was the new Elizabeth I and his – traditional, Protestant – triumphs were in contrast to the shameful pro-Catholicism and incompetence of the Stuarts. The triumph was used as proof that the Spanish war was working, despite the anger of the mercantile community at the seizure of shipping in the Channel by Spanish-funded Dunkirker pirates (which Cromwell's French alliance was intended to halt by conquering that port). MPs were encouraged to pay up by a government able to show that the war was a success – and a full £1 million was needed. Following delays, Parliament voted on 30 January 1657 to raise £400,000 taxes in four instalments.

There were useful political implications in the government playing up the danger of anarchy to MPs. So it was at least a happy coincidence that the desperate royalist hardliners, some now allied to angry Leveller republicans in a bizarre link, were now supposed to be plotting to kill Cromwell. Thurloe now revealed to the House on 19 January the apparent plot by an ex-royalist soldier linked to the Levellers, Miles Sindercombe, to assassinate Cromwell by starting a major fire in the chapel at Whitehall Palace and attacking him in the confusion. Sindercombe had supposedly tried to shoot the Protector on his way to Westminster Abbey at the opening of Parliament in the autumn from the window of a nearby house but the crowds had been too dense to aim properly, and had also planned an ambush on the road en route to Hampton Court (as William III's enemies were to do in 1696). Taken into custody after the second attempt, Sindercombe, the potential Lee Harvey Oswald of the Protectorate, was conveniently dead by suicide (arsenic) after questioning so he could not be tried openly or reveal more about the plot. Leveller militant Colonel Sexby was supposed to have been up to his neck in it and impatient at Sindercombe's hesitation. Ambassador Bordeaux was probably not the only person to suspect that Thurloe exaggerated the danger in order to scare MPs into backing the forthcoming government legislation in the House; as with the Gunpowder Plot in 1605, the sensational details could be used to whip up pro-regime opinion. But was Sindercombe cynically put up to the plot by Thurloe and his agents to scare MPs into voting for government measures, or just allowed to go ahead with a genuine plot rather than being quickly rounded up? We have only Thurloe's word for it that the details were as he said, though they do not seem unlikely. Sindercombe's (convenient?) death prevented him confirming the regime's version of events (or 'going rogue' and denying it) at his trial. Was Sindercombe silenced?

Parliament now moved onto the subject of the constitution. The first formal suggestion of a monarchy was made by a backbench Somerset Presbyterian MP, John Ashe, on 23 January 1657. The occasion was the wording to be put in the Speaker's formal speech of congratulations to Cromwell on escaping the recent Sindercombe assassination-plot – a sharp reminder to all of what chaos could follow if the Protector was suddenly removed. The regime would be much more secure if its leader was king and the form of government fixed, presumably hereditarily, as Ashe pointed out; but this was not followed up. Bordeaux, reporting it, said that 'Master of Ceremonies' Fleming (Cromwell's cousin) had told him that the idea was expected to be adopted by Parliament shortly.[16] It was revived on 23 February by one of the City of London MPs, Sir Christopher Pack – a far more substantial and well-connected figure, who sat on a number of government committees and had been suggested as Ambassador to the German Protestants in 1656 and spring 1657. He put in a formal 'Humble Petition and Remonstrance'.[17] If the proposal had any senior sponsors close to Cromwell, the likeliest figures (though not necessarily its originators) included Cromwell's cousin and original Parliamentary patron (1640–2) Oliver St John, a senior lawyer and former solicitor-general at the time of the Long Parliament's demolition of Charles I's prerogative powers who had led this legislation and the prosecution of the king's hated chief minister the earl of Strafford in 1641. A champion of Parliament against the monarchy before and during the Civil War, he had however refused to assist the king's trial and execution in 1649 and had preferred to retain a reined-in monarchy – or so he was able to allege to save himself from prosecution in 1660. He may have been lobbying for a Cromwellian monarchy now along with Cromwell's moderate Yorkshire gentry friend William Pierrepont, as both men were reported as having secret conferences with the Protector in early February. Lord Broghill was also apparently advising Cromwell on political matters at this time. There may also have been support from Cromwell's son Henry, who thanked Broghill for his advice (which he said could avoid chaos for the Cromwell family, i.e. presumably the effects of losing their exalted position and the Stuarts returning) and sent Cromwell a top-secret letter from Ireland which his father read and destroyed.[18]

The 'Humble Petition and Advice' was debated during the following month, and it was duly agreed by 123 votes to 62 to request Cromwell to accept the crown on 25 March.[19] On 31 March a Parliamentary delegation led by Speaker Widdrington waited on Cromwell in the Banqueting House to formally present the request, within yards of the site of the late king's execution.[20] One pro-kingship MP, Robert Peake of Coventry, is quoted in a letter as saying that his group hoped to use the prestige of their being a majority of the elected Commons – representing the will of the country – to prevail with Cromwell over the will of the army, who represented a mere faction.[21] This faction was, however, more ideologically attuned to Cromwell than the ordinary citizen or MP – and would Cromwell want to be dependent on the MPs after their attacks on his executive in 1654? The officers were expected to resort to a personal appeal to Cromwell to ignore the MPs' request[22] – as in fact happened.

Cumbrian monarchist MP Sir Thomas Widdrington, now Speaker of the House, was joined by the government's main City financier,

Sir Christopher Pack; by Cromwell's junior supporter and immanent ambassador to Denmark, William Jephson; and probably also by behind-the-scenes civilian advisers such as Lord Broghill, Irish civilian head of the Scottish council from 1656. Given Henry Cromwell's letter to Broghill of 3 February mentioned above, the latter was clearly using the argument that a Cromwellian monarchy would prevent the danger of chaos after the Protector died, and would protect Cromwell's family. Some of Cromwell's non-Council advisers, conservatives like William Pierrepont, as well as Oliver St John can be presumed to have been in favour and it is reckoned from the prevalent attitudes of Councillors in 1658–9 that the 'civilian' faction, centred on Thurloe and South Wales strongman Colonel Philip Jones, were in support and hoped to marginalise the generals' influence.[23] Thurloe was to stay silent about this aspect of Protectoral politics in his review of past policy for Charles II's ministers in 1660/1, but his strong stand in favour of the new Protector Richard Cromwell (Cromwell's second but eldest surviving son) against the republican generals in spring 1659 makes it probable that he was a major backer of the scheme. The implication is that the revival of the hereditary principle would make untried and marginal Hampshire squire Richard Cromwell, who was shortly to join the Council, the next ruler – with his father currently aged 58 as of April 1657 and sporadically in poor health. (No male English King had reached that age since Edward III in 1370.) This time it seemed that Cromwell was in favour, as close advisers believed, and when around 100 officers made a personal appeal to him a few days later he told them smartly that they had not objected to the suggestion of the royal title being revived in the 'Instrument of Government'. Then it had been him, not them, who had objected – presumably a reference to what happened in the secret talks at Whitehall of 10–14 December 1653. The army had made him 'their drudge upon all occasions' since the eviction of the Rump, and now 'it is time to come to a settlement and lay aside arbitrary proceedings so unacceptable to the nation'.[24]

Cromwell was briefly able to accept the theory that the needs of political stability, legal acceptability, and national reconciliation must come first whatever his alleged religious doubts over God's favour for monarchy. If so, this decision was only temporary and was to be reversed – and his airy statement that the crown was only 'a feather in a hat' could be used as an argument against as well as for taking it. Given his ever-active conscience and brooding sense of waiting on indications from Providence of what course to pursue, the appeals of religious congregations against him becoming king may have had most effect. They could present the moral case – that him becoming king would betray their cause and show that he had fallen to the temptation of worldly vanity. Rejecting temptation may have seemed more vital to a wavering Cromwell than listening to his ungrateful army colleagues. Those who warned him against assuming the crown included George Fox, to whom he always listened with respect and who implied that it would endanger his life (from army assassins?).[25] The abuse of long-term foe William Prynne, whose latest pamphlet compared him to similarly 'invited' regal usurper Richard III, was more to be expected.

The first attempt to lure Cromwell into becoming king failed through Cromwell's hesitations and senior army criticism, and on 3 April he told a Parliamentary delegation that he could not accept the crown out of his 'duty to God and to you'.[26] Notice the priorities in that statement. He was prepared to accept the rest of their political package for a monarchic constitution – although the 31 March delegation had sought to tie him to accepting the title by adopting an 'all or nothing' approach.

(iii) The second attempt: the arguments.

The Commons made a second attempt to persuade Cromwell to take the crown in a face-to-face meeting at the Banqueting House on 8 April, presenting it as the wish of the representatives of the three nations (England, Scotland and Ireland). He assured them that no man put a higher value on the wishes of Parliament than him, but that it was a matter of conscience – would him becoming king meet with Divine approval? He said that there were many other points than the kingship on which he needed elucidation, and only the MPs could answer them; he would have to consider the good of the nation in his decision, as well as the good of himself and them.[27] A grand committee of MPs was duly set up to consider his detailed requests and draw up Parliament's replies, and ten of them (including the two Lords Chief Justice, several Councillors, and Lord Broghill) dealt with Cromwell directly in successive discussions over the next few weeks. They argued that the nation's peace and safety, civil and spiritual, and its rights and liberties depended on him taking the royal title; the December 1653 constitution with the Protectoral title would not suffice. The royal title was 'known by the law of England ... and more conformable to the laws of the nation', so there was 'more of certainty and stability, and, of the supreme authority, civil sanction upon that title than upon any other'.[28] The argument that any change in the existing royal title was far too dangerous and would invalidate future laws issued by the new title's holder had been used before, when James VI and I had endeavoured to transform his title from 'King of England' and 'King of Scotland' to 'King of Great Britain'. The latter title had duly been accepted only for limited use. The legal problems of the Protectoral title were put bluntly by leading Councillors. Nathaniel Fiennes (a legal expert as Commissioner of the Great Seal) said that:

> everyone knows that it does not relate to him that hath the chief magistracy, but to he who is tutor or guardian to another.

Sir Charles Wolseley, the youngest Councillor and the man who had set in motion the fall of the Nominated Parliament, said that:

> The law knows not a Protector and requires no obedience from the people to him. The Parliament desires a settlement whereby the people may know your duty to them and their duty to you. ... God hath by his providence put a general desire of it in the nation.

The fact that the statute law did not accept the office of Protector encouraged juries to acquit people arrested for treason against Cromwell, Wolseley pointed out. Refusing the Crown would not only 'deny yourself the honour' which the people wished him to have but 'deny the people their honour which by right they ought to have'. It would 'deny the nation their due when their representatives challenge it from you'.[29]

Wolseley used all the correct practical, legal and moral arguments to impress Cromwell, and his arguments were more powerful than most 'where it mattered' as an intimate of the latter's. When it came to Lord Broghill's turn he added the practical point that at present it was as if there was a divorce between Charles II and the supreme legal authority of the state – the crown. If Cromwell was to occupy the crown it would cut off Charles from it permanently, as effectively as a divorced person's ex-partner's remarriage ends their hopes of restoring their first marriage. (This would imply the separation of the monarchy – the legal headship of state – from the existing Royal Family, which by implication meant an elective rulership.) In addition, the large numbers of people who were happiest giving their loyalty to the chief magistracy of the nation in the form of a king would now have no possible cause to seek an alternative ruler. Cromwell's own replies to the committee at their various discussions were frequently obscure as usual, and reflected his uncertainties as well as an exhaustive examination of all the arguments and precedents. He did not come to his decision to reject the crown lightly. But among his more important arguments were that:

(i) general obedience had been given to the new order in 1649–57 without its use of the royal title;
(ii) honest and loyal soldiers, 'true to the great things of government, to wit, the liberty of the people', had spilt their blood against the Stuarts and would feel it had been for nothing. (But had they all spilt their blood against the institution of monarchy or against Charles I as a bad monarch?) It would be 'contrary to civil and gospel liberties'.
(iii) 'God hath seemed providential not only to strike at the family but at the name… It is blotted out. It is a thing cast out by Act of Parliament'. This had been done 'not by sudden humour or passion but by the issue of ten or twelve years' and after the shedding of much blood. (This ignored the small number of elected MPs who had voted to abolish the monarchy in 1649, a minority of the anti-Stuart coalition of 1640–6.)

The committee's reply to (i) was that this had been due to God's favour and the beneficent nature of the post-1649 governments. On (iii), the fault had lain with the family not with the title; now that the Stuarts had lost Divine favour and been dispossessed there was nothing to stop Parliament restoring the monarchy under a new dynasty.[30] Both these arguments were perfectly valid, had Cromwell chosen to listen to them.

(iv) Cromwell's last-minute change of mind, 6–8 May 1657: principle or panic? Was he threatened with a military mutiny?

After prolonged meetings between the committee and Cromwell in the first half of April, several weeks of hesitation by him followed before his reply. Some of his close friends like Sir Francis Russell of Chippenham (Cambridgeshire), father of his second son Henry's wife, thought he would accept; Russell semi-jokingly wrote to Henry on 27 April that his next letter to Henry would be directed to the 'Duke of York' (i.e. the usual title for the king's second son). 'Your father begins to come out of the clouds, and it appears that he will take the kingly power upon him.'[31] Illness may also have delayed Cromwell's decision – though intimations of his declining physical state would logically have made him more anxious to secure a stable government for his and Richard's future, pointing to a monarchy. On 20 April he received the committee in a state of undress at Whitehall, and complained at the fact that they were concentrating on the crown (i.e secular glory) not religion in their plans for the constitution, adding a jibe at royalist licentiousness as exemplified by young nobles travelling to France to pick up immoral habits.[32] Bordeaux believed that the argument being used to persuade some obstinate Army officers in their discussions with MPs was that Cromwell was constitutionally obliged to follow the advice of Parliament[33] – which argument could be counter-productive. The main contemporary source for the Protector's and the petitioners' comments throughout this crisis is a publication of 1660, *Monarchy Asserted*, attributed to Whitelocke who is reliable enough on other matters to be an accurate source – though he may have written with an eye to his self-preservation after the Restoration.

By 6 May Thurloe believed Cromwell would announce his acceptance at the reception arranged for the MPs in the Painted Chamber at Westminster next morning. He believed that many soldiers were content with Cromwell becoming king and 'some indeed grumble but that's the most for all that I perceive', 'there being nothing from without that should be any constraint upon him either to take or to refuse it'. The advice of Parliament was the most important factor – at least to Thurloe.[34] But the meeting set for 11 a.m. on 7 May at Westminster was postponed unexpectedly; instead it was scheduled for the 8th at the Banqueting House. In the interim, on the afternoon of the 6th Cromwell unexpectedly encountered his brother-in-law Desborough and son-in-law Fleetwood while he was walking in St James' Park, told them that he would accept the crown, and was informed by Desborough that if he did so he (Desborough) would sever all relations with the Cromwells. The general said that those who urged Cromwell to accept were closet royalists.[35] Meanwhile, as Parliament waited to meet Cromwell on the 7th a military petition (signed by two colonels, seven lieutenant-colonels, seven majors, and sixteen captains) was delivered to the Commons – requesting that they stay loyal to the 'old cause' by abandoning kingship. It was apparently organised by Colonel Pride, the veteran of Parliamentary coercion, who had been alerted to the threat that Cromwell would accept the crown by Desborough.[36] A delegation of MPs who turned up at Whitehall on the evening of the 7th hoping to see Cromwell found him on his way, in informal dress, to see a new horse and not inclined to deal with them. He was only alerted to the petition next morning, and sent Fleetwood to the Commons to ask the MPs to postpone a debate. A Commons declaration of anger at the army's meddling would have inflamed military opinions.

Ominous signs of discontent from the army – one from two of the most senior officers, backed by Lambert, and one from their juniors – must have given Cromwell pause. The threat of military instability if Cromwell persisted in his plan turned the argument that the Crown represented a return to stability on its head, and he apparently changed his mind. Accordingly, when he received the MPs at the Banqueting House on 8 May he regretted that the proposals in the 'Humble Petition and Advice' had 'many excellent parts in all but that one thing, the title as to me'; he could not accept the crown. Given what Thurloe had written earlier, the decision was unexpected to his closest associates. The author of *Monarchy Asserted* (Whitelocke?) wrote that 'Lambert and some leading officers would not consent' so Cromwell had second thoughts about accepting the title despite enjoying the powers associated with it.[37]

(v) A way round the impasse – a marital tie between Cromwell and a restored Charles II? The Broghill plan.

Another solution to the dilemma of restoring the monarchy was allegedly promoted by Lord Broghhill some time during the 'Humble Petition and Advice' crisis. The exact date of it is unclear, it is only known from two accounts later given by Broghill to associates (his chaplain Thomas Morice and Bishop Gilbert Burnet), and Broghill would appear to have been acting on his own – as far as the London side of planning was concerned. One of the few pro-Commonwealth Irish Protestant 'settler' peers who had rallied to the occupier in his homeland, he had family ties to major royalist dynasties and was to continue as a state adviser after 1660. He was trusted by Cromwell as a senior Cromwellian adviser on Scottish policy, a proposed Second House peer, and a personal intimate, and according to his account was close enough to the Cromwell family to approach the Protector's wife and daughter to promote his proposals. The incident occurred at the time that for the first time a number of important aristocrats were starting to appear at Cromwell's court, with the veteran Parliamentarian power-broker Warwick (now seventy) re-emerging in politics and about to carry the Sword of State at Cromwell's second Protectoral investiture. Broghill's suggestion was that Cromwell should marry his youngest daughter Frances to Charles II rather than the current favoured candidate, Warwick's grandson Robert Rich. Broghill's plan would thus bring about a reconciliation of the Cromwell and Stuart dynasties by a personal marital link – a favoured manner of creating family and political alliances among the aristocracy at the time. Cromwell would then back the restoration of the legitimate king rather than making himself sovereign. Broghill said that he cleared the proposal with Charles II, who was willing to countenance it as his hopes of a military restoration or foreign help had been dashed; this was at the time that he was living in Bruges as a Spanish pensioner, short of cash from his heavily-indebted foreign paymasters and with no immediate prospect of a royalist revolt. Broghill then told Cromwell's wife Elizabeth and the proposed bride Frances, who agreed to it, and spread rumours about the plan around London; they duly reached Cromwell who summoned him to explain what he proposed. He told Cromwell that it was more logical to place the Crown on the head of its legal owner than take it himself, pointed out that even if he could hold it for his lifetime his heir (i.e. the untried Richard Cromwell) would have difficulties, and assured that an indebted Charles II would be so grateful that he would pardon Cromwell and make him 'Lord General' for his lifetime. He would thus be safe from retaliation from regicide as commander-in-chief, and could hope to see his grandchild on the British throne. (Charles II had already shown his fertility, as the Protectorate knew due to the recent appearance in London of his ex-mistress Lucy Walter and her son James 'Crofts', later Duke of Monmouth. They had been arrested briefly, and Cromwell was supposed to have joked about James' resemblance to Charles II.) Allegedly Cromwell refused to believe that Charles would ever forgive him for killing the late king, and expressed doubts over Charles' reliability as a son-in-law – he was 'so damnably debauched he would undo us all'.[38] Cromwell was also said to have asked the veteran moderate royalist Earl of Hertford, head of the Seymour dynasty and former husband of the royal claimant Arbella Stuart, for advice about how to restore stability at a private dinner. Hertford advised him to restore Charles, and was told that Cromwell feared the king would never forgive him for executing Charles I. The story of the Frances Cromwell – Charles II marriage proposal was also mentioned by a former Protectoral chaplain to Samuel Pepys, with the statement that Cromwell had turned it down.[39] It would seem to be more than a post-1660 attempt by Broghill to reassure Royalist 'ultras' that he had only served Cromwell in order to help Charles get his throne back.

Cromwell's fears about Charles' morals were prescient, seeing the way that Charles was to treat his wife Catherine of Braganza by flaunting his mistresses in front of her; an English 'Queen Frances' with powerful relations ready to avenge slights would have been more of a problem than an isolated foreign Catholic queen. The remark is not unlikely, seeing that when Lucy Walter was picked up by Thurloe's 'secret police' in London and accused of meddling with local royalists on Charles' behalf she was openly referred to by the State authorities as 'Charles Stuart's whore'. Broghill's account was given after the Restoration, when he had every political reason to make it clear that he had planned the marriage to facilitate Charles' quick restoration and it was politically correct to emphasize Cromwell's sense of guilt for the sin of killing his king, a man now hailed in the 1660s as a martyr. The slighting references to Charles' immorality were politically and morally welcome to the man to whom Broghill allegedly told the references, the future Bishop Gilbert Burnet – a Scots Whig critic of Charles' debauchery (and autocracy) and so relatively sympathetic to Cromwell's agendas. But this is not to say that Broghill invented the story, which served no notable post-1660 political purpose. The notion of Cromwell being bribed to restore the king as direct action by royalist rebels had failed, the means to be used, and the dilemma over how best to restore political stability under a monarchy fit in with what is known of moderate aristocratic royalists and Cromwellian conservatives in 1657. There had been suggestions of bribing Lambert to undertake this role in a Restoration earlier, and other military leaders were to be considered in these terms in 1659–60. It is significant that the suggestion of Cromwell being made commander-in-chief for life, reassuring him and binding the New Model Army to the king, was virtually the successful offer made to General Monck in 1660.

The alleged comment Cromwell made about the king never forgiving him for killing his father was also prescient, seeing the pains that the restored monarchy made to hunt down regicides in 1660–1; Broghill said that Charles would not have arrested his wife's father, but that still placed the responsibility for keeping any terms of pardon on the notoriously unreliable Charles (who had already sacrificed his military supremo Montrose to the Scots Covenanters in 1650). It cannot be argued that the vindictive hunt for the regicides was to be entirely the fault of Parliament, not Charles, as he made no effort to halt it although he did excuse a few of the senior regicides who had proved useful to him (e.g. Colonel Ingoldsby, Cromwell's cousin). If Broghill reported him accurately and Charles' critic Burnet did so too, Cromwell was accurate about not trusting Charles.

(vi) A monarchic constitution without a monarch: an uneasy compromise. The resignation of Lambert.

The revised constitution that was adopted without the royal title was submitted by Parliament to Cromwell and accepted on 25 May. It was more 'monarchic' than that of 1653 and it kept the issue of a future monarchic title open. The Protector now assumed quasi-royal powers, with the limitations imposed on him to seek the consent of the Council removed, although all new Councillors were still technically subject to Parliamentary approval of their appointment. The Protector would now have to take an oath of office, a revised version of the Coronation Oath for monarchs – to uphold the 'True Reformed Protestant Christian Religion' as set out in the Bible, and to maintain the peace, safety, rights, and privileges of the people. He would name his successor in his lifetime. A Second House was restored as a check on the Commons – though not the hereditary House of Lords. As Cromwell told the objecting army officers:

> Unless you have some such thing as a balance, we cannot be safe. By the proceedings of this Parliament, you see that they stand in need of a check or a balance for the case of James Nayler might happen to be your case.[40]

Socially and religiously conservative MPs had queued up to express their outrage at the blasphemy committed by the radical Quaker Nayler for riding into Bristol in 1656 in a manner echoing that of Christ's entry into Jerusalem. All sorts of savage punishments were proposed for his offences against religion and public decency, and the unforgiving atmosphere alarmed Cromwell and other more tolerant Independents. Cromwell had always taken a tolerant attitude to Quakers and others who offended against the social order (e.g. by refusing to doff their hats to superiors), and the violence of the MPs indicated the prevailing attitude among their social grouping against his 'godly' protégés – the sects whose rights he defended against a disciplinarian state church. It awoke echoes of the attacks on the Independents by the dominant faction of Presbyterian MPs in 1646–8, which the Army march on London in June 1647 and later 'Pride's Purge' had been carried out to thwart. What would a supreme and untrammelled Commons do to heretic Independent Army personnel in future if it was not tied down by political checks? A Second House composed of pro-tolerance peers could thus prevent these MPs from using their 'power of the purse' over Government to demand that their intolerant bills be accepted. Arguably Cromwell's mention of Nayler showed prescience, as the rabidly Anglican Commons of 1661–5 was to tear up the religious toleration plans of 1660 and drive the Independents 'underground' as Dissenters. The anti-Anglican, Presbyterian peers who returned to the restored Lords in 1660 were never numerous or bold enough to stand up to the Anglican majority of MPs – and the Cromwellians who Oliver Cromwell put in his Second House were unlikely to have been allowed to or wanted to stay in a restored Stuart king's House of Lords.

The Second House was to consist of between forty and seventy peers, nominated by the Protector; sixty-three were eventually chosen but only forty-two of these accepted. Cromwell, not Parliament, had the right to fill vacancies; the questions of whether this House had a right to initiate legislation or to veto Commons bills were never resolved. There had been talk of allowing the pro-Parliamentary peers of the 1640s to resume their seats, but in the event only seven hereditary peers were chosen for the new House, including Warwick and Saye, and only three took their seats. (These included Cromwell's sole creation of a hereditary peer, his young Life Guard commander Charles Howard; Warwick did not turn up.) But the creation of 'life peers', next used in 1958, brought problems which were to be familiar to later centuries. As in the 1990s and 2000s, the prospect of an entirely appointed body was to lead to charges of government cronyism in selecting the membership which included a suspiciously high number of Cromwell relations and senior generals. The nominees included his brother-in-law Colonel John Jones and cousin Colonel Richard Ingoldsby, two 'Major-Generals' (Whalley and Berry), long-time Cromwellian ally William Goffe, Cromwell's son Henry's father-in-law Sir Francis Russell, the 'Humble Petition and Advice' proposer Sir Christopher Pack, senior judges, and perhaps surprisingly republican officers Colonels Pride and Hewson.[41] Pride might be a republican, but he was fond of acquiring the benefits of status; his list of expropriated ex-Royalist estates included Nonsuch Palace in Surrey and the Corfe Castle estate in Dorset The incorporation of some senior officers implies an intention to try to lure the Army leadership into participating in the government in a civilian guise – which flattery probably worked on the acquisitive Pride but failed to win over other officers. The new constitution also technically required Councillors to be subject to Parliamentary approval, as in the 'Instrument' of December 1653, but unlike then allowed the Protector to name his successor.

The coinage now took a further step back towards that of the Stuarts – with a design apparently set in motion when the Spanish bullion, from which the new coins were cast, was seized in September 1656 but delayed by the constitutional crisis. Cromwell's head appeared on the obverse like a monarch's, surmountd with a Roman-style laurel wreath; the Commonwealth's coins had placed the cross of St George there. On the reverse, the Protectoral arms (the crosses of St George and St Andrew and the harp of Ireland) replaced the cross of St George and the harp, with the whole surmounted by the imperial crown of England. The use of a Latin inscription on the reverse was also restored, based on the coins of Charles I; the Protectoral motto was '*Pax Quaeritur Bello*', 'Peace is Sought Through War'.[42] The regime's 'publicity men' were thus doing all that they could to make Cromwell seem as legally legitimate as any king.

A suitably royal inauguration ceremony in was carried out in Westminster Hall on 26 June, where Cromwell used the royal robes and sceptre without a crown. (The closest parallels, which may have been used as a model, were those of the assumptions of authority by Edward IV in March 1461 and by Richard III in June 1483.) The coronation-chair was used, the Earl of Warwick (Parliamentary Lord Admiral in 1642–8 and instrumental in the fall of Charles I) not Lambert carried the Sword of State (did Lambert refuse?), and the symbols of state were presented by the Speaker of the Commons. The use of Warwick was highly ironic, given his role in the overthrow of Charles I; the nephew of the man who had tried to overthrow Elizabeth I in 1601 (the Earl of Essex) now ended his career as a stalwart of the House of Cromwell, with his grandson currently engaged to Cromwell's daughter Frances. The oath of office was administered by the Speaker, a chaplain issued prayers recommending the Protector to the Almighty, and Cromwell took his seat in the thirteenth-century Coronation Chair – which was thus taken out of the Abbey for the only time. Then Cromwell was proclaimed by the heralds and left the Hall in a procession (all based on the coronation procedure). As Clarendon wrote, all that was missing from a normal coronation were the crown and an archbishop[43] (and the anointing which would have been seen as Popish).

The exclusion of political opponents of the new constitution from politics was reinforced – by requiring oaths of loyalty. It now included Cromwell's own deputy Lambert. He refused to take the oath and was duly excluded from the Council; his scruples were logical on religious grounds but other Councillors better known for their religious fervour, e.g. Fleetwood, saw no need to walk out. One or two other Councillors such as William Sydenham had to overcome scruples about swearing an oath,[44] but did so. It is possible that Lambert chose to take a stand on this issue as a means of abandoning the Council where his influence was diminishing, laying down a marker as having done so on religious grounds for future rallying of army opposition. He had scared off Thurloe's plan to make Cromwell king, but the accoutrements and effectively the political institution of monarchy had been restored minus the title. Did he walk out of government as he believed Thurloe had won, and position himself for a future republican challenge? His political position was not consistent, given that he had already framed one semi-monarchic (not hereditary) constitution in 1653; but he had then avoided any monarchic symbols and had hedged the Protectorate in by a requirement to take the Council's advice. As Cromwell had pointed out to the anti-monarchic army delegation around 1 April, the creators of the 'Instrument of 'Government' (led by Lambert) had not cavilled at using the title 'King' then so why was it so important now? Thurloe was also apparently wary of Lambert for alleged plans to meddle with the Army that spring during the kingship debates.[45] Lambert may have resigned out of pique that Cromwell's nominee, i.e Richard, not an elected leader (himself?) would now succeed the Protector; he was to remain quietly on his estate at Wimbledon until Cromwell died, more interested in gardening than plotting, but was to resume his ambitions in 1659.

Aftermath: uneasy equilibrium or the calm before the storm?

(i) Cromwell and the Royalists – marital ties used in broadening the Protectoral elite. A riposte to Army vetoes on the monarchy?

Though Cromwell had moved towards a monarchy, his execution of the king and reliance on military rule meant that he was personally unacceptable to large numbers of royalists. More senior peers – and members of the younger generation with no personal involvement in the clashes of the 1640s – now attended Cromwell's Court, but what little evidence we have indicates that important figures such as the Dowager Countess of Devonshire continued to hope for Charles' restoration. The clamour and political manoeuvres for a monarchy in spring 1657 were seen by them as a way to coax the elite into choosing the most legally secure option, i.e. restoring the legal king – or so they were to claim after 1660. It is quite likely that some of them were less zealous for the King's restoration at the time than they pretended later, not least as it seemed unlikely to occur by military means after the failure of the Penruddock Revolt and Charles' foreign backers in 1656–8, Spain, were weak. Lady Devonshire, for example, was the maternal grandmother of Robert Rich, the intended bridegroom of Frances Cromwell, and her promotion of the match indicates that she was hedging her bets and was anxious to secure her family's alliance with the Cromwells at the time.[46] This need not exclude a desire to use her newly favourable position with the court to work for the 'real' king's restoration – but only as Cromwell's successor, not his supplanter?

Senior royalist figures may have been less anti-Cromwell in 1657 than they pretended after the Restoration, with reconciliation to a Cromwell dynasty possible; Warwick, a Presbyterian and from his 1640–8 activities clearly in favour of a limited (or puppet?) monarchy, probably saw the Rich-Cromwell marriage as a final chance to secure influence at the new court. He had initially cavilled at Cromwell's financial demands so he was not desperate to cement it at any price, and Cromwell himself was supposed to have been suspicious of Robert Rich's character; there was also the question of a supposed promise of Frances to a Mr. William Dutton to be sorted out first. The wedding duly took place with quasi-royal festivirties at Whitehall on 11 November 1657, with Warwick and the Dowager Countess prominent – and an orchestra and dancing, contrary to the general myth of Cromwellian Puritan austerity.[47] Unluckily, Robert Rich was to die within months of the wedding. Frances' sister Mary Cromwell also married into a royalist dynasty, with the young Lord Fauconberg (in Paris) conducting negotiations with Cromwell's ambassador – and nephew-in-law – Lockhart. A widower travelling abroad, Fauconberg was too young to have been involved in the Civil Wars but the family estate had been fined by the 'Compounding Committee' for his father's royalism and he had Catholic relatives. His uncle Lord Belasyse was a leading member of the Sealed Knot, the royalist underground organization which had been plotting rebellion since 1653 and had launched a dangerous military revolt in March 1655 – as Thurloe, who had infiltrated it, would have told Cromwell. Fauconberg was recalled to England to marry Mary a week after her sister's marriage in November.

Mary had been talked of seriously as a potential bride for another and far more senior royalist, Charles' boyhood friend, the Duke of Buckingham, who returned (illegally) to England early in 1657 to open talks. Charles supposedly approved, though he may have had no choice if he wished to retain his friendship and made the best of it; the acquisitive and rakish Buckingham presumably saw the marriage as a way to end his penurious exile. He clearly calculated that his prospects were better if he became reconciled to the Cromwells with Charles' hopes of restoration by force of arms much reduced, and his cynical plan is an indication of poor royalist morale (at least among impatient young spendthrifts). The marriage was seen as a distinct possibility by observers, and was not quickly rejected out-of-hand by the government. In the event, the talks broke down and he had to return to Paris empty-handed. Mary's name was also linked to that of another former royalist, Philip Stanhope, Lord Chesterfield – who allegedly turned her down and whose eventual fiancée, Mary Fairfax, was the daughter of Cromwell's ex-commander. (The arrangement broke down and she married none other than Buckingham.) Given the louche reputations of Charles and Buckingham, Frances and Mary Cromwell probably had lucky escapes from a lifetime of humiliation. But the political point is that this talk of marital alliances was part of a general move towards tentative royalist-Cromwellian reconciliation in 1656–8, which was to be airbrushed from history due to its embarrassing nature for the royalist participants after 1660. As Thurloe was to point out to the restored Stuart regime in 1660 when threatened with prosecution, many so-called royalists had offered their services to Cromwell in the 1650s (of which he retained written evidence in order to protect himself by blackmailing them if Charles was restored). And as Charles II said sarcastically after his Restoration, if everyone who said they had always worked for his return was telling the truth he was a fool not to have returned earlier.[48]

Did the marital alliance with Warwick, that veteran advocate of a limited, 'godly' monarchy, indicate a move to bring in the 1640s Parliamentarian peers to back Cromwell? The re-emergence of a Second House would suggest a political plan to use peers as a curb on the troublesome Commons, possibly over-confidently concerning their willingness to take part. As it was, the House was mainly staffed by ennobled Cromwellians, including reliable conservative military figures such as Monck, Pride, Berry, and Hewson as well as Cromwell's relations (his sons-in-law and his brother-in-law John Jones) and assorted Councillors, judges, and City figures. But even if the majority of Royalists remained disaffected this was not a serious military threat, given the effect on morale of the Penruddock Revolt in 1655 and lack of a serious foreign military backer for any plots. It was up to Secretary Thurloe's intelligence service to see that discontent did not turn into plotting, though – as with anti-terrorist actions today – pre-emptive raids on or restrictions of suspects ran the risk of driving them into open action. Thurloe had to admit in winter 1657–8 that the new royalist plot by Slingsby's group had included some men who had never been active before, in which government repression in 1655–6 must have been a factor. As with British state measures to contain the potentially dangerous elements of disaffection in the Muslim community after 11 September 2001, drastic repression and/or close supervision only made the problem worse by involving new malcontents angry at harassment. The ban on Anglican clergy serving as private chaplains and tutors in 1655–6 was also likely to encourage resentment and breed hostility, as with the similar government mistrust of plotting by subversive 'radical imams' in the 2000s.

Using spies to detect plots was problematic, given that they could exaggerate stories to make themselves seem more important (and worth better rewards) or 'finger' personal enemies out of spite. The ultimate loyalties of many of them were suspect, with regular payments and an appreciation of which side was likely to prevail being important factors. Nor were Cromwell's so-called allies abroad seen as trustworthy. Bishop Burnet later wrote that Cromwell (and thus Thurloe) believed that France could have used a military expedition of Huguenots – less offensive to English Protestant rebels than French Catholics – to aid the King if it had not been rendered harmless in 1657 by a close alliance.[49]

(ii) The military and diplomatic situation, 1657–8. Seeming British invincibility masks the regime's serious internal weaknesses?

When Cromwell was at war with Spain (1656–8) the latter was unable to lend Charles II an effective fleet for invasion. Spain could only use two Flemish ports, Dunkirk and Ostend, to harass English shipping or launch an invasion, whereas France had all its Channel and Bay of Biscay coast to chose from; and in 1657–8 the Cromwellian expeditionary force in Flanders blockaded and later took over Dunkirk. The expedition was initially commanded by Sir Henry Reynolds, a notable siege-expert from the war in Ireland (and brother-in-law to Henry Cromwell). He was drowned in the Channel while visiting England and succeeded by his deputy, Sir Henry Morgan, with Ambassador Lockhart taking command of the English forces for the crucial military clash with

Spain in spring 1658. Cromwell insisted on the alliance concentrating on the occupation of Dunkirk, as it was a potential royalist invasion-port as well as a privateer base; Mazarin failed to fob him off with the (harbourless) nearby fortress of Mardyke in 1657. When the 1657 Anglo-French expedition failed to move in on Dunkirk quickly due to French procrastination, there were dark rumours of it being a deliberate ploy to avoid carrying out the treaty.[50] Indeed, the majority of the Council were said by Lockhart to oppose the diversion of English troops to Flanders as a waste of men and money[51] – though Lockhart may have been trying to scare Mazarin into thinking Cromwell would call off the campaign if his wishes were not met. In the meantime, a new royalist plot was underway in England, in which Charles II could land to assist with Spanish troops if the Flemish campaign did not stop him – and Thurloe believed that it was especially serious as people who were not known from past involvement to be royalists were involved.[52] As with modern 'domestic self-starter' terrorists, this sort of plotter was particularly difficult to detect and could be missed. The French also tried to distract England militarily into helping out their threatened mutual ally, Sweden, which the Dutch and Danes might attack.

The Anglo-French army did not reach the coast until late in the season and the Dunkirk attack was postponed. Suspicion did not abate when the expedition finally took the small fortress of Mardyke, near Dunkirk, that autumn and handed it over to England. Thurloe grumbled that the treaty specifically said that both Mardyke and Dunkirk should be handed over together[53] which had not happened (deliberately?). The fort was nearly retaken in a surprise raid by Spanish troops in which Charles II participated, and after this Mazarin tried to panic Cromwell into agreeing to evacuate it; he refused to budge. The threat of a royalist invasion from Flanders that winter, which the capture of Dunkirk would have minimised, added to Anglo-French tension and recriminations; luckily the English Royalist plans came to nothing. As the king's secretary Sir Henry Bennet wrote, while the Royalists waited for a Spanish expedition before committing themselves and the Spaniards waited for a royalist rising, Charles would 'fall between two stools'.[54] Spain would only assist the king to hire a small fleet of five ships, and as these finally arrived at Ostend harbour in March the Cromwellian Admiral Goodson attacked and sunk three of them.[55] The others were blockaded in Ostend. The threat of invasion or a Royalist revolt was clearly exaggerated, and Cromwell made the most of it in addressing Parliament on 5 January 1658 as an inducement to MPs to think the country at maximum risk and so induce co-operation. Quite apart from Charles II being 'at the waterside' ready to invade, he alleged that Spain had been England's 'avowed designed enemy' since the time of Queen Elizabeth and was ever-ready to 'rout you from the face of the earth' by open war or secret subversion.[56] This was a distorted and paranoid view of recent history, based on the 'Black Legend' of Popish cunning, cruelty, and subversion, but to a providentialist like Cromwell the way events had turned out would seem to argue that it was God's plan that he should fight the Spanish menace.

The Anglo-French treaty was renewed for another year on 18 March 1658, promising an attack on Dunkirk by 10 May.[57] The defeat of the Spanish army (and Charles II's force of Anglo-Irish exiles led by him in person) at the battle of the Dunes on 4 June was followed by the surrender of Dunkirk on the 14th. The terms granted to the citizens allowed them to stay unmolested and practise their Catholic worship if they desired – which was anathema to the 'godly' troops of the New Model. Army. The occupation of a Popish stronghold in the English and Irish wars had usually been followed by enthusiastic iconoclasm and assaults on the local Catholics, occasionally by massacres.There was patriotic French indignation at the Catholic citizens being harassed by zealous New Model Army troops, which Mazarin's enemies stirred up. Lockhart had to keep them in check and stop Cromwell from accepting suggestions that they should be thrown out of their Catholic church so it could be Protestantised, asking his employer if he thought it useful to stir up Catholic Dunkirkers when there were two Catholic armies (French and Spanish) nearby ready to save them if they revolted.[58] The town was considered as a useful site for a colony of loyal Protestants, a move which would have inflamed French opinion. Thurloe's analysis also hopefully presumed that local Protestants in Spanish Flanders would be inspired to revolt. Giving Cromwell control of both sides of the Channel, it was a 'bridle upon the Dutch', and a 'sally-port' for enabling English troops to operate easily on the Continent. As enthusiasts for a new religious war in Europe saw it, Dunkirk would serve Cromwell as a centre for a Protestant offensive against the Catholics.[59] Cromwell was now seeking to tie the aggressive Charles X of Sweden and his large army down to a joint Anglo-Swedish attack on the Habsburgs in Spain (England's main naval target) and Germany (Sweden's main land target).[60] Each Power would aid the other against its enemies – and against its own allies if they attacked its co-signatory. This would have the practical usefulness of requiring Sweden to join England if the latter was at war with any other Northern Power such as the Dutch or Denmark, and distract Charles from attacking such states rather than the Habsburgs and thus causing disruption to Baltic shipping-supplies – a perennial fear for England

Cromwell's rant to Parliament in January 1658 about the existential threat from Spain was far from the cool calculations of the Council in spring-summer 1654 that a Spanish colonial war was the most profitable option for England and France a more dangerous enemy.[61] The 'Black Legend' of Spanish cunning, treachery, and relentless Counter-Reformationary zeal was called into action to justify the war, presenting Spain in the terminology of the 1610s and 1620s when Cromwell had been an impressionable young man seeking a religious purpose. Spain had been far more powerful then, and been accused of meddling in England's affairs (and bribing the Stuart Court) via its ambassador Gondomar. The apocalyptic English Protestant view of the German crisis of the early 1620s as a final battle between Protestantism and Catholicism had led to calls in Parliament for English intervention on the Protestant side, and its language was now echoed in Cromwell's interpretation of the current European crisis. It was the 1620s rather than solely the Elizabethan nostalgia of which his anti-French 1670s detractor Slingsby Bethel was to accuse him[62] that inspired Cromwell's world outlook. Presenting the conflict between himself and Spain (and its allies in Germany) and the concurrent Franco-Spanish conflict as a narrative of inevitable and continent-wide religious warfare – with the Catholics as the aggressors – had pressing reasons. It would justify his expensive foreign policy to MPs and excuse the unpopular losses of English shipping to Spanish-funded privateers.It should thus encourage MPs to vote for higher subsidies to his government, ending current reluctance. However, the reasons for presenting such an approach do not excuse the fact that his portrayal of Charles X as 'a poor prince… driven into a corner' by a Catholic coalition[63] was wide of the truth. Sweden's many foes, nervous at its domination of the Baltic, included Protestants (Denmark and Brandenburg, backed by the Dutch) as well as Catholics, and Charles had wasted his resources and alarmed his neighbours by pursuing his family's claim to the Polish throne with a recent gamble on a major invasion of inland Poland which had failed to come off (and led to devastation and a local backlash against Protestants). They were afraid for their lands and their free trading-access to the Baltic rather than having been foolishly induced to attack a fellow-Protestant by scheming Papists, although Cromwell chose to take the latter moral reasoning.

Cromwell's main aim of preventing the Austrian Habsburgs from sending aid to Spain was met in the terms of the new Emperor Leopold's election capitulations with the German Protestant princes in July 1658, as these required him not to make war on or fund opponents of their ally France (i.e. Spain). This was the crucial clause which England's security required be imposed on Leopold if he was elected, though Cromwell unrealistically wanted the Electors to vote for a Protestant.[64] England lacked the money or the military-diplomatic clout in Germany to influence the election, and had to act as a minor observer and a distrustful supporter of France. Arguably Elizabethan Protestant enthusiast Cromwell was too dogmatic to be flexible in his European diplomacy, and was lucky that he did not increase Habsburg hostility and thus aid to Charles II.

The rapid Anglo-French advance of summer 1658 resulted in the nearest coastal town to Dunkirk, Gravelines, being taken and handed over according to the treaty, and Ostend seemed likely to follow. The invasion threat was thus ended, but the government's financial difficulties meant that garrisoning all these places was very costly and existing funds had to go to the higher priority of army back-pay. Dunkirk alone was believed to cost £60,000 per annum, and its customs receipts were lower than expected.[65] Money had to be sought from the City after Parliament was dissolved early, Cromwell was rumoured to have 'hijacked' the money raised for the relief of overseas Protestant refugees, and it all added to the financial strain which was to make Charles II's government eager to return Dunkirk in 1662. In France, Mazarin was roundly abused (including by Cromwell's one-time contact Cardinal Retz) for handing Catholics over to the heretic English and was obliged to issue a literary defence of his duty to keep up ancient commercial alliances no matter who was in power in England. In typical English political fashion, once Charles II had rid England of the now strategically unimportant burden of Dunkirk there were complaints at the indignity of surrendering conquests to the French and rumours that the latter had bribed Lord Chancellor Clarendon to sell it.

All this made Cromwell's strong military position in 1658 one that was still subject to serious difficulties, but not serious enough to give much hope to Charles II. Constitutionally, the abandonment of the plan to make Cromwell king in 1657 meant that he was denied the legal (and psychological) bonus that using the traditional title would have given him with the citizenry. The surprise failure to persuade him to take the title stymied his more determinedly conservative supporters in the Commons, who hopefully expected 'King Oliver' to serve as the sort of dependable king at the head of a just and stable constitution that Charles I had failed to be – though the constitution was as monarchic as if Cromwell had taken the crown and Cromwell probably regarded assuming the formal title as not worth the problems. The backers of a Cromwellian monarchy, allied with Councillors such as Sir Charles Wolseley, Philip Jones, and Edward Montague and private advisers of the Protector like Broghill, seem to have hoped to use Cromwell's assumption of the kingship to detach him from his senior military allies (e.g. Desborough and Fleetwood) and their militant sectary backers. The dismissal of a second Parliament after deadlock on supply in February 1658 added to the sense that the regime had run out of ideas and energy, and Cromwell and his over-worked Council struggled to keep up with administration. On the occasions when the Protector was ill business came to a standstill, though it appears that his declining energies did not lead to serious worries until August 1658. The delays while Cromwell and/or Thurloe were ill notably infuriated foreign ambassadors in 1656, and logic would imply that an ageing Protector was bound to suffer worse health-problems in the coming years. There was no effective deputy who could take his place, the capable and militarily popular Lambert having withdrawn from the Government in July 1657. The grants of honours and the quick promotion of Richard Cromwell to the Council – with Thurloe, until then only a 'back-stage' figure – in summer 1657 suggests that he was being groomed for such a position, and if Cromwell had lived longer Richard could have been expected to take on more duties. It was perhaps ominous that Richard had been content to live as a country gentleman in Hampshire since his marriage to local girl Dorothy Major of Hursley Park (near Winchester) in 1649. His younger brother, Henry, now serving in Ireland, was more involved in administration, and the senior generals knew little of him – but Richard could still have been a constitutional sovereign guided by his Council.

(iii) Political stalemate?

The revised constitution envisaged a Parliament free from executive interference about who should sit, so the MPs excluded from the first session of the current Parliament in September 1656 were readmitted for the next session. Another problem was that the leading English hereditary peers summoned to the Second House – Warwick, Councillor Fiennes' father Lord Saye and Sele, Cumbrian reformist Lord Wharton, and Cromwell's ex-foe the Earl of Manchester (plus one Scottish peer, the Earl of Cassilis), all linked to the Presbyterians, failed to take their seats. This was apparently mainly on the grounds of doubt about the legality of a non-hereditary second chamber, at least on the part of Saye and Sele who was certainly not hostile to Cromwell's regime per se. They were thus holding out for a restoration of the 'proper' House of Lords as part of the legal ancient constitution, which logically could accompany the restoration of the monarchy (for the House of Cromwell). If one part of the ancient constitution of 'King, Lords and Commons' had been restored already in essence if not name, why not another? The lack of a hereditary element in the Second House also meant debate over whether the new Second House was entitled to use the name and hold the privileges of the old House of Lords; republican MPs now readmitted to the Commons were violently opposed to this. Nor were they enamoured of the concept of a second chamber made up of government nominees, which gave too great a weight in the constitution to unelected patronage. (The arguments recurred in the Labour Party plans to reform the Lords in 1968 and 1998.) This unelected body would be able to delay or veto legislation passed by elected MPs if it inherited the role of the old Lords – and it is likely that Cromwell envisaged using the Second House to prevent MPs voting for unwelcome religious legislation threatening the sects.

On 4 February 1658 Cromwell suddenly lost his patience with MPs and hastened to Westminster in his coach to dissolve Parliament, without the usual entourage of Councillors and other officials who it appears were taken by surprise. His action was a personal initiative on the spur of the moment rather than a pre-determined plan, and indeed both Fiennes (a leading civilian Councillor) and Fleetwood (the leading military Councillor after Lambert's resignation) were at Parliament at the time and tried to talk him out of his action when he arrived. They were ignored, as Cromwell repeated his hasty shutdown of the Rump of April 1653.[66] But the surprise dissolution of this Parliament did not signal any autocratic intention to rule without Parliament in the manner of Charles I, as opposed to frustration with the current body of MPs (who Cromwell could no longer legally purge of dissidents). It was still rumoured that he intended to restore the ancient constitution with a king (i.e. Cromwell), the old-style hereditary Lords, and the Commons.[67] Indeed, the Government 'spokesman' and editor Marchamont Nedham was among observers who had expected the just-dissolved Parliament to proclaim Cromwell as king. This was rumoured to be intended to take place in tandem with restoring the hereditary House of Lords, with its temporary title of 'The Other House' a short-term expedient.[68]

'King Oliver' – the rationale and justification for this constitutional gamble.

The constitutional situation in 1658–9 had nearly looked very different from what really happened, and the fact that there was a Protector not a king was more due to a last-minute decision by Cromwell in early May 1657 than to any inevitable political process. Cromwell very nearly took on the title of king. Would a stronger Second House with hereditary peers (and officers) have vitally aided Richard Cromwell in the 1659 showdown, or been brushed aside by the generals? Thurloe expected him to take the title, as he told Henry Cromwell – and, as Cromwell reminded anti-monarchic officers at the time, there had already been an option of him taking the title in December 1653 when they had not protested. On that first occasion Lambert, framer of the 'Instrument of Government', had supported the move if not originated it and it had been Cromwell that hesitated. Had Cromwell agreed, the need for the army to put on a united front against the threat of instability or radical plots might have given the kingship proposal a better chance than in 1657. There was nothing inevitable about his rejecting it, though in each case he appears to have been swayed by the argument that it would be a sin to use the title which God had struck down in the fall of the Stuarts. The counter-argument put to him was that God had abandoned the family that held the Royal title, not the notion of kingship.

The *'Humble Petition and Advice'* sought to carry the growing conservatism of the 1650s administration a step further along the same line of logic, restoring the Royal title and the House of Lords to rebuild the ancient constitution. It had the advantage of ending the ambiguity over the legal status of the Lord Protectorship – was it treason to plot against a head of state who did not owe his authority to a traditional title? This legal argument had been aired at the time of the trials of the Penruddock conspirators, and had never been satisfactorily resolved. The legal right for a non-royal head of state to impose taxes had been questioned in Cony's case, and even Chief Justice Rolle had not been satisfied of the government's legal rights and had retired rather than act on a de facto not *de iure* principle.

The Protectorship as an office did have historical precedent, as the title of an effective regent for an under-age sovereign n 1483 (Richard, Duke of Gloucester) and 1547–9 (Edward Seymour, Duke of Somerset). Both had ended up dead by violence, one in battle and one on the execution-block, so it was not a promising precedent; and the Presbyterian controversialist Wiliam Prynne duly enjoyed comparing Cromwell to Richard III as a monster of ambition. But the title's emergence at the head of the first written constitution in Great Britain, the 'Instrument of Government', owed its success to an ad hoc compromise organised by Cromwell's party on the failure of the April – December 1653 experiment of rule by Council of State and a nominated 'godly' Parliament. Cromwell had backed this experiment, out of idealistic enthusiasm for (temporary) rule by a select body of the virtuous in place of the Parliament he had dismissed in April 1653 – but it had broken down into deadlock between contending parties by December. A solution was thus needed, and with the religious radicals like General Harrison blamed by Cromwell's close and moderate advisers (e.g. Lambert) for the Parliamentary paralysis rule by a Single Person was seen as producing action and stability. This duly excused the drastic action of shutting down the radicals' 'godly' Parliament in Cromwell's mind – and coincidentally or not the new constitution produced in December 1653 had similarities to the moderate constitutional monarchy plans by civilian conservatives in 1648 which the Army had then vetoed. Cromwell had stood with the army against the majority of MPs then; now Harrison and his radicals had botched their chance to show what their 'godly' non-elected Parliament could do and Cromwell was to back a form of monarchy without that tainted name. But it is unclear (as usual for him) what exactly Cromwell had intended as a political solution and if he had hung the radicals out to dry deliberately in autumn 1653 as Lambert did – or if he was waiting for Providence to show him the way to move.

There was a legal argument for a monarchic settlement, and this appealed to Cromwell's legally-trained, politically moderate allies like Bulstrode Whitelocke as well as to the regime's judges. Royalists could be tried for treason with more hope of conservative judges' support if they had offended against a king, and if the Stuarts were ever restored arrested Cromwellians would stand a better chance of amnesty if they could argue that they had acted on the orders of the legal sovereign. The precedent for this was the 1495 De Facto Act, excusing people who had 'only obeyed orders' for Richard III and protecting Henry VII's adherents in case of his overthrow by Perkin Warbeck. Obeying the legal authority at the time of the defendant's actions was a legitimate argument – leading Henry VII to date his reign from the day before the battle of Bosworth so that he could accuse those who had fought for Richard III of treason. Kingship would add to the sense of domestic stability, reassure foreign powers that Cromwell's regime was there to stay, and enable a smooth transition to his legal successor – now presumed to be his eldest surviving son Richard.

As the charismatic and prestigious leader of the army in its wars in Scotland and Ireland and an undoubted Protestant zealot, Cromwell had the personal position to maintain the support of most of his officers even as king. No doubt he could have found appropriate Old Testament quotations to use in support of a properly-chosen godly general as king. The most obvious precedent was Jehu, displacer of the tyrant Ahab – whose notoriously godless idol-worshipper wife Jezebel would have provided a template to Puritans for Charles I's widow Henrietta Maria as a Catholic. The sycophantic efforts of admirers to find an appropriate genealogy for him as a descendant of early British kings would have been redoubled – his mother had been a Stewart, if with no Scottish links, and his father's South Welsh family were tentatively linked to early Welsh dynasties via the Glamorgan gentry.[69] The first of them to come to England was an archer in the service of Henry VII' suncle Jasper Tudor, Duke of Bedford, soon after 1485 – putting them in the same group of

Anglicised South Wales 'arrivistes' as the Cecils. The royalists did their best to denigrate his origins, and the post-1660 smears of the Cromwell family began with James Heath's hostile biography in 1663 where he and they were portrayed as shameless jumped-up adventurers. Even had he become king they would have continued to emphasize the lowly origins of his only prominent – indirect – ancestor, the Tudor minister Thomas Cromwell, as son of a Putney brewer, and use his own brief spell as leassee of a Fenland brewery against him. But it is still debated by recent analysts such as Jonathan Fitzgibbon whether the 'shift' from creating a hereditary Protectorate to a full monarchy in winter 1656–7 was pre-planned or an 'on the spot' gamble by reinvigorated conservatives – and if this went too far for Cromwell as well as the generals to stomach.

Cromwell died at only 59, albeit after a slow physical decline over the previous year or two and several serious illnesses. Despite the late fifties being a greater age in the seventeenth century than it is today (among other English rulers, James I died at 58, Charles II at 54, and James II at 67), the Cromwells were a long-lived family. His grandfather Sir Henry lived to 67, his uncle Sir Oliver to 69, and his second son Richard (the longest-lived male English Head of State to date) to 85; among the womenfolk his mother Elizabeth lived to around 90 and two daughters to 83 and 75. Apart from the alleged premonition of George Fox on seeing him for the last time riding in his coach in Hampton Court park in August 1658, his condition had given no cause for immediate alarm and there is no hint of concern in the ever-watchful Thurloe's correspondence. It is possible that his daughter Elizabeth Claypole's unexpected death had fatally undermined his will to continue. But if he had been spared for a few more years the amount of offices granted to Richard in 1657–8 suggests that his dutiful if unassuming heir, now over thirty and being brought out of earlier obscurity as a Hampshire landowner onto the Council of State, would have taken on more of a political role under Thurloe's tutelage. The longer Richard had to earn the respect of the army, the more chance he would have stood of surviving once his father was gone. There is a parallel with the equally dangerous transition from a 'military' government, officially civilianised but with an ultimate army veto, to a civilian regime in Spain post-1975. In that case, a ruler raised by and dependent on the Army not legitimacy, General Franco, had six years to accustom his untried chosen heir from 1969 – Prince Juan Carlos

– to the army before he died, and in the crucial test of loyalties during the 1981 military mutiny the majority of the Army backed the new ruler. (The parallel is not exact as Juan Carlos had the advantage of being the legitimate king by birth, provided that his father's renunciation of rights in his favour was recognised; Richard had no legitimate claims.) Richard's lack of military service was a vital problem, given that a common line of abuse for Cromwellian civilian ministers by the Army radicals was their lack of proven dedication to 'the Cause'. His younger brother Henry – who had held military rank – could have returned from Ireland to assist him, though the crucial role he was playing as a loyal 'viceroy' there made this less likely.

With Oliver Cromwell still alive as the lynch-pin of the regime, it would not have collapsed into factional strife in 1659 – especially if he had not risked senior military resignations and a radical army mutiny (in Ireland?) by assuming the Crown. Charles II, isolated in Brussels as a Spanish pensioner in 1658, would have stood no chance of restoration as the guarantor of order – even in summer 1659 the failure of the Booth Rising showed the lack of active royalist plotters after years of failures. The immediate resentment caused by the 'Major-Generals' rule in 1655–6 had been met by abolishing them, albeit with Parliament taking the lead (by refusing to carry on funding them) not from Cromwell's own initiative. After this, the lack of major royalist activity in 1657–8 was shown by the poor amount of participation in that winter's plotted invasion – though it was a problem for the government that some new figures not on Thurloe's intelligence radar were involved, as the alarmed secretary conceded. The efficiency of Thurloe's secret service had made the success of a revolt very unlikely and so put people off running the risk of revolting, although there was always a danger of unsuspected new entrants to the royalist plotters' circles being undetected and so having a chance to strike. Also Cromwell's regime was feared across Europe as a military power, putting off foreign help to Royalist plots. He was able to re-establish English troops on the Continent for the first time since 1558, at Dunkirk which the French had to hand over as the terms of their alliance against Spain; the regime's main danger was now of internal splits.

Chapter Two

1658–9: The Collapse of Richard Cromwell's Protectorate. Inevitably Doomed – Or Is This Only Hindsight?

The situation in August-September 1658. A smooth succession.

The political situation was at a stalemate when Cromwell fell ill, with no new Protectoral initiatives to resolve the intrinsic hostility of many MPs to the nature of the reformed constitution. More rumours that Cromwell would take the crown followed the apparent manufacture of two Royal-style 'caps of estate' (which a king normally wore in lieu of a crown at state occasions) in mid-May.[1] The Protector continued sporadic creations of peerages for relatives and observed royal-style 'purple mourning' when his son-in-law Robert Rich died of scrofula (the 'King's Evil', ironically considering recent events) on 16 February.[2] Rumours of him changing his title, via a new Parliament or otherwise, reached a royalist correspondent in late April.[3] There was also an interesting sign of the regime reaching out to a prominent former opponent (unusually, successfully) as on 1 May Cromwell appointed the prominent Presbyterian lawyer John Maynard, one of those MPs secluded by the army in 1648, as his 'Protector's Sergeant' (i.e. at Law). Maynard had been the defence lawyer for the obstreperous merchant George Cony when the latter refused to pay customs duties in 1655 as they were only legally owed to a king, not to a Protector – the trial was thus a crucial test case of the legality of Cromwell's authority and its loss by the regime had helped to impel it towards the creation of a Cromwellian monarchy by the 'Humble Petition and Advice'. (The case had famously seen Maynard call on Magna Carta as the bulwark of the subjects' liberty and Cromwell retort crudely that he cared not a jot for 'Magna Farta'.) As an MP Maynard had strongly backed the idea of a Cromwellian monarchy, saying that a king unlike a Protector had to govern within the traditional law so it would

1658–9: The Collapse of the Protectorate 43

help restore good government – and now he took office to help shore up the Cromwellian unofficial monarchy.[4] Officially the Protectorate was behaving like a monarchy without a king, but without any of the political will to grasp the nettle and resolve the situation of spring 1657. Given the nearness of Cromwell's death, it could be assumed in retrospect that the political paralysis came from exhaustion on Cromwell's own part – or the greater urgency of the Flemish expedition and the plan to occupy (and pay for) Dunkirk. The distractions of burdensome Council business is just as likely, as long delays in decisions had been seen before at times of overwork (and/or Cromwell's illnesses) and the vital Dunkirk campaign had to be overseen that spring and early summer. Once Dunkirk was occupied there was the business of arranging its garrison and their payment and supplies, and also making provision for further occupations of Flemish coastal towns as the allied army advanced Eastwards.

Cromwell may not have had the will or the energy to contemplate the domestic constitutional problems or take any new initiatives, but there was no concern about his health among observers until mid-August. As was exhaustively documented at the time, his decline only appears to have begun after the death of his favourite daughter Elizabeth Claypole on 6 August. Notably, rumours of a plan for a coronation were still circulating in London – though the extreme heat, likely to start an epidemic and affect those already exhausted or depressed like the Protector, was probably more important.[5] Cromwell's decline initially only took the form of his prolonged withdrawal to Hampton Court, normally a 'weekend retreat', for weeks on end and slowness in doing business by him there and by the Council in Whitehall – no more alarming to observers than the situation at other times when he had been ill. The length of his indisposition was not new either; what was new was his failure to recover from it. The famous encounter with George Fox in the park at Hampton Court, when the Quaker leader said that Cromwell looked like a dead man and he 'saw and felt a waft of death', was on 17 August; Thurloe reported that Cromwell was much improved for that day's outing but he suffered a relapse that evening.[6] From mid-August there were regular bouts of a 'quartan' fever, classified at the time as the ubiquitous gout but probably malaria. The later allegation by Cromwell's (and Charles I's) physician George Bate that he had poisoned Cromwell, with Charles II's agreement, is very implausible given the timing and context of the allegation; Bate was delusional and suffering from syphilis by this point and at best was endeavouring to earn royal gratitude.[7] Cromwell's decline appears to have been perfectly natural, as was the unexpected nature of its outcome as his exhausted frame gave way.

The Protectorate's international reputation was at an all-time peak following the conquest of Dunkirk, with a large English garrison in a town on the Continent for the first time since 1558 and Spain and its client Charles II in no position to challenge Cromwell. The English regime may have been heavily in debt and in political deadlock, but its power – and durability – seemed unchallengable. Significantly, there was no sense that things would change quickly when Cromwell died (on 3 September, the anniversary of the battles of Dunbar and Worcester on 3 September). There was no sign of an enthusiasm for or expectation of change in the following weeks, even among Royalists,[8] and the usual loyal addresses were made to the new ruler in the provinces with no obvious sign of this being co-ordinated. The government continued to function normally as it would when a monarch died, with the Council meeting as quickly as possible to confirm the succession and his eldest surviving son Richard, aged thirty-two, being proclaimed Protector in public places by the State heralds like a king.[9] The decision had evidently been made by the Council to stress the legitimacy of the new regime by behaving as if a monarch had died, and possibly there was some wishful thinking by moderate civilian advisers like Thurloe and Wolseley that they would now behave as if Cromwell had taken the crown as they had wished – he could no longer stop them with protests that this was unseemly or 'ungodly'. The Protectoral funeral could be delayed for over two months while a splendid State pageant was arranged as it would be for a king or a hero like the first Parliamentary commander-in-chief the Earl of Essex who had died in 1646, with a lifelike effigy made for the lying-in-state at a royal residence, Somerset House. The barge-procession downriver to Somerset House was probably modelled on that for Elizabeth I (who had died at Richmond), and the obsequies were probably based on those for James I. 'Godly' restraint and avoidance of Popish pageantry – which Cromwell himself might have preferred – was less important than sending out a message about the equivalence of his (and now Richard's) political position to a king's.

In fact, it appears that Cromwell's physical burial took place quietly at night in a private ceremony (as was thought appropriate for a Puritan burial) before the state funeral. This was on 10 November. The official funeral took place on 23 November.[10] The choice of site, Westminster Abbey, was of course another sign of Cromwell's royal status and Queen Elizabeth and King James had been buried there; but so had prominent Commonwealth and Protectorate figures (e.g. Admiral Blake in 1657) and Cromwell's own family, most recently Elizbeth Claypole. The Abbey was being used as a parish church for the Whitehall Palace and Westminster residents, supplementing St Margaret's next door (the church for Parliament), as well as a State mausoleum in the 1650s; the first of these reasons could be cited if religious zealots complained at its use for the ungodly practice of high-profile funerals.

The most notable element of the two-month lying-in-state – apart from the cost – was the appearance of a crown there, placed equivocally beside the effigy not on its head as Cromwell had refused a crown in life. The question must arise of where it had come from, given that all the Royal Regalia was supposed to have been melted down on Parliamentary orders in 1649 and only the sceptres and swords-of-state had been re-made for the second Protectoral inauguration in 1657. Had a crown been made in secret by the 'official' state jeweller in the City, Alderman Blackwell, ready for a coronation in 1657 which never happened? Or did the Council commission a crown especially for the funeral? The Imperial and St Edward's Crowns were officially re-made for Charles II's coronation in April 1661 as if from scratch, though apparently with some original jewels in them. There was no mention of the new regime – surely too short of money to pass over the chance of using an existing crown? – re-using Cromwell's mysterious crown, though that would have been politically embarrassing and so needed to be suppressed. But it is possible that Blackwell, who also made Charles' crowns, had to re-cast one in 1660–1 from the crown which suddenly appeared in November 1658, all mention of whose existence was then suppressed as the new Stuart crowns would be tainted to have any association with the detested usurper.[11] Did Blackwell even secretly base his design of Charles II's crown in 1660–1 on Cromwell's crown? The royal regime was also to exhume and remove all the 'inappropriately' buried bodies of commoners that had been placed in Westminster Abbey in 1660–1, not only those of the posthumously condemned 'criminal' Cromwell – an act of snobbery and spite traceable either to the returned Anglican clergy at the Abbey or to Parliament. Technically the evicted deceased were non-Anglicans, but the decision was to say the least a bad omen for the possibilities of reconciliation.

The fact that the Protectorate was gone within eight months of Cromwell's death and the king back on his throne a little over a year after that was not anticipated when Cromwell died, and could be played up by the royalists in retrospect as miraculous. It had logical political reasons, which the Royal mythographers would have preferred to ignore – partly to play up the Divine intervention on Charles II's side and partly to hide his political weakness in 1660. As shown below, it was the quarrels among the senior ranks of political and military figures in the Commonwealth in 1659–60 that restored the king, not royalist efforts. This was, however, sidelined by ruthless post-1660 monarchic spin which sought to present the new order as a natural continuation of the old pre-1642 order, not a political bargain between two stalemated factions to restore stability.

Political deadlock between a head of state and the dominant part of the political nation represented in the Commons – the situation as of February–August 1658 – was not unusual for the early-mid-seventeenth century. The Parliaments of 1614 and 1621 under James I had broken up as a result of Royal impatience with defiance by the Commons (over a financial settlement on the first occasion, on foreign policy on the second). The repeated problems of Charles I in 1625–9 are well-known, but the point to remember here is that the more politically astute James – and Elizabeth in 1563 and 1566 – had faced similar deadlock over an issue on which MPs felt strongly and would not give way. These had often been constitutional if not as fundamental as the issue of legislative or executive primacy that the Commons fought over in early 1658. MPs (backed by certain Court peers wishing to pressure the monarch) had sought to force the naming of a successor in the 1560s and to register their concerns on foreign policy in 1621, infuriating the sovereign, and in 1610 and 1614 they had refused to accept royal plans on reforming finance.

The political embarrassment in February 1658 – an embattled Government left needing tax-revenues that had had to dismiss Parliament and seek temporary alleviation elsewhere – was a frequent problem for early seventeenth-century sovereigns. Cromwell faced no more serious financial problems in doing without a Parliamentary grant in 1658 than James had in 1611 and 1614, or Charles I had done in 1626–9 and 1640 (when he too had been at war). The addition of a fundamental constitutional dimension to the problem in February 1658 was unusual, as on these previous occasions the nature of the constitution had not been under challenge but in 1658 some dogged Commonwealthsmen MPs (e.g the republican faction led by ex-Civil War commander/ MP Sir Arthur Haselrig) had never really accepted the army-imposed 'Instrument of Government' or the Protectorate set up in December 1653 by Cromwell's fiat. The elected House of Commons (or what was left of it) had been evicted by Cromwell at gunpoint in April 1653, with Haselrig among the MPs left in the political wilderness as the army and its radical religious allies decided on the form of the next, nominated Parliament ('Barebones Parliament', so-called) and then on the form of the Protectorate. The latter, a mixture of monarchic and elective Parliamentary government but headed by a Single Person and his Council of State, had been created by 'Cromwell's understudy', his politically moderate but religiously radical deputy General John Lambert. These two men had subsequently blocked any attempt by Cromwell's Parliaments in 1654–5 and 1656–8 to assert their authority over the Protector and his Council – the legislature was not to control the executive, possibly due to Cromwell's fears of the MPs voting for a persecuting state church that would oppress the radical sectaries who he patronised. But the disgruntled proponents of civilian/ legislative supremacy over the executive were not prepared to give in yet. Challenging the nominated Second House was a means to preventing the Protector using it – and the weapon of patronage against the elected Commons; it did not look back to 'executive vs. legislature' clashes of the early seventeenth-century so much as forward to the attacks on placemen in the 1690s and 1700s.

Cromwell's regime rested on insecure legal foundations, as had been the argument of those moderates like Lord Broghill, Sir Christopher Pack, and Whitelocke who sought to restore a fully legal monarchy. But in strict matters of politico-military power Cromwell was safe in possession of authority as long as the army did not fracture, and he showed assiduous attention in courting its officers throughout 1657–8 (as with a special meeting soon after the early 1658 dissolution of Parliament).[12] The Council could continue to rule by administrative order without Parliament, and the local county authorities cooperated with this; the

Penrudock Rebellion's shambles had shown that rebellion was not an option unlike it had been to 'anti-centralisers' resenting taxes and County Committees in 1648. As had been shown with the regime of the 'Major-Generals', in an emergency Cromwell could rely on government by the sword as long as he had the structure of a loyal standing army in existence – and after 1660 MPs were to be hostile to a standing army as a threat to their power for many decades.

The break-up of the Protectorate and resulting domestic upheavals among the republican leadership – leading to the struggle among army and Rump partisans in 1659 and the growing calls for a Restoration and political stability – only followed Cromwell's death. Since the revision of the constitution in 1657 the succession had been hereditary rather than subject to the initial, 1653, choice of the Council and a Parliamentary ratification.[13] This prevented a conflict but opened the office to the hazards of kingship without giving it the benefits. Presumably Cromwell gave little thought to the future beyond assuming that it was in God's hands and he had time for his heir to grow into more experience. Given his complex personal religion and fondness for interpreting the Bible as a basis for his actions, he probably argued to himself that God had shown His disfavour for hereditary monarchy – this had been his reasoning in 1647–8 – so a hereditary Protectorate was safer from divine displeasure than kingship. As usual, once he had made the decision not to become king (which could have gone the other way as Thurloe expected) he justified it in retrospect as inevitable or at least Divinely-assisted, without mention of the political advantages it would have brought him. God had decided against the continuation of kingship in 1649, and it was not for him to question this. But his eldest surviving son Richard (born in 1626) had only been a councillor for a year and had no military prestige for his father's former officers or men or a personal ascendancy over the senior officers, a necessity for the Protector's survival whatever the constitution laid down. Richard's character and supposed impassivity were mercilessly ridiculed in retrospect, with the fact that 'Tumbledown Dick' only lasted in power for seven months combining with the lack of any powerful constituency having a reason to uphold his reputation.

Richard's poor reputation may well reflect his lack of post-regime defenders. The senior generals wanted to control him at best and once they had dismissed him had no wish to reconsider their verdict; crucially the less decisive Fleetwood, who was of Richard's own generation but had a far stronger religious reputation with the junior officers and men as a devout Baptist, chose to stand with the older and more ruthless Desborough. The more politically radical officers and MPs regarded the Protectorate as illegitimate, wished to see it abolished as soon as they had the chance in spring 1659, and had no interest in restoring it. The Fifth Monarchists had been deeply sceptical if not violently hostile to the secular government of the Protectorate ('King Oliver' not 'King Jesus'); other religious radicals who had accepted Oliver Cromwell's 'godly' credentials and work for their cause had no common ground with the unknown Richard; and the royalists wanted King Charles not Protector Richard as the monarchic Head of State. In retrospect after 1660, the royalists needed to stress the argument that a stable, hereditary headship of state could not exist except with a Stuart king; Richard's rule thus had to be marginalised and ridiculed. Richard's own backers in 1658–9 (led by the Council) had no influence over events after May 1660; although very few of them were to be prosecuted, only Edward Mountague among the Councillors, and outside the Council General Monck, held real power in the restored monarchy. They had played no role in Charles I's death and had too much military power in the crucial months of constitutional decision-making in early 1660 to be driven to the political sidelines as civilian Cromwelians were. Monck continued as commander-in-chief and acquired a dukedom, and Mountague (as Earl of Sandwich) held senior naval commands until his death in battle in 1672. However the tension between ex-Cromwellians and former royalist exiles at the new court meant that they had to play down their Cromwellian past, not attempt to defend the now discredited regime. Among Richard's main civilian allies Thurloe escaped prosecution (possibly by threatening to expose those royalists who had secretly betrayed their king to him in the 1650s) but had to retire to private life and ended up living quietly in Chancery Lane, where his papers were later discovered in a hidden attic. The Protectoral 'Steward of the Household' and senior Councillor Philip Jones, a South Wales farmer's son who like Essex vicar's son Thurloe had pushed his way into the upper gentry with a large mansion in the 1650s, had to retire to the country. He faced lawsuits from his local enemies, as did fellow-Councillor Sir Gilbert Pickering (a Northamptonshire squire of zealous and shifting religious opinions), and Cromwell's unofficial adviser, Buckinghamshire lawyer Bulstrode Whitelocke. (The latter also had to fend off vengeful and extortionate royalists, including his own former friend Lord Clarendon.) Richard could be impugned as the hapless and incompetent 'Queen Dick' by semi-official royalist writers without being able to defend himself or rely on others to do so, and was so nervous of malicious legal prosecution that he kept a very low profile, moved abroad for some years, and on his return used a false name. But the reputation of Richard and his regime has to be seen in its context of a swift collapse and post-1660 vilification; it was vengeful spin, not honest contemporary analysis. Where Oliver had received support out of grudging acceptance of his remarkable politico-military record and/or his de facto power, Richard lacked any basis for support except as his father's heir and had no powerful defenders after 1659.

The creation of a hereditary Protectorate in 1657 provided a fillip for the old principle of hereditary power, although it led to the most probable candidate for a future Protectorship on the grounds of talent/army support, Lambert (at least as he saw it), resigning. From then on, Lambert was a potential challenger to the next Protector. But the inevitable beneficiary of backing the hereditary principle would be the legitimate king – unless Richard was aided by the powerful factor of sheer inertia. Few people had dared rise against the large united and well-trained army in 1649–58, so why should that be altered now – unless the Army fractured? The disaster of the first royalist revolt after Oliver Cromwell's death, the 'Booth Rising' in late summer 1659 (when Richard and the hereditary principle had already been removed), shows that the republican government in 1659 could still defeat outright external challenges easily. The main question as of autumn 1658 was whether the untried Richard could hold together the coalition of vested interests that had supported his father. He failed as soon as he faced his first major crisis with another Parliament in session and the army officers restive, but was this inevitable? Is too much made in hindsight of his alleged incompetence or misjudgements? Would he have stood a better chance had he possessed more experience of dealing with and loyalty from his father's senior military colleagues? Arguably a large degree of fault lay with his father for not preparing him better, and with Thurloe for not warning the less clear-sighted Oliver that a stable succession needed to bind the military to Richard more closely. But until

Oliver's physical decline became noticeable in early-mid August 1658 neither of them probably thought there was any urgency.

The narrative of events after Oliver Cromwell's death in the seemingly stable – if unpopular and financially rocky – Protectorate now developed into a downward spiral, leading to its swift collapse. But was this inevitable? It can be argued that if Cromwell's first son, Oliver, had not died of smallpox while serving at Newport Pagnell in 1644 the latter might have had more authority over the generals as he had at least served in the army in the Civil War and so was a comrade-in-arms, which Richard was not. (He would have been thirty-five in 1658.) Richard was merely a country gentleman without a military record, lacking even the crucial administrative role given to his younger brother Henry as joint Commissioner for Ireland from 1655 (with the military men Tomlinson and Okey) and Lord Lieutenant there from November 1655. In this role Henry had had to deal with a body of senior officers of republican sentiments (though when it came to a crisis in 1659 he could not command their loyalty). Richard had lived a retired life on his father-in-law Richard Major's Hampshire estate at Hursley, near Romsey, until brought to prominence by the Protectorate's newly hereditary status in summer 1657. His wife had been selected for him by Oliver in 1648–9 due to his friend and correspondent Major's religious credentials, but that was not unusual for the time; her Hampshire gentry family had no army or political connections He had then joined the Council and replaced his father as Chancellor of Oxford University. He had nothing in common with the officers and seems to have been unknown to most of them, which his retiring nature and preference for the life of a country gentleman no doubt aided. A surviving letter of the young Oliver's contains a complaint against some of his troopers as 'dishonourers of God's cause', suggesting a degree of religious enthusiasm which generals like the Baptist zealot Fleetwood, his sister's husband, would have appreciated.[14] By contrast, we shall see that Fleetwood undermined – or did nothing to save – Richard.

Richard was of unclear religious adherence and was supposed by rumour in 1658–9 to favour Presbyterian preachers.[15] He was also accused by worried Army militants of seeking to reconcile the Protectorate with civilian MPs in order to bring in Charles II[16] – which was a possibility given that he was free of that fear of vengeance for regicide which allegedly prevented his father from accepting overtures to the king.[17] The allegation may have been intentional slander designed to stir up Army feeling against him and in support of his treacherous senior officers, but it was logical – if not for Richard, then for senior civilian advisers like Lord Broghill who had hankered after settlement with the Stuarts. His main political allies seem to have been Thurloe, Philip Jones, Edward Mountague, and his own brother-in-law Lord Fauconberg who was a valuable conduit to the peerage but who he could not force onto the Council against the generals' wishes. Significantly, when Richard sought to give his contemporary and ally Mountague an army colonelcy to add to his naval rank in autumn 1658 this was complained of by a group of current officers, who went to him and demanded that he only make such appointments with the advice of senior officers. He refused, and they got up a petition demanding that he abdicate control over the army. They took it to and were backed by Fleetwood, who Richard offered at a meeting with army personnel on 18 October to make 'Lieutenant-General' (i.e. effective commander of the army). Richard would retain the right to make appointments himself, and Fleetwood accepted the offer and duly addressed the soldiers a few days later appealing for unity. The fact that a draft of Richard's speech exists in Thurloe's papers probably indicates that the compromise division of authority was the latter's idea; it was probably necessary to satisfy the soldiers but was still a sign of weakness.[18] But Fleetwood had the credibility with the army that Richard lacked, so logically he could be used to channel their complaints and in return persuade them to obey orders – was this Thurloe's plan? And did Richard lean on the wrong man – an ambitious one who came to want Richard's job or a broken reed who was too wary of mutiny to stand up to his grumbling juniors?

Henry Cromwell was now made full Lord Lieutenant of Ireland and the troops there were exempted from coming under his brother-in-law Fleetwood's command. Either brother, however, was at risk from Fleetwood, an experienced general from the Worcester campaign and a fervent sectary fond of using Biblical language though from his actions in 1659–60 apparently not a strong leader.

Richard's abdication of full control of the army was an ominous sign that the latter would not obey him if he seemed to threaten or ignore their interests – they would only follow men who had some repute from past service and godliness. This had already been seen in the officers' address presented to the new Protector on 18 September, which offered only a conditional allegiance and had a hint of menace as it referred to backing him as long as he promoted godly officers and clerics and protected peaceful Protestant sects. The deputation was led by Fleetwood, a sign that he was putting himself forward as the spokesperson for the discontented as well as of his own sincere sectarian zeal. Its language referred to the 'Good Old Cause', the term which was now appearing as a nostalgic rallying-call to the ideals of the New Model Army in 1645–8 though it may have been coined by a royalist, and implied that the Army had as important a role as guardian of the constitution as the Privy Council.[19] Such claims have a habit of leading to military coups, and if the petition was organised by a clique rather than spontaneously at a lower level, Fleetwood was undoubtedly involved; in either case he made the most of it. At the most charitable, it can be guessed that he did not want to risk his new authority by clamping down on dissent; a more cynical view would have it that the growing complaints among the soldiers encouraged him to pose as their supporter to aid his increasing ambition to rule. The provincial civilian 'grass roots' religious organizations of most of those moderate sects who were comprehended in the current church, Presbyterians excluded, seem to have been mainly concerned that autumn with the alleged threat to 'law and order' from and presumed blasphemy of the Quakers as the latter continued to grow in numbers. A grand meeting of these groups' representatives was held at the Savoy in London (including some of the regime's selectors of state clergy, the 'Triers') and produced a statement of faith making clear their divergence from and detestation of both Quakers and Presbyterians, and the new Protector made a conciliatory speech to them.[20] Another moderate sectaries' organization was formed in Essex to resist and dissociate themselves from the feared Quakers. Efforts to unite the moderate sectaries and Baptists and Presbyterians by the veteran Protestant theologian John Durie, a widely-travelled thinker of European stature who had lived in and been Cromwell's ambassador to Switzerland, foundered on mutual suspicion. Seen in the knowledge of what was to come, the failure to create any sort of common front among the moderate sectaries in 1658–9 was dangerous in that it left them exposed to the stronger and more determined revanchism of the Anglicans in 1660–4.

It also failed to make it clear to alarmed social conservatives who feared sectarian anarchy (now symbolised by the 'Quaker scare') that all sects were not to be lumped in with 'fanatics' as a threat to law and order and would-be revolutionaries. The ultra royalists were to be able to blame all the sects as dangerous fanatics and push Parliament into legislation to marginalise them once the king was back in office, and peaceful quietists such as the writer John Bunyan were to be regarded as being no different from the extremists who refused to doff their hats to their superiors and had wild millenarian fantasies about the Second Coming. It ended up with men like Bunyan dumped in prison for years as 'dangerous fanatics' by paranoid local gentry MPs after 1660. But from the perspective of autumn 1658 such a bleak future was unimaginable to the moderate sectaries.

The Quakers now petitioned the government against a new round of arrests of their sect in the provinces on various excuses, e.g. their non-payment of tithes to support the state church. They believed they had a right to 'opt out' of paying for a church they did not support; the social elites who provided most JPs regarded this as dangerous subversion. The Council ordered some releases but hung back from antagonizing local elites by being firmer for toleration – and recommended that the Quakers stop being publicly provocative to social 'mores' by refusing to doff their hats to their betters.[21] But the number and alarming size of the Quaker meetings across the country were an ongoing argument for worried political and religious moderates to back up whoever in authority would keep these apparent anarchists and blasphemers under control, as a 'backdrop' to the choices that most MPs would make for stability and conservatism in Parliament in 1659–60. This would tap into the sense of panic and desire for repression that the High Anglicans were to use to create the 'Clarendon Code' in Parliament in 1662–6 and ban their rivals from public life. At the least, did this panic inhibit religiously 'moderate' MPs from objecting to the 'Code' as it was a force for stability ?

The pomp of Cromwell's funeral and the smoothness of Richard'a accession hid serious political conflict. The ninety-four loyal addresses that Richard received from the provinces, and the apparent goodwill of the Presbyterians who regarded him as a more hopeful ally than his father, were countered by the lack of obedience that Richard could command from his father's officers. A new wave of petitioning by soldiers soon began once Richard had assumed power. The conservative nature of the political order of 1657–8 (which now seemed to have a monarch and a Second House) was the main target, with virulent criticism that it was a return to ungodly and oppressive Stuart despotism. The mutterings in the army about this were exacerbated by the perennial problem of the soldiers' pay being in arrears, with Richard endeavouring to satisfy the soldiers based around London (who were the most dangerous) and personally appealing to an army 'prayer-meeting' for unity in November.[22] The basic rate of pay for the whole Army was raised, though it was another thing to find the money to carry it out[23] and some regiments could not be reduced in size to cut costs as this would mean having to pay off the dismissed men. The feverish atmosphere and Richard's lack of rapport with the army were certainly a bonus for those who had grumbled at the conservative constitutional moves of 1657–8 but been unable to halt Cromwell himself, e.g. over the Second House, and the lack of money for soldiers gave them an audience to be worked on. Also some civilian councillors were said to be unhappy at the extent of the Protector's powers and to be prepared to link up with the regime's republican critics, presumably men like Vane and Haselrig, so army and civilians might combine. But the situation was not hopeless, and even in the regiment of Richard's religious radical uncle General John Desborough (who can be presumed to be opposing the Protectorate's political powers given his attitude to the 'Humble Petition and Advice' in 1657) the soldiers' current petition was mainly concerned with suppressing the 'blaspheming' Quakers.[24] Richard took firm action against some conspicuous individuals, notably Colonel Ashfield in the latter's quarrel with the senior Cromwellian loyalist officer Edmund Whalley in early March 1659. Whalley had confronted his junior over allegedly holding secret and seditious meetings of malcontents in his regiment, Ashfield denied it and was insubordinate, and Whalley reported him to Richard who had him court-martialled. Richard could or would not press the case to a conviction though apparently Desborough and Fleetwood refused to back Ashfield to the point of sedition as the latter's friends asked.[25] Desborough had earlier (6 December) tried to have the young, civilian, and conservative Fauconberg thrown off the Council for allegedly conspiring against him, possibly a reference to the latter being more prepared to stand up to his pressure and consider prosecution for it than Richard was. But the Protector stood firm and Desborough, a blunt ex-farmer in his early fifties who clearly despised the young civilian aristocrat, backed down temporarily.[26]

The Spanish war – an unnecessary result of the old Protector's miscalculation of Spain's reaction to a colonial attack – was causing a financial deficit due to the slump in trade, a risk that Lambert had warned Oliver Cromwell of when he first contemplated the war back in 1654. This enabled Richard's new Parliament of spring 1659 to attempt to use the 'power of the purse' against the indebted government which could not rely on a good stream of income from the customs; when the new regime's Parliament set up a committee to assess the current public revenue it reckoned (as of 7 April 1659) that the government was around £2,500,000 in debt and its revenue was falling short by nearly £333,000. Oddly, the government cancelled the 1653–4 reallocation of English constituencies and abolition of some rotten boroughs, one of the few constitutional innovations of the Protectorate – presumably as a gesture to conservatives who would be sitting in this Parliament, but at the cost of annoying reformers (including in the army such as Edmund Ludlow) further. The French ambassador Bordeaux reckoned it was due to a desire to restore smaller-franchised boroughs and to more easily control the latter. The Commons proved far more unruly than anticipated after a turbulent mid-winter election, showing the regime's comparative lack of organising ability (or willpower?) to control elections across the counties. The government could control a major bloc of MPs sent by Scotland and Ireland and put Fleetwood and Richard's uncle Desborough in charge of the Cinque Ports to control their patronage while Richard replaced eight of the sheriffs (who supervised the county elections), but many MPs were minor gentry without previous experience or obvious connections and seem to have been the choice of local communities. Greater rivalry and open confrontations between rival groupings (eg in Caernarfonshire) plus public shouts against the army (at the hustings in Yorkshire) testified to a more open atmosphere and less intimidation than under Richard's father. The radical republicans like Thomas Scot (former head of intelligence before Thurloe) and Edmund Ludlow (a lifelong republican) and other troublemakers secured election and took the required oath of loyalty to the Protectorate but then proceeded to undermine it – as republican thinker and Councillor Algernon Sidney, maverick son of the Earl of Leicester, had warned about the similar oath (the Engagement) required

1658–9: The Collapse of the Protectorate   57

in 1649, and such men would willingly perjure themselves to gain access to power. Haselrig, a leader of the Rump attempts to curb Army power and leading foe of Cromwell in 1651–3 (and a Presbyterian feared by the Army for his anti-toleration policy), and veteran mid-1640s Independent leader Sir Henry Vane – who had stressed the primacy of the legislature and the rule of law in 'A Healing Question' in 1656 – were allowed to take their seats, an evident attempt at conciliation. The government had attempted to keep Vane (who had been an ally of Cromwell in the late 1640s but had broken with him over the expulsion of the Rump) out by blocking his candidature at the open boroughs of Hull and Bristol. But he secured a pocket borough (Whitchurch, Hampshire) in the gift of a sympathiser, ex-Rumper Robert Wallop. Haselrig, who had a long pedigree as a senior – Presbyterian – MP in the 1640s and who had led his own regiment into battle (and nearly been killed at Roundway Down in 1643), had been banned from public life by Cromwell in 1653, and an attempt to lure Vane back into supporting the Protectorate had failed due to his principled condemnation of its defiance of the law and the dismissal of Parliament by military force in April 1653. The coup then had ended their co-operation with Cromwell. It was presumably hoped that now their main objection to the Protectorate – Cromwell – was gone they would give his successor the benefit of the doubt. Instead, they joined the republican 'ultras' (e.g. Scot and Ludlow) in demanding that the constitution be revised and the army curbed, re-fighting the battles of the mid-late 1640s and early 1650s. This time everyone who sought political change took the required oath of loyalty to the Protectorate in order to secure their seats, and then proceeded to attack the government from the House. A decision had clearly been taken beforehand to put strict principle aside and use their power in the Commons, not continue their years in the political wilderness since 1653. In that sense, Richard's sincere and passionate call for unity and mutual co-operation in his opening address to the Commons on 27 January 1659 was a vain hope.

The vital choice of Speaker was down to MPs not the government, but with a pro-Cromwellian majority a useful government ally could be chosen – as Sir Thomas Widdrington, a moderate Cromwellian lawyer from an old Northumbrian gentry family, had been in 1656. This time the choice was the obscure Chaloner Chute, a sixtyish senior Chancery lawyer who had been a JP in his native Middlesex since 1638 and more recently for his adopted Hampshire. A self-made man, he had purchased the estate of The Vyne near Basingstoke on 1649 and was thus from the same area as Richard and may have known him socially. More importantly, he had taken the principled and politically dangerous course of acting as counsel for eleven impeached Presbyterian MPs in 1648 and for the defeated royalist general Hamilton in his treason trial in 1649. He was reckoned an unlikely but sincere convert to the Protectoral regime, but unfortunately his health now failed so he was unable to give much direction to the MPs from March. Vainly requesting permission to resign, he died on 15 April.

Thurloe attempted to secure official legislative acceptance of the new regime's legality by a Bill of Recognition – which would mean accepting the constitution as it stood and not restricting the Protector's powers. This was 'talked out' by the veteran Rumper Haselrig,[27] who showed his intransigence. The civilian and military radicals introduced a portentously-named 'Humble Petition of Many Thousand Citizens' listing their grievances on 15 February, and this was also talked out but by many more speakers – the petitioners were not helped by the number of well-known sectaries in their deputation.[28] The recognition of Richard as commander-in-chief on 24 February owed more to immediate practicality than to a sensible constitutional compromise, given that orders had to be issued to the navy to sail to the Sound to deal with another Swedish attack on Denmark. This time, Charles X was feared to be intending to swallow up the whole of Norway or even Denmark too to round off his Scandinavian 'empire', which Cromwell had spent years vainly urging to attack the Catholic Habsburgs, not his and Charles' Protestant co-religionists. A small force had been sent under Admiral Goodson in November, but had proved inadequate. With access to Baltic naval supplies threatened the MPs put nation above faction and gave way to Thurloe's request, and Richard deputed Councillor Mountague to sail to the Sound in March. This removed a major political ally from his side but kept the fleet safe from a resurgence of republicanism by any more radical commander, who could have appointed sympathetic officers and thus added the fleet to the balance of forces against the government. The choice of Mountague reflected his experience at sea, most recently off Dunkirk leading the blockade in 1657–8 – and also his awareness of Dutch duplicity in the Baltic as he had been used to warn the Dutch from assisting Frederick

III of Denmark against Sweden in 1657. The choice had the advantage of removing one source of 'civilian vs. officers' conflict from the Council at a time of tension, as he had a personal quarrel with Desborough who late in 1658 had accused him and Lord Fauconberg of plotting to kill him and Fleetwood. Desborough may have heard exaggerated rumours of a genuine attempt by Mountague and his allies to remove the senior Cromwellian generals from power – were they trying to strike first and prevent any coups?

An example was made of an army officer (Colonel Boteler) who was accused of illegal mistreatment of an accused royalist – indicating the MPs' priorities. They returned to attempting to secure control over the militia as in 1654, and showed their attitude to toleration for sectaries by rejecting a Quaker petition for relief for prisoners. They also annoyed the military and their sect allies by a vote of 5 April censuring JPs for their slackness in punishing heretics, which category particularly encompassed militant and publicly scandalous sectaries, and talk in the Commons of re-establishing a formal Presbyterian structure for the national church revived the fears of intolerance by the latter which had partly caused the army to mutiny against the Commons majority in 1647. Ironically, on that occasion Cromwell and his civilian allies such as Vane had backed the army; Oliver Cromwell had had a reputation for always putting the 'godly's' right to free worship above administrative coercion but – dangerously – Richard now did not.

The regime however managed to secure the MPs' recognition of the controversial Second House as legal, which Cromwell had failed to do in 1658, and pro-government moderate Presbyterian Arthur Annesley (an Irish Protestant 'settler' MP and post-1660 royal minister) secured an invitation to peers loyal to Parliament in the 1640s to take their seats.[29] As far as conservative MPs were concerned, this would both add to the House's legal legitimacy – by allowing in hereditary peers as well as those created by Cromwell – and out-vote the religious radical Cromwellian generals in the House. Similarly, an attempt by republican critics of the Protectorate to deny the right of Scots and Irish MPs – more likely than English ones to be placemen selected carefully for election by those countries' loyalist governments – to sit in the Commons was defeated after a fortnight of argument. Both successes would add to pro-regime votes. The MPs also obeyed the government in quickly setting up a committee to look into the revenue, and required the customs-farmers to explain why income was not higher. Raising money quickly would ease army arrears of pay and decrease the soldiers' threat to the House, in which MPs had common cause with Richard. As of the finance committee report referred to earlier on 7 April, the government was reckoned to owe £890,000 in arrears of Army pay. The sooner some of this money could be found and passed on to the soldiers, the less the latter would have to grumble about, and the Commons' revenue committee began pressurising the 'farmers' of the Excise tax to hurry up with collecting overdue arrears. One crucial opposition figure with great prestige who anti-army MPs might follow, Vane, argued that they should co-operate with Richard to lure him into rejecting such monarchic powers as a veto on legislation, unfettered command of the army, and accepting a grant of revenue for life.[30] This marked an advance on his refusal to deal with Cromwell after 1656, and he clearly thought Richard more winnable to the principle of legislative supremacy.The MPs' order to JPs to act agaisnt heresy[31] – aimed squarely at the Quakers and a sign of social conservatives not sectaries being in the ascendant – would however add to soldierly sectaries' alarm and boost grumbling at the Commons' 'ungodliness' that could extend to Richard too.

MPs' religious conservatism was thus unlikely to please the army, whose 'General Council' of officers resumed sitting at this crucial point thanks to an apparent miscalculation by Richard and his advisers that it would air grievances, not exacerbate them. The likeliest explanation is that Richard and his ministers hoped a formal General Council-organised petition could be diluted in its antagonism to Parliament, unlike a spontaneous grass-roots one. This was a crucial mistake, as the senior officers did not have the same agenda as Richard. The hints of religious intolerance in the Commons raised the threat of a disciplinarian state church, and the attempts to assert legality over military power threatened their group interests – both of which they could trust Oliver but not Richard to protect. They could be persuaded or overawed in personal debate by Oliver Cromwell, their old commander to whom they felt ties of sentiment and of whose devotion to the cause and godliness they were assured. They were not going to treat the untried Richard, who had no military record, with similar respect unless they placed loyalty in his office – a new one which lacked the traditional respect and superstitious awe given to kingship.

The officers had rallied round Lambert in the creation of the Protectorate in December 1653 and religious zealots who objected to it (especially Fifth Monarchists) had been weeded out, and the 'Three Colonels' who had tried to protest about a semi-monarchical regime in 1654 had been cashiered successfully. But that had been when the war-winner generals Cromwell and Lambert were in control, and Richard would be on shaky grounds if it came to a trial of strength. He had not fought in the war and so had little claim on the soldiers' loyalty, and would need to rely on the ageing veteran Desborough, his uncle by marriage and a Civil War hero who had been opposed to kingship to the point of resignation in 1657, and the younger Fleetwood, his Baptist brother-in-law who had fought in the 1651 campaign and commanded in Ireland. Desborough apparently believed that younger civilian Cromwellian courtiers would stick at nothing to attack the army leadership. For the moment, the generals backed Richard as he turned up unexpectedly at a meeting at Fleetwood's house, Wallingford House up Whitehall from the Palace, to make a personal appeal to the officers not to back the radical City-army petition to Parliament. They pulled back from doing so, the petition 'flopped' and was ignored, and uneasy co-operation was evident through March. But once the army General Council met the junior officers and soldiers had a forum for agitation, and the risk rose of this getting out of hand as it had done in confronting the then Presbyterian-led Parliament and kidnapping Charles I from their custody in June 1647. Even the trusted Cromwell and his then senior, commander-in-chief General Fairfax, had let the soldiers have their heads sooner than risk disobedience in the first flush of democratic Leveller agitation in the army in summer-autumn 1647, and had openly debated the future constitution with the radicals at Putney Church in an unprecedented situation for England's (or any) army. This had involved open discussions on the extension of the franchise, long before the agitation that led up to the Great Reform Act of 1832, the rights of the citizens' representatives in the Commons to supervise the executive, and the need for annual elections to keep MPs responsive to their voters. The radical Colonel Rainsborough had even dared to suggest that all citizens, even the poor, had as much stake in the government as the richest gentlemen so they deserved the vote – though this sort of talk had soon been 'shut down' by the alarmed senior officers led by Cromwell and his son-in-law Henry Ireton. The military radicals had been encouraged to stand up to their officers by ever-busy civilian democrat pamphleteers in London led by 'Freeborn John' Lilburne, generally known as the Levellers – and who had been infiltrating the Army in 1647–8. There was always a danger of this sort of Army democracy resuming (or soldiers demanding a return to their 1647 practice of electing delegates to the Army Council) if the soldiers and various idealist junior officers were not controlled, and any vacuum in the Army leadership could cause this. But Cromwell had had the ruthlessness to confront seditious soldiers in a crisis that men such as Fleetwood lacked, ending up having pro-Leveller mutineers shot at Corkbush Field in 1647 after the 'Putney Debates' and at Burford after a major low-level military refusal to go to Ireland rather than enact constitutional reform in 1649.

The chances of the nervous senior officers reining in their men were thus not high, and the General Council now showed their attitude by setting up a committee (to frame their proposed petition to Parliament) full of troublemakers. The most prominent of these was Colonel Ashfield, who had been court-martialled by Richard's orders in March for apparent anti-government remarks made to the loyalist Colonel Whalley in Westminster Hall. The dissident officers succeeded in getting the General Council to adopt their petition to Parliament on 6 April, demanding that 'insolent' royalists who were openly appearing in London (presumably in support of Parliament) be sent packing as in earlier Cromwellian security clampdowns and the Army's demands for arrears of pay be met.[32] Fleetwood managed to tone the wording down a little to make it less menacing, but another petition – to him this time – from Colonel Thomas Pride's regiment on the 8th stressed the promoters' loyalty to the 'Good Old Cause', implicitly now under threat.[33] Ominously, Pride was the man who had led the eponymous 'Pride's Purge' of the Commons in December 1648, standing at the House's door with a list of reliable MPs to let in – and banning those MPs who did not favour the king's trial and execution from sitting with levelled guns. According to republican officer Edmund Ludlow's (edited) later account, the senior officers of Desborough and Fleetwood's group now entered into political dialogue with republican Commonwealthsmen in Parliament[34] – possibly to hold up conservative legislation, or to protect their own position from Haselrig's civilian group meddling with their more radical juniors.³⁵ The possibility thus arises that the fall of the Protectorate with the accompanying move of former regime loyalists to what would be called in post-1790 politics the 'left', like its mirror image the political shift by Monck and co. to the 'right' in early 1660, was a defensive move by the main actors. Were they in both cases driven to act by fear of losing control of their mutinous subordinates? The threat was latent for the moment, but at a similar moment of threats of mutiny Cromwell had quickly isolated any army-civilian republican associations (e.g. Overton's group's 'Petition of the Three Colonels' in 1654) and prevented lateral links between his potential challengers. Richard could and would not do this; thus the senior officers could be encouraged to think of disloyal actions by their civilian allies and desert their first duty to their commander-in-chief.

Old battles were refought at the General Council as it met on 14 April and Desborough endeavoured to secure a requirement that all officers subscribe to a statement approving of the regicide. This was probably intended to isolate and remove moderate supporters of the monarchic proposals of 1657, and reassert the army's coherence against infiltration by such moderate Cromwellian appointees as the Life Guard commander and deputy major-general, Charles Howard (a member of the aristocratic Howard clan and later a Restoration peer). Parliament in turn sought a compulsory declaration by all officers accepting their supremacy and disavowing military coercion, reviving the attempts of the 'Rump' and Cromwell's first Parliament to secure the principle of the supremacy of the legislature, and then ordered the army's General Council not to meet without its permission. Colonels Whalley and Goffe, two of the most loyal Cromwellians in the army high command (and of impeccable military record and 'godly' credentials unlike Howard), came to Richard's rescue by demanding an oath of loyalty from all officers to the Protectorate.³⁶ All these proposals were eventually dropped. Richard sought a vote by both Houses to settle the army's grievances on overdue pay, to couple with the Commons' motions to send the troops back to their duties outside the capital and require the officers to publicly swear denunciation of coercing Parliament. Broghill claimed to have been the brains behind this, others blamed Thurloe. But the Cromwellian generals in the Upper House defeated the motions in that body.³⁷

Cromwell's Second House thus served to aid the cause of political radicals not the pro-Richard conservatives due to the personnel who Cromwell had placed in that body. A quick invitation by the Protector or the Second House to moderate peers who had not sat in the Lords since 1648 to come and join the body, following the earlier (contentious) vote to accept such men as members, would have won that vote for Richard. But even if a vote to send the soldiers out of London had been passed the soldiers were capable of defying it in the tradition of their defiance of the Presbyterian majority in the Commons in summer 1647 and autumn 1648, provided that they had leadership capable of standing up to the generals. If there were 'old' peers who had not backed the army in 1648–9 among the Second House, this would have further inflamed opinion. Richard went ahead anyway, and summoned the officers to say that as Parliament was now voting for payment of the arrears the soldiers could leave London and he was dismissing the General Council. Desborough complained that the General Council was channelling discontent, showing his fear that it would be worse (and more of a threat to his control of it) if subterranean; Ashfield said he dared not go back to his troops without money. Richard ignored them, showing that he did not lack courage on this occasion .

The General Council did not meet on the 20th as planned, but the soldiers did not prepare to leave London either and Richard called his Life Guard to arms and sought declarations of support from the Lord Mayor and City of London (as controlling their militia). Desborough and Fleetwood visited him that evening and received assurances of goodwill to take to the army, but evidently did not consider this sufficient. Richard was expecting the army to obey orders (e.g. in not holding illegal meetings and in leaving London) and if the soldiers refused to do so the generals would publicly lose control. There was no point in obeying Richard if the upshot was that their men defied them. The crisis moved to a climax out of the generals' desire for self-preservation as much as due to a bid for power; but in either case the crucial fact was the lack of army loyalty to its commander-in-chief. On 21 April 1659 the Commons started debating setting up a militia force, i.e. a potential replacement for the current army that would be under their control – the crucial issue of legislative not executive control of the military that the Commons had attempted in vain to force on Charles I in 1641–2 and 1646. This was poor timing to say the least. Richard's brother-in-law Fleetwood and his uncle Desborough now deserted the Cromwell dynasty and joined other senior generals in demanding that he dissolve Parliament. Doing this would protect their own position from mutiny, as they could show their juniors that they had taken drastic action. On his refusal they defied him to his face by calling a military assembly at St James' Palace. It was supposed by uncommitted observers that Richard could call on at least a third of the army, led by his Life Guards (now commanded by Howard's successor James Beke), but the vast majority abandoned him and ignored the pleas of loyal officers. Even the veteran Whalley could not control his men; the defiance of those Cromwellian officers who had not seen service in the Civil War (e.g the American colonist Stephen Winthrop, successor to the cashiered General Harrison) was more to be expected. Richard was left with only around 200 men facing a much larger rival rendezvous at St James' Palace, with mutinous soldiers breaking into the Whitehall wine-cellars. He clearly could not hope to hold out until Monck could be contacted in Edinburgh or Henry Cromwell in Dublin to send loyal troops to London, and had to give way. (It must be asked why he or Thurloe did not consider the chances of trouble ahead of the notoriously anti-Army Parliament meeting and call some more reliable regiments to London in February or March.) Despite the constitutional position Richard held as Protector after Oliver he could be brushed aside by his father's old comrades and did not have enough loyal troops to arrest the dissidents. Forced by the officers to dissolve Parliament on the 22nd as Desborough threatened to lead his men there and do so himself if he did not, Richard was reduced to a figurehead in Whitehall as Parliament bravely locked its doors rather than obeying Richard at once and debated what to do but as it lacked force decided to disperse. Armed might had won as in 1648 and 1653, and policy was now decided by Fleetwood's junto meeting up the street in Wallingford House (now the site of the Admiralty building). The Army Council met from the 23rd to run the country, ordering royalists out of London and setting up a committee to raise revenues which Parliament would not now be granting.[38] Fleetwood secured the temporary loyalty of the army in Scotland by writing to Monck pretending that all this had been agreed by Richard, and by the time the only commander on the British mainland able to intervene had discovered the truth the new regime was secure and the MPs had tamely gone home. It was a return to the naked military rule of April-July 1653, but now with a junto (a contemporary term for a small council, derived from the Spanish government bodies), not one man (Cromwell) in charge.

Events now assumed their own momentum, as is common in times of upheaval; once the 'dam' of a conservative Protectorate had been broken all sorts of political possibilities raised themselves. Richard was apparently backed by Fleetwood against an immediate call for his removal by Desborough, but the more radical junior officers were now meeting on their own at St James' so the generals had to be wary of offending them. The removal of Parliament led to an outbreak of republican propaganda by the civilian Commonwealthsmen who were hostile to a Protectorate, with over twenty-eight pamphlets being printed in the two weeks after the 22nd. They promised arrears of pay, religious liberty, 'godly' government, and other notions attractive to the Army if it had the Rump recalled. The primacy of a properly elected Parliament – i.e. the Long Parliament, shorn of its untrustworthy royalist and Presbyterian members as of December 1648 – was thus to be restored by military power. This irony was no block to men like Haselrig and Vane now using the army to reverse the coup of April 1653. In the meantime, the senior officers made sure of their full control of the army on 28 April by cancelling the military commissions of their enemies from the Cromwellian faction, led by Richard, his brother-in-law Lord Fauconberg (a young nobleman with no army links), his father's cousin Richard Ingoldsby (an army veteran who was later able to show that he had a considerable level of support from ordinary soldiers even against Lambert), and Lord Broghill (a moderate political Anglo-Irish nobleman who had helped to rein in the army radicals in both Ireland and Scotland). Those who filled the vacant posts included Lambert (a miscalculation by his potential rival Fleetwood, but presumably too popular to be ignored) and Haselrig (another potential threat to the generals).[39]

Left isolated at Whitehall, Richard survived as titular Protector until 24 May when he had to sign a paper of abdication given to him by Rump Parliamentary delegates (including his father's cousin and political patron Oliver St John). His main concern appears to have been negotiating an adequate pension and payment for his debts, once he found that his written appeal to General Monck in Scotland to send troops was apologetically ignored. Even Monck could not coerce his officers, who had accepted the General Council explanation that the Army had had to remove Parliament for its self-preservation; the garrison of Dunkirk and the fleet in the Sound were too far away to act. Possibly if Mountague and his ships had been in English waters Richard could have asked him for help, given his moderate political views and future pro-royalist actions – but the question of the admiral's views at this point are too murky to be sure although he clearly preferred a single head of state to republican military rule. In the event, when he returned from the Sound to find the republicans in power he caused no trouble and retired to his Huntingdonshire estates, while keeping in touch with Richard. Richard now apparently attempted to contact the Royalists for support, but for the moment had to accept the allegedly inadequate payment offered by the Rump (which had other financial priorities) and retire to his Hampshire estate near Winchester.[40] Mocked by the Army as 'Queen Dick' and by the Royalists as 'Tumbledown Dick',[41] he survived in obscurity until 1712. Ironically, the ruler to hold power for the shortest time since Jane Grey became the longest-lived head of the government in any part of the current United Kingdom until 2011, dying at eighty-five, and nearly outlived the Stuart Restoration. In the meantime, the junto – now rejoined by the crucial figure of Lambert – proved no more able than either of the Cromwells to secure a lasting settlement with the civilian Parliamentarians, and a bewildering succession of events led to the collapse of the Commonwealth within a year of Richard's eviction. The old battles of 1647–8 about civilian or military primacy were re-fought, the civilian and military leaders could not work together, and neither would concede on points of ultimate authority. To be fair to the junto, men like Fleetwood and Desborough were zealous Independent sectaries and as concerned for their co-religionists as Cromwell had been when Parliament challenged his power to enforce religious toleration for the sects in 1655. They could not trust the Rump – or Richard once the rumours of Presbyterian support for him emerged? – to maintain religious toleration. Ever since the time when a majority of MPs had been Presbyterians and had sought to impose a hardline state church that did not accept the sects' right to freedom of worship in 1644–8, there had been a fear among the sects' Army patrons that religious toleration was under threat from their religious rivals, Presbytrians as well as Anglicans. Cromwell's senior officers also had personal differences with the Presbyterian leadership in the 1659 Parliament – they had purged this faction from the Commons in December 1648 and forced the remaining MPs to accept regicide and a republic.

The nominally civilian regime set up by the 'Instrument of Government' in December 1653, and amended by the 'Humble Petition and Advice' in 1657, ultimately rested on the veto of the army leadership. The officers could overthrow it, though it is unclear whether or not Cromwell dared not take the crown and formalise the civilianisation of his authority on traditional lines for fear of the senior officers. Once he was dead, his old comrades could show their disquiet with the constitutional solution of 1657 – or even of 1653 – and prevent Richard from acting freely, and when he challenged them remove him and start to tinker with a new form of the 1649–53 Commonwealth. The question remains, however, if Fleetwood and his allies would have been so quick to act against Richard if pressure had not been building up among their juniors. (Desborough was more likely to have acted; back in December he had accused Mountague of trying to have him arrested and dismissed.) The burst of petitions, attitudes within the General Council, and hostility to Richard's regime as a nest of pro-royalists betraying all that the army had fought for indicated that the officers were expecting their seniors to take drastic measures. If they had not, would some radical officers have repeated Pride's Purge on Richard's Parliament, or even have marched on Whitehall to remove Richard? It is possible that Lambert, not yet reinstated as a senior commander after his resignation on principle in July 1657 but popular within the army for the action he had taken then to refuse to join the new order, was capable of leading a mutiny – or was anyway feared as such? Had Fleetwood and Desborough allowed a more conciliatory Richard to talk them out of action, would a mutiny have broken out anyway?

The return of the Rump, 1659. Reasserting 'legality' – but with a military 'junta' behind the scenes.

It was symptomatic of the divisions between the generals and their allies in the restored Rump (which met on 7 May), civilians such as Vane, Haselrig, and the veteran republican Henry Marten (a lone wolf alienated from 'godly' colleagues by his debts and mistresses), that they could not even agree on the precise nature of the new government. The regimental commanders loyal to Richard, e.g. Goffe and Whalley, were removed and Fleetwood made commander-in-chief with Lambert as his deputy; the contentious Cromwellian grants of titles of nobility were cancelled; and an Act of Indemnity was passed which eventually included all the Cromwellians criticised by the Army. This in effect put Fleetwood at Lambert's mercy by removing his own connections within the wider Cromwellian family circle, but he was presumably reacting to grass-roots pressure within the army to sideline Goffe and Whalley as stalwarts of the ousted Protectorate and political conservatives. The army officers put forward their requests as early as 12 May. Their petition for religious freedom for all Protestants except Episcopalians (i.e. Anglicans) was accepted by the House, but not their request for a Senate (the less contentious term for a Second House) including themselves – with some veto-powers over the Commons. The religious request was passed on 20 May,[42] but was not that contentious as it was barely different from Cromwell's declaration on religion of 1657; the questions of a national ministry, tithes, and the right of Quakers not to accept Scripture as essential to faith were left vague. Some Quakers in prison were released as requested, with the Commons committee (led by Vane) allowing the Quaker witnesses they were examining to keep their hats on rather than upset their consciences by demanding that they take them off respectfully. But clergy were to be protected from disruption of services (which was mostly done by Quakers) and tithes were kept in force until an adequate replacement could be found. Potentially anti-Army MPs excluded by Pride's Purge in 1648 were not allowed to take their seats despite a petition on their behalf, and when the arch-Presbyterian pamphleteer William Prynne slipped in anyway after lunch on 9 May, he was ejected by soldiers. Given his fierce anti-sectary views as a Presbyterian hardliner, mastery of invective, and inability to keep his opinions to himself Prynne was a destructive (though hugely prestigious) figure who would only have disrupted attempts at conciliation. Both he and the other Presbyterian leader who was kept out by force, Arthur Annesley, would end up as royalists a year later – Prynne as implacable towards regicides as he had been earlier towards Charles I – but their views at this stage are more likely to have been just anti-army given military control of State politics and religion since 1653. At this point, Prynne's main public declarations were in favour of a state church imposing tithes as sanctioned by scripture – always a marker for conservative or radical religious views in the Interregnum, with the abolition of tithes having been proposed by the Nominated Parliament in 1653 but blocked. Pride's Purge's legality was confirmed, a necessary sop to the Army, and the Commons faced mutually contradictory pressure for anti-persecution action by the Quakers, from Vane for full religious toleration, and for an anti-'Protectorate elite' purge by Commonwealthsmen reformers who had been thwarted in 1653.[43] The huge petitions against payment of tithes brought to the Commons in mid-May (from western England) and on 27 June (national) showed the strength and organising ability of the sects and other critics of a centralised state church, but suffered from having been organised by the Quakers (especially the latter, in which women played a major role too) so they could be written off as a fanatic campaign that needed to be resisted. The 'Rump' was supposed to sit for not more than a year, with the new executive Council consisting of a temporary 'Committee of Safety' (7 May) on which Vane was the main civilian in the original membership.

From 19 May there was a 31-member Council of State led by Fleetwood, Desborough, Lambert, Haselrig, Vane, and Ludlow. The body included two senior civilian Cromwellians – Anthony Ashley Cooper, who had left the Council in 1654 (out of objections to Army executive power?) and the monarchic supporter and moderate lawyer Bulstrode Whitelocke, though Scot tried to keep both out.[44] Members were also allowed to affirm rather than swear loyalty to the Commonwealth in order to keep them on side, in contrast to the government's actions in 1657; this enabled Fleetwood and Scot to join the Council. The thorny question of ultimate legal power over the military was solved by having Speaker Lenthall – official head of the government under the Commonwealth in 1649–53 – sign all military commissions, though this probably annoyed Fleetwood and military radicals. The resignation of Henry Cromwell, Richard's more dynamic younger brother, as Lord Lieutenant of Ireland on 14 June, as requested by letter by the Speaker, placed the army in that country in the hands of safe military officers – a commission including the republicans Edmund Ludlow, Miles Corbet, and Matthew Tomlinson.[45] Unlike in Scotland the army in Ireland would not be a force for moderation in 1659–60, though that was perhaps inevitable given the number of religious zealots who had gone to Ireland in the 1650s to colonise it and keep it safe from

Catholics. But the existence of a group of radical officers in command in Dublin would also keep these men out of politics in London, a bonus for Monck as he sought to neuter the army in the latter in early spring 1660.

The civilian and military leadership seemed willing to work together, and discussions in the Commons proceeded on the basis of a seemingly cooperative mood to receive and examine the multitude of petitions for secular and religious reform. Anger by disgruntled provincials and egalitarian soldiers and sectaries at the pretensions, self-appointed titles, and supposed embezzlement of the Cromwellian elite led to the technical cancellation of the titles awarded by Cromwell as Lord Protector (though they continued to be used without prosecution in a typical British political compromise). Office-holders were allowed to continue in their roles provided they swore allegiance to the new regime (without any noticeable refusals or vigorous checks), and past salaries were excused and continued as long as they were seen to be necessary (which was not specified).[46] In reality, the petitioners' anger was being sidelined as was necessary to avoid a rupture in the ruling circles; any prosecutions of past Cromwellians could well have driven important figures to link up to the Royalists. One of the two leading civilians on the Council of State, Vane, had politico-religious goals in common with the army, unlike the other (Haselrig). He regarded wide religious toleration for the sects as essential and a foundation-stone of a 'godly' future for England, and back in 1644–7 had been a leader of the pro-toleration 'Independents' in the Commons who objected to the setting up of a rigorously disciplinarian Presbyterian state church. He had also been among the first to suggest the idea of deposing the untrustworthy king, and despite his principles, capability as an administrator, and struggle for religious toleration had put the rule of law above army rights in 1653 and had broken with Cromwell over his coup. He was concerned to effect rule by the most virtuous citizens rather than by the usual body of conservative county gentry and townsmen in the Commons, and had that in common with religious-minded military sectarians like Fleetwood (and even with the Fifth Monarchists). The Presbyterians loathed him for his opposition to their religious plans in 1644–8. He was also at odds with the principle of military supremacy over the civilian authority, as seen by his stand in 1653–6, but not with the aims that military power sought to achieve; ironically, his views in

1659 made him close to those of the enthusiasts for the 'Nominated Parliament' he had boycotted in 1653.

Vane was also at odds with the other main civilian propounder of constitutions in summer 1659, the 'Roman Republic' enthusiast philosopher James Harrington, and with Harrington's principal Parliamentary ally Henry Neville. They were too secular-minded in their classicism, and too naïve about the propensity of unreformed mankind for sinning for Vane to back them. In his written reply to Harrington's proposals, 'A Needful Corrective or Balance in the Commonwealth', he insisted on the creation of a ruling elite of the 'godly' to organise both the Senate and the Representatives for the new legislative body; they would secure the rule of virtue as in the ancient Commonwealth of Israel. In due course an appropriately educated and reformed public could be admitted to government, once it could be assured that they would carry out the desired will of the Lord rather than of Man. This desire for a religious elite, in practice led by the sects, placed Vane with the generals and against both the Neville-Harrington bloc and the MPs around Haselrig (mostly Presbyterians loyal to the principles of the 1649–53 regime) in the clashes of autumn 1659. The fact that the army's administrative commission for appointments now chose to restore known military troublemakers dismissed by Oliver Cromwell, such as Colonels Rich and Alured, to their regiments stored up trouble for the future but was probably necessary as a temporary sop to low-level Army pressure, balancing the radicals who backed these men with the moderates in the senior ranks. Some senior Cromwellians in the latter, e.g. Goffe and Whalley, were sacked to make way for them – but even if they had been retained their men might have refused to obey them. This second remodelling of army commissions in 1659 was carried out supposedly by co-operation between the army and Commons, but mostly by army action before their list of approved officers was handed to Parliament for confirmation.This stored up trouble by restoring men like the republican Alured and the Fifth Monarchists Overton and Rich – but grass-roots pressure won. It is probable that radical MPs encouraged the reappointment of known enemies of Fleetwood and Desborough on the principle of 'divide and rule'. So far Fleetwood and his allies could 'ride the tiger' of militant junior officers' discontent by such gestures – but for how long?

On the crucial question of finance, the Commons agreed on 20 May to confirm the current assessment and speed up its date of payment, but in the meantime the lack of money was to be remedied by squeezing out more from the customs and excise. The farmers were summoned and intimidated to that end, but with no visible results – thus meaning that soldiers became disillusioned with the Rump. Indemnity was granted to Cromwellian officer-holders, albeit largely due to the various factions of MPs sidelined or prosecuted in 1653–8 being unable to agree who to prosecute, and the Protector's palaces were supposed to be sold off to raise money but failed to find any buyers. The nature of the permanent constitution to be arranged was as contentious as in 1649–53 and the eruption of pamphleteering in London (and James Harrington's new 'Rota Club' of constitutional enthusiasts) showing the degree of public interest in the matter. There was also a revival of hopes by religious radicals that the contentious issue of tithes would be settled by their abolition, to which end two large provincial petitions were delivered to Parliament on 14 May and 27 June. The Quakers' reputation as dangerous anarchists led to continuing attacks on them by angry crowds in the provinces after they vociferously interrupted church services, this ostentatious 'direct action' of repeatedly disrupting the main religious activity of the week not exactly winning them toleration.[47] On other matters, the City radicals handed in a petition for a purge of the City militia (9 May) and the City radical Samuel Moyer, a stalwart of the Nominated Parliament, led a petition for promotion of the 'Good Old Cause' (12 May); the London radicals who had stood firm for Parliament against the king in 1642–8 were not yet so worried at army power that they would consider restoring the monarchy as was to occur that winter.[48]

There was thus a return to some of the political and religious hopes of 1649–53. But the crucial question was whether the alliance of generals and civilian republicans could last – a matter which would have emperilled the post-Cromwell government at whatever date this emerged. The allies were united in their antagonism to a Protectorate and civilians like Vane had as much nostalgia for the 'Good Old Cause' (which was never clearly defined) as the soldiers had by 1659. But they were not united in much else. Despite the civilian MPs having formally approved of Pride's Purge, i.e. military coercion, this was not an indication that the Commonwealthsmen accepted a military veto on their actions but necessary to keep Presbyterian opponents of religious toleration (and republicanism) out of the Commons. Haselrig and Vane had both stood against the post-20 April 1653 regimes on the grounds of their illegality, and would not accept coercion by the generals. Nor was restoring the king an option yet for most of the county communities, though it is apparent that local conservatism was given a boost by panic in early summer 1659 over the renewed prominence of religious radicals in London. There were fears of a rising by either Fifth Monarchists or Quakers, with wild rumours of fanatics planning a massacre,[48] and as a result renewed legal ferocity against Quaker prisoners by JPs. The Independent sects' London branches sought the ideas of their provincial counterparts on the future of the country, stimulating a degree of enthusiasm and extra meetings among the latter – and alarm among their critics. The new regime's purge of the local militia and county government added to the potential for disruption by removing 'suspect' pro-Cromwellian conservatives in favour of obscure local supporters of the republican Commonwealthsmen, men who lacked local support or prestige and could not count on loyalty from the gentry or townsmen. Worse, some of the new commissioners even included Quakers – vocal support for whom by Vane did not exactly endear him to the moderate MPs who he would need for votes if his planned reforms were ever to be passed by the Commons. This added to the prospects for the royalists as the best guarantors of stability – though when the latter decided to act they were to prove to lack the necessary tipping-point of armed backing when faced with the well-armed and co-ordinated army. At a less politically significant non-elite level the Army were as unpopular for perceived arrogance and excesses of power as they had been in 1648 when their prominence and intimidation rallied support to the royalists, as seen by the popular disturbances against local military commissioners illegally enclosing fields from common land in Enfield in Essex that summer. The locals rose against the soldiers' bullying tactics and scuffles led to deaths, soldiers arrested rioters who a local jury acquitted, and both sides petitioned the Commons; Parliament backed the forces of law and order. This case ominously became a cause celebre.[49]

The Royalist failure, August 1659: jumping the gun? 'Regime change' is shown to be from within only, not from external action.

The royalist 'Booth Rising' of summer 1659 was a fiasco as the rising in 1655 had been, though worryingly this time it included some Presbyterians among its leaders (most notably the eponymous Sir George Booth and his ally Sir Thomas Myddleton, 1640s Parliamentarian officers, in Cheshire) as well as the Cromwellian Lord Fauconberg. Fauconberg's participation reflected an antagonism to the generals seen back in late 1658, with his family's royalist ties making it easier for him to join them than it was for other Cromwellians. Presumably the overthrow of his friend Richard Cromwell and his personal clash with Desborough drove him to revert from Cromwellian to Stuart royalism as he had no hopes of the increasingly radical new regime – and any overt decisions for full religious toleration or abolishing tithes by the Rump would have increased the number of Cromwellians who joined him. Even without them, this coalition of summer 1659 combined the same deadly mixture of 'old' royalists (or younger members of their families) and ex-Parliamentarians who believed in a limited monarchy as had threatened the army in 1648, with the extra addition of Cromwellians. Unlike in 1648 the king who was to be restored was not tainted by a long career of treachery and double-dealing, though Charles II had invaded England from Scotland in 1651 and been condemned to death for treason by the ruling regime – and as in 1648 a long army of occupation of the country had raised tax-burdens and irritated the civilians who had to put up with their depredations. The lack of serious foreign support from Charles' patron, war-exhausted Spain which was preoccupied with its peace-talks with France, was no more damaging than French hesitation had been to the 1648 risings. As with that occasion and in 1655, a network of simultaneous revolts were intended to tie down the army (which would not know which revolt to tackle first) until a large enough royalist force could assemble to challenge it. The coalition that came together under the auspices of the young but experienced royalist plotter John Mordaunt, brother of the Earl of Peterborough, and already tried for treason for his part in a January 1658 plot, was thus impressively wide in membership. It overcame the usual distrust of the more hesitant noble leadership of the Sealed Knot, the senior (in social rank and length of service) royalist grouping, for the risky gambles of Mordaunt's 'Action Party'. It also had the backing of Charles II's senior civilian adviser and secretary, Sir Edward Hyde, who sent agents from the Spanish Netherlands to assist the Mordaunt group, though the latter were on uneasy terms with the other main group of younger royalists who had not been involved in the 1640s struggles, the Oxfordshire circle around Lord Falkland (son of the distinguished royalist ex-secretary of state killed in battle at Newbury in 1643). For once the groupings of older and younger royalists worked together, reinforced by moderate Presbyterians who had fought for Parliament in 1642–6 but had wanted Charles I to keep his throne as a puppet-ruler at the head of a modified monarchy and had opposed Pride's Purge and regicide. They were now alienated from the new regime of spring-summer 1659 by the return to power of their foes from a decade before, and when Charles II and Hyde sent two royalist Anglican clerics to England in May 1659 to rally their fellow-clergy and consecrate new priests they were instructed to co-operate with (and consecrate) Presbyterians too. The fear of Quakers and sectaries aided by a rampant army could thus boost royalist support – and it appears that the alarmed ex-Cromwellian stalwart Colonel Ingoldsby approached the plotters too on behalf of Richard Cromwell (with or without his permission). The royalists' main foe Thurloe – who had suborned some of the 'Knot's membership to feed him information years before – had recently been sacked by the 'Rump' as a Cromwellian. His replacement Scot was equally zealous but lacking in experience – or in willingness to co-opt his predecessor for help. The Council of State apparently only had three days' notice of the date set for the revolt – 1 August – which suggests a less reliable spy-system than Thurloe's.[50] As in 1648, Presbyterian clergy came out in open support of the king.

The participation of both Parliamentarians-turned-royalists and a few Cromwellians in the plot indicated that the danger of socially and religiously conservative Presbyterians turning to the king as a safer ally than the sectaries, already seen in 1648, was reviving. Charles II promised pardon for all ex-rebels except regicides, who would be allowed to emigrate if they so preferred before they were prosecuted (as was to occur in practice for some of the less dangerous regicides, e.g. Goffe and Whalley, in 1660–1). But, as in 1655, lack of confidence or mutual communications between the groups of rebels meant that on the appointed date to revolt some lost heart and failed to take part, fearing that it would fizzle out and so it was useless to proceed. This affected the two most crucial groups in the south, Mordaunt's in Surrey and Viscount Falkland's in Oxfordshire. The rebels in the south-west, north-east, and midlands decided similarly, and in the south-west midlands small groups failed to coalesce and were quickly routed by local army garrisons and militia. In 1655 this had left Penruddock's group in Dorset/Wiltshire as the sole rebel army to make a viable but outnumbered stand; in August 1659 it was the turn of Sir George Booth and the mixture of 'old' royalists and Presbyterians in Cheshire. Possibly the serious and even nature of the Civil War in 1643–5 in Cheshire between two nearly-matched political/religious groups meant that there was more of a willingness by experienced ex-soldiers to make a fight of it, with men on both sides from 1643–5 now fighting for the King. Booth himself had defended Nantwich for Parliament then, been secluded from Parliament as a Presbyterian distrusted by the army at Pride's Purge, and sat in Richard's Parliament. Significant members of the militia joined this senior local magnate as he rose in the name of a free Parliament, and the local ex-Parliamentarians from the 1640s evidently believed that he favoured the sort of limited monarchy and state church which his allies had intended to impose on Charles I. This was far from the programme of the Sealed Knot or the Action Party of Mordaunt, but close to that of the Presbyterian wing of the 1648 rebellion.

As an ex-Parliamentarian general, Booth was in the same league as his more nationally known colleagues Massey and Waller who had been involved in the 1648 Royalist/Presbyterian revolt. It was enough to secure him local support, but not national success. The Rump quickly voted on 2 August to renew the powers of the wartime committees for sequestration (and to award rebels' lands to those of their tenants who stayed loyal, giving the latter reason to desert their landlords). It had already told the army in Flanders to return home at the end of July, and now summoned 1,500 Irish troops to take the Cheshire rebels in the rear, called out the militia, and initiated the raising of new regiments. Desborough was placed in charge of the west of England, as in 1655, and on the 7th Lambert left London with five regiments to deal with Booth. The news of the rebels' success spurred their allies in the East Midlands to revolt belatedly, though with small enough members for the militia to disperse, while Sir Thomas Myddelton proclaimed the king in Denbighshire, Fauconberg made an unsuccessful attempt to raise

Yorkshire, and Mordaunt and his friends were arrested or driven into flight before they could stir up London. While Lambert was raising enough men to tackle Booth, who had around 1,000 men in control of most of Cheshire, the main rebel force went unmolested, but it lacked the nerve or the numbers of allies elsewhere to take the initiative. As soon as Lambert was ready he marched on them, and his better-disciplined soldiers routed the royalists at a clash at Winnington Bridge on 19 August. Booth escaped to be captured later in Buckinghamshire and put in the Tower charged with treason, and the other rebel groups quickly dispersed. Quite apart from the disheartening effect of a repeat of 1655, the royalists were now hampered by belated discovery that the 'Sealed Knot' leader Sir Richard Willis had been corresponding with Thurloe for years, which ruined his reputation.[51]

Charles II was en route to Brest in Brittany to board a ship to join Booth in Cheshire when he heard news of the rebels' defeat. Had he landed, he would have been too late to be any use (as his nephew the 'Old Pretender' was to be in Scotland in 1715) and might well have ended up humiliatingly 'on the run' as in 1651. Luckily he was still at St Malo waiting the arrival of Ormonde, who had been sent to Paris in the vain hope of French support. He now set off to the Franco-Spanish peace-conference at the River Bidassoa in the Pyrenees to seek aid from one or both kingdoms, and was promised help there by Philip IV's chief minister De Haro but not by the French chief minister Cardinal Mazarin. The threat of a peace-treaty and Catholic (French?) European aid for Charles had seemed a major menace to English interests by Thurloe in 1653–8, but was now virtually ignored by the preoccupied 'Rump'. Their main overseas concern was the joint Anglo-Dutch naval demonstration in the Sound to force Charles X of Sweden to cease threatening Denmark's independence. The two parties were not in agreement, England being broadly pro-Swedish and the Dutch close to Denmark, but were assisted by a third and more neutral party – France, under its ambassador to Denmark (Terlon). The most the English navy would do was to interpose itself between an outnumbered Swedish squadron and its Dutch attackers, to Charles' disappointment.

Their joint naval demonstration duly made the belligerent Charles X, disappointed of hopes of English aid, give way to peace-talks with Denmark. The two kings, Charles and Frederick, met outside

Copenhagen. The crisis had a domestic factor, given that the English admiral Mountague was a senior Cromwellian and might defy the 'Rump' and/or join the August 1659 rebellion. Retained in his naval command in May 1659, Mountague was a close ally of Richard, feared by the new regime as a potential rebel and Richard appears to have kept up contact with him as a possible ally; ironically the admiral was informed of Richard's deposition by the future Restoration diarist Samuel Pepys, his cousin and at the time his aide. Mountague's position at the Anglo-Dutch naval force at Copenhagen during the negotiations had been made difficult by the arrival of three commissioners from the Rump to 'assist' him, with the well-founded fear that the new regime distrusted him and the trio were empowered to replace him if necessary. (Their secret instructions did include this option.) The most important, experienced and forthright of the commissioners, the republican zealot Algernon Sidney (the estranged brother of Mountague's ex-Council colleague Lord Lisle) was described by him as 'my mortal enemy'. A second commissioner, Sir Robert Honeywood, was Vane's relative and so presumably his nominee.[52]

Fearing arrest or denunciation by a grudge-driven Sidney, might Mountague defect to the King and take his fleet to join in the rebellion? Charles II is supposed to have offered him an earldom to defect to the royal cause which he did, along with Monck, in 1660. His choice of an agent to go to royalists in Copenhagen was ironically Cromwell's nephew, disgraced young Captain Thomas Whetstone. This swashbuckling bravo was more in the mould of a typical royalist officer than a Cromwellian, owing his political allegiances solely to family, and had been thrown out of the Navy for making allegations about his superior officer Captain Stokes (Cromwell's Mediterranean commander in 1658). His mission was apparently suggested by Thurloe's ex-deputy in the intelligence service Samuel Morland, another disgruntled Cromwellian now in touch with the king. Mountague's decision to return home in mid-August, with the diplomatic talks still going on, was a source of anxiety although the fleet was genuinely running short of supplies as he alleged. It undermined the Rump commissioners' ability to coerce Sweden if Charles X broke off negotiations, which he did; but was it timed to assist the rebellion? The rebellion collapsed before Mountague's fleet arrived (he landed on 7 September), so he was spared a choice of loyalties and fulsomely assured his support to the Council on 9 September. He also defiantly gave a written account to his former employer Richard Cromwell, showing that he regarded him as the rightful head of State as he explicitly stated in his letter. The suspicious Rump Admiralty Commissioners, now led by republican Colonel Valentine Walton (Mountague's defeated rival at a Parliamentary election in 1654), set up a committee to investigate why Mountague had returned home early. Nothing was proved, but he lost his regimental command to the radical Colonel Alured. Already the Council had handed the Channel Squadron over to the veteran 'Leveller' ally and plotter dismissed for suspected disloyalty in 1656, Vice-Admiral John Lawson.[53] Ironically, Mountague's quick return after a successful expedition added to the government's problems, as it meant that the now idle squadrons he had commanded had to be stood down and the men aboard sent home but there was not enough money to pay them; the Franco-Spanish peace also meant the return (for payment of overdue salaries) of the Protectorate's garrisons in Flanders. This all compounded the financial crisis and the threat of disorder by unpaid soldiers; the militia (stood down after the revolt's failure, on 7 September) could not be fully paid either and some angry militiamen kidnapped government commissioners as surety for payment. There was also a potential threat from Lawson, who had tolerated or even encouraged mutinous officers opposing the Protectorate in 1656 and now was to prove equally disloyal to the Rump – but he was presumably chosen as a popular commander and a proven republican.

The republican alliance breaks up: the showdown between Army and Rump, October 1659.

The 'Commonwealthsmen' needed to show unity and reach agreement on the nature of the next government. But in the event, they threw away their strong position with continual bickering. Fleetwood was supposed to prefer a moderated Protectorate; Lambert a form of oligarchy by the well-affected (which would include some Cromwellians and possibly pro-toleration moderates); some radical MPs like Vane and officers a government of the godly; and other MPs a single-chamber Parliament. Vane had now withdrawn from the 'Committee of Safety' (along with the Cromwellian stalwart Richard Salwey) out of dissatisfaction with military rule, but stayed on its sub-committee on government (so as to put forward his own schemes for the future of the regime) and on the Admiralty Committee to help direct the response to the Baltic crisis. Significantly, the idea of a Senate of senior figures to steer Parliament the right way as the top Councils did the legislature in Venice now had popular military backing as it featured in petitions for the nature of a future regime by soldiers. This probably reflected contemporary classical enthusiasms as much as interest in the oligarchy of Venice, and would entrench a collective executive as a check on the Commons. The most detailed and coherent civilian thinker, Harrington, favoured a bicameral Parliament elected by the property-holders, parts of it being elected in rotation.[54] When Parliament set up a committee to look into the future constitution on 8 September Harrington's proposals were submitted by Sir Arthur Haselrig, and were said to have Fleetwood's backing too; Harrington practically wanted some form of clause to inhibit future governments from changing the constitution again at whim, which was contentious but a clear-sighted warning of what the Restoration's second Parliament after 1661 was to do to the initial plans made by the Convention in 1660. Vane, who had the best record as a defender of both legal civilian government and of free religious expression and who was now urging impatient officers like Lambert to respect the legality that the Rump represented, preferred a nominated government by 'Saints'.[55] Petitioning for this by Independent congregations had revived after the Booth rebellion, helped by the lapse in government censorship that spring which had led to a flurry of pamphleteering as seen earlier in similar circumstances in 1640–1, and Vane was connected to their role in pressurising the government that autumn. Vane's plans however reflected the overwhelming importance he, like Cromwell, placed on religious toleration at a time when there was little hope of that from a 'free Parliament' of alarmed conservative country gentry dominated by Haselrig's Presbyterians. His religious idealism arguably doomed his chances of getting any of his preferred forms of republic accepted by enough allies to be workable.

As the conservative gentry held the advantage of numbers in any Commons elected under the usual political system, enforcing toleration to protect the 'godly' would require curtailing elective democracy. Already there was growing alarm among Presbyterians at the Quaker threat and an added fear that the defeat of Booth's rising had emboldened the latter and other radicals, and in London that autumn a common front began to appear with talks between Presbyterian, Anglican, and even moderate Baptist religious ministers. Indeed, after the revolt was suppressed Lambert's triumphant army showed open sympathy for the Quakers in the north-west, attending their meetings in Liverpool, giving them the keys of the town hall in Manchester for a meeting, and protecting them from angry locals in Cheshire. (This was not yet useful to the King, though, as hardline Anglican royalists like the diarist John Evelyn were angry at the Booth rising's leaders for co-operating with republican Presbyterians.) A sects' petition to the Commons on 17 September favoured formal and firm legal toleration led by the House; so did the millenarian Fifth Monarchists who wanted to impose Mosaic law as in holy ancient Israel.[56] Vane was now opposed to the Haselrig faction's proposal to enforce an oath of loyalty on all office-holders before deciding on the form of the new constitution they were supposed to swear allegiance to. Lambert, the sects, and the army were in sympathy with the requirement for wide religious toleration, but the committee on religious measures voted against it. This raised alarm among the sects, but in any case Parliament's vote on 3 October to delay the crucial constitutional debates while it arranged by-elections for vacant seats showed its priorities. As in April 1653, the MPs seemed more concerned with self-perpetuation than with reform – and the continuing army anger at arrears of pay made any sign of dilatoriness or self-seeking an explosive issue.

The civilian moderates in the Rump seemed prepared to take on the Army, precipitating confrontation in October, and Haselrig led an attempt to respond vigorously to a petition by members of Lambert's army demanding swift action and reform. (Lambert's part in this is unclear.) This 'Derby Petition', arranged by troops in Lambert's force in the field on 17 September at Derby after suppressing the Booth revolt, required godly reforms, a senate (as a check on the Commons), and promotion to generalship for all senior officers. Courts-martial, not Parliament, were to dismiss military personnel.[57] This revived fears of an attempt to coerce or expel the Rump, and on 22 September Haselrig read a copy of the petition to the Commons behind closed doors in the best conspiratorial manner useful for whipping up hysteria. (Ludlow later accused Fleetwood of leaking it to Haselrig to embarrass and hopefully ruin Lambert; this has no evidence.) It was proposed to send Lambert to the Tower, but

Vane and Fleetwood succeeded in heading this off and he remained at large when he returned to London a few days later.[58] Not all his troops were recalled to London, but some of the others slipped back anyway and probably stirred up anti-Rump feelings among their colleagues; nor is it clear what Lambert and Thurloe were doing holding a private meeting.[59] Was Thurloe seeking to ask the popular Lambert to restore Richard? And if he had succeeded would this have provided the Cromwellians with the military muscle they needed for a come-back? But if this was Thurloe's intention, Lambert put his own ambition or his republican principles first.

Fleetwood sought to regain control of the army by holding a meeting of the senior officers at his house where he asked them to help draw up a – controllable – army address to the Commons, presumably mentioning some complaints (especially arrears) but not inflaming the MPs. But on 3 October the meeting of the Army General Council to do this, at Somerset House chapel, got out of hand and the raucously insistent majority of officers secured a more inflammatory petition, demanding most of the ideas in the 'Derby Petition' (e.g. no dismissal except by courts-martial) as well as payment of arrears. Desborough delivered this to the Commons on the 5th, with predictable results.[60] The MPs were initially conciliatory, albeit in practice only over arrears so their refusal to play into the radicals' hands only postponed a clash. But they were annoyed as rumours spread of army talks about closing the House, and on the 11th they voted it to be treason to levy a tax without Parliamentary approval. This meant that a military regime that had expelled them would be starved of funds, as well as invalidating Cromwell's grants of revenues to various officers. An attempt was made to dismiss Lambert and other officers who were encouraging soldiers in various provincial garrisons to sign up to the Derby petition, as the House was presented with written evidence of this apparent 'call to arms' by Colonel Okey on the 12th. The military move to gather support for the petition was probably designed to put pressure on the Commons, not stage a coup – but was taken as the latter. By a new order of the panicking House, Lambert and the other troublemakers were to be replaced in senior command by a mixed commission of loyal officers – at this stage including Fleetwood and Ludlow. In retaliation, Lambert marched his men on the House on 13 October. Haselrig, like Richard in the confrontation in April, relied on loyal officers – this time

Colonels Okey and Hacker and Herbert Morley – controlling their men, but enough soldiers deserted to enable Lambert to prevail. The latter bravely marched up to loyal Horse Guards defending Scotland Yard to order their commander to surrender, risking being shot and trusting that his reputation would prevail as Napoleon was to do with ex-Napoleonic troops in the Bourbon army in 1815. Like Napoleon, he had his way; the City militia did not move, Speaker Lenthall vainly asserted his rights as their commander to sceptical soldiers, and eventually Sussex ex-officer MP Herbert Morley's few loyal troops defending Parliament against Lambert's men had to give in.

As in April 1653, the elected House was shut down by the troops. For the moment, Lambert's gamble had succeeded – but like Cromwell in April 1653 he now had to build up a stable coalition of allies and find a new government. The Council of State remained in session unlike its predecessor had done in 1653, but after the army General Council sacked all pro-Rump officers (14 October) a final political breach occurred. On the 17th Haselrig and his Council of State allies walked out. This left Vane as the principal civilian MP retained in power by the army, the field cleared of his rivals, and indeed French Ambassador Bordeaux was to reckon him the new regime's principal minister; in effect he took over control of foreign policy for the rest of 1659. On the 20th the Council of Officers declared Fleetwood as commander-in-chief, Lambert his deputy, and Desborough and the absentee Monck as the 'Generals of Horse and Foot'. They then set up another 'Committee of Safety' to supersede the Council of State, which ceased to meet on 25 October; ten of the former Council joined the military-led Committee which in turn co-opted some more respectable and politically reliable civilians to join them. This even included conservatives such as Whitelocke, and was clearly designed to appeal to as many factions loyal to the Commonwealth as possible.

Fleetwood and Desborough did not challenge Lambert, who probably took them by surprise, over expelling the Rump. They presumably decided that opinion in the ranks was on his side so it was unrealistic – but the triumphant Lambert had too little civilian support to prevail for long. The main advantages he had as of late October 1659 were inertia and fear of the consequences of defiance, and the forthcoming split in the army was to overcome both factors. The crucial factor was to be the attitude of Monck in Scotland, the only man with an adequate military force to challenge the army in England. Cromwell's coup in April 1653 had kept the armies in Scotland and Ireland on-side, but Lambert – who lacked his late master's overwhelming prestige as the 'war-winner' – failed. Also, once the officers had lost patience with and expelled the Rump, their decline in popular support accelerated and desire for a stable government rose. Those political actors who put stable government first and were not yet focussed on the king were vital; they included both Whitelocke, the conservative lawyer who in 1652 had been pushing Cromwell for a monarchical settlement featuring Charles I's youngest son Prince Henry as a puppet-king, and the Cromwellian councillor and admiral Mountague. Some minor Cromwellian figures, e.g. Morland, seem to have been assisting the king already. Could they swing back to Richard Cromwell? But the earlier call for a free Parliament began to be coupled with that for the King, and crucially Monck in Scotland chose to intervene and lead his men south to overthrow the discredited and directionless Junto of generals in Westminster. This was not yet a pro-Royalist move, as far as can be worked out from Monck's deliberately opaque pronouncements, but it was not a pro-Richard one either. Widening the support for the crumbling regime by readmitting all members of the Long Parliament excluded in December 1648 – as backed by Monck – meant readmitting Presbyterian MPs who had opposed regicide and would logically favour Charles II. Many of them had indeed been involved in the abortive Presbyterian 'Treaty of Newport' with Charles I in November 1648, providing for the king to keep nominal power as the front-man of a powerful Presbyterian-led Parliament and church. Any calls for a freely-elected Parliament would run a risk of pro-royalist MPs being elected, so just using legally-elected 1640s MPs instead was safer.

By this point, the tide of events was clearly moving fast against the supporters of a republic – though it is probable that this took Monck, who had been away from London in Scotland for many years, by surprise. The figure of Monck would now be the crucial factor in how events developed, first in overthrowing the military junto in London and then in guiding the restored Rump into a position where it was widened to include the 1646-8 'Royal Presbyterian' faction who were prepared to back a Stuart monarchy. The ambiguity with which Monck operated was so successful that this ultimate military professional's motives and ultimate plans were not known in 1659-60 and have been argued about ever since. He may well be an example of Cromwell's words about the equally surprise moves towards regicide: 'Nobody goes as far as he who knows not where he is going'. Monck had a mixed past record that suggests a man with a sense of self-preservation as well as principle – he had started off as a royalist officer in Ireland in the 1640s but had insisted on a transfer to England so as not to be tainted by having to work with ex-rebel Catholics, had been captured by Parliamentary soldiers in battle in Cheshire, and had eventually joined the Parliamentary army to secure his liberty. Cromwell then chose him for promotion as a competent and loyal officer in the late 1640s. Whether or not he chose to drift with the tide and see where it went in 1659–60, without compromising his own safety by expressing definite views, Monck was in a special position by virtue of having been absent in Scotland for most of the period 1652–9 – he had not taken part in Cromwellian or post-Cromwellian politics and his views were unknown. Accordingly people of disparate views could hope that he really favoured their own opinions – and he could play up to this expectation successfully. It helped his forthcoming relations with the royalists that he had originally fought for them, and despite his humble (Devonshire farm) origins this meant that he did not have a network of well-placed relatives to have to look after. He was also independent-minded enough to have committed the unusual social solecism of marrying his laundress (in captivity). He had not fought against, or for that matter with, any of Cromwell's generals who now dominated the junto in the 1640s. But he was also a firm Protestant, who had served France and the Dutch against Spain on the Continent in the 1630s which argues for his commitment to combating the Papist menace; and in Ireland in 1643 he had asked the royalist 'high command' to be sent to England so he did not have to serve with their Catholic recruits who he found distasteful as former rebels connected to the notorious October 1641 massacres. The latter had involved a sudden and co-ordinated rising by supposedly peaceful Catholics (to some extent across Ireland, but mainly in Ulster) to evict incoming English Protestant settlers, hundreds of whom had been killed with others driven to flee destitute to England – where stories of their sufferings at the hands of 'murderous Papists' had multiplied. The supposed massacre of many thousands, laid out in lurid pamphlets, had had a major effect on public opinion in England and had tainted the reputation of Catholics in general and Irish ones in particular ever since, so no loyal Protestant Englishman was supposed to have anything to do with the latter. Indeed captured Irish Catholics (women as well as men) had been shot *en masse* by some of the Parliamentary armies. Now, in summer 1659 Monck was supposed to have formed a secret plan to join Booth's rising if it showed signs of success but to have covered this up when it failed – as three of his friends claimed to recall after the Restoration.[61] Monck was a blank slate, at least as far as English politics went, and under his image of a bluff, hard-drinking infantry veteran (Lambert and Fleetwood had served as cavalrymen, most of whom came from a higher social class) he was to prove both shrewd and ruthless. The fact of Restoration and the form that it would take owed most to him – to his omissions as well as to his actions. Monck's apparent willingness to link up with the Booth rebellion may indicate more than self-preservation – ie a lack of objections to working with those Presbyterians who had sought to retain a monarchy in 1648. A pointer for 1660 alliances? The longer the inter-republican wranglings went on, the more attractive the monarchic option was.

Section Two

The Return of the King: October 1659 to the Early 1660s

Chapter Three

From Military/Parliamentary Rule to Stuart Monarchy: Events to the Recall of Charles II

The moves towards a restored monarchy: inevitable to avoid chaos, or avoidable? How fear of the radicals led to sidelined 1640s moderate Parliamentarians re-emerging in politics.

Seen from the perspective of autumn 1658 at the time of Richard Cromwell's smooth succession, the situation eighteen months later was astounding. As the diarist John Evelyn wrote after watching Charles II's entry to London on 29 May 1660, it was a miracle that the king had been restored by the very army that had evicted his father, and without one drop of blood being spilt[1] – though that was to change once the king and the new Parliament were freer from constraint. The king had been in a hopeless short-term position as of 1658, reduced to being a pensioner of Spain which lacked the military power to restore him, and even after Richard's overthrow the Booth Rising was a fiasco. Not enough Presbyterians – mostly backers of a (restricted) monarchy until the last minute in December 1648 – were prepared to join the Thurloe-infiltrated royalist networks to revolt against the generals' Junto, and it was not until winter 1659–60 that even the City of London crowds – supporters of a royalist-Presbyterian alliance at the time of the 1648 revolts – came out in favour of the king again.

The march south by General Monck and his Scottish garrisons of the New Model Army was heralded by them and their supporters as being for the restoration of the Rump – those MPs allowed to stay in the Commons by Colonel Pride as in favour of prosecuting Charles I in December 1648 – not for the return of the king. Both radicals and royalists were excluded from participation in the political process by this group, and in Monck's initial political moves. The agitation for a free Parliament among the soldiers who deserted Lambert's army for the pro-Rump rebels at

Portsmouth (joined by Haselrig) in December 1659 was not aligned to royalism; nor was the rioting by City apprentices. The Army had been purged of conservative Cromwellian senior officers by the Junto in late spring 1659, and Monck could not afford to alienate many of these new officers as he arrived in London (though some were purged). Few of the Cromwellians who he and the Rump duly restored to military command were yet known as royalists; their candidate to head a stable government might well by their ex-ruler Richard Cromwell, still a factor. Hyde and other senior exiles had hopes of Monck's ultimate intentions, but based on guesswork rather than firm intelligence – he had been a royalist in 1642 but so had other Cromwellian/Commonwealth trusties, such as Anthony Ashley Cooper. An added factor was the devious ex-Cromwellian spymaster Thurloe, lurking in the shadows and as far as we can tell active on Richard's behalf in autumn 1659 – but he seems to have been stymied by Monck's lack of interest in his candidate for power.

As of winter 1659–60 Monck's contacts with royalist agents could be argued as being only a political move to widen his base of support, and wean royalists away from an alliance with the Presbyterians – and the same applies to the equally moderate Mountague, former navy commander and Cromwellian Councillor, who was to be put in charge of the fleet again (in place of fierce republican Admiral Lawson) and back the king in spring 1660. Latent royalist feelings across the country, and potential willingness to deal with the king among the elite in power in Westminster, are difficult to assess as of winter 1659–60 – not least due to the nature of the evidence. As the outcome was the King's return, in hindsight every ambitious politician seeking office in the 1660s – and every republican fearing prosecution for past misdeeds – was to be eager to assure that they were really royalists all along. Thus what major political actors claimed to have wanted in 1659–60, and what they did in reality, may have been widely different. As Charles II said cynically afterwards, he should really have returned earlier as everyone claimed that they had been longing for his return for years.

(i) The instability of spring – autumn 1659: generals vs. civilians?

As explored in the previous chapter, the summer and autumn of 1659 saw the leadership of the Commonwealth prove completely unable to forget old grievances or to work together as they sought to establish a new political settlement once the Protectorate had been ended. The generals removed Richard Cromwell and recalled the Rump that spring, returning the situation to that of early April 1653 – and for legalists resuming the chain of constitutional authority which Cromwell had broken on 20 April 1653. This allowed men like Vane, Holles, and Haselrig to resume political activity after boycotting Cromwell's 'illegal' regime, and there was widespread political discussion about a new constitution. Classical enthusiasts like Harrington and his Rota Club debated high principles and appropriate constitutional precedents, there was much talk of a Senate (ancient Roman or modern Venetian) to balance the democratic legislature with a powerful body of permanent elders, and in practical terms senior Army officers talked of institutionalising their own position in a Second House. In practical terms, a Second House filled with army men and loyal Cromwellian moderates would have served as a brake on rampant royalist triumphalism by the majority of pro-royalist MPs elected to a free Parliament in 1661, even if it had included restored royalist peers too. Even if the backers of this idea in 1659 had no idea of the king ever returning to power, there was a coherent argument for a Second House institutionalising religious toleration against the threat of a persecutory Presbyterian-led Commons as seen in 1646–8.

The Cromwellian Second House had been derided as a nest of what the early eighteenth-century would refer to as 'place-men', bribed hirelings on the government payroll – as was to be said about an appointed House of Lords as 'Tony's cronies' after 1997. It included loyal Cromwellian officers as well as civilians and a few genuine Lords, with trustability the main criteria for membership. But a Second Chamber would serve to check the abuse of power by the legislature, with a wider membership than the 1649–59 (temporary) Councils of State possessed, and would preserve army power – and the safety of a tolerant and comprehensive church including Independents – from the revenge of elected Presbyterian MPs. (Army men in the Senate would also be operating as civilians, not as generals – a sop to current dislike of military power?) The one element of the constitution which seemed to have fallen into disrepute was the 'Single Person', monarch or Protector, an inevitable reaction to what most of the civilian non-Cromwellians active in power in summer 1659 felt they had suffered under Cromwell. The illegality of Cromwell's dissolution of the

Rump (and the way he had dissolved his two Protectoral Parliaments) weighed heavily with the restored Rumpers and affected perceptions of the need for a chief executive; those Commonwealthsmen who had taken seats in Cromwell's Parliaments had been continually endeavouring to secure the control of the executive by the legislature. They now had a chance to force their point. But after the disillusionment caused by the bickering of MPs and generals in summer-autumn 1659, followed by the second dismissal of the Rump, there was a reaction in favour of a stronger chief executive. Indeed, among one group of opinion this took the form of a movement to restore Richard Cromwell to power – though it was to be overtaken by Royalist revival.[2]

Parliament's attempt to assert its authority by dismissing the most threatening of the generals, Lambert, from his post led to him marching on Westminster and evicting it on 13 October. The move seems to have taken other senior generals, led by Fleetwood and Desborough, by surprise. Lambert was the framer of the semi-monarchical 'Instrument of Government' in December 1653 so he was thoughtful and experienced in creating new constitutions and was not inimical to one-man rule. Military feeling in the lower ranks was in Lambert's favour, so the senior generals could not disavow him; it is uncertain how much of Lambert's current boldness was due to principle as opposed to a personal bid to assume military leadership and outflank Fleetwood's supporters. Fleetwood was now said to resent Lambert's new prominence[3] – but it was Lambert who was the bolder and the more effective soldier despite Fleetwood's impressive public piety. The 'hard grinding' of the struggle for power that winter and next spring would be between Lambert and Monck, two more determined and ruthless men than Fleetwood, with the latter left lamenting his faction's eclipse as an unexpected punishment by God. The brief chance of a reconciliation between the generals and the Rump now passed, and the army commanders created a new Committee of Safety on 20–22 October to take over power from the current Council of State. The Army Council assisted in naming members, and thirteen of the twenty-three were military men.[4] They included the main leadership, such as Fleetwood, Lambert, Vane, and Haselrig, and their allies, but also a number of minor figures committed to republicanism – ex-Cromwellian loyalists Colonels William Sydenham (a 1653–8 Councillor and before that a leading Parliamentarian figure in 1640s Dorset) and

James Berry (an East Anglian ex-ranker protégé of Cromwell's in the latter's regiment), and civilian Richard Salwey, radical non-Cromwellian army officers Colonels Ludlow (who refused to sit and only served as an adviser) and (John) Jones from Ireland, and radical ex-Rumper Thomas Scot. Bulstrode Whitelocke represented the moderate Cromwellian lawyers, claiming later that he had agreed to sit in order to help keep radical Vane in check, and Archibald Johnston represented those Scots Calvinists that had thrown in their lot with the Commonwealth after 1651.

The new regime had the military might to cow London, as had all changes in power since the army took over the City and expelled the leading Presbyterian MPs in June 1647. But for the first time the army split over it – the crucial action which opened the floodgates to the current instability turning lethal. There had been murmurings in the army in Scotland and Ireland – both containing religious and secular radicals banished from service in England as troublemakers – about the autocratic nature of the Protectorate, but these had been kept under control in Cromwell's lifetime. After Richard's fall, the radicals in Ireland (who Fleetwood had promoted during his mid-1650s Lord Lieutenancy but had been marginalised by Henry Cromwell from 1657) enthusiastically removed Henry and declared allegiance to the military junto. George Monck, commander of the army in Scotland, now declared his allegiance to the Rump and demanded its restoration. An ex-royalist prisoner-of-war recruited to the winning side by Cromwell, a bluff and ruthless 'career' soldier from a minor Devon gentry family with no discernible political preferences or involvement through the 1650s but ready to crack down on local army radicals for Cromwell, he had not been involved in the army politico-religious manoeuvrings of the late 1640s. According to his pro-Royalist Presbyterian clergyman brother Nicholas, sent to lure him into Royalist action in summer 1659, he had expressed his support then for Rump rather than the generals but preferred a free Parliament to either.[5] He later told the army leadership in Ireland a few months later that he had acted in attacking Lambert to save the country from blasphemers (i.e., the extreme sectaries) and they should trust neither Cavaliers nor Anabaptists.[6] He may even have considered joining Booth's rising, whch involved Presbyterians (some ex-Parliamentarians alarmed at army threats to the monarchy and state church) as well as hardline royalists.

He may have been personally at odds with Lambert, or alternatively been more worried at the spread of seemingly anarchic Quaker sectarian zeal across England in 1659 – perceived at the time, especially by socially conservative JPs, as a serious threat to order – and feared the junto would not control it, thanks to their sectarian sympathies. (Fleetwood had actively encouraged Baptists in Ireland and so was not seen as a figure to entrust with power.) Lambert was believed to be in the pockets of the more extreme sectarians, who Monck – and his wife, Anne (who was later claimed to have secret Royalist sympathies, along with spiteful remarks about her plain appearance and manners)' now a Presbyterian – rejected. Accordingly Barry Reay ('Early Quaker Activity and the Reaction to It', 1980 Oxford D. Phil. thesis) has suggested that fear of the 'fanatics' was his main motivation. Austin Woolrych would prefer to suggest dislike of the army's unfettered power in London – which indeed had a religious element given their leaders' sectarian allegiances.[7] The truth has been muddied by hindsight, given what Monck's action led to – but did he intend that outcome from the start or was he 'playing it by ear'? After 1660 he and his apologists had every reason to portray his defiance of the coup as a principled 'first step' in restoring the king, to reassure the new royalist government of his unshakeable loyalty and distance himself from his former colleagues who were now in disgrace. But as of 17 October 1659, when he heard of the expulsion of the Rump, the king's quick return was not considered plausible and the pragmatic Monck undoubtedly put his own preservation first. Dislike of the junto, and fears that he would be removed as Henry Cromwell had been in Ireland, are more likely motivators whatever his private sympathies for Charles II. Moreover, his purge of officers in Scotland before he set out for London in December 1659 shows that he could not be sure of all his subordinates' loyalty despite his strong grip on power; he could not afford provocative measures that seemed to betray the 'Good Old Cause', such as open sympathy for the king. If the popular mood he found in London had not been running so strongly for a monarchy in early 1660 Monck was not likely to take a gamble on Charles' behalf.

The news of the Rump's expulsion by the junto of generals luckily reached Edinburgh before the current round of dismissals of anti-junto officers had had time to take effect and while some of their allies were down in London. This enabled Monck to secure control of the remaining officers for his revolt – which would have been more difficult a month later. Timing was thus crucial – possibly Monck would not have dared to revolt if the Rump had been expelled later that autumn, although pressure for its return would have been building up elsewhere even without his involvement. The likeliest rebel against the junto if Monck had not moved was Lawson, new and doctrinaire republican commander of the fleet – a popular and outspoken officer who had defied Cromwell himself in assisting Leveller agitation among his men in 1655–6 and was not intimidated by authority or afraid to take risks. Monck's remaining quiescent would not have ensured the junto's success in the long term; would Lawson have stirred up his notoriously unruly men and blockaded the Thames to cut off supplies to London? The new Committee of Safety now commissioned Lambert to march against Monck.[8] He was to take most of the local troops, which had its own problems as it emboldened the uncommitted and potential defectors in London to turn against him once he had left. This was what had sunk the shaky regime of the usurper Lady Jane Grey in London in 1553, with her father-in-law the Duke of Northumberland abandoned by his wavering colleagues once he had led the troops north to tackle their challenger Princess Mary. Lambert was the junto's best general, Cromwell's lieutenant at Worcester in 1651, and had experience of command in his native Yorkshire from the 1648 civil war so he was an expert in the likely area to be fought over. But once Lambert left London the divisions in the Committee became apparent – Colonel Ludlow, as a principled republican, refused to take up his seat in the Committee of Safety over the illegal coup (but offered unofficial advice), as did others; Fleetwood was jealous of Lambert's rising power which posed a threat to him as commander-in-chief; and Vane's godly enthusiasm for the regime's potential was shared by few. The fact that Vane told the equally zealous but more doctrinaire Archibald Johnston that the recent events heralded the Second Coming indicates his lack of political sense – Johnston's reply that they were rather the result of sinful pride was more to the point (in the sense of pride causing the republican leadership to fight each other, not unite). Luckily for the London regime, the commander on the Borders, General Robert Lilburne, backed them not Monck so there was no danger of Monck's war-ready army (more used to being on the alert due to the security threat in the Highlands) marching quickly on London and catching Lambert before he could gather his regiments together. With Lilburne holding Newcastle in strength, Monck had to wait for developments and offer to negotiate. Once Lambert left London on 3 November with most of its garrison, the moderates had their chance. The restoration of the Protectorate to secure stability was seriously considered, Richard Cromwell was invited to London, and his debts were paid off, but the junior officers are supposed to have opposed it and the Committee – narrowly – voted against it. Royalist reports said that the junior officers stopped it.[9] If the vote had gone the other way or Fleetwood had had the nerve and the prestige to force the junior officers to submit, the crisis could have ended in a return to the situation of March-April 1659 with Richard nominally in power, and as a Cromwellian loyalist Monck could well have accepted him as his choice of chief executive – though Lambert was more likely to challenge Richard had he defeated Monck.

Vane proposed a model for his new government to the sub-committee on 1 November, guaranteeing religious toleration and thus annoying the rigid Calvinist Johnston. The junior officers' suggestions for abolishing the tithes – thus opening the weakened Church, stripped of State funding, to autonomy for local congregations – and the Court of Chancery revived their main enthusiasms of 1653, but were rejected as too radical and likely to alienate moderate opinion.[10] Neither Monck or Lambert being ready to fight and Lilburne holding the border fortresses of Newcastle and Carlisle for Lambert, Monck's officers' suggestion for a truce and talks (with the restoration of Parliament and preservation of a national Church on the agenda) at a council-of-war on 3 November was accepted.[11] This delayed a confrontation, but worked for Monck as he had time to order all his own garrisons across Scotland to sign a declaration of support for him and dismissed dissenting officers. He also produced two pamphlets promoting his 'stand' for military consumption, arguing that he was for justice by restoring Parliament and for putting down the sects.[12] This delay put him in a position to march well into England at the New Year, which he would have found far more risky at an earlier date. But the question arises of whether his desire for a truce was just a 'stop-gap' measure to buy time for a planned invasion later, or was sincere and could have led to a settlement. If the latter is correct, could a more flexible attitude in London have staved off the confrontation between the English and Scottish armies of December 1659/January 1660? The likelihood is that his insistence on a state church plus his contacts with potential allies within England (as below) indicates that the only way to have kept him friendly to the London regime – and thus possibly avoided his march on London – would have been to press ahead quickly with a 'moderate' settlement of the constitutional/ religious questions in London. This would have risked a military mutiny. Monck sent representatives to secure support within England, including from ex-commander-in-chief Sir Thomas Fairfax (now in retirement in Yorkshire), some of Lambert's officers, and the Common Council of London.[13] The restoration of a Parliament (Rump or freely-elected) and civil supremacy over the army was a popular cause, not least due to the fears of army religious radicalism – which the 'Quaker panic' stoked – arbitrary government, and high taxes. It had worked for the king when the radical army was coercing Parliament, abusing its local authority in garrisons, and swallowing up supplies and taxes in 1648; it worked for Monck now. The longer Monck waited, the stronger his position – though there was one moment of panic when his representatives in London agreed to a (fortunately for him abortive) plan to disband his and Lambert's armies and summon military representatives from all three kingdoms to London around 6 December to work out a settlement. Lambert took no notice of this and stayed with his (around 8,000) troops at Newcastle where he had just arrived and was in a strong position,[14] so Monck could ignore it on that excuse. The Irish army showed no signs of intervening on either side, and what evidence we have from the provinces shows that military and civilian radicals were disheartened at the current lack of enthusiasm for rallying to the 'Good Old Cause'.[15] Usefully for Monck, the Fifth Monarchists were divided over whether to back Parliament or the military, while the leading reformist pamphleteers John Canne and Livewell Chapman put out pamphlets backing Parliament and local gentry committeemen in North Wales and Northumberland, and sacked generals Goffe and Walley all raised volunteers for Monck.[16] Lambert and the London regime would not be saved by a spontaneous rally of armed supporters ready to defy Monck – possibly due to the 'Quaker panic' that was making many waverers fear the sects and so feel more sympathetic to Monck.

There was significant trouble in the emboldened City, especially over entrusting militia control to the pro-junto sects which Fleetwood was forced to reverse, and a ban on the Lord Mayor's Show for fear of riots –

London, as in 1648, was broadly sympathetic to the conservative cause. Fleetwood was concerned enough to agree to replace the radical sectary militiamen guarding the City with regular soldiers following complaints, and on 8 November he, Desborough and Whitelocke came to the Guildhall to make conciliatory speeches about a national settlement and appeal for unity; the new Lord Mayor replied in favour of a free Parliament, with crowds shouting the same as the regime delegates left. Next day the Common Council voted for a free Parliament.[17] Moreover, unlike in 1647–8 the radical civilian 'left' – alienated from the army leadership that had prosecuted their late champion, General Lilburne's ultra-democratic pamphleteer brother John Lilburne – was hostile to the generals for dissolving Parliament and the republican ex-MPs Haselrig and Scot continued to meet with junior army allies like Colonels Okey and Alured. Unlike in April 1653, the hardliners in the expelled Rump had a chance of overturning the coup due to the split in the Army. They were joined in their plot by the already veteran (ex-royalist and ex-Cromwellian) intriguer Anthony Ashley Cooper, whose political line remained broadly in favour of a democratically accountable constitutional chief executive and against the generals whose power had probably led to his resignation as a Councillor in 1654. The religious radicals were split over whether to back the coup, unlike they had been in April 1653[18] – their most famous and eloquent pamphleteer John Milton for one was against it and the Fifth Monarchists were divided. It is likely that the open support of the new regime by some activist Quakers, e.g. those at Brecon who took over the corporation and imposed their own bailiff, alarmed many of the sect's detractors into deciding for the Rump.

The new regime did seek to head off political opposition by declaring that it would frame a new constitution and inviting the armies in England, Scotland, and Ireland, the Dunkirk garrison, and the Navy to send delegates to a conference in the near future. This might have headed off military discontent in a normal situation, even with arrears of pay causing extra impatience among the men. But events were moving too fast for this to be a practical solution, and the way in which soldiers and sailors were to join in the immanent mutinies shows that they did not trust their senior officers. It may be significant that the Junto's main opponent in the confrontation of early December 1659, Haselrig, was a man that the potential mutineers could trust as an implacable republican

St. James' Park, London. Where Oliver Cromwell was successfully 'warned off' taking the Crown in 1657 by a group of his senior republican army officers, arguably halting the Commonwealth's political moves towards reconciliation and stability. (© *Paul Gillett/Creative Commons*)

Westminster Hall, London. The site of the royal coronation banquets and many medieval ceremonies, where Cromwell carried out his semi-royal inauguration as a hereditary 'Protector' in summer 1657. Making the best of a botched political compromise that failed in its purpose? (© *Paul Gillett/ Creative Commons*)

Winnington Bridge, Nantwich, Cheshire. The modern bridge at the site of the decisive defeat by General Lambert of the abortive Presbyterian/Royalist rebellion against the republican 'Junto' in 1659. But within months the deep fissures among the republicans and hostility to army rule had brought the 'losers' here back into play on the winning side of British politics. (© *Christine Johnstone Creative Commons*)

The River Tweed by Coldstream bridge. Where General Monck 'crossed the Rubicon' to march his army into England and overthrow the republican military 'Junto' in January 1660, paving the way for the Restoration. But did he really intend a monarchic solution at this point? (© *Jennifer Petrie Creative Commons*)

Tower Wharf and the Southern exterior wall of the Tower of London. Irreconcilable republican General Lambert escaped from custody here in April 1660 in a last-ditch bid to halt the Restoration by force. (© *David Dixon/Creative Commons*)

The historic battlefield of Naseby, Northants. The site of Parliament's decisive victory over the King in 1645, chosen by Lambert for his rally of military opponents of the Restoration in April 1660. Unfortunately not enough men turned up to mount a proper rebellion, and pro-Monck troops led by Cromwell's cousin Colonel Ingoldsby arrested him instead as his horse got stuck in the mud. (© *Philip Halling/Creative Commons*)

Dover Castle and beach. Where Charles II landed at the Restoration, on 25 May 1670. A decade later it was the site of his secret talks and treaty with the emissaries of his autocratic and ultra-Catholic cousin Louis XIV of France. He supposedly promised to convert to Catholicism in return for military aid, contradicting all that he had promised in 1660 – but was he serious or not? (© *Chris Downer: Creative Commons*)

Blackheath, SE London. The then open hillside near Greenwich, site of many earlier rebel rallies where on 29 May 1660 Charles II reviewed the New Model Army which had twice driven him out of England. Now it tamely accepted his return as a lesser evil than chaos and (mostly) quietly disbanded (© *Chris Downer/Creative Commons*)

Highgate Wood, North London. In January 1661 this was the site of the chaotic last stand of the militant millenarian 'Fifth Monarchist' foes of Charles II, at the end of the underwhelming 'Venner's Revolt'. This was too small to be a serious challenge to the King, but caused panic and was used as the excuse for draconian repression. (© *Malc McDonald/Creative Commons*)

Chepstow Castle, Gwent. The usefully remote and secure medieval fortress where the republican regicide MP Henry Marten was imprisoned for life by the Royalists as a potential security threat. It was the principled republicans like him that could not be trusted who headed the King's 'hit-list'. (© *Rob Farrow/Creative Commons*)

Drake's Island, Plymouth Sound, Devon. A 'top-security' location near a naval base where Charles II had General Lambert interned for life after his trial, and kept him there even when his mental health declined. The facts that Lambert had not been a regicide or been listed as a target for prosecution in 1660 mattered less than his attempt to stop the Restoration or his high profile for military dissidents © *Jeff Clarke /Creative Commons*)

Sir Robert Holmes' house as 1660s Governor of the Isle of Wight (now the 'George' Hotel), Yarmouth. The home of the flamboyant and swashbuckling Royalist ex-privateer, a protégé of Prince Rupert, who was chosen in 1663–4 to renew the Cromwellian colonial challenge to the Dutch – by attacking them in West Africa. (© *Christine Matthews /Creative Commons*)

Swarthmoor Hall, near Ulverston, Cumbria. The home of Quaker founder George Fox's wife Mar
where they set up their sect's effective headquarters after their marriage. The growing numbers, ant
State Church principles, and social disruptiveness of this movement scandalised local gentry JPs in th
1660s, and helped to propel both local repression of 'Dissenters' and support for the King's 'strong-arm
tactics. (© *David Gearing/Creative Commons*)

River Medway, North of Chatham. The Dutch fleet were able to sail up here to raid Charles II's ma
naval dockyards during the Anglo-Dutch war in 1667, largely due to slackness and complacency
defence. The sharp contrast of this humiliation with the successes of Cromwell's fleets was a bonus
critics of the new order – as the flagship that had brought the King back to England in 1660 was tow
off to Holland as a trophy. (© *Robin Webster/Creative Commons*)

and he had also raised and led a regiment himself, fighting at the head of his 'Lobsters' (so-called because of their red jackets) in the South-Western campaign of summer 1643. The revolt was also to be joined by credible and well-known second-ranking officers, especially the regicide Colonel Okey; it was not just a protest by civilian MPs who had no support in the ranks and/or ideologically dubious pro-Cromwellians.

When the junto heard rumours of Haselrig's plots and ordered him out of London he set about organising his provincial allies, moderate Presbyterian gentry, to refuse to pay taxes in order to starve the army of funds and stir up trouble among the unpaid soldiery. This was backed publicly by his allies in the counties of central Southern England.[18] It showed the plotters' reliance on that provincial revolt against the Army's central command in London which had broken out in 1648, but with the added danger to the regime of unpaid provincial garrisons – including radical soldiery alarmed at the dissolution of Parliament, a factor missing in 1648 – revolting. Sending distrusted ex-MPs like Haselrig out of London meant that they could now meddle with this disaffection. On 3–4 December a mutiny duly broke out in Portsmouth, a major garrison town as well as the navy's main base and close enough to threaten London but too far to be suppressed quickly. The disaffected commander, Colonel Whetham, a new appointment lacking backing from his divided garrison, had reason to seek outside help to bolster his position. He admitted Haselrig's ally Herbert Morley, a leading Rumper and central figure of the pro-Commonwealth network of local MPs in his native Sussex; they declared for the Rump on the 4th and arrested officers loyal to the Junto.[19]

The revolt in Portsmouth showed the greater danger that the generals faced in 1659 than they had when confronting local resistance and a hostile London in 1648 – trouble in their own ranks. The news sparked off large demonstrations in London on the 5th, as an apprentices' petition for a free Parliament was presented to the Common Council in defiance of the regime, and a military order banning it was read out to jeers and a hail of stones. The troops restored order by shooting some rioters, only to be indicted for murder by the City legal authorities.[20] In modern political terms, both the 'left' (the radical officers and men) and 'right' (the Presbyterian conservatives) were now against the regime, reducing its chances of survival. In the north, Lambert was still unready for battle with his troops starved of pay or supplies due to the crisis in London, though Monck faced disaffection among his men too and had had to purge his officers. Monck moved forward to Coldstream on the Tweed on the 8th, ready to advance over the Border. In response to the demands for a Parliament, the Army Council announced on 10 December that they would call a freely-elected Commons and an army-chosen Upper House. Liberty of conscience and an executive council independent of the Commons were promised and the document was passed on to the Committee of Safety, with the Parliament's sitting set for 24 January.[21] But this was too long a timetable and was overtaken by events, as on the 13th Lawson's fleet declared for the Rump and on the 16th they sailed into the Thames to blockade London. The flight of the anti-Junto Colonel Okey and the Council of State's Secretary, radical MP Thomas Scot, to Lawson and the presence of his friend Colonel Rich with the Portsmouth mutineers were vital in determining his course of action. The regime could only rely on a few naval officers – mostly absent from their ships in London – like Vice-Admiral Goodson to stay loyal, and Lawson commanded far more affection among the sailors than they did.

The revolt in the fleet came from a different political trajectory from that on the mainland, at least as far as its leadership was concerned. Lawson and men like Morley were politically poles apart. Due to Lawson's own radical sympathies as a critic of Cromwell and autocracy, and Leveller and religious radical feelings among the officers and men, this was partly a 'radical' declaration in the hope of further reform – religious toleration and secular constitutional reform were expected of the Rump. Indeed, Lawson and his officers had protested to Monck in November about how his defiance of the Junto might lead to civil war and the unwelcome return of monarchy – and been assured that Monck was as opposed to that as they were.[22] As the potential head and/or beneficiary of a mixed radical and moderate revolt, Monck had every reason to promise contradictory results to the two 'wings' of his allies – and his real intentions cannot be disentangled from what was politically possible at that moment. The naval blockade of the Thames, halting trade and squeezing revenues further, put more pressure on the government and emboldened the City, which declared for a free Parliament – i.e. not the same terms as the fleet were demanding – on the 20th. The Committee of Safety now abandoned both Vane's proposed redistribution of Parliamentary seats for the next election – in Vane's absence while he was treating with Lawson – and the proposed controls over who should be elected, thus reducing exclusion to royalists and giving in most of the way to demands for a free Parliament. The Army Council abandoned their demand for an executive council, while still insisting on a second House to guarantee them some influence.

With the new City Common Council elected on the 21st strongly in favour of a free Parliament, and the troops sent to besiege Portsmouth having mutinied and deserted to Haselrig, all the Army Council could do was to issue a futile statement of principle on the 22nd. This supported a 'free' Parliament, of two chambers, but required it to restrict freedom of conscience to non-Anglicans and non-Catholics (the latter uncontroversial but the former unlikely to be agreed given the number of pro-Anglican, ex-royalist gentry likely to be elected to any free Parliament). They also wanted separation of executive and legislature, implying a Council of State unconnected to the Commons and so open to their control[23] – also contentious to civilian MPs tired of army and sectarian influence but arguably important to preserve their own influence on a settlement. They had no means left of enforcing their demands, unlike in the army confrontation with the Commons in autumn 1648, given the alarming spread of defections among their ranks which was losing them the monopoly of force. Some of Colonel Berry's regiment had deserted to Haselrig's army, now strong enough to march on London. For the first time officers and soldiers were rallying to Parliament and to former 'enemy' Presbyterians of 1648 like Haselrig, not to their generals – a major boost for the cause of civilian government and a reflection both of low morale (aided by the loss of pay due to financial meltdown) and of the low esteem that the ranks and their superiors had for Fleetwood as opposed to Cromwell. Parliament as of December 1659 did not stand for religious intolerance and a dodgy deal with an unrepentant king, as it had in 1648; it stood for a chance to be paid and hope of a religious and constitutional settlement which the junto had shown neither will nor ability to arrange. In 1648 Fairfax had led a united army in London against rebels; Lambert and Fleetwood now could not.

Lacking either money or leadership, the troops now started to defy their pro-regime officers and mutiny spread. Such actions are often infectious and if potential mutineers in one regiment saw others getting away with defiance it would encourage them; the lack of inspiring central direction from the 'high command' was important as it left initiative to their juniors. Fleetwood seems to have been in a state of depressed shock in mid-December and took on no major new initiatives, and the more vigorous Lambert's absence on the Scots border was vital. Was sending charismatic Lambert rather than Desborough to confront Monck a disaster? The Army Council officers returned to their regiments after the meeting on the 22nd, only to find that their men demonstrated for a free Parliament; Desborough's regiment, sent south by Lambert to assist its commander in London, deserted and on the 24th most regiments based around London obeyed orders from Rump Speaker Lenthall and senior MPs to muster under pro-Rump officers led by Colonel Okey. They duly rallied at Lenthall's house in Chancery Lane to declare their allegiance, an ironic reversal of how the troops had deserted Lenthall in Lambert's favour on 12–13 October. In constitutional terms, the restored Rump of May-October had given Lenthall the right to sign all regimental commissions so he was legally joint commander with Fleetwood. The latter did not intervene, probably to save himself the humiliation of being defied – showing that he had less nerve than Lambert but saving his personal safety. Instead, having spent the past few days praying in his house, he gave in. As the Tower garrison declared its allegiance Fleetwood had to hand over the keys of Parliament to their representatives, declaring tearfully that God had spat in the faces of his party. His authority and career as commander of the Army were thus ended; his depressed reaction showed his bewilderment. He had had the nominal authority to take on Cromwell's role as supreme military and political commander in autumn 1659, though he had been in a weaker position due to his fractious and mutually antagonistic subordinates. But, as the outcome now showed, he lacked Cromwell's determination or strength of character – and so let others take the initiative. Desborough, tougher and more experienced in battle, did not resist either and most of his personal regiment had declared for the Rump anyway. Most of the provincial garrisons followed the London regiments in surrendering to the authority of Parliament via the local civilian authorities, though there was some disorder as hardliners resisted and were either overcome by other soldiers or by pro-Parliament vigilante groups raised by the civic authorities and gentry.[24] It was an ironic return to the '*force majeure*' seizure of various areas for either king or Parliament by the best-armed and largest grouping of supporters on the spot in 1642, involving some veterans of the 1640s such as South Wales' Bussy Mansell. The activists were usually gentry or the higher classes of townsmen – thus, social and political conservatives – and their targets the mixture of radical soldiers and sectaries loyal to the 'junto'. That spelt disaster for those sectaries now linked in the public mind with the hated military regime by their physical support for its garrisons, e.g. the Quakers at Exeter. The lack of army pay that autumn had made the garrisons in towns more hated than usual, given that no money was coming to them from London and the civic authorities had to buy the troops off to stop them plundering the citizens (as at Bristol and Gloucester). As far as future MPs and JPs were to be concerned, the sects were the agents of oppressive military despots – and arguably the crisis of autumn 1659 encouraged decades of retaliation against them by lawmakers and magistrates.

Once Desborough, who retained prestige as Cromwell's brother-in-law, had submitted the only focus for resistance was Lambert, who was isolated in the north confronting Monck. He was already hampered by the fact that his men had not received their promised pay and were having to live off 'free quarter' from the annoyed locals in Northumberland. Hearing of the revolt in the south, he endeavoured to march there via York and sent Robert Lilburne ahead to secure the city (27 December). The Quakers offered him support – which was not to be forgotten by indignant local JPs. His marching south left the Border open to invasion by Monck, thus starting the chain of events that led to the securing of London by the man who was to turn to the king for stable government. Lambert was intercepted by a pro-Parliament revolt led by the retired 1645–50 New Model Army commander-in-chief General Fairfax – already preparing to rise when Monck arrived but now doing so ahead of schedule, on the 28th, and retaining local military prestige as the Yorkshire Parliamentary commander of 1642–4 and army prestige ascommander of the New Model. To be fair to him, he was not just climbing on a bandwagon for his own advantage as he had never favoured the Commonwealth, having opposed the king's execution in 1649 and then retired from service rather than fight the Scots – and he and his wife were Presbyterians. They had sat it out at their mansion at Nun Appleton through the Protectorate and had no sympathy for radical soldiers or Lambert's allies the Quakers. Robert Lilburne's force at York fell to pieces as part of it defected to Fairfax's advancing army, and on the 30th Fairfax arrived at York with some of his own 1640s veterans and defectors from Lilburne's army. Lilburne surrendered to him with the 'face-saving' formula that he would only admit those who would sign allegiance to the Commonwealth (which meant his Army colleagues, not the Royalist part of Fairfax's support). In a supreme irony considering events in the mid-1640s, the former commander of the New Model Army thus took the decisive action in neutering its most 'political' general and thus aiding Monck's advance on London – though the modest, 'un-political' Fairfax had never been a radical anyway.

As Lambert and his dwindling force moved South from Newcastle, Monck crossed the Tweed into England behind them at Coldstream on 4 January. Cut off from London by the rising at York and with Monck to his rear, all Lambert and his men could do was give in and submit to the restored 'Rump' as his army began to desert. He halted his march at Northallerton and opened negotiations; the troops duly obeyed Lenthall's orders to disperse, leaving their irreconcilable commander with no means to resist.[25] On 11 January Monck entered York, with the locally-revered Fairfax to keep the area 'on side' while he advanced south to London. The capital had already gone over to the cause of the 'Rump', with Haselrig arriving from Portsmouth on 29 December.

(ii) Winter 1659–60: Monck and the 'Rump'. An uneasy alliance of moderates and radicals against military rule and the sectaries?

For the first time since April 1653 the army now recognised civilian control, and unlike the situation in 1645–53 it technically owed its allegiance to a civilian commander-in-chief (the Speaker) with no supreme military authority. Fleetwood had been shown up as unable to command obedience and had been forcibly retired, and Haselrig's group had recognised Monck as acting commander-in-chief even before he crossed the Border. The temporarily powerless Lambert lacked means to defy the 'Rump' – and events that spring were to show that he could not command widespread backing from the troops even to defend the republic they had supported for a decade. There was no obvious military commander to replace these two eclipsed figures – a hiatus which Monck now filled as he arrived in London on 2 February with his large and coherent army. Technically, both religious radicals like Overton and political radicals like

Alured and Okey, retained their rank for the moment, and Monck lacked any recent service with the English troops and so ability to command personal support. His coherent body of over 5,000 Scots veterans could overawe dissidents for the moment, and his cautiously 'minimalist' politico-religious position of backing a free Parliament and a state church left all factions with a hope of his support. Also important was Admiral Lawson, who had a less ambiguous politically radical reputation than Monck's; he remained irrevocably opposed to Restoration. Placed on the remodelled Council of State on 2 January, and unlike his fellow-recruit Monck able to attend in person, he was the regime's most senior military defender through January and significantly received Lambert's Whitehall lodgings. He and his radical acolytes were successful in defeating royalist attempts to win over Navy officers and men, as Hyde's and Mordaunt's frustration shows. His republican determination undoubtably added to Monck's initial equivocations on the future of government. But ultimately the navy was less vital to events in London than the combined mood of MPs, the London populace, and the provinces.

Monck and the restored 'Rump' proceeded to neutralise the potential of the army for a further round of mutinies. Commands were given to December 1659 insurgents who had seized control of the localities, and some Ricardian loyalists were returned to their posts and other commands given to men like Cooper (though army opposition kept Ingoldsby out), with the Tower placed under the command of Sussex veteran MP Herbert Morley. The delayed bill for a new assessment to pay the army was swiftly passed. Three-eighths of the officers were replaced, including half of the field officers and two-thirds of the captains, with political and religious radicals the main targets, although the new loyalist appointments were often not familiar with their regiments and might face trouble from the men if it came to a crisis. The lands of the Booth rebels of 1659 were sold off to provide funds and satisfy the unpaid soldiers. Monck, as the new commander-in-chief, thus secured control of a reasonably disciplined and reliable army under loyal officers with no evident challengers to his authority, last seen under Cromwell's rule in 1650–8. He only had a few radical republican officers left, including Okey and Alured, but many pro-Cromwellian officers (who had backed the conservative semi-monarchic goverment of 1653–8 and been purged in 1659) returned. The most powerful non-civilian voice for republicanism was the navy commander,

Lawson. The new Council of State was also purged of members of dubious loyalty (such as Vane). The potential danger to the restored 'Rump' lay in Monck's interests and theirs continuing to coincide, such as over religious toleration, the exclusion of pro-Royalist Presbyterians from the next Parliament, and the form of the new constitution. Vane had thrown in his lot with the Committee of Safety in autumn 1659 as had his fellow-radical Scot, and they were thus in political eclipse and not trusted by Monck. But could Monck and the Haselrig clique continue to work together without yet another 'Army vs. civilian' clash?

Monck had been promoting the more conservative Scottish gentry, those who had been prepared to work with Cromwell and had thus been sidelined by the 'junto' in 1659, after he seized control of Scotland. This had restored the 'civilian' moderate group used by Broghill to build Cromwellian support, and a similar group – including Broghill himself – now took over in Ireland as well, removing the pro-'junto' radicals led by Ludlow. In London, the sectaries and their preachers were sidelined and a proposal by the still-republican Haselrig that all MPs have to sign up to denunciation of the Stuarts was defeated – the victors being led by Cooper and Morley.[26] The latter were backed by a significant group of Councillors of State, including Fairfax; it now seemed that the political 'clock' was moving backwards and that the men who had supported the abolition of the monarchy and Pride's Purge, the 'Rumpers', would be challenged by those loyal to the proposed settlements of 1646–8 which had included monarchy. Given the widespread support from such people (and royalists) for the restoration of the 'Rump' in December 1659, they needed to be appeased; the 'Rumpers', now bereft of radical political or religious Army backing with the more fervent officers mostly purged, could not call on the latter for support. The Army once again acted to keep out Prynne and Annesley's group of Presbyterian MPs as they turned up demanding readmission to Parliament, but this time the latter had public opinion in the City running in their favour. The apprentices noisily backed readmission, with Prynne resorting to abusive pamphleteering – indeed it was at this point that the epithet 'Rump', coined in May 1659, appeared in public use. The crowds booed Monck's soldiers as they marched threateningly through the City, the Common Council remodelled the militia to remove pro-'Rumpers' and voted for a free Parliament, and Lord Mayor Allen's official support for the new regime seemed increasingly out of touch with the public mood.²⁷ Indeed, the government's action to reduce the military threat in London by sending troops away only increased dissension in the towns where the troops were now billeted. Petitions for a free Parliament flooded in from the affected areas, e.g. Bristol and Canterbury, and the City Common Council's threat of not paying taxes until a free Parliament was summoned spread to other places. For the moment, civic authorities remained loyal to their masters in London, aided by local regiments, as in Bristol (where an apprentices' riot was put down) and Leicester (whose leadership disassociated themselves from the local petition for a free Parliament.) Only in the long-time Parliamentarian stronghold of Taunton, heroic redoubt of the cause through sieges in 1644–5, and allied Bath did semi-official civic demonstrations take place as shown by their ability to ring the bells and light bonfires unchallenged. But in Cornwall, always a bastion of independent action far from London intimidation, a gathering of those gentry who had backed Parliament until Pride's Purge (i.e. hose free from accusations of 1642–6 Royalism by the current regime) came out in favour of a free Parliament and duly petitioned the government for this. The local mayor stopped a riot by the Exeter apprentices in favour of a free Parliament as the Epiphany Quarter Sessions opened, but a petition for it was set up by the gentry anyway.²⁸

Monck kept his counsel about his desired politico-religious settlement, not having known views on a republic or on backing radical sectaries as his predecessors as commanders-in-chief had done; alarmed 'Rumpers' could not count on him in a confrontation either. The idea of an army coercion of the moderates was in any case unlikely to be popular, given the well-known provincial attitude to military rule and its accompanying discomforts – and the local elites had acted with vigour to neutralise army resistance to the restoration of the 'Rump' in December 1659. Thus any MPs alarmed at the growing political moves towards accommodating that section of the political 'nation' excluded from power since Pride's Purge (ie Parliamentarians in favour of a limited monarchy) had no means of halting it. The momentum lay with the forces acting for stability. This helps to explain how the most dominant figure of the restored 'Rump', Haselrig, a republican, was unable to halt the slide towards opening the possibility of accommodation with those who unlike him would accept the king's restoration. Haselrig's political position, seemingly stronger than when he had led Parliamentary attempts to curtail the executive in 1654 as he had no Cromwell or united army to face, was thus illusory. The Army 'rank-and-file' had accepted allegiance to a civilian leadership when they rallied to him, Morley, and Lenthall in December 1659, but the triumph was temporary – particularly once Monck arrived from the Borders to take control.

The Commons now voted to expel secluded members (e.g. the 1647–8 evicted Presbyterian leadership) and fill their seats by by-election, while keeping to their timetables of dissolving in June 1660.[29] This combined the desirable cause of increasing their legitimacy – and showing that a 'proper' Commons had to include MPs thrown out by the army, which was thus snubbed – and the useful politics of bringing in more moderates to help win votes. Vane and Lambert were ordered out of London, to prevent plots. The result of this was to bring in more conservative MPs from the victorious Parliamentary alliance of 1642–6 and 'swamp' less reliable radicals – but it also brought in men who had been trying to arrange a new constitution saving the monarchy in November 1648 when the army intervened. In the long run, this was a double-edged sword for the chances of saving the Commonwealth. The Commons could not agree, however, on the qualifications for electability in the forthcoming general election, a crucial matter which could see the next House swamped with Presbyterians (royalist Presbyterians included) or straightforward royalists. City public opinion remained noisily in favour of a free Parliament, raising the possibility of pressure from demonstrations – which were already underway in favour of the secluded and now banned Presbyterian leadership who the City crowds had backed through the 1640s. The veteran Presbyterian controversialist William Prynne, a celebrated victim of both Charles I and the Army and as vicious in his attitude to the Anglican Church in the 1640s as it had been to him in the 1630s, launched a pamphleteering campaign for his readmission as an MP, with popular backing.[30] He was a powerful potential ally and a master propagandist, who had notoriously undermined Charles I and his 'Popish' Church on behalf of the Presbyterian cause and called Henrietta Maria a 'whore' for acting in public in the late 1630s – so he was safer as an ally in the Commons than left ranting outside it. His unruliness made him a 'loose cannon', but he had shied away from backing regicide or a republic so he could now back a (controlled) monarchy. A public campaign of vilification began in London against the 'Rump' – a term of coarse abuse among the apprentices in 1659, now generally adopted – and drove Haselrig's faction to rely on military protection which only heightened their unpopularity.[31] Monck would now be the ultimate determining factor in deciding who would sit in Parliament. The "secluded' members purged by the army in 1648 and the Independent churches (both of them opposed to Haselrig's republicans) thus sent envoys to Monck for support on his arrival and were given hope by their reception, though he expressed opinions against the sectaries to St John.[32] He was constrained from immediate expression of his real opinions for a future settlement, whatever they were, by the presence in his entourage en route to London of two watchful radical MPs sent by the 'Rump' (Thomas Scot and Luke Robinson) and by the hostility of some officers to a free Parliament, but gained in confidence over the weeks following his arrival on 2 February. However, he initially ruled out readmitting the secluded MPs as unacceptable to the Army, and announced his preference for gradual broadening of the House's membership through by-elections.[33] This could let in secluded MPs by the 'back door', one by one and so hopefully not noticed by the army.

A crucial difference between Monck and his 'strongmen' predecessors was that he had thr nerve and the organizational ability to quietly take on the soldiers in London rather than following their whims. He understood that breaking up the body of unruly soldiers in the capital was the key to improving stability, and had enough men at his disposal from his Scottish forces to deter open resistance – provided that he did not alarm his own men. The New Model regiments quartered around London were paid from what money the government could scrape together and sent to quarters across the provinces, at Monck's request, thus reducing the danger of any tension between them and either the House or Monck's Scottish regiments. As they left London on 2 February Monck's troops entered Westminster to take over guarding Parliament, and Monck attended the Commons on the 6th to receive their thanks for his intervention. His official speech of reply denounced both royalists and sectaries (his men had helpfully attacked a party of Quakers on their arrival on 2nd) and requested abandonment of the anti-monarchic oath and some speedy by-elections. Provincial petitions for a free Parliament and threats of a provincial 'tax strike' to starve the army of funds[34] led to the Council of State having to order the troops to suppress rowdy demonstrations.

Indeed the arrival of fresh troops ordered out of London at Monck's request was stimulating those same demonstrations and putting on pressure for a conservative and army-free settlement. (Arguably this also boosted the royalists in the provinces by reminding future voters in the 1660 and 1661 elections that republicanism meant military misrule.) The continued defiance in the City by Presbyterian crowds who disliked both the 'Rump' and the Army led to the Council of State asking Monck on 9 February to march his men into the City to overawe protesters, arrest named ringleaders, and demolish the chains erected over the streets and the gates, and arrange for the dissolution of the Common Council; the militia were to be take over by their own nominees. This form of intimidation of a defiantly pro-Presbyterian City had worked in 1647 and 1648, but had been carried out by a largely Independent army and an unequivocally pro-Independent officer-corps led by Cromwell. Now, however, the religious sympathies of the commander, officers, and men were not so reliable. Monck duly arrested the ringleaders, demolished the illegal chains, and required the Lord Mayor and aldermen to recognise the 'Rump', but after consulting with his (evidently unhappy) officers requested Parliament to keep the gates in place as a conciliatory gesture. The House refused and repeated their order; he obeyed this on the 10th, but after a meeting with his officers, Herbert Morley (now controlling the Tower), and a few intimates he made a stand. On the 11th he sent the House requiring them to issue writs for new by-elections within a week and to dissolve once the vacant seats were filled; the army then moved its quarters into the City, not to intimidate but to support the stand taken by the citizenry.

Another military confrontation with the House was now underway, but this time with popular opinion in both London and the provinces backing the Army which was in alliance with 'moderate' political and religious opinion. Indeed, unlike in 1647–8 the Army was allied with the Presbyterians in the City. Some MPs such as Morley were with Monck, those MPs allied to Haselrig (who was supposed to have been having talks with Ludlow and Lambert) and the City sects could not call on the support of the troops, and the 'Rump' would have been advised to give in. Instead Haselrig's faction proceeded to replace Monck as commander-in-chief by a commission of five loyalists, without any means of carrying it out or any expectation that the troops or officers would act on their

From Military/Parliamentary Rule to Stuart Monarchy 113

orders. Monck ignored them and they had to back down; he thus avoided the rash and provocative demonstrations of military might that Cromwell had carried out in April 1653 and Lambert had in autumn 1659. However, he undertook no immediate retaliatory measures and allowed the House to proceed with their promised arrangements for a new general election, which were completed on the 18th. This provided for the exclusion of royalists and Catholics, but allowed all secluded members (mainly the Presbyterians of 1647–8, many of whom had then favoured a controlled monarchy) to stand.[35] Public opinion in the provinces was loudly in favour of Monck's stand, with rowdy demonstrations in favour of a free Parliament (suppressed by the local units of the English New Model, but not where Monck's men were in charge). Significantly, most of the local Sequestration Commissioners due to carry out the next batch of sales of 1659 rebel lands now failed to show up or start work –as with the failure of the local elite to pay the Ship-Money tax in 1640, a sign that people believed the legislation would soon be redundant and its supporters in political trouble.[36] But Monck remained cautious, with no sign that his political or religious position had moved since December. Monck was publicly conciliatory to Ludlow, one dangerous republican radical with army links, and assured him that he would not allow the secluded MPs readmission to this Parliament, though he did arrange for them to meet current MPs for a conference; but he told Fairfax that as the secluded MPs could stand for the new Parliament the issue of their readmission was academic anyway.[37]

The conferences between current and secluded MPs were a failure, and on the 20th Monck decided for readmission– apparently encouraged by his wife, brother-in-law, and chaplain, and a few other intimates (including Colonel Clobery, who had royalist sympathies) and backed by the London Presbyterian clergy. Technically, the argument may have been that these excluded Presbyterian MPs would provide the voting-numbers necessary to force a swift dissolution and elections, which Monck could not trust the Haselrig faction to accept. Next morning, having secured his officers' backing, he received the secluded MPs at Whitehall and warned them of the divisive dangers of monarchy and the necessity of a republic and of a Presbyterian church (i.e. one tolerating Independent sects). He wished to remain as commander-in-chief and Lawson to be retained as naval commander. Once they had assured him of their agreement his men let them into the House; Haselrig and his allies protested to him but were told that the measure had been necessary for political stability. This was a perfectly logical argument, given the public agitation for the dissolution of this and election of a new Parliament which Haselrig's group had been holding up and the fact that Monck could not rely on men who had recently tried to dismiss him. His own political survival as well as national stability were involved, but that does not mean that his decision was only taken for self-interest. There is no reason to assume that his declarations about a republic and a tolerant Presbyterian church as the desired outcome were not genuine either – at the time. In retrospect both disappointed current allies and the royalists who benefited from his actions were to claim that it was all part of a deep-laid plan to restore the monarchy, and both he and Charles II had every reason to play up his monarchist intentions after June 1660. But as of 21 February it was far more likely that he was at best playing a waiting game to see what came of the elections and that his main aim was to restore stability within the camp of those loyal to the Commonwealth. The same could be said of the more ideologically reliable Admiral Lawson, who was explicitly anti-monarchic but stayed loyal to Monck throughout the crises of February 1660.[38]

(ii) The regime widened: readmission of those excluded in December 1648 and its pro-royalist consequences. Only possible due to the 'Rump' overplaying its hand with Monck?

The tide of political power now shifted in favour of those moderate Parliamentarians known for backing a monarchy in the 1640s joining in the regime – but would this actually lead to restoring the king? The current regime's body of political support was widened as Parliament readmitted the secluded MPs of 1647–8 who had then attempted to secure a monarchy as well as a Presbyterian state church. They also included some MPs who would have tolerated a modified form of Anglican episcopacy which included presbyters, had Charles I been prepared to definitively support this. They were all 'Parliamentarian', as understood by their loyalties of 1642–8, but the republican section of this body was now diminishing and Monck's actions had isolated the Haselrig faction. Anthony Ashley Cooper, Herbert Morley, Oliver St

John, and three other former Councillors of State excluded from power by the army were admitted to the new Council of State set up on 23 February, along with Edward Mountague (Cromwellian commander of the navy until 1659), the Cromwellian Richard Norton, and the moderate Presbyterian Arthur Annesley.[39] The successful dispersal of regiments out of London in early February neutralised the potential for military resistance to this 'betrayal' of what they had done in 1648. Among the now isolated republican military officers who could be expected to resist the reversal of Pride's Purge, Colonel Okey, recently sent off to Bristol (no doubt to keep this avowed republican out of London lest he cause trouble), gave in tamely on finding that his fellow-republican Lawson was supporting the readmission. Colonel Nathaniel Rich, who had backed the December 1659 Portsmouth mutiny in the name of Parliament and was a friend of Lawson, was now stationed in Suffolk; he attempted to resist his summons to London but was abandoned by his men as Colonel Ingoldsby advanced on him and surrendered; Colonel Overton (an anti-Cromwellian protester cashiered in 1654), commanding in Hull, protested at the readmission but was persuaded to give in by Monck's emissaries.[40] None of the three was geographically close to the others so able to contact them, and their scattered locations were clearly a shrewd move by Monck anticipating trouble; Rich in particular could have incited Lawson to revolt had he been near London. Two of them were talked round by men of impeccable republican credentials who had backed Monck (and who were trusted by their targets as Commonwealth loyalists). Thus the army was preserved intact to accept the reversal of their political actions of December 1648, and the potential opened up for a tentative alliance of most of the Parliamentary cause of 1642–8. Monck had showed a degree of shrewdness and determination that Fleetwood had lacked in supreme command. Arguably this strategic vision and ability to play off one faction against another was what made his attempts to forge a stable new regime in early 1660 successful, whereas Fleetwood's efforts in summer – autumn 1659 had failed, and Monck's experience in military and political command of the army in Scotland had given him invaluable experience that he was now using. He had sidelined radicals successfully in Scotland in 1652–9; Fleetwood, by contrast, had been a (religious) radical ally of his own army's sectaries in Ireland and had never wanted or bothered to run a purge. Also, Monck was looking for (and needed) new allies in London and the provincial elites in early 1660, and so was prepared to 'reach out' to the long-sidelined moderate (royalist and non-royalist) Presbyterians who the army had driven from power in autumn 1648.

The new, enlarged Commons started to fulfil its part of the bargain by voting large new taxes to pay the army, confirming Monck's and Lawson's appointments, and preparing a bill for itself to dissolve. The Haselrig faction did not follow Ludlow's advice to try to gather soldiers in the provinces for a counter-coup, and for the moment continued in their seats in the Commons. Given the recent turbulence, they may well have decided to opt for stability quite apart from fearing the results of a challenge to the ruthless Monck. Some MPs favoured restoring Richard Cromwell, whose partisan Thurloe returned as (co-) Secretary of State on 27 February, and St John – a cousin of the Cromwells – was supposed to be in favour of Richard but Cooper preferred a continued Commonwealth. Pepys heard from his cousin and employer Mountague around this date that there were great endeavours to bring back Richard, but nothing came of this.[41] This suggests that Thurloe was still active in this cause. The difficulties of reconciling those MPs prepared to countenance a monarchy or a Protectorate with the republicans remained, with the arrival of assorted demobilised officers from the provincial garrisons in the capital adding to the potential backing of the latter.

On 3 March the minor issue of the wording for instructions to the committee on revenue dropped the specific reference to the Commonwealth – which could be interpreted as a hint that the form of government was negotiable. A bill to place the militia under new, non-republican commanders was held up in the Commons due to republican objections by Haselrig's group, who still had a solid 'bloc' of MPs to rely on; some of the readmitted conservative MPs had not taken up their seats yet. Okey, now back in London without his regiment but still capable of stirring up trouble, organised an officers' petition on 7 March for all MPs to swear that they opposed both monarchy and a House of Lords. This was the 'grass-roots' agitation which had toppled Richard Cromwell a year previously, but unlike him, Monck was a respected officer of known republican and 'godly' reputation and he had managed to purge many of the most radical officers and to send the main regiments of the turbulent English military establishment out of London. An officers' meeting at St James' accepted his opinion that the oath would only delay MPs from voting for a dissolution and a new House which would be able to meet their financial requirements. He also arranged a conference on the evening of 8 March between concerned officers and a delegation of MPs including Presbyterians Prynne and Annesley, who replied to the military demands for an indemnity, arrears of pay, and security of lands which they had acquired since 1646 that these would be guaranteed by the next Parliament.[42] The meeting was a success, and with Monck repeating his loyalty to the republic Okey was unable to muster support for his petition. When those officers who had left their provincial commands to come up to London and lobby Monck were ordered back to their posts they obeyed.[43]

Monck had faced down the potential military challenge, aided by a mixture of greater personal authority with the officers than Richard Cromwell had possessed and a large degree of political skill. The Commons now voted for a tolerant Presbyterian church, without bishops but including the sects, and for a new set of 'Triers' to select clergy – mainly Presbyterians but also some Independents who had not backed the 'junto in 1659. This isolated the most feared or irreconcilable 'fanatics', such as the City sectaries and the Fifth Monarchists (and the Quakers). Tithes were to continue, thus providing for a publicly-maintained and centrally-controlled ministry (which the radicals had sought to abolish in the Nominated Parliament in 1653); all current Church clergy were retained in their posts. The more controversial Militia Bill, which took control of the local committees away from the men of lesser status but greater political loyalty appointed in 1653–9 in favour of the gentry who had used to command it, was held up by Haselrig/army opposition but eventually passed after intervention by Monck.[44] The writs for the next general election were issued on 13 March in the usual Commonwealth form, thus appeasing republicans, but the Commons voted to abolish the declaration of allegiance to the republic required of new MPs. Royalists and their sons were banned from standing, unless known as repentant – which left a lot to local latitude by the county and borough electoral authorities – and Catholics and Quakers were banned from voting. It was clear which way the Commons was moving as it finally dissolved.[45] The way that the tide was flowing now caused the late republican regimes' principal literary defender, John Milton, to write and issue an anguished plea, 'The Ready and Easy Way To Establish A Free Commonwealth';

warning against any attempt to restore monarchy as inevitably leading to a gradual and complete erosion of all that had been fought for since 1642. He sent a copy to Monck, but it is unknown if it was read. It was ignored by Milton's former political allies of the 1650s, but his return to the literary arena would have reminded his Royalist enemies of his potential danger to them and so increased the probability of punishment after the king's restoration.

There had been no sign of any accommodation with the Anglican faction yet, and the new state church was firmly Presbyterian while accepting toleration of the Independent congregations – the compromise which even Cromwell had been prepared to accept at one point in the mid-1640s, but which the Presbyterian hardliners had turned down with disastrous consequences in 1647. Some of their leaders then, including Denzel Holles (one of the 'Five Members' who Charles I had tried to arrest in January 1642 but a proponent of a negotiated settlement in 1643) and Sir Harbottle Grimston, now sat on the new Council of State with their then republican and/or Independent foes. There was no guarantee that the elections would return a majority of MPs loyal to this religious solution or to the Commonwealth, although as far as the concerned army looked at it both were to be preserved by the power of Monck as commander-in-chief in case of Commons treachery. The officers who had backed a republic and opposed the Presbyterians in 1647–9 but had now refused to support Okey – and who would fail to rally to Lambert that spring – would have argued that if necessary Monck could dissolve a troublesome Commons as Cromwell had done in 1653. But the real situation was far different from that of 1648, not least due to Monck's purge of the more politically active officers in February 1660. Moreover, some of the restored MPs who had been secluded in 1647–8 were more than passive and /or lapsed royalists; Holles, Grimston, and others were in contact with Charles II, as were their former allies in the abolished Lords like the Earl of Northumberland, the veteran Parliamentarian commander of the fleet in 1642, and (Cromwell's original commander in East Anglia in 1643–4 and later foe) the Presbyterian Earl of Manchester. Linked together by Royalist conspirator Lord Mordaunt in what became known as the 'Presbyterian Knot' since November 1659, they were aiming for the king's restoration on the terms which Charles I had hesitated over at the talks in Newport in November 1648 – centred round the creation of a Presbyterian state church. This had initially been intended for the result of another rising like Booth's, hopefully with more support as the Commonwealth fell into chaos, and the restoration of order and discipline by Monck had been deeply disappointing to them as he was a capable military foe and seemingly loyal to the republic. But the surprise readmission of the secluded MPs gave these Presbyterian royalists access to power in the Commons for the first time for over eleven years as of March 1660, and the immanent elections opened the possibility that they could elect Presbyterian royalist MPs. The exclusion of – Anglican – royalists who had been in arms against Parliament in 1642–6 served their requirements as well as it did Monck's, by keeping the Anglican church (and bishops') supporters out of the Commons. That would duly help them to push for a Presbyterian church settlement in the Commons – though arguably they failed to realise that any interim settlement created by a 'tame' Commons could be revoked by a subsequent one with a wider electoral base. Some of their faction – e.g. Presbyterian officers such as Edward Massey, Parliamentarian governor of Gloucester in 1643–4 – had risen against the Parliamentary army in 1648 or 1651 and so were included on the proscribed list, but this was not an insuperable obstacle.

Crucially, the 'Presbyterian Knot' was extending its support to new recruits from previously impeccable republican and/ or Cromwellian backgrounds that spring, most notably Speaker Lenthall and the restored fleet-commander Mountague (son-in-law of a Presbyterian MP, John Crew).[46] Crew indeed put forward a motion on the final day of Parliament's meeting to condemn the regicide, which worried ex-republicans seeking to save their skins hastened to support. Principled regicide Thomas Scot boldly protested that his heart as well as his head had been in the act and he would be proud to have it inscribed on his tomb, which amounted to inviting royalist vengeance on him. The situation had also stabilised in Ireland despite its 1650s legacy of radical officers in senior ranks in the army there – Lord Broghill (the main pro-government landowner in Munster), an initially Cromwellian monarchist but a potential royalist, and his ally Sir Charles Coote of Connacht were in control of Dublin, and the latter was indeed to invite Charles II to Ireland before the Convention Parliament voted to restore the monarchy. Their 'linkman' in London was Annesley. The list of senior figures prepared to use the new Parliament to work for the restoration of Charles II was growing, not least as a source of stability after the recent upheavals, and the opponents of a monarchy (who probably still included Monck at this point) were having the ground cut from under their feet. The question would now arise – if the new Parliament turned out to be dominated by men prepared to accept Charles II back (on conditions or not), did the republicans have the will to resist it if this would lead to another bout of political turbulence? And now that Monck had neutered the Army, would its officers be able to resist if he did not?

(iii) The 'Convention' Parliament: the moves towards 'Restoration' gather unstoppable momentum.

The debate about Monck's ultimate intentions as of early 1660 is partly irrelevant, as what mattered to this canny political survivor – a man lacking Cromwell's religious rhetoric or Lambert's constitutional planning – was 'the art of the possible'. As far as his own principles go, it is apparent that he detested the 'fanatics' (his preferred term for sectaries) and so was a natural ally of any stable and conservative political order. He was also a personal rival of Lambert and Fleetwood and, unlike the latter, was prepared to purge the Army and reach out to moderate civilian supporters of the Parliamentarian cause in 1642–8 to bolster his support even if these men included supporters of monarchy. Compared to Fleetwood, he was both ruthless and unsentimental; the latter, as we have seen, was left in bemused shock by the collapse of the 'Good Old Cause' in early 1660. His own past as a former royalist in the army fighting the Catholic rebels in Ireland, who had been captured on arrival in England and turned Parliamentarian, was a hint as to his pragmatism. He had also allied with moderate Calvinist Scots against the more extreme anti-English, anti-monarchist faction in the 1650s – and so had had to work with men who had initially backed Charles II (then at the head of a Presbyterian regime in Scotland) against the English in 1650–1. His targets then had included truculent semi-autonomous military radical commanders who would not accept those orders they disapproved of, such as the inflexible Covenanter ally Colonel Strachan – forerunners of his 1660 military foes? Did his political flexibility in Scotland in the 1650s present him with a hint as to what model to follow in England in 1660? But even if he had now accepted his wife's and friends' suggestions that a restored monarchy need not be a disaster in 1660, not least for a stable and comprehensive state church on the model planned by the moderate Presbyterians in 1647–8, there were still military qualms at the re-emergence of monarchism. As seen above, he had to reassure these worries with declarations of his devotion to the Commonwealth during early spring 1660, with the recent past indicating the danger of a split in the army and Colonel Okey still able to stir up trouble in the purged ranks. The spontaneous assembly of officers in London – including those Monck had sent out of the way into the provinces, i.e. those he could not trust – was probably the most dangerous moment for him. The military reaction to local provincial petitions for a free Parliament – which could easily set up a Presbyterian church and end toleration of the sects – shows that even the purged, dispersed army of February-March 1660 could maintain military control of the country. This would not have lasted in the long term, given that pay was short and only Parliament could grant a new assessment to raise more money, but if properly organised and led the Army was capable of staving off an unwanted Parliament temporarily. What if the more senior Lambert, not Okey, had been leading the petition? But Monck managed to win the officers over and prevent Okey's agitation from going further, and the elections went ahead.

Contemporaries placed emphasis on the way that Monck relied on advice from a mixture of family, friends, and officers in the crucial confrontation of 9–11 February with the 'Rump'; he did not rush to defy their order to coerce the City. The popular mood in the provinces – or indeed in the City itself – was not the deciding factor, as both were strongly against the much-reviled 'Rump' although generally in favour of a free Parliament. He only moved when he sensed he had his men's support. This was not the behaviour of a determined idealist ready to demand a free Parliament and gamble his authority, but of a careful commander wary of his position and needing to be sure that his men would follow him. It is most probable that he did not decide what to aim for until he was sure it would work (and not threaten his own position), and this applies to his attitude to the king too. Whatever he ultimately believed was a desirable politico-religious solution, he reacted to events and did nothing without assessing its consequences. Even if his religious sympathies were broadly Presbyterian, this did not drive him immediately to insist on any actions – the readmission of the secluded MPs, most notably – which would aid the creation of a (tolerant) Presbyterian church. But he and the restored secluded royalist Presbyterian MPs of March 1660 had one agenda in common, namely broadening the base of their support. The risks of mutiny in the army and the danger of stalemate with a surviving 'Rump' encouraged Monck to press for a new Parliament and a permanent resolution of the politico-religious impasse. In the meantime, the dismissal of the government newsletter editor Marchamont Nedham and the arrest of the republican bookseller Livewell Chapman at the end of March showed that Monck would not permit the uncontrolled literary agitation that had encouraged republican dissidents through 1659.

The danger of their own politico-religious 'left wing', the 'Commonwealthsmen' around Haselrig, linking up with men like Vane and Ludlow encouraged the readmitted civilian MPs to arrange for a broadly-based new Parliament; this would add to their own strength as well as arrange a sympathetic Church and pay off the nuisancesome army. Both Monck and the civilian MPs had every reason to fear the radicals, and the extent of socially conservative 'moderates' fearing the alleged anarchic threat of sects like the Quakers in 1659–60 needs to be emphasised. In this situation, an alliance with the royalists (hardline Anglicans excepted) to restore the king became attractive – and would have done so even without the busy lobbying of Mordaunt's 'Presbyterian Knot' to win over doubters. The outcome led to self-serving assurances from former Parliamentarians fearing revenge in 1660–2 that they had been active in helping to restore the king and thus deserved exemption from prosecution, and so it is difficult to untangle the genuineness of their claims to have worked for the Restoration. The claim that figures were supporting the king before it became the safest course of action to take is difficult to substantiate, even with figures like Mountague who had been approached byCharles in 1659 and had committed ambiguous actions then. Until the mood of the Convention Parliament became known, supporting a stable, conservative monarchic regime could mean a willingness to restore Richard Cromwell, a course of action still backed in early 1660 by Thurloe (a Cromwellian protégé) and St John (a Cromwellian relative). In the first week of March an approving Mountague told his cousin, the diarist Pepys, that 'there was great endeavours to bring in the Protector again'. Probably, as with careful politicians keeping in touch with the exiled court of James II while serving Wiliam III in the 1690s, many people were anxious to back the winning side and would have backed away from the king if the attempts to restore him had stalled. The attitude of the army – a block to any Stuart restoration – was vital here, and the military failure of the 'hard left' republicans in March–April 1660 may well have enabled cautious political actors to step down off the fence. But Charles was undeniably a force for stability, when the question of the form the new executive power should take was considered. On past experience, a military head of state like Monck would be capable of using the army to close Parliament as Cromwell had done. The weariness of the nation with the cost and intrusiveness of the army into civilian life was another factor arguing for its abolition – which the civilian Presbyterian MPs had been attempting to arrange in 1647–8. If there was no need for an army, someone other than a general would need to fill the vacancy for chief executive and govern when there was no Parliament; the question was whether this should be one man or a Council of State. The experience of rule by the latter in 1659 was not promising – and a king would guarantee legal authority for the government, as Whitelocke and others had argued in endeavouring to persuade Cromwell to take the crown.

The omens were thus good for the re-establishment of a limited monarchy as of April 1660, even without the ulterior motives of Mordaunt's recruits and of past royalist Presbyterians in the 'Long Parliament' (many of them leading local gentry and so controlling the electoral process). The royalists were now able to use the lack of public knowledge of Charles II's character to launch a propaganda blitz about his pleasing personality, good intentions, and desire for reconciliation. This was masterminded by Samuel Tuke.[47] All the country had seen of Charles since he left for the Scillies as Cornwall fell to the New Model Army in 1646 had been his heroic but futile invasion of 1651, which usefully for current purposes had been in alliance with royalist Presbyterians against the rule of 'fanatics' and the army, and his romantic escape after the battle of Worcester. The part played by Catholics in this was not generally known, and neither was his louche private life in exile. His mistress and alleged 'wife' Lucy Walter, mother of the Duke of Monmouth, had been arrested on royalist business in London in 1657 by Cromwell's secret police and exposed in the State press as 'Charles Stuart's whore'[48] but this had limited impact. Indeed, Charles had even taken the Covenant to secure his admission to Scotland in 1650 and so could be portrayed to Presbyterians as more sympathetic to their religion than his father had been. As far as political declarations went, his last offers had been made after the end of the Booth revolt and involved a pardon for all but seven regicides, a free Parliament and regular triennial elections, and vastly reduced taxation (which meant no large standing army). The more cynical or vengeful royalists could excuse themselves from being tied to this programme indefinitely by arguing that what one Parliament could grant another – its elections now manipulated by royalist gentry – could revoke.

The way that the political 'tide' was flowing was now shown by the first direct contact between Monck and Charles. The king arranged for a distant cousin of Monck's, Sir John Grenville (nephew of the 1640s royalist commander Sir Richard), a 'passive' royalist from a major Cornish royalist dynasty who had kept out of trouble in the 1650s, to deliver a letter to his and Monck's mutual cousin, Long Parliament MP William Morice (a victim of 'Pride's Purge) for onward transmission to Monck. Morice had also sat in Richard's Parliament, so was not implacably anti-Cromwellian despite his treatment in 1648; he had put his loyalty to civilian rule above distaste for the Cromwells. It made the predictable offers of high office and lucrative grants in return for support, as offered to Mountague and other senior figures earlier. The commander-in-chief received Grenville some time after the 'Rump' dissolved in March, on the evening of Saturday 17 March at his current quarters at St James' Palace, and assured him that he had always favoured Restoration. He accepted an offer of £100,000 from the king to distribute to people he needed to win over at his discretion, and Greville's account has it that Monck then pledged his life for the king but advised that the latter make no open calls for vengeance on the regicides and other opponents.[49] Two days later, after more talks between Monck, Grenville, and Morice, Grenville returned to receive a paper in which Monck provided his terms, but was advised by him to commit these to memory; in fact once Grenville had done this Monck checked that he had memorised them and burnt the paper in front of him for reasons of safety and secrecy. Monck's terms by his account were – full amnesty, arrears of pay for the army and navy, guarantees of current legal titles to the purchasers of Church and Crown lands, and extensive but unspecified religious toleration. (Given Monck's attitude he was unlikely to mind if the king excluded the more radical sects.) All this was delivered verbally to Charles at Breda. Charles agreed, and also followed Monck's suggestion that he should not stay in Spanish territory due to his ally's unsavoury Catholic and oppressive reputation in England. Monck wanted him to abandon his Spanish alliance, but the King preferred a public gesture to such a drastic act; he told the Spanish authorities that he was going to visit his sister Princess Mary in Holland. He then removed his court from Brussels to the Protestant territory of the Dutch state, taking up residence at Breda at the beginning of April.[50]

The elections led to a strong royalist showing in the provinces and in London, despite the public exclusion of their 'party' from the process. As usual for elections except when Cromwell's army had had a firm grip on the country in 1653–8, who was nominated and who was elected reflected the current control of the local electoral process. The machinery of administration remained as in the mid-1650s, but there was no central state power to direct the election of suitable candidates as in Cromwell's time. Monck was unused to the English political process as he had served in Scotland throughout the Protectorate; the purge of the army and removal of most of its more 'political' officers had neutralised the chances of senior officers opposed to Presbyterians and/or royalists interposing vetoes. It is clear that the revolt against the 'junto' in December 1659 had restored much local political power to the traditional elites of gentry and urban corporations, who could thus elect their own choices – certainly the control of the local militia, as sign of political power, had returned to them that winter. Thus there was no authority to see that the ban on royalists was enforced, with the ex-rebel Booth being returned as MP for Cheshire and his colleagues Myddelton and Massey being elected too, Massey for his former governorate of Gloucester. The local troops tried to arrest the latter but the citizens rescued him. Monck and his allies Clobery, Colonel Ingoldsby (Cromwell's regicide cousin), Charles Howard (Cromwell's Guards commander), Mountague, and Lord Broghill were all elected; at least sixty-one MPs were either royalist veterans or their sons despite the ban, and they did particularly well in the more 'open' county elections.

Haselrig was denied a seat by concerted action by the local gentry in Leicestershire; Vane did not try to stand, recognising that it was hopeless; Lambert had been thrown in prison and stood in *absentia* but was not elected; and Ludlow and Scot managed to secure election in boroughs where they had built up influence in the 1650s but faced petitions to disqualify them by their opponents who would have likely backing from most MPs. Ludlow stood in Hinden in Somerset, with an indication of royalist plans in the way that the latter published a list of the late king's judges for the voters to peruse and hinted that any who backed these men would face Charles II's wrath shortly; his opponent who evicted him on petition was local royalist Thomas Thynne of Longleat. Scot was accused of producing a bastard to put 'godly' voters off him, achieved an equal number of votes to his opponent in the 'count', but then faced the new Commons disqualifying some of his voters in order to give his opponent the seat; the mayor who had proclaimed him elected was arrested.[51] The shenanigans were normal for the era, and served to point out where the local power lay as for once there was little 'government' direction to the presiding officers at the counts. Notably, where there is evidence of popular participation this was strongly in favour of the king's restoration without conditions;[52] the more royalist a candidate was the better. There seems to have been no co-ordinated effort by the royalists across the country; as far as can be determined there was not a 'party' election strategy as there was to be in the 1670s or 1680s. The results were an expression of the popular mood and of the desires of the restored local elites, and the makeup of the new House duly reflected the mood of the country. Monck had taken no chances with the army's reaction, requiring all serving officers to take an oath to respect the results as he had discussed with leading moderates Cooper, Annesley, and Charles Howard; this new 'Engagment' was imposed on the more reliable regiments under Monck's eyes in London first and then in the provinces.[53] Former 'junto' propagandist Marchamont Nedham was sacked lest he stir up trouble in writing, official tracts urged the soldiers to obey orders and stand by Parliament, and the Council issued orders for the arrest of 'hit-and-run' agitators who were touring the regions inciting military mutiny. On 9 April the regiments' officers duly announced their acceptance of the election results.[54]

Lambert's last stand.

There was one abortive military challenge after the election that could have caused disaster, as the well-regarded Lambert escaped from the Tower of London and fled to the midlands to try to raise a military mutiny. The escape, on the night of 9–10 April, came within hours of the delivery of a signed agreement by the regiments in and around London to abide by the result of the elections, arranged by Monck and his allies, to the commander-in-chief at St James'. In typical daring fashion, Lambert left his maidservant in his bed in his night-cap to deceive any patrolling guards, then shinned down a rope from an outer wall of the Tower onto Tower Wharf to flee by ship. The threat of mutiny now revived under a charismatic leader who had the prestige and skills to challenge Monck. Lambert's reputation, prestige, and determination made this the most serious threat that Monck faced after the Okey petition was halted, though the dispersal of pro-Commonwealth regiments from London and the cashiering of many officers meant that Lambert had no instrument ready to hand to win over for a coup. He was still a danger, and Monck hastily issued assurances that all arrears of pay would be met quickly and required the troops to sign up to the 9 April declaration accepting the elections or be dismissed.

Lambert had to travel well away from London into the Midlands to look for support, with the soldiers nearer London, more subject to Monck's attentions, being less likely to revolt (having had their arrears met quickly). He was hotly pursued by the reliable Colonels Streater, Rossiter, and Ingoldsby, and while he was in hiding contacting his allies Monck had time to disband the unreliable regiment of Colonel Mills and arrest suspect sectaries. Due to the distances involved in contacting other malcontents Lambert suffered from the same problem as Booth had in August 1659, although (as with royalists) the same factor meant that once a revolt occurred far from London it could have time to spread if not quickly checked. One potentially disloyal isolated garrison who could resist loyal troops for weeks, on St Michael's Mount, was caught unawares by Monck's agents and purged in time; the potentially disloyal radical-led militia in Caernarfonshire was also purged quickly by their pro-government replacements. Lambert could not count on pro-Richard officers, such as Goffe and Whalley, who followed Council orders to report to London, and the delay in rising (twelve days from Lambert's escape) gave Streater time to set up a central base in Coventry ready to pounce on the first sign of trouble from the midlands garrisons. Even so some radical garrisons, including Warwick Castle, declared for Lambert and men from six regiments mutinied and attempted to join him. His name and his cause attracted widespread if scattered support even in the purged army, though no civilian radicals (primarily Vane and Haselrig) or former Cromwellian senior officers joined the rebel.

There were revolts by civilian radicals in three counties, including Somerset (worryingly far from London and easy defeat) and – led by 1647 military Leveller leader Lockyer – in Nottinghamshire. The latter, back stirring up subversion in his old regiment at Nottingham before Lambert's escape, broke his parole to behave and caused many of his sympathisers to join in the rising, thus lending experienced military support to the local civilian rebels. Luckily there was no co-ordination with the activities of Ludlow, who was plotting revolt among the militia in his local district (Wiltshire) but was taken by surprise and had to react to Lambert's timetable. In fact, according to Ludlow's later account he had been planning since late February to bring together the sacked military members of the 1659 military Council of State to go to their local commands and raise them in revolt. But he had had less support than he anticipated, and when he had sent Slingsby Bethel to Haselrig – a civilian and a principled republican but also a former, 1643–4 regimental commander used to leading troops – the latter had been in a panic and had refused to help. According to what Monck later said when successfully trying to save arrested Haselrig from execution, Haselrig had at around this time (after the readmission of the secluded 'Rump' MPs) gone to Monck to ask for help as he believed that Restoration was now inevitable. Monck agreed to help, explaining subsequently to Parliament later in 1660 that Haselrig was technically in command of the regimental troops at Newcastle-upon-Tyne, Berwick, and Tynemouth so he could cause revolt across this region if he so chose and was obeyed; but he would only promise to speak up to the king for Haselrig's life if the latter remained passive throughout the coming months. Haselrig so promised, and kept his word – and if Monck was accurate this would have kept one major prestigious figure from aiding Lambert in March – April 1660 and also undermined Ludlow's plans. Was this crucial to the revolt turning into a 'flop'?

The Quakers and other religious radicals were rumoured to be involved in the plans, which would have done them no good with alarmed local provincial gentry elites for months to come. Lambert planned a general rendezvous at the Edgehill battlefield for the 22nd (Easter Day) and then to march South to Oxford to link up with the south-western rebels, but the government's quick response caught him in time. Cromwell's cousin Ingoldsby took charge of hunting him down, and arrived at the rendezvous with enough men to outnumber Lambert's small force. Lambert offered to restore Richard, but what might have worked to win over Ingoldsby in summer 1659 was now out of date and the loyal forces attacked; the rebels were dispersed and Lambert was ignominiously caught as his horse floundered in mud while he was fleeing across a field. The risings elsewhere collapsed with rebel-held Warwick Castle and Red Castle (Montgomeryshire) being surrounded, and Ludlow had to call his revolt off and flee to the Continent. Lambert was taken back to the Tower.[55]

The 'Convention' opens: setting a course for the king to respond to.

The 'Convention' Parliament opened on 23 April with military resistance now shown to be impracticable even if it decided to call the king back without conditions. To that extent the nature and timing of Lambert's challenge emboldened the MPs, and enabled Monck to risk taking a firmer line than in February in facing down any army complaints at what the MPs proposed. Indeed, the strength of royalist feelings in the electoral nation added to arguments that his own position as commander-in-chief would be more secure by following rather than intimidating Parliament if it voted for monarchy. What good was closing it for defying his previous promises about the security of the Commonwealth when he would have no means of paying off his army? There were thus practical reasons for allying with the royalist Presbyterians – now reinforced and emboldened in the new House by straightforward Royalists who would not put conditions on the king's return – even if he had not been convinced yet of the need for a monarchy. The 'Presbyterian Knot' group, now reinforced by AnthonyAshley Cooper and Thurloe, now proposed to Monck that they work together for a limited monarchy, influencing Parliament by excluding MPs who would not accept the current Commonwealth (an echo of Cromwell's tactics in 1654 and 1656), keeping the Second House for their own reliable Presbyterian peers, and electing a reliable Speaker. The exclusion of Scottish and Irish MPs and abandonment of the more democratic electoral reforms of 1654 – opposed by Monck but insisted on by his allies – also made the commons more manageable. The intention of the 'Knot' group was thus for a controllable monarchy based on that planned by the moderate Presbyterian Parliamentarians in 1646–8; the new and uncontrolled factor in the Commons was the attitude of those MPs who were young newcomers to politics since the 1640s. The 'Knot' had the advantage over Monck in that he could not fall back on military republican allies, having 'burnt his boats' with them in February–April 1660; but they themselves were not united and one senior member of the group, Lord Annesley, was keeping the king informed of their plans.

The dominant faction in the House now moved to assert conservatism, securing the election of a sympathetic Speaker (the veteran Presbyterian Sir Harbottle Grimston) on 25 April. Their peer allies – led by Manchester, who Cromwell had scorned for his unwillingness to confront his king in 1644 – forcibly occupied the House of Lords. Manchester, elected Speaker, proposed to redmit sixteen carefully-vetted peers backing the Presbyterian faction to the second House. This was accepted by the Commons despite some opposition, the decisive argument (by Heneage Finch, a future 1670s Lord Chancellor) being that it would widen conciliation and reconciliation. Now, however, the Presbyterian Lords were outflanked by the 'no-conditions' Royalists, apparently led by Mordaunt, who proposed that the sons of former peers who had come of age since the abolition of the House in 1649 should be allowed to sit. These men were almost all untainted by past royalism, and so exempt from Monck's stricture and attempted ban, but could be expected to vote for Restoration. Opinion in the Commons was divided, but the 'no-conditions' royalists favoured them as they would swamp the votes of Manchester's more cautious Presbyterian peers; Monck temporised, told the young peers to stay away for two days, and sought the opinions of MPs. Once it was clear that most favoured admitting the new peers he gave way, and they took their seats on 27 April.[56] It was now those Presbyterians who favoured a limited monarchy and a disciplinarian church, on the lines proposed in 1646–8, who looked likely to be outflanked – and the crucial point is that Monck had abandoned them (when pushed by Mordaunt). This was probably due to a mixture of not risking unpopularity (i.e. self-preservation) and the likelihood that the inexperienced new peers and their allies would be more malleable (and grateful) politically than their rivals. The political wheel had come full circle, and the Commons and Lords were more royalist in sentiment than they had been in spring 1642 – with Lambert's defeat showing the radicals still in the army that there was no chance of taking unilateral action to halt the drift of events. For the first time Monck appeared to be losing control of events and being outflanked by his civilian allies – and he, unlike Lambert, had no apparent objection to working with a coalition containing an increasingly hardline royalist element.

The results of the elections, and the resultant strength of royalist sentiment in the Commons in April 1660, was clearly unexpected to those who had been responsible for calling them – above all to Monck. The lack of any central control over the elections, as seen in the 1650s, enabled royalists to defy or evade his requirements; the local county authorities (e.g. the sheriffs) and the senior figures in boroughs where voting was fairly open were wary of defying the popular will even where they were not now pro-royalist themselves. The local gentry, most of whom had been excluded from office by the 'Rump' and Cromwell in favour of 'baser' but more politically trustworthy figures, had regained their influence in their areas in winter 1659–60 as the army's power weakened. The army veto on participation in local politics by 'unacceptable' personnel – royalists, those pro-Parliamentarians unprepared to accept regicide, and/or Presbyterians likely to persecute the sects if allowed to run Parliament – had been ended by the collapse of army power in winter 1659–60. The latter could still stop demonstrations for a free Parliament early in 1660, but could not stop royalists being elected in March-April; and the removal of most of their most zealous republican senior officers by Monck weakened their will and ability to act. As of April 1660 the hardliners were considering whether to join Lambert or Ludlow in revolt, not how to intimidate the voters; and the defeat of the rebellion disheartened those who were not implicated and cashiered from attempting any further resistance. In practical terms, the new Parliament would offer a firm chance of meeting all arrears of pay and there was no inkling that it would back an Anglican rather than a comprehensively pro-Independent Church.

The chance of 'grass-roots' action to intimidate Parliament, as in 1647 or 1648, was thus much reduced; and with Monck not Cromwell or Fleetwood in the supreme command there would be no 'lead' to do so from the central leadership.His personal security as much as religious disagreement had required Monck to sideline the senior personnel of Cromwell's 'high command' in winter 1659–60, and luckily only Lambert chose to attempt military resistance – at a point by which the army had been dispersed across the country so staging a takeover was difficult.

Attitudes to an Anglican church were not all favourable, as seen by the attitude of representatives of the local gentry (in pro-Parliamentarian counties at least) in 1640–6. The MPs excluded from sitting in 1647–8 had been attempting to force a disciplinarian, anti-Independent state church without bishops on the king, and had refused to concede his request for bishops. They had little choice in backing a free election for the next free Parliamnt when they returned to the House in 1660, as popular opinion – especially among the intimidatory crowds in London – and the resolute Monck both insisted on it. Such secluded MPs as Holles would hope for a full new House to represent their politico-religious views rather than 1642–6 royalist views, and they were duly taken by surprise by the election-results. But those MPs with broadly Presbyterian sympathies – whether excluded or not in 1647–8 – had been in favour of retaining a monarchy, and all had been suspicious of the radical sects and unwilling to accept them in a new church. This fear of 'anarchic' sectaries was still potent, as seen by the 'scare' over the potential of the Quakers in 1659–60 – and the latter had been conspicuous by their support for the army in coercing Parliament in so they were regarded as dangerous. Seen in retrospect, it would appear that this panic was exaggerated – but as seen by the socially conservative civilian MPs in 1660 the sects were the mainstay of their army enemies and had done their best to prevent a free Parliament sitting. The oppressive and intrusive nature of army rule in the provinces in 1646–60, plus the high taxation needed to pay it, made it essential to use any chance of ridding the country of it and its radical political and religious allies. In this context, it was politically advantageous for the 'Parliamentary Presbyterian moderates' of 1646–8 who were now back in Parliament, seeking a resolution to the long years of resented pro-Independent military rule, to accept support from even royalist MPs who were now returned to the House. Putting up with the latter was preferable to more instability and the threat of a return of army power, as graphically shown by the spectre of Lambert's revolt as Parliament prepared to sit. In any case, the large numbers of known or suspected royalist MPs would make it difficult to evict them all, even if this was not guaranteed to launch disturbances in London and the localities.The legal way to keep them out – listening to and approving election-petitions from their defeated opponents – would be time-consuming and detract from the need to meet army requirements on pay and to frame the next constitution and religious settlement. Technically the Presbyterian leadership and Monck could have denied them entry by posting soldiers at the doors, as Pride and Cromwell had done to secure a trustworthy House – but this would entail reliance on the army which civilian MPs now sought to curtail, quite apart from the thtreat of riots.

The number of 'Presbyterian' gentry opposed to royal rule – be it conditional or unconditional – in principle was small; the leader of the principled republicans among them, Haselrig, had been sidelined and driven out of politics by his resistance to Monck. Even the 'Cromwellian' gentry, those who had been prepared to take part in local or national politics and back the Protectorate in 1653–9, had supported it as a force for conservatism. The 'Humble Petition and Advice', a Cromwellian kingship, had been designed by or for these men (and for noble allies, like Broghill and Howard, and Presbyterian allies like Crew and Pierrepoint). They had been against army rule and in favour of Richard in 1659, but hopes for his restoration had faded so their requirement for a civilian 'Single Person' as head of state would be transferred to Charles II out of necessity. Neither 'Cromwellians' nor 1642–8 Parliamentarians had any reason to stand in the way of strongly-expressed public opinion and back the army dissidents and sectaries in spring 1660, with the latter a proven source of instability (as seen in 1659) and full of feared zealots.

Accordingly, those MPs of Holles' faction who could be expected to favour a careful, negotiated 'Restoration', were unwilling to try to control the Commons, and the unexpectedly large numbers of MPs who favoured an unconditional recognition of Charles as king could use their numbers to win the necessary votes. Co-ordinated from behind the scenes by determined organsiers led by Mordaunt, the latter now proceeded to move swiftly to recognise the king without preconditions – helped by his prudent move from the Catholic Spanish Netherlands to the Protestant (Dutch) United Provinces. Charles seemed to be willing to grant both a nearly-full amnesty, confirmation of grants of Crown Land made since 1642, settlement of arrears and indemnity for the soldiery, and a guarantee of religious toleration – as suggested unofficially by Monck in his contacts with Charles. Charles was to be understood as being bound by what terms of settlement Parliament decided on, though cynics or hardline royalists could argue that technically any terms set by the 'Convention' could be cast aside later as it had not been called by a king and was therefore illegal. The 'Declaration of Breda' made by Charles from Holland on 4 April, addressed and sent to the Commons, Lords, army, fleet, and City of London, duly encouraged optimistic attitudes of his generosity. Indemnity, guarantees of confirmation of current ownership of Church and Crown Lands, payment of arrears to the army and Fleet, and religious toleration for all 'peaceful' Christians were to be arranged by Parliament and confirmed by the king.[57] By now senior figures in the Council of State like Annesley and Charles Howard and the fleet's commander Mountague were dealing with the king independently and offering their services, hopeful Englishmen were flocking to Breda to offer their services and seek royal grants, and even the Protectoral ambassador to the Dutch, George Downing, changed sides after years of harassing his next master. The States-General, who had been tolerating but not encouraging Charles while he was on their soil, now invited him to The Hague and put on lavish receptions for him. Parliament set no conditions for Restoration, and on 8 May Charles was formally recognised as king[58] – though he was to continue to date his reign from his father's execution on 30 January 1649, a significant snub to notions of deriving his power from anyone but God. Notably, Parliament did not seek to lay down the law as to when his reign had begun, which would have had the advantage of securing in writing its position of legal authority – either this was overlooked or (more likely) both veteran MPs from the 1640s who had not wanted regicide and new royalist MPs regarded that sort of declaration as an insult to their favoured governmental form of monarchy. This, however, was more than a question of semantics and should have been recognised as such by past participants in politics under the Interregnum – as with Henry VII dating his reign from the day before the battle of Bosworth in 1485, it implied that all who had served the late regime were potential traitors to the current one and so open to prosecution. Nor did an attempt by the Presbyterian Earl of Manchester and Lord Wharton (the latter a personal friend of Cromwell) to have the terms of the 'Charles I/Presbyterian MPs' Treaty of Newport of November 1648 voted as the basis for the new political structure get far; it received a proposer and seconder but was not voted on. One contemporary account has it that Monck was 'instructed' (by who? Grenville on the King's behalf?) to stop it and did so, by making a speech warning of the danger of more revolts unless the new, royal order was definitively put in place quickly.[59] Was this treachery to Monck's Presbyterian allies, ingratiating himself with Charles, or genuine fear of more Lambert-style risings?

Parliamentary debates continued to include efforts to control the king's freedom of manoeuvre, with the appointment of ministers an obvious 'front-line'. The most senior politico-legal office, that of Lord Chancellor, was vested in a commission headed by the Presbyterian leader Manchester despite Charles' intentions of handing it to its royalist holder in exile, Hyde, and 'Long Parliament' Presbyterian MP Sir Walter Earle (Parliamentarian commander in Dorset 1644–5) proposed that all ministers be subject to a Parliamentary confirmation as his faction had wanted in 1646–8. But the plan to control the ministers was subject to defeat should its opponents collect enough votes in the Commons and Lords, ambitious men and nervous ex-republicans would not want to risk offending the king, and already senior 'moderate' figures such as Howard and Cooper were expressing objections. The political tide was flowing in Charles' favour, and the plan to control appointments was not passed.[60] This was another political 'mistake' by the moderates in the long term. To emphasize the royalist triumph, the Lords voted to readmit all peers who had sat in 1642 – thus swamping the Upper as well as Lower House with royalists.[61] This would complete a constitutional 'coup' by meaning that there was no formal, legal constraint on a king and a Commons both intent on vengeance in 1661.

Chapter Four

The Restoration, 1660: a missed opportunity for moderation? If so, who was to blame?

There was still much to sort out in the form and the policies of the new government, particularly the vexed questions of royal powers and royalist revenge – but for most people the main reaction to the Restoration seems to have been relief at the end of chaos and a constant military presence in national and local life. This was shown by the size of the crowds that turned out to see the king return to his kingdom in triumph – ten and a half years after he had skulked off on a sailing-ship from Brighthelmstone (Brighton) in disguise and in fear of his life. Charles was welcomed to The Hague on 15 May by the ruling Dutch States-General with all the honours that he had been denied for years, and a week of celebratory banquets and displays followed. Among the large number of prominent Englishmen who flocked to express their delight at his restoration was the ex-Parliamentary commander-in-chief, Fairfax (who Charles apparently consulted in private). Assorted delegations from English civic bodies joined those of the Lords and Commons who now arrived to confirm the offer of the throne, and all were received graciously whatever the king's private cynicism about their sincerity. On the 23rd he went aboard Admiral Mountague's fleet which was waiting off the port of Scheveningen, with the bulwark of the Commonwealth's and Cromwell's successful efforts to keep Charles abroad now being used to transport his entourage home. Among many ironies, the republican ships had been given patriotic names reflecting on the glories of their government's record, such as their victories over the royalists; thus Charles sailed home on the flagship that had been christened '*Naseby*', now hastily renamed the '*Royal Charles*'. (The monarchy's sensitivity about naval names was to continue for over 250 years, with George V refusing to name a ship after Cromwell as suggested by Winston Churchill.) Luckily for posterity, one of the witnesses of the royal return on Mountague's flagship was the Admiral's protégé and secretary, the diarist Samuel Pepys, who had commenced his nine-year record of events that January. On 25 May Charles landed at Dover to start his journey to London, reviewing the carefully-tamed army en route at Blackheath. The extent of wild popular rejoicing across the country appears to have taken the authorities by surprise, and led to vigilante attacks on the now-powerless sectaries (especially Quakers) and the forcible ejection of current, 1650s-appointed clergy from their parishes by Anglican parishioners. Already privately he had written to Monck on 10/20 May warning him not to continue to indulge 'many persons still contriving… against me and you who must be rather suppressed by your authority and power than won and reconciled by your indulgences'.[1] This may principally refer to genuinely feared plotters, but Charles was to show his desire for vengeance on foes of his father who were not a serious threat as of 1660 as well.

On Charles' memorable arrival in London on 29 May he still chose to be prudent in allocating offices. The new Privy Council included sixteen royalists led by Sir Edward Hyde (royalist Lord Chancellor and ex-Secretary of State, now confirmed in office), royalist Secretary from the 1640s Edward Nicholas (ditto), the veteran Irish royalist commander the Marquis of Ormonde, the Earls of Norwich (father of the late royalist general George Goring), Berkshire, and Leicester (the latter a moderate Parliamentarian in the 1640s as Lord Lieutenant of Ireland), the veteran moderate royalist Earl of Hertford, Lord Wentworth, and the royalist Channel Islands commander Sir George Carteret. (Leicester had looked after Charles' interned brother and sister for the Commons in 1649.) There were four Cromwellians: Monck (confirmed as commander-in-chief and given the Dukedom of Albemarle); Mountague (deputy naval commander and given the Earldom of Sandwich); Cromwell's ex-ally Charles Howard, who was a cousin of the royalist Earls of Arundel and Suffolk; and the ex-royalist turned Parliamentarian Anthony Ashley Cooper. There were eight members from the 1642–8 'moderate', Parliamentarian faction opposed to the creation of the Commonwealth, mostly Presbyterians – such as the Earl of Southampton (Lord Treasurer later in 1660), Monck's associate William Morice (the second Secretary of State), Annesley, Holles (who had been abused by Vane's radicals in 1644–5 for his efforts for peace), Lord Saye and Sele (a moderate Parliamentarian peer in the 1640s and major backer of 'godly' colonies in

North America), and the Earl of Northumberland. The latter and Saye and Sele had been 1630s courtiers from ancient noble families (Percy and Fiennes) who supported Parliament in 1642 out of disquiet over Charles I's contentiously autocratic and 'Popish' leanings. Fiennes was also to end up as father to the pioneering late seventeenth-century female travel-writer Celia Fiennes, and Northumberland was brother to the 'behind the scenes' plotter and intriguer Lucy, Lady Carlisle. Denzel Holles was the only senior anti-Charles I Commons figure of 1640–2 to be fully rehabilitated, despite being one of the 'Five Members', a leading royal critic in the 1628–9 Parliament, and a fearsome critic of Charles I in 1640–2. He and Manchester, who as Lord Mandeville had also faced impeachment by the king in January 1642, were lucky in their current vital political role as royalist Presbyterian leaders but had both opposed the Commonwealth in 1649 which would have earned Royal approval. Manchester had been sacked by Parliament as a military commander via the Self-Denying Ordinance in 1645 after complaints about his lack of zeal for winning by Cromwell. 1642–6 Cornish (Presbyterian) Parliamentarian commander Lord Robartes, a leader of the 'Presbyterian Knot', was made deputy to and soon replacement for Ormonde in governing Ireland. Of these, only Morice among non-royalists was reckoned to be close to Charles as he started to rely more on an 'inner circle' of Councillors;[2] Morice had been Monck's 'go-between' with Charles' representative Grenville in early 1660 and was to be politically isolated before he lost office in 1668.

The court offices, still important for their access to the king, included Northumberland as Constable, Manchester as Lord Chamberlain, and Mountague as Master of the Wardrobe; the former royalist commander-in-chief in Ireland, the Marquis of Ormonde (head of the major Anglo-Norman landed dynasty of Butler) became Lord Steward and the veteran moderate royalist Earl of Hertford (head of the Seymours, descended from Queen Jane Seymour's brother) the Groom of the Stool and thus the official with the closest personal contact with the king each day. Seven of the eleven closest Royal personal attendants, the Grooms of the Bedchamber, had served the King in that role in exile and were thus from reliable royalist families and deserved reward for either being exiled by the Commonwealth or risking their wrath by going to join their enemy. The Duke of York, the king's next brother and heir presumptive, took control of the navy as Lord Admiral. Two Royalist lawyers became Attorney-

General (Geoffrey Palmer) and Solicitor-General (Heneage Finch), with the latter more politically key as sitting in the Commons too. The 'ultra' royalist views of the occupants of these two posts were perhaps ominous, seeing as who was to have control of political prosecutions – though even an ex-Parliamentarian officer could hardly have defied the wills of both king and 'Cavalier' Commons in launching prosecutions of their enemies in 1661–2. Their main lawyer ally Orlando Bridgeman, already in his early fifties and the son of a bishop, had been attorney for the pre-war Court of Wards and for the current king as Earl of Chester in 1640; he had also spoken up for Strafford in the Long Parliament and been an unswerving royalist but had annoyed Hyde by being prepared to compromise drastically to secure peace at the Uxbridge talks in 1645. His reputation was as a learned legal theorist, albeit as a backer of the pre-war monarchy, rather than as a partisan – for which Finch more than made up. Finch had no previous history of backing any faction, but his father (Sir Heneage Finch) had been Speaker in the first Parliament of Charles I and his uncle Sir John, subsequently Lord Keeper, was the hardline Speaker who Holles and fellow-radicals had physically constrained as Parliament was closed down in March 1629. He duly lived up to his ultra-royalist relations' past record as MP for Canterbury in the Convention, defending full powers for the bishops in the first (6 July 1660) Commons debate on the church as legally correct and opposing any special relief for 'tender consciences' with jeering words about 'ranting after Cromwell'. (The word 'ranting' in that context was a dig at non-Anglicans as being linked to the notoriously eccentric 1650s sect of 'Ranters'.) On 30 July he backed expelling all intruded ministers who would not turn Anglican from the church. He was named as chairman of the crucial Commons committee arranging the extent of pardons to be allowed under the Act of Indemnity, and insisted on a full list of regicides to be prosecuted in the Commons/Lords conference on this matter on 16 August, presumably following his masters' orders. Significantly, in the 1661 Parliament he was to sit for Oxford, a seat within the gift of the University Chancellor – Hyde/Clarendon. As far as the tone of the crucial regicide trials went, he and Bridgeman must bear responsibility for their hardline, 1630s-style 'Divine Right of Kings' rhetoric of outrage adding to the sense of a show trial, though it is unlikely that Finch was the prime hardline organiser for retribution (despite his evident keenness for this action) given his long-term role as a legal functionary rather than a political leader. Notably, as soon as the initial batch of regicide trials were over in October 1660 the hardliner Bridgeman was made Chief Justice of the Common Pleas, presumably as a reward and as he could be trusted to appoint congenial subordinates to supervise London and provincial trials. In the distribution of judicial offices, four Commonwealth and two Protectoral senior judges were retained and the two surviving pre-1642 royalists were restored.[3]

In military matters Monck restored royalist officers to command of half the regiments and around half the garrison posts; the navy saw a similar restoration of royalists to some senior posts, with commanders distinguished for service for Charles in the 1650s (e.g. Sir Robert Holmes, an officer in Prince Rupert's privateering fleet in the Mediterranean and Caribbean) sharing office with their old foes. The ex-Cromwellian Navy captains were mostly purged by the Duke of York's administration in 1661–4, but to be fair to the duke this was not so much revenge as uneasiness at continued anti-royal murmurings among them. Imposing an oath of loyalty to the new order was only continuing Commonwealth practice; weeding out unreliable fanatic chaplains was essential to stop seditious preaching. Some captains were reliably reported to be in a state of shock at the king's return and self-disgust that they had allowed it; this could be inflammable material given the right leader, but none emerged. Many of the officers had been appointed in 1659 after the remodelling of Cromwell's navy command by Lawson, and were thus politically radical Rump/junto nominees. Ironically Lawson himself survived in office for life (to 1665), having remained conspicuously loyal to the king since 1660 – a surprise considering his Leveller sympathies and earlier disloyalty to the equally conservative Cromwell. Lawson's survival is proof that unswerving loyalty to the new regime could outmatch a dubious earlier record and preserve a grip on patronage into the mid-1660s. The new Comptroller of the Navy was Sir John Mennes, a protégé of Prince Rupert; the Navy Board's new secretary Pepys, as is well-known, owed his appointment to his cousin Mountague.

The local militia was crucial to government security. It was placed under senior local landed magnates without partiality for either 'party' and where none was obvious was transferred to figures notable for backing Charles in 1659–60; the ranks of JPs were varied from county to county with a large number of Cromwellians retaining office in some areas (even in largely pro-royalist Devon) but very few in others. Some courtiers – including ex-Cromwellians – were able to secure local posts for their clients, others not; a dominant position in recent county affairs, an impeccable royalist record, or a court patron were not sufficient to ensure office as a JP, deputy lieutenant, or sheriff.[4] Notably moderate leader Anthony Ashley Cooper failed to become lord lieutenant of his native Dorset, presumably due to royalist bitterness at his past defection to the Parliamentarians in 1644. Attempts were made to keep Cromwell's former Attorney-General Edmund Prideaux (owner of Forde Abbey near Yeovil) off the Somerset list of JPs, though his well-connected friends stopped this. Among the financially rewarding and prestigious posts of relatively minor political import, most were used as 'pay-offs' and marks of thanks for good service for leading royalists (also given new peerages, which added to the King's votes in the Lords). Sir John Grenville, the king's messenger to Monck and son and nephew of the two main Cornish royalist commanders (Sir Bevil and Sir Richard Grenville), became Earl of Bath and Steward of the duchy of Cornwall – thus helping to ensure that that Duchy, merged with the monarchy as the King had no legitimate son to give it to, returned reliable MPs. Ormonde became Lord Lieutenant of Somerset with estates there, though he was mostly absent in Ireland after a year or two; initially his expected role as Lord Lieutenant there went to Monck but only titularly as he usually stayed in London. The real Irish 'strongman' was Monck's Lord Deputy, Lord Robartes, a leading Cornish Presbyterian figure (who as the former Parliamentarian commander there in 1643–4 may have been sent abroad to mollify the royalist Cornish veterans).

The veteran royalist Secretary of State Sir Edward Nicholas, politically eclipsed by Hyde and ageing, took over the same post in England until his retirement in 1662 (with Morice as his colleague) and became Keeper of the Game of Hampton Court Park and Ranger of Windsor Great Park, with more posts for his sons (the Clerkship of the Council for the elder and financial offices for the second) and the Latin Secretaryship, once held by Milton, for his protégé Joseph Williamson (later Secretary of State himself). The Keepership of the Privy Purse, the senior court financial post and with valuable access to the king, went to Hyde's current ally Sir Henry Bennet when he returned from his royalist ambassadorial post in Madrid early in 1661. He was also to take over the second secretaryship of state from Nicholas in 1662, though by that date Hyde's refusal to secure him any of the senior ambassadorial posts he wanted (e.g. Paris) had turned him against Hyde. The complex relationship between Hyde and Bennet was a symptom of the tensions surviving from the senior figures among the exiled royalist court in the 1650s, which helped to bring Hyde down in 1667. The way in which Bennet had aided Hyde against his former friend Sir John Berkeley in a successful intrigue to disgrace the latter in 1656–7 had resulted in Berkeley's furious patron Prince James (Duke of York) having to be placated by sending Bennet away to Madrid as ambassador. Bennet was also to clash with Hyde over the extent of religious toleration in 1662–3, backing the right of the king to dispense with the law to exempt individuals from the ban on non-Anglicans from corporations and the ministry, and in that cause lined up with Cooper and another ex-Parliamentarian, Lord Robartes against the High Anglicans. Bennet's knowledge of foreign languages and goings-on at intrigue-ridden courts like Madrid made him invaluable in helping to organise and sift intelligence, in which matter Thurloe was not allowed to continue in any position of influence. It is not known if, like Downing, he offered his services or if he made a principled retreat; he ended up living quietly in Chancery Lane. Although he was not prosecuted (reputedly due to his threat to use his collection of letters from allegedly loyal royalists offering him their services against Charles II) he was probably regarded with too much unease to be employable.[5] Downing, equally unpalatable to royalists, was working abroad until 1665 so he did not have to come into contact with his former victims as Thurloe would have done had he been at court.

Among the minor-ranking but crucial royalist diplomats who had served the king in exile in the late 1640s and 50s, Sir Henry De Vic became 'Secretary for the French Tongue' and Chancellor of the Order of the Garter. The diarist Evelyn's father-in-law Sir Richard Browne (envoy in Paris throughout the Civil War) became Muster-Master General. Sir John (now Lord) Berkeley, one of Charles I's last attendants and political advisers in 1647–8 before being a leading supporter of Prince James' hardliner faction in exile, became Keeper of Nonsuch Palace and a commssioner for the navy; his colleague John Ashburnham became a peer, as did the 1659 rebel Booth (Lord Delamere). Berkeley and Ashburnham had notably escorted the late king as he fled from

Hampton Court towards the south coast in November 1647 but had been too unlucky or poorly organised to get him to the Continent safely; Charles II nevertheless owed them a debt of gratitude for the attempt. Lord Mordaunt, the king's co-ordinator in England in 1657–60, became Governor of Windsor Castle; the Scots Engager leaders who had assisted the 1648 invasion to try to assist the late king, Middleton (Charles II's senior commander in Scotland in 1653–4 and a close and alcohol-loving friend of his in exile) and Newburgh received Scots peerages. Middleton was made the King's Commissioner to the Scots Parliament and the effective chief minister of that country, with the king's other 1650s commander Glencairn (head of the Cunningham family) as Lord Chancellor; the Scots Lord Treasurership went to the Earl of Crawford (head of the Lindsays) who Charles I had given that office in the 1640s. The 'moderate Presbyterians' Lord Cassilis became Justice-General and Lord Rothes (son of the leader of the 1637 'Prayer-Book' rebellion) Lord President of the Council. Alexander Leslie, Lord Leven, commander-in-chief of the Scots rebel army in 1637–46 and their leader against Charles I in England in 1644–6, became governor of Edinburgh Castle but was too old to be a threat although his past record in ruining the late king's cause must have made some of his fellow-officials uncomfortable. Nor had he atoned for that with evidence of royalist enthusiasm in 1659–60 like his fellow-Presbyterian general Manchester. John Maitland, Lord Lauderdale became secretary of state; he had a past record as a 'rebel' from the 1640s and had been a Scots commissioner to the Parliamentarians in 1644–8 but had tried to save a (politically neutered) monarchy in both kingdoms for Charles I. He was also lucky in having a useful link to the Stuarts via his wife Elizabeth (nee Murray), Countess of Dysart, the daughter of former royalist activist Will Murray (Charles I's page) and chatelaine of Ham House near Richmond in Surrey.

In Ireland Broghill, a moderate Cromwellian and also an adviser to Monck in Scotland in the mid-1650s, became Earl of Orrery, president of the council governing Munster, and governor of Limerick, and his ally Sir Charles Coote, president of the council governing Connacht in western Ireland, became Earl of Mountrath and Constable of Athlone. These two were the 'strongmen' in provincial Ireland. Coote had been involved with the Booth Rising plot in 1659 so he was an early defector from the Cromwellian leadership of 1653–8 to the king, but had not managed to rise in revolt against his distrustful superior Edmund Ludlow as the latter had ordered him to stay in Dublin. But he had been the senior commander in Dublin in February 1660 who declared for a free Parliament in support of Monck, so the latter and the King owed him thanks for his help. Coote, Broghill, and the aged new Irish Lord Chancellor Sir Maurice Eustace (a survivor from 1630s politics) became the Irish Lords Justices despite the first two hating each other which inhibited their co-operation; Eustace was made Lord Treasurer with Annesley, a Presbyterian to balance his Anglicanism, as his deputy. The Scots general David Leslie, who had destroyed Montrose's royalist army in Scotland in September 1645 at Philiphaugh and equivocated between king and Covenanter leadership in 1650–1 but fought for Charles at Dunbar and Worcester, got a peerage but no useful office; the same sort of payoff went to ex-Covenanter leader and Commissioner to Parliament Lord Loudoun who had served with Maitland in attempting to retain but politically constrain Charles I in 1646–8. The (Douglas) husband of the executed Hamilton brothers' heiress, the first Duke's daughter, had their dukedom restored for him.

Henrietta Maria's principal adviser Sir Henry Jermyn, stalwart of her hardline Louvre faction in exile (enemies of Hyde's moderates) which had encouraged politically dangerous international Catholic alliances, became Earl of St Albans and resumed control of her court when she eventually returned to England to reside at Somerset House. He had a reputation for unscrupulousness as a plotter who had attempted to raise an army plot to close down Parliament for Charles I in 1641, but had a major East Anglian dynasty (the Suffolk Jermyns) behind him as a useful provider of tame MPs in the Commons. He was, however, politically marginalised and was kept happy with grants of land, especially the lucrative soon-to-be residential sites north of St James' Palace which he made a fortune developing (e.g. St James' Square and Jermyn Street). The peerages created by Charles I after 1642 (i.e. without Parliamentary approval) were all recognised despite Monck's disapproval and their holders admitted to the Lords, and two more promised but never created by Charles I were now granted. At least 159 former royalist army officers and the families of around 30 deceased ones received rewards, over 70 royalists received grants of Crown lands, and 54 who had loaned money to the late king and never been repaid were now paid out of Charles' personal income. The most prestigious prizes in terms of grants of residences, land, and/or rewarding offices (often useful military governorships or royal heraldic/ household sinecures) went to a mixture of past royalists and those who had aided the king's restoration in 1659–60, headed by Monck. Morice, for example, became governor of Plymouth and 'avenor' of the Duchy of Cornwall; Sir John Grenville became Earl of Bath and Steward of the Duchy of Cornwall, Groom of the Stole and Under-Keeper of St James' Palace; Berkeley joined the new Naval Commission (balanced between two Cromwellians and two royalists) and became Keeper of Nonsuch Palace in Surrey, a half-ruinous Renaissance 'folly' built by Henry VIII; Secretary of State Nicholas became Ranger of Windsor Park; ex-diplomat De Vic became Secretary for the French Tongues (i.e. he replaced Thurloe in charge of day-to-day diplomacy with French diplomats) and Chancellor of the Order of the Garter; the 'Presbyterian Knot' leader Mordaunt became Governor of Windsor Castle; and all of Mordaunt's group except the suspect Willis acquired peerages. The King generously drew up his own list of those who had helped him to escape after the battle of Worcester and made sure that they all received something. Those who received nothing were often minor figures (usually with no record of distinguished service) with nobody important to promote their case, such as the poet Abraham Cowley, or known equivocators such as the only unrewarded Sealed Knot veteran, Sir Richard Willys. The poet Edmund Waller (distrusted by both sides over his Civil War plot to hand London over to the king in 1643) was also ignored for preferment or rewards, which his now-embarrassing flattery of Cromwell in the mid-1650s made unlikely. His fellow-panegyricist Andrew Marvell, now Convention MP for Hull, escaped censure (but ceased publishing his pro-Cromwellian 1650s poems) and dared to speak up in Parliament for his ex-colleague John Milton's protest in December 1660 at being charged extortionate gaol fees.[6] Marvell received no rewards in 1660–1, but was high-minded and may not have sought any. By 1663 Marvell, an assiduous and popular MP who reported back regularly to his constituents, was undertaking a secret government mission to Holland, probably arranged by his patron the Earl of Carlisle (aka Charles Howard, Cromwell's Life Guard commander).

The overall impression is of the lack of a dominant 'party' or interest in arranging for local, as for national, office and a genuine degree of accommodation between differing interests. There was usually exclusion of those of socially inferior degree or no local connections who had risen to power as pro-Cromwell or pro-republican loyalists in the 1650s, apart from occasional lucky or skilled characters like the Cromwellian Thomas Birch (Herefordshire) and Philip Jones (Glamorgan).[7] Both were politically useful and had no clear and well-connected local royalist rivals who were more useful than them to the king, although Jones faced numerous attempts to slander him or bring prosecutions for his past local 'fixing' as a Cromwellian stalwart. In civic matters, some but not all Royalists managed to regain their positions on town corporations lost in 1642–6, and if necessary the king required reclacitrant corporations to restore expelled royalists and expel pro-republicans – often by means of requiring the members to take an oath of allegiance, which sectaries found it difficult to do on principle. The restoration of expelled incumbents from purged colleges in Cambridge, usually by written request from its (retained) Parliamentarian Chancellor, Manchester, was managed with less bitterness and resistance than the situation in Oxford, where both the Chancellor (Hertford) and many more Fellows had been purged. The problem in Oxford was exacerbated by the fact that it had been the royalist capital in 1642–6, thus causing an exodus of pro-Parliamentarian figures from its colleges – a situation reversed forcibly on its occupation in 1646. Cromwell, as the new Chancellor, and his vigorous deputy John Owen (the intruded Dean of Christ Church) had purged the colleges and installed more reliable Independent claimants. Anglicanism had in any case been stronger in Oxford (with Laud, a former Head of St John's College, being its Chancellor and a vigorous purger of the theologically suspect) in the 1630s than in Cambridge, and a large body of expelled fellows from there now expected restitution. Hertford, returned to office and on his swift death later in 1660 succeeded by Hyde, had to order a more extensive restoration of expelled Fellows and at times have the incumbents physically ejected.[8] The drastic action taken included figures with good connections among the restored court and a willingness to go over to the Anglican church such as John Wilkins, Cromwell's brother-in-law and Warden of Wadham College. One of the most intellectually brilliant and well-connected Oxford academics, Wilkins was a founding member of the circle of scientific and philiosphical experimenters who were soon to form the Royal Society – but that did not save his Oxford post. (He was later to become Bishop of Lincoln.) As with the corporations, there was some coercion by orders from the King and Hyde/Clarendon against local resistance, auguring badly for the future.

Punishment of the defeated: politically necessary or did it get out of hand?

The main efforts of the Convention were now devoted to the questions of the civil and religious settlement, with a boost to royalist determination – and to possible breaches of the initial understandings of spring 1660 – from the king's return. Deciding on bills and daring to punish republicans and sectaries was easier once the king was restored as chief executive and Monck was no longer able to coerce the Commons with his troops. The most symbolic measure was the Act for Indemnity and Oblivion, and it duly concentrated on the symbolic act of regicide in selecting the principal victims to be excluded from amnesty. Usefully, the personnel of the regicide court of January 1649 had been mainly military republicans in or trusted by the then army leadership, plus a few radical MPs who had been on the losing side in the 'Rump vs Monck' confrontations. They did not include any of the main actors of the Restoration – the only important military regicide to be prominent in the confrontations then was Cromwell's cousin Colonel Ingoldsby, who had backed firstly Richard Cromwell and then Monck and had provided invaluable services in capturing Lambert in April 1660. The Restoration owed a debt of gratitude to Ingoldsby, and he duly received a pardon – having ingeniously claimed when summoned before the Commons to explain his part in regicide on 14 May that he had tried to avoid signing the king's death-warrant but Cromwell had seized his hand and made him do it. (The document shows no sign of this.) Charles initially excluded only seven regicides from pardon in his first offer of September 1659; Monck attempted to cut the number to five but the Commons insisted on seven (14 May 1660). Helpfully, the new military strongman in Ireland, Sir Charles Coote, had already rounded up the late king's prosecutor, John Cook, and Colonels Huncks, Phayre, and Tomlinson, officers of the guard at the regicide trial, at Athlone even before the king was proclaimed.[9] Technically he had no legal right to do so as the regicide had not yet been declared a crime again, and it appears that he was prompted by Charles' agent Sir Arthur Forbes but was eager to assure the king of his usefulness by rounding up his late father's enemies in any case. Cook had indeed already warned in a pamphlet defending his ally Ludlow that Coote's support for readmitting the MPs excluded in 1648 was but a feint intended to proceed further to a Stuart restoration, so Coote may have wanted revenge on him in particular for 'blowing his cover'. Regicide Sir Hardress Waller was also already in custody, in Dublin, but for his attempt to stop the city garrison going over to Monck in February 1660 by arresting those officers who were about to declare for him and the readmission of the excluded MPs. (They were warned in time and blockaded him in the Castle until he surrendered.)[10] It was an ominous sign for the future prosecutions that at the first meetings between the king's new Attorney-Gerneral (Sir Geoffrey Palmer) and Solicitor-General (Heneage Finch), plus the Duke of York's lawyer, with leading judges around early June it was decided to charge the regicides with the traditional crime of treason and to reduce the number of witnesses needed to produce acceptable evidence of treason from two to one. The accused could now be charged with 'imagining' the death of the late king, a vague accusation susceptible to interpretation as required by political circumstance.

The Commons had named General Harrison as the first regicide to be exempted from amnesty and arrested on 4 June, which was to be expected given both his extreme hostility to Charles I in November-December 1648 (he had led the king's escort from Hurst Castle to Windsor) and his leadership of the fanatical and republican Fifth Monarchists. Harrison was also supposed to have been in favour of a trial or royal murder back in 1647 and so to have encouraged Charles I's flight from Hampton Court to the Isle of Wight, and the late king's then attendants Berkeley and Ashburnham would have warned Charles II of this. In any case, as a radical millenarian he was capable of regarding it as his duty to God to intrigue and fight against the Stuart restoration so he needed to be silenced. The next named accused, on the 5th, were Colonels John Jones (a dangerous republican leader in Ireland in the 1650s so a politcal threat too) and John Barkstead (governor of the Tower of London and as such hated for blackmailing money out of prisoners' relatives) plus the leading anti-royal lawyer John Lisle (republican Commissioner of the Great Seal in 1649–54) and politicians Scot, Cornelius Holland, and William Say. Lisle and Scot were demonstrable republican idealists, so especially dangerous to a nervous new king. This made up the initial list of seven, but on 8 June Parliament added non-judges who had been involved with the trial – the prosecuting counsel John Cook, the clerk of the court Andrew Broughton, the sergeant-at-arms Edward Dendy, and the nameless executioners. The 'small fry' who had officiated in minor roles by carrying out their usual jobs thus joined the political targets;[11] in this sense the Commons was clearly keen to play up the treasonous illegality of trying the king and lay down a marker that 'only obeying orders' was no excuse. In fact, all of these named accused non-judges except Cook appear to have left the country already, and so had Broughton and Dendy; Scot was in Brussels and Barkstead in Germany. Sir Hardress Waller had also used his release in Dublin as a chance to flee to the Continent. There was a grass-roots campaign to round up the regicides, incited by pamphlets such as 'A Hue And Cry Against the High Court of Injustice' which used semi-religious terminology in reminding the public of the details of the martyrdom of Charles I and blatantly tried to whip up a wave of outrage. This could duly serve as an excuse for those in power who were determined on or too terrified of their own past records to oppose a hunt for scapegoats, and those rounded up on local initiatives without their having signed the late king's death-warrant included the ex-Keeper of the King's Jewel-House, Sir Henry Mildmay (a turncoat who had attended the trial and helped Parliament to sell off the king's goods) and Colonel Francis Hacker (in attendance on the king at the trial and so open to a charge of constraining him). Prynne's Parliamentary committee meanwhile examined the evidence as to whether the City hangman in 1649, Francis Brandon (who luckily for himself was dead), had executed the king – this was inconclusive.[12] Some evidence from one alleged witness pointed to a junior officer called William Hulet having been recognised as the executioner (despite his mask) on the day of the regicide, so he and another possible (though unlikely) candidate, the preacher Hugh Peter, were added to the list to be executed on 18 June. Peter was plausibly said to have boasted to his doctor in 1649/50 that he and Cromwell alone had made the initial decision to kill the king, and he had a long history as an inflammatory preacher to the New Model Army so he could soon be plotting revolt if not dealt with.

The expanding list of regicides to be prosecuted was discussed in a conference between the Lords (where some were literally talking of 'an eye for an eye' over all executions of 1640s-50s royalist leaders, especially peers) and the Commons on 16 August, with the former more bitter and demanding that forty-three judges be executed along with Vane, Lambert, and Colonels Axtell and Hacker. Solicitor-General Finch delivered a 'compromise' proposal over the numbers, presumably as per the King's and Clarendon's wishes, which made it clear to reconciliatory MPs that more men would have to be executed than originally planned in order to get the Lords to vote for the measure.[13] This was probably due to a sincere desire to unblock the 'log-jam' and 'get the ball rolling' on the trials to avoid embarrassing squabbles, but was hard luck on those caught by suddenly extending the list of the men to face trial. The issue of making fair allowances for the co-operation of those regicides who had given themselves up in expectation of escaping with their lives while the hit list was still small was raised by the Commons but not accepted. Accordingly, some who had not fled but surrendered while their names were not yet on the list to be prosecuted had reason to complain of bad faith. The number to be tried was finally fixed at thirty-two in the finalised bill of 29 August; the Commons preferred to pardon those who had surrendered so far (nineteen in all) and the Lords did not so as a compromise a separate bill was to be introduced to cover them. In other words, they could be condemned quickly as the Lords wished (preserving the Lords' desire to punish as many men as possible for killing their king) but could only be executed if this second bill was passed. It was not, so they remained alive but in prison.

The Lords persuaded the Commons to punish nineteen others (including Fleetwood, Desborough, Alderman Robert Ireton, and Speaker Lenthall) with a ban from office, in return for them accepting the Commons' request for similar leniency[14] for other republicans who had sat on tribunals where royalists had been executed. Some regicides were saved individually by the efforts of their friends and relatives in the Commons, e.g. Colonel Hutchinson, whose sudden arrest had surprised Clarendon (who assured the victim's messenger sent to him for help that he had no idea what the charge was) and who was imprisoned in Sandown Castle, Kent[15] Given that Hutchinson had been politically inactive for years and was no threat to the Restoration, spite by personal foes from his eastern Midlands army campaigns in the 1640s was possible – and he was shut up in a cold and draughty Tudor fortress and had trouble securing permission to take exercise outside. General

Fleetwood's brother George, formerly Cromwell's go-between with and recruiter of mercenaries for the King of Sweden but not involved in British politics, was possibly another victim of spite; he was imprisoned for life but reprieved from execution after testimony from Monck and Cooper that he had aided the Restoration. He was deported to an isolated fortress in Tangier, presumably as a potential security risk whose friends could rescue him. A mixture of lobbying and bribery saved Bulstrode Whitelocke, who had made enemies from chairing the Sequestrations Committee that had imposed fines on and/or seized land from royalists. He was being threatened by the Earl of Berkshire with being put on the 'partial exception from amnesty' list of those who were 'delinquent' but not regicides unless he handed over £500, and Prynne, as chairman of a Commons committee into adding new names to be punished, was also out for vengeance (presumably from past clashes in the law-courts). Worse, Whitelocke had accused Monck of aiming at a restoration of monarchy back in late 1659, which could be construed as trying to ruin both his and the king's chances. Given Whitelocke's services to the cause of a conservative monarchy – Cromwellian as well as Stuart – in the 1650s, he might have expected more honourable treatment from the regime. But his personal friendship with Cromwell (and his support for the idea of Charles' brother Henry as a puppet-king?) made him an embarrassment. He found it advisable to bribe a courtier to secure a meeting with the king so he could assure his loyalty; Charles advised him to retire to the country. His vindictive former friend Hyde/Clarendon made the most of the reversal in their fortunes to launch what amounted to a campaign of blackmail to mulct him of money in return for immunity in the 1660s.[16] But Hyde's activities were moderate compared to the enthusiasm of Prynne for vengeance, with the latter unsuccessfully attempting to have all involved in the creation of the semi-monarchical 'Instrument of Government' constitution and all senior Cromwellian office-holders barred from office.[17] Was Prynne just bitter and spiteful about his being sidelined in the 1650s despite his service to the Parliamentary cause in 1635–42, or fearful of Royal vengeance for his insulting the current king's mother and hounding Archbishop Laud? There was also the matter of Governor John Robinson of the Tower charging his prisoners and their visitors excessive fees and using them as a milch-cow to build up his funds as the Cromwellian Barkstead had done in the 1650s, though this was par for the course for slackly-supervised contemporary gaolers.

Younger close friends of Cromwell not yet active in 1648–9, such as Sir Charles Wolseley and William Pierrepont, survived unscathed; their support for the idea of monarchy (e.g. in 1657) and their antagonism towards the Cromwellian military high command probably helped to have them considered to be harmless. Cromwellian panegyricist and unrepentant republican Milton had done himself no good by warning against the danger of a restored Stuart monarchy leading to revenge in February – blind or not, he was as principled and thus unbribeable a foe as Vane or Haslerig. As early as 7 May he left his house in Petty France, close to Parliament, to 'go to ground' with £400 of ready cash in the City; on 16 June a proclamation was issued for his arrest. His 'Eikonoklastes' and 'Pro Populo Anglicano Defensio', his most notable and well-argued idealistic attacks on the monarchy, were ordered to be burnt by the public hangman, with their contents condemned in the order as treasonably justifying the 'murder' of Charles I. Some time around the book-burnings (which have an ominous ring nowadays but were normal for treasonable or blasphemous writings in this period) in late August Milton was captured, and was lodged in prison for a few months but eventually released for lack of evidence to royalist surprise.[18] Despite his open and fluent republicanism and justification of regicide, he was evidently not accounted a political threat – his fate shows clearly that it was usually only active potential plotters who were to be physically eliminated.

One senior Parliamentarian who might have expected prosecution, Cromwell's cousin Oliver St John who had led the prosecution of Strafford in 1641 and was one of the few senior remaining Independent MPs of the mid-1640s (thus a rival of the moderate Presbyterians), had taken no part in the late king's trial and stood aside from post-1648 politics, serving as a Lord Chief Justice. This probably saved him from Royalist revenge; the professional judges of the 1650s were spared prosecution, unlike the more political – and junior – lawyer John Cook who had prosecuted the late King. Cook was the only serving lawyer of the 'show-trials' by the victors in 1648–51 to be executed, with his uncompromising republican and legally reformist views isolating him (as had his 1650s residence in Ireland with the hardline military Cromwellians). Cook, an individualist concerned for the welfare of poor litigants and savagely critical of the failures of the Law, was always liable to be sacrificed by his fellow-lawyers as an embarrassment, unlike the well-connected and socially conservative St John. He had been personally abrupt to Charles I at the trial and asserted that nobody was above the Law, which was enough to damn him; and he was not at all apologetic in 1660. The two assistant clerks at the king's trial, more practical than Cook, made themselves scarce at the Restoration and fled to the Continent. It seems that personal behaviour towards Charles I was a deciding factor in awakening the king's hostility apart from a few special cases of political fear of the accused (e.g. Lambert and Vane). The commander of the guard at the late King's trial, Colonel Axtell, was not technically a regicide as he had not signed the death-warrant but was put on trial with them and then executed anyway. (The judge Orlando Bridgeman excused adding non-signatories to the list of accused by saying that they had all 'levied war on the King' which was treason.) Quite apart from Axtell's role during the trial where he had supposedly had muskets levelled at pro-royalist protesters, he had taken part in the execution which made punishing him essential. He denied the incident of having his men aim muskets into the gallery, which relied on one witness and was not recorded in the official record of the trial by one of the clerks, and also denied the accusation of his fellow-officer Colonel Hercules Hunckes (who had a royalist family and was pardoned, presumably in return for his useful evidence) that on the morning of the execution he had been touting for signatures in the 'Painted Chamber'. He also mischievously and bravely raised the issue of 'only obeying orders' as a loyal soldier, claiming that he had been carrying out the instructions of the legally-appointed Lords and Commons in Decmber 1648 – January 1649 and had taken part in the trial – and allegedly later gone to collect the City of London public executioner to carry out the sentence – on the orders of his legal superior, 'Lord General' Fairfax. The latter, of course, was not on trial or even under investigation – but Bridgeman got round that issue by having Axtell admit that he had been told the orders came from Fairfax by Cromwell rather than having actually received them direct. Cromwell, of course, was dead so he could not testify, and was assumed for political purposes to have lied – thus clearing Fairfax in a whitewash. Axtell was condemned and executed with the first main group of regicides on 16–19 October; the actual executioner was never identified.[19] Among various indications of a stitch-up, one of the civilian

'Rump' MPs and religious radicals trusted by the Army who had sat as a judge and signed the death-warrant, William Heveningham, had been considered important enough to join General Harrison and Sir Hardress Waller in the first group to be brought to court and was duly condemned but was not executed. His panicking claims that he had been tricked into joining the judges and was sincerely repentant were not such as to win others who grovelled like this a reprieve. But Bridgeman personally asked for a delay in carrying out the sentence – the only such submission – and he was not executed; coincidentally or not, his father-in-law was the Earl of Dover.

Some MPs with personal animosities, such as the typically vicious Prynne (who had previously used his abusive talents to call the present King's mother a whore in his 1630s pamphlet 'Histriomastix' and to prosecute Archbishop Laud) and assorted sons of ruined royalists, were noticeably vindictive, either generally or against individual enemies; members of the government tended to concentrate on particular personal foes but also to support other individuals. Hyde was noted for his financial extortion, which was to add to his problems in the mid-1660s from younger rivals as his large new mansion in Piccadilly could be portrayed as the fruits of corruption. Eventually the MPs and Lords agreed on eleven regicides who had sought to evade arrest and – in absentia – all twenty-two who had prudently fled abroad; the latter included some of the most politically irreconcilable and thus dangerous individuals, such as Ludlow and Okey.[20]

Four had fled to Switzerland, a decentralised collection of Catholic and Protestant cantons which were less likely than the Dutch state to be willing to succumb to English diplomatic pressure for extradition; five more went to the Netherlands or Germany. Three, including Cromwell's military sectary allies Colonels Whalley and Goffe, swiftly and ingeniously fled to sympathetic Independent congregations at New Haven in North America – who reputedly hid those two in a cave from royalist pursuers who the King sent there with orders to hunt them down in 1661.[21] The thoroughness of the latter's search shows the King's determination to find and make an example of these two, who were by no stretch of the imagination a security risk (unlike Lisle and Ludlow were on the Continent) but were as inflexibly anti-Stuart as the similarly hounded Sir Henry Vane.

All the regicides currently in custody were tried, and all but one of the eleven executed, during the Parliamentary early autumn recess in October. The House of Lords had wanted a longer list for prosecution in the August debates with forty-three regicide judges plus Vane, Lambert, Haselrig, and Colonels Axtell and Hacker, but the Commons had managed to talk this down to a list of thirty and have Vane and Lambert taken off the list.[22] Both royalist and Parliamentarian judges sat on the tribunals, though the latter (including Monck, the Earl of Manchester, Lord Saye and Sele, Denzel Holles, and Sir Arthur Annesley) were hardly likely to stand up for their former colleagues for fear of reprisals, and a jury sat as well. The prosecution case was led by Solictor-General Heneage Finch with the usual vindictiveness of a prosecuting State attorney in this era, as seen at Tudor and Early Stuart 'show trials' – interrupting and threatening witnesses, ignoring contradictory or weak evidence, and skating over blatant unlikelihoods in the interest of a swift condemnation, were not invented by the later Carolean Judge Jeffreys though he is the most famous exponent of this. There are modern parallels with the procedure of Stalinist show trials in the lax procedure and blatantly rigged evidence and verdicts of the regicide trials, but this was hardly the only instance of this in the era. As with a modern 'political' trial in a 'police state', the trials were about spectacle as much as justice, with the state being presented as above criticism and its attackers as wicked and disgusting in order to impress the public with the need for obedience. The indictments claimed that the act of regicide had been horrible wickedness inspired by the Devil, and the notion of it being a formal and open judicial process by the then legal authorities – which Harrison and others insisted – was evaded. More unusually, Finch waxed lyrical about the Divine Right of Kings and the wickedness of levying rebellion against them in a sign of the likely autocratic ideology of the new regime – and thus indicated that revenge would trump mercy. The constitutional gains of restricting royal power of the 1640s and 1650s were to be brushed aside as a horrid and impious innovation, at least in the mindset of the judiciary, and the king clearly did not set out to limit this return to the attitudes of the 1630s. His enthusiasm for reviving the old mystical ceremony of 'touching for the King's evil' (scrofula), which it was popularly believed could be cured by the laying-on of hands by the king as God's vicegerent, showed where his own views on an unconstrained monarchy lay.

The executions were attended by jubilant and insulting crowds and no attempt was made to show dignity to the victims or their bodies (though this was normal for the period's treatment of traitors).[23] Few of the condemned royalist 'traitors' had been hanged like this rather than shot or beheaded in 1649–59, the exception being Montrose in Scotland, so the punishment was arguably disproportionate in retaliation; the king could have granted the condemned a different form of execution had he wished. General Harrison – a political danger as the irreconcilable leader of the Fifth Monarchists who believed in Christ not Charles as his king – was the first notable victim, being executed on 16 October. He was also the first of the accused to point out that at least he and his colleagues had not killed the king privately but had done it as an open act of public justice; this was brushed aside like most awkward arguments were in the trials. His dignity on the scaffold and sincere defence of his actions earned him grudging respect from the crowds, and served to present him as a martyr for his cause despite the outlandishness of his Fifth Monarchist world outlook.[24] His co-religionist John Jones (second husband of Cromwell's sister Catherine and stepfather of the Cromwellian-turned-royalist Thomas Whetstone) was the only member of the Cromwell connection to be executed. A third and unrepentant Fifth Monarchist regicide, John Carew, was also hung, drawn and quartered (having tried to argue that Charles I's crimes had been laid out by the 'Grand Remonstrance' passed by two Houses of Pariament in 1640). So were the radical preacher Hugh Peters and Thomas Scot, a civilian radical Rumper and replacement Secretary in Thurloe's place in 1659. Scot initially fled to Germany but incautiously decided to return; his fellow-radical Rumper regicide MP Thomas Chaloner and the military radical regicide Ludlow did not return and survived. Ludlow had to stay abroad until 1689 – and such was Stuart fear of his potential and uncompromising republicanism that even when he did return he was not welcomed by William III. Haselrig, whose Presbyterianism and antagonism to the army were potentially helpful for his chances, was more of a danger to the new regime than the other Presbyterian leaders due to his republicanism. Like his fellow-radicals Vane and Marten, he was a loner and thus a safer target for prosecution. He was left to suffer royalist and Anglican revenge by the more moderate Presbyterians, but his apparent deal with Monck to save his life by keeping out of the rebellion in March 1660 was honoured by the

Commons (by a vote of 141 to 116) once Monck had sent a letter testify to this. Haselrig was put in the Tower instead, dying on 7 January 1661 before his case came to trial. Given the Royalist pamphleteering abuse of him as a 'church-thief', he would have been likely to be imprisoned for life at best had he lived.

When Parliament resumed, the fugitive regicides, and those who had died before the Restoration, were placed under attainder (which meant that there was no need for a new trial involving such matters as proveable evidence) and had their property confiscated. It was at this point that the Commons had the three principal deceased regicides, Cromwell, Henry Ireton, and Bradshaw, dug up at Westminster Abbey following a proposal by the returned royalist exile, MP Captain Titus, on 4 December. Secret agent Titus had not scrupled to assist the intended assassin of Cromwell, Miles Sindercombe, on the king's behalf in 1656; now he was a bloodthirsty Convention MP who busied himself hardening the evidence and securing convictions in regicide cases such as that of MP Adrian Scrope. The three dead regicides' bodies were drawn through London on hurdles and hung at Tyburn to commemorate the twelfth anniversary of the king's execution in January 1661 – with Bradshaw, not Cromwell, in central place as the senior regicide judge.[25] It has been argued that Cromwell's body may have been smuggled away and a substitute used, whether by connivance or not. The likeliest occasion for this to have been done was during the overnight halt for the procession at Red Lion Square, Holborn (which Cromwell was later supposed to haunt), with an alternative narrative tradition having it that Cromwell was not actually buried at Westminster at all but had requested that he be buried in secret on the battlefield of Naseby. The head what was said to be Cromwell's body was then stuck on a spike above Westminster Hall, blown down in a gale in the 1680s, and taken away by a private trophy-hunter. It was supposed to have ended up in an eighteenth-century 'freak-show' and been gifted by a later owner to Sidney Sussex College, Cambrdige, Cromwell's amla mater where it is still kept. The body was either thrown into a common pit at Tyburn, the normal fate for traitors, or secretly removed by Cromwell's daughter Mary to her husband Lord Fauconberg's local church at Newburgh in Yorkshire.[26] The public message of the long arm of royal law for regicide was uncompromising, and used as a deterrent for future rebels, whatever concessions the regime may have given the Cromwell family in private.

More legally dubious was the disinterment of all the Commonwealth's elite dead from Westminster Abbey, by the Dean of Westminster without official sanction – an indication of Anglican revenge and royal disinclination to halt it. It would have been more impressive for the ex-Parliamentarians in the Privy Council to protest to the king, even if their MP colleagues were too afraid of royalist MPs turning on them in the House as 'traitors' to do so.

On the issue of restitution of lands and other property confiscated from or sold off by ruined royalists, the government's record was more positive. As an anonymous royalist complained in June 1660, indemnity and oblivion meant indemnity for the king's enemies and oblivion for his friends.[27] This question of too many rewards for those perceived by disgruntled loyal Royalists as ex-traitors was not an isolated complaint, and the Venetian ambassador both heard it and judged it to be correct,[28] and hardline royalist journalist Roger l'Estrange wrote a pamphlet, 'A Caveat to the Cavaliers', in support of it. A popular series of ballads on this theme followed, presumably feeding off a viable audience of royalists. In fact, Charles rewarded some 159 ex-Royalist officers in 1660–3, along with around 30 families of deceased royalists, and granted land or pensions to around 70 more; he also paid back loans made to his father by 54 royalists. Lord Treasurer Southampton was disturbed at his improvidence.[29] To be fair to the king, he had restricted resources to grant out and a crowd of supplicants gathering at court to lay their claims before him, many of them undoubtedly exaggerated; Clarendon sourly reckoned that the noisiest were the least deserving.[30] The complaints were probably exacerbated by the prominence of 'new men' who had risen to political and financial fortune in the 1650s and who survived without any requirement to pay back lands or offices they had gained. The ex-Cromwellians Monck, Mountague, Cooper, and Howard – all luckily major actors in the Restoration – kept up their position at Court and were rewarded with peerages. (Cooper's and Howard's descendants, the Earls of Shaftesbury and Carlisle, have survived as aristocratic dynasties to this day.) Only Cooper, as a royal opponent in 1679–81, suffered any political reversal of fortune and accusations of unrepentant republicanism – and that only when he endeavoured to use MPs and the London mob to coerce the king. Manchester remained Lord Chamberlain until he died in 1671, though with no input into politics on behalf of his marginalised and arguably double-crossed Presbyterian co-religionists. Howard/ Carlisle later became Governor of Jamaica. Towards Cromwell's own family, there was less post-1660 vindictiveness than towards politically dangerous republicans, though as early as May 1660 the Commons was voting to impound the late Protector's widow's property in order to search it for missing items removed from the royal family's homes. Henry Cromwell survived unmolested without confiscation of his lands though he lost some honorary posts from local bodies now seeking a more suitable and useful patron. Richard Cromwell, a potential rival to the king in winter 1659–60, but lacking enough support, did not have his debts paid as promised in 1659 and found it prudent to retire under an assumed name to the Continent in early summer 1660. He kept to his false name and anonymity on his return in 1666, probably due to fear of royalist malevolence and the likely unwillingness of the King to protect him as due to a desire for a quiet life. He nearly survived the Stuart dynasty, dying at eighty-five in 1712 after outliving his son Oliver and disputing the latter's estate (under his own name so no longer in fear of using the Cromwell surname) with Oliver's daughter. Fleetwood, who had proved a broken reed as an army commander in 1659 and so was not much of a threat, survived, banned from office; he was able to continue as a local patron of the Baptists in retirement at Stoke Newington, Middlesex until he died in 1692. Desborough, arrested en route to Holland in June 1660, found it safer to flee than rely on any Royal pardon but obeyed an order to return home from this now hostile nation in 1665 sooner than be proclaimed a traitor. Temporarily held in Dover Castle, he was evidently judged 'safe' and was allowed to retire to the country. Most of Cromwell's Councillors had avoided supporting the king in 1660 but taken no action to resist him and were not touched, though some (e.g. Pickering) faced local harassment from triumphant royalist gentry rivals.[31] The main danger these ex-Cromwellians, and army officers in particular, faced was local harassment from zealous royalists and professional troublemakers keen to gain from denunciations – especially if they kept up links with 'seditious' Independent congregations. The new laws still permitted arrest and prosecution for post-May 1660 disaffection, and assorted real or imaginary denunciations were common although the first wave of arrests of supposed plotters in summer 1660 was followed by Council orders to release those held without viable evidence.[32]

Notably the official reaction in Whitehall after the 'White's Plot' that winter and the Venner Fifth Monarchist revolt was harsher and/or more paranoid. The threat of military conspiracy also impelled an anxious government to watch out for Lambert-style uprisings, in which respect the early 1660s were full of rumours of sinister New Model veterans' conspiracies. The rash of arrests in and after 1660 – most notably the mysterious 'White's Plot' to seize London in December 1660 – were not entirely imaginary or invented by local royalists to ruin their old enemies, and some of the 'low-level' harassment of ex-army officers was inevitable. Suspicious new and ex-royalist JPs were not acting entirely out of spite, though some old scores were undoubtedly settled.

In practical terms, the crown's personal possessions (as sold off to raise money in 1649–50) could be restored by adminstrative order and in any case purchasers were hurrying to return them for fear of prosecution. Participating in an illegal purchase of items from the royal art collection was as legally suspicious as benefiting from regicide, although overseas buyers of Charles I's possessions could only be asked to return them and not many showed that goodwill.[33] On 14 August a proclamation ordered all British subjects who had acquired goods belonging to Charles I to surrender them to the new Master of the Royal Wardrobe, the Earl of Sandwich (i.e. the ex-Cromwellian Edward Mountague) by 29 September or else, and Cromwell's former household manager and arranger of looted Royal goods in the Protector's palaces, Clement Kinnersley, now had the task of drawing up a list of everything that had gone missing and receiving it when it was handed in. A commission headed by zealous (and greedy) royalist Colonel Hawley took charge of finding missing goods, with 20 per cent of the value to be paid to any citizen who could help locate them. This duly encouraged both informers and a black market, with Hawley running a racket in blackmailing those who were 'fingered' (often by personal enemies).[34] The Spanish government, Charles II's hosts in 1656–60, were particularly reluctant to return works of art bought in good faith in 1649–51, and in 1662 agreed to stall any English requests for information or a handover. Their ambassador Cardenas kept quiet about his participation in the great Interregnum sell-off of looted royal artworks, as did art-dealer Emmanuel De Critz – who now sought a reward from Charles II for 'saving' part of his late father's collection in his personal custody. (He did not mention all the other paintings and statues which he had sold to foreign buyers, or return the profits from this.) Infuriated Hyde reckoned that not one foreign government had handed any of the loot back.[35] The restoration of Crown, Bishops', and Dean and Chapter Lands to their former owners was equally problematic, not least as they had been purchased by men whose political goodwill was essential – and by army personnel. Charles had initially proposed unspecified compensation for returning them in 1659, and Monck had suggested that the purchasers be granted long leases so they retained the lands but the king and church regained their official title.[36] The initial Convention bill for long leases was defeated, being abandoned by supporters including Howard, and the replacement bill just granting unspecified compensation was modified to exclude the Crown lands; these were returned to the king unconditionally in July.[37] The reacquisition of Church Lands was more haphazard, with no bill setting out the terms for it being agreed; individual seizures of specific estates by royal and church agents proceeded that summer with the current owners receiving varied settlements. Unilateral action to grant new leases by the Dean of Peterborough before any Church Lands had been returned by statute led to successful protests to the Commons and a royal order to halt his actions, but while a bill was delayed local agreements were sorted out between church and current possessors. Leases were granted to many important purchasers, and Charles set up a body of MPs and peers to arbitrate in cases of dispute in October.[38] In settling with military purchasers of Crown Lands, preferential terms (over when current ownership with full rents was to be converted to a less lucrative lease) were given to soldiers who had been in Monck's army at Coldstream or had otherwise been involved in the Restoration, and behind them to those who swore the oath of allegiance to Charles. Current or previous tenants were next in line behind the soldierly occupants to receive the new leases; those soldiers purged as unreliable by Monck in 1660, plus regicides, lost all title to their lands.[39] Meanwhile eleven of the most senior royalists who had lost all or some of their lands, by confiscation or by forced sale to pay fines, had them returned by Act of Parliament. A large proportion of the others had managed to regain their lands since the confiscations or sales by direct repurchase or through sales to their friends and relatives. The rest had to rely on a clause in the Church Lands bill which failed to get through the Commons in summer 1660 and were left stranded. They were reduced to lawsuits for individual cases (most of these succeeded but it was a slow and costly process) or waiting for another bill. The same frustration faced those who had not had land directly confiscated but had had to sell it to meet fines or general hardship after 1646; they had to resort to law, albeit with more prospect of sympathetic judges as new royalist judges were appointed, or to seek redress from a second bill.[40] This added to the number of Royalists who were dissatisfied with the settlement and had reason to agitate for punitive action against their foes and/or to vote for hardline royalists (new or old) in the next Parliamentary general election.

It can be seen in hindsight that the unsatisfactory (non-)resolution of the land issue in 1660 inflamed royalist opinion, causing people denied quick and guaranteed compensation for their sufferings to invest political energy in a more resolute Parliament at the next election. This worked to the detriment of moderate, ex-1642–8 Parliamentarian MPs – and of their ability to design a comprehensive Church settlement, as many of them were not re-elected in 1661. But at the time the Commons was clearly without any centralised direction, which would on past Tudor and early Stuart experience be supplied by privy councillors, the monarch via his ability to influence elections in some seats (e.g. the Duchy of Cornwall), and aristocratic borough patrons. The king, most of the Privy Council, and many local magnates had been in exile or at least political eclipse since 1646/8; they were inexperienced and had their restored or new roles (and their personal patrimonies in many cases) to sort out. No Commons 'managers' from the 1650s remained in power in June 1660, and most MPs were new to the role. Managing the Commons was not a priority for the inexperienced new government, and the MPs as well as the council were divided over what line to take on matters such as compensation and arranging the return of landed property. Some chaos and delay naturally resulted. Muddle was equally apparent in Ireland, where around seven-eighths of Catholic landowners (both royalist and rebel Confederacy Catholic as of 1646) had been dispossessed. The major beneficiaries of the 'hell or Connacht' confiscations by the victors of 1649–50 included Cromwellians who had played a leading role in restoring Charles in 1660, led by Monck, Broghill, and Coote. They could not be mulcted of their gains, and dispossessing military settlers would be dangerous – Cromwell and Fleetwood had both encouraged idealistic republicans and sectaries to settle in Ireland, from different motives, and the military leadership there in 1659 had been keen to remove moderate Henry Cromwell. Broghill,

Charles Coote, and their allies had secured Ireland for Monck and eventually Charles, but had also built up vast estates; the Convention proposed to leave lands with all who had possessed them in 1659 except for regicides. (That would neutralise most of the 1659 radical leadership, such as Ludlow and Miles Corbet.) Only Ormonde – bought off to stop him lobbying for his ruined royalist subordinates from the 1640s? – and two or three other leading royalists would have their estates restored by individual orders – the Irish equivalent of the list of top royalists granted their confiscated lands in England. Coote in Connacht sought an urgent ruling by the English Privy Council as returning exiled royalists started to occupy their old estates by force, and Charles' correspondence with Hyde on the issue shows that the king was more sympathetic than his minister to giving lenient terms to the Catholics among them even if they had technically been rebels and might thus threaten the Dublin Anglican regime again.

On 30 November Charles announced that most current occupiers would retain their land, led specifically by a named list of Monck's and Broghill's supporters, but that Church Lands had to be returned. So did those of Protestant royalists and Catholics not implicated in the 1641–9 rebellion, provided that land was found elsewhere to compensate those dispossessed; thirty-eight royalists were thus immediately restored on request, and others later by individual application to the king. The problem here was that Charles lacked enough land to pay off all those who were now dispossessed, and compensation was therefore inadequate. Ignorance of the amount of land available was the reason, rather than deliberate fraud.[41] The Episcopal church in Ireland was restored quickly as already approved by the local royalist-led Convention meeting in Dublin, with no Persbyterians admitted to the firmly royalist Anglican list of bishops; all the Scots Presbyterians in Ulster could secure was a royal promise that they could worship unmolested outside the church.

A generously inclusive church settlement hits the buffers – were the Presbyterians too reluctant? But was the popular mood such that any quick agreement would still have been undermined by resurgent Anglicans?

The Church of England had lost its disciplinary powers and mechanism of enforcement at Parliament's hands in 1641, with MPs waxing lyrical about its wicked Popish persecution of 'godly' Presbyterian and sectary ministers and the obsessive sackings and prosecutions of non-Anglicans by Archbishop Laud. The latter had ended up in the Tower of London, and in 1645 he was subjected to a 'show-trial' and execution with the fulminating lead prosecutor being none other than William Prynne. Charles I had regarded Laud as a martyr, and the unusual experiences of marginalisation and prolonged lack of office for sacked Anglican clerics in 1646–60 had hardened and embittered many of them and their gentry patrons. For every thoughtful and generous moderate cleric and lay ally aware that the oppressive church of the 1630s had brought its troubles on itself, there were many more keen to obtain revenge and reconstitute a 'fortress' church that excluded all the hated 'heretic' Presbyterians and sectaries. The closest clerics to Charles II (not exactly a religious enthusiast, unlike his devout and moral father) and his senior ministers had been those loyal and/or hardline clergy who chose to go into exile and follow the court around Western Europe in the 1650s, not those who had stayed in England as private citizens or as tutors to the children of friendly members of the gentry and as such had often had dealings with the sectary clergy who had taken their parishes. The more accommodating Anglicans who were prepared to reach out to the other sects were the minority, and Cromwell had not exactly helped by banning Anglican clergy from becoming schoolmasters in the mid-1650s as alleged subversives. To him and his clerical allies such as John Owen (intruded Dean of Christ Church, Oxford) and Hugh Peter, Anglicans were semi-Catholic 'Papists' who committed unseemly and unholy ceremonies in their over-decorated churches and were to be avoided. There had even been difficulty in keeping up the ordination of enough 'underground' Anglican clergy to be ready to repopulate the church in office if and when it was recreated – though the long wait for this from 1646–60 had meant that many hardline figures of the 1630s, led by most of its bishops, had died in the interim period.

Reconstituting the church as it had been in 1640 would be controversial among the current political elite and would require a majority for hardline Anglicanism in both houses of Parliament. King Charles I and his post-1644 negotiators had been prepared to consider an Anglican church with its bishops assisted by presbyters to secure agreement with the moderate Presbyterians dominating the Commons then, and when the bishops were abolished in 1646 the financial advantages of this (seizing their lands) had been the paramount reason. The same applied to Deans and Chapters. As of 1660 there was a possibility that this compromise could be used again to satisfy both Anglicans and Presbyterians, both of whom wanted an ordered church hierarchy and had an overwhelming interest in keeping at bay the more radical sectaries – tarred as they were with the brush of republicanism as well as socio-religious anarchy in 1649–59. The gentry who dominated Parliament in 1660 reflected the return of local power to the traditional elite from the fanatic sectaries who had run rampant in politics in the 1650s, though they were often also friends and relatives of clergy sacked in 1642–6 who now wanted their jobs back. In addition to this, assorted Presbyterian clerics who had been given parishes by Parliament's commissioners in the mid-1640s to replace Anglican clerics had been removed later as disloyal to the Commonwealth – and they also had a claim to clerical office. Satisfying everyone would be impossible. Hopefully, some grass-roots Presbyterians like Richard Baxter had been working for this sort of comprehensive church model in the 1650s, and after eighteen years of neglect (fourteen in royalist areas) the physical fabric of the Anglican cathedrals and deaneries would need expensive repairs if they were restored to pre-1642/6 use. The sacked bishops of 1646 would be expecting restoration, but fourteen of them had died and only three hardline allies of Laud (led by Matthew Wren of Norwich, the later architect Sir Christopher Wren's uncle) were still alive.

Hyde had sent his clerical envoy George Morley to persuade Presbyterian clergy to accept modified episcopacy in March 1660 and to consult moderate Anglican ex-clergy, and a Presbyterian delegation led by Edward Reynolds had visited The Hague a little earlier to see Charles and express their willingness to enter a tolerant Church of England. In May the Presbyterians conceded use of the old Anglican Prayer Book used pre-1646, provided that clerical objectors could omit contentious passages of it.[42] Both MPs and Councillors represented both parties, as did the new chaplains who Charles selected for himself, and the attitudes of most Anglican clergy in their initial sermons after the Restoration seemed to be conciliatory. The majority of a London meeting of Presbyterian leaders duly conceded the acceptance of bishops, provided that they were assisted by presbyters, and the use of the Prayer Book provided three contentious ceremonies accused of 'Popery' were made optional. Parliament, as in secular matters, acted to guarantee the positions of men in office in the 1650s who were not doctrinaire fanatics and could be assumed to be friendly to the King – all current clergy who were not 'baptisers' (i.e. Baptists or allied enthusiasts), had not preached against the king, and were not occupying parishes where a deposed royalist had requested readmission were confirmed. (The length of the vacancies, since 1642/6, added to the chances that many deprived clergy would have died or be in search of a new post away from their original parish.) This led to around six-sevenths of expelled royalist clergy either returning to their old posts or receiving new ones; 345 current 1650s clergy were expelled in 1660–2, most for real or suspected political disloyalty, and at least 161 of these acquired new parishes elsewhere; only 134 were reported as continuing to preach illegally.[43] The implication is that unpopular 1650s appointees were often removed for specious reasons thanks to local enemies, but most were not certified radicals and they were fitted in elsewhere as perfectly acceptable to the church authorities. Even where they held views inimical to Anglicanism (and had been promoted for such in the 1650s) they were either prepared to keep quiet to keep their jobs or had no local royalist enemies denouncing them. While the settlement of parish incumbencies was being arranged by local initiatives, often driven by personal feuds or outright jobbery, the Commons remained divided over the issue of theological and administrative settlement. Zealous Presbyterians like Prynne continued to argue fiercely for a church on the lines of that which his faction had tried to force on Charles I in 1646–8, no doubt encouraged by the absence this time of a powerful and sectary-favouring army. He was fighting the intellectual battles of the 1640s, not looking to the threat from embittered Anglicans. His model of church would embrace boards of presbyters to run local affairs and Presbyterian theology but might accept the office of bishop if the bishoprics were shorn of disciplinary authority and kept away from hardline Anglicans. The number of royalist MPs, or men from old royalist families who could be presumed to be Anglicans, did not give these Presbyterians pause for more sensible consideration. The government and its allied MPs preferred to leave the form of a church settlement to an ecclesiastical conference of the various parties – which Charles I had conceded to Parliament, provided that a few Anglicans could be added to the then sitting Presbyterian-dominated Westminster Assembly. This gave the advantage of the current king graciously securing agreement from the religious factions involved, with evidence suggesting ready Presbyterian acceptance of the main Anglican demands, rather than imposing a settlement. After heated debates the Presbyterian hardliners, outvoted, had to accept it.

As with the secular punishment of regicides in 1660, it was the numbers of activists favouring particular courses that would decide the outcome. The impatience of the royalist grass roots for a resolution in late summer led to government moves, led by Hyde, to chivvy the clerical rivals into an agreement. The restored pre-1646 bishops and the first new ones appointed were invited to discuss the Presbyterian proposals and to show their goodwill by filling vacant livings with men of both parties. The intention was to name a number of Presbyterian bishops to fill vacant sees, the religious equivalent of the civil settlement at both national and local level of offices; but only one of the Presbyterians approached, Edward Reynolds, accepted – after he had consulted with senior clerical allies in his sect such as Edmund Calamy. The case of Reynolds (vicar of St Lawrence Jewry in London and in 1648–50 and 1659 Dean of Christ Church in Oxford) showed his unusual status, as he had been an Anglican clergyman back in the 1630s and had moved to the Presbyterian faction by joining the Westminster Assembly in 1643 and taking the Covenant in 1644; his past activities show that he was unusually open-minded. But his influence over other Presbyterians was limited; one of the most famous (at least in retrospect) and well-regarded of the Presbyterian ministers, the 'non-political' Richard Baxter of Kidderminster, notably refused Hyde's offer to arrange the grant of the bishopric of Hereford to him. Allegedly he feared the local royalist reaction to this and doubted that he could prevail in enforcing his own religious views and appointing his allies to parishes. Similarly, Edmund Calamy refused an offer of the bishopric of Coventry and Lichfield. There were some gentry Presbyterians in the West Midlands to back up such a potentially controversial bishop as Baxter (e.g. the Harleys of Brampton Bryan near Hereford), and Baxter's personal holiness and abilities as an organizer and an inspiring preacher had been apparent through the 1640s and 1650s. But had he accepted his ability to reconcile the regional religious antagonisms must be doubted. Usefully, he had opposed regicide and the expulsion of bishops from the 1640s Church – but he had been a New Model Army chaplain (briefly). Baxter did speak up for comprehension in the new church at the forthcoming Savoy Conference, but he also called for the continuation of penal laws against the Catholics (against the king's express wishes) which shows that comprehending him and other like-minded Presbyterian leaders in the church would have had its own problems.[44] In modern terminology, broadening the church to let in the 'left wing' (the Presbyterians) would have damaged attempts to resolve the exclusion of the 'right wing' (Catholics). Memories of the 1620s and 1630s with their alleged aggressive Catholic proselytization at court and the rise of semi-Catholic ceremonial in Laud's Church were too strong to enable the Presbyterians to accept that times had changed and loyal Catholics needed to be thanked for helping their king. (For that matter, even in the House of Lords with its resident bloc of twenty-four Catholic peers, a royally-backed plea in summer 1661 for abolishing anti-Catholic legislation only led to a failed bill to cancel restrictions on secular priests.) It would have been more useful if other senior Presbyterians such as Calamy had not left the country for Holland in 1660–1 but gone to the conference to negotiate en bloc; however the extent of panic in the ranks of what belligerent Anglicans called 'fanatic preachers' over the purge and trials of their secular radical allies in the Long Parliament (would they be next?) explains why many of them took the safe course of leaving England. The best hope of their party was now to reform the church from within and use senior officers to press their agenda and promote their own loyalists to junior rank, and the failure to take this course argues for a lack of realism (or awareness of the threat from the Commons) whatever their theological qualms about having to use the Prayer Book. Theologically, their doctrinal equivalents in Scotland had taken part in an episcopal church and even served as bishops in Scotland under James I; this mixture of bishops and presbyters within a broadly Calvinist theological framework was indeed now reconstituted successfully in Scotland. Possibly the reconstitution – and aggressive demands for the return of their old lands and privileges – of the deans and chapters had alarmed them about the high Anglican tone being taken within the 1660 English church. The old membership of the Chapters, where surviving, spontaneously reconstituted themselves. Nor did current lay leaders of moderate Presbyterianism in the Lords, e.g. Manchester, take the initiative to forcibly ask their clerical allies to take a gamble and enter the new state church; did they not realise the danger of hardline Anglicans having their own way in this body?

Charles thus had to fill the vacant sees from Anglican personnel, ranging from the pro-Independent moderate John Gauden (ex-chaplain to the late Earl of Warwick, the Calvinist leader, an ally of pro-reconciliation Archbishop Ussher in the 1650s, and now a favoured Convention preacher) to the Laudian ally John Cosin. Most had been royalist clergy in the 1640s. The see of Canterbury was given to the elderly Bishop Juxon, formerly a Laudian ally and Charles I's Lord Treasurer and owed a debt of honour for attending the late king on the scaffold. The latter's lack of effort in assuming leadership of the senior Anglican clerics, or writing on the current problems to be faced in restoring the church, in the turmoil of 1660 show that he was too old and exhausted to take a major (as opposed to symbolic) role. The most politically prominent bishop, and his successor in 1663, was Gilbert Sheldon who arrived in London in mid-May 1660, a few weeks before the king, and initially aided but soon pushed aside the senior, more moderate Anglican 'man on the spot', Morley. Sheldon received the turbulent see of sectary-filled London; he was more of a competent adminstrator than a theologian, as was needed to sort out the chaos left by the long eccelesiastical interregnum.[45] Dean of All Souls College, Oxford in 1626–42 and a pro-Laudian disciplinarian in the University of Oxford in the 1630s, Sheldon had been one of the late king's religious 'trusties' at the Court in 1642–6, and was the man to whom Charles had allegedly passed his written vow to restore all Church Lands and impropriations if he had the chance in March 1646. Imprisoned in Oxford gaol in 1646–8 and then banned from going anywhere near Oxford or the king, he had kept out of trouble during the Interregnum but been well-regarded enough to be one of those Anglican clerics considered for an 'underground' bishopric in 1656. The aged Laudian Bishop Duppa duly regarded him as the main hope for the 1630s-style Anglican church's cause with the king in 1660. His commitment to the church as established in the 1630s was as unwavering as was the new king's trust in him as a confidante of his late father; in this his loyalist pedigree from the 1630s-40s far outmatched those of more tolerant senior clerics. His main task was to purge his see of sectaries, in the manner in which he had aided Laud to do so in Oxford colleges in the 1630s. His administrative abilities were also to prove politically vital in helping to elect and co-ordinate the measures proposed by MPs in seats where the church had influence in the 1661 election. Arguably he was the best man available to assemble an ordered and confident new state church and to assuage the feelings of angry grass-roots Anglican clergy who had spent years in the wilderness (and poverty) since 1646; but he was not the man to compromise and in modern terminology be inclusive. The more senior Juxon (born 1582) had also operated as a (senior) assistant to Laud's disciplinarian purges in the 1630s, as Bishop of London – Sheldon's current role – so hardliners could respect his record too. He was however too old (seventy-eight in 1660) and soon too sick to make much impact and he was in effect a front man for Sheldon. The more tolerant new Archbishop of York, Accepted Frewen (whose Christian name shows his family's 'Puritan' godliness), was both usually absent from London rebuilding his archdiocesan structure in the North, and sidelined.[46]

Given the political threat of the turbulent City crowds to the government in Whitehall – and to Parliament, as remembered by MPs fom 1641 and 1647–8 – it was essential for the regime to appoint a ruthless and effective operator as Bishop of London, and to choose a man who could tame the local 'fanatic' congregations. An impeccably loyal Anglican was needed to ensure that he would fulfil the requirement of driving seditious clergy out of the parishes and marginalising the danger of their parishioners mobilising to intimidate the government (which, as of 1661–5, did not have many troops on hand for riots). Sheldon was thus an obvious choice, and his success in London invaluable in winning him the see of Canterbury and ability to lead the way – in a firmly Laudian direction – in the church after 1663. Quite apart from the King's desire to reward loyalty from the men who had stayed faithful to him and his 'canonised' father in 1646–60, the political imperatives of the early 1660s made it impractical to risk including too many candidates of doubtful royalist commitment – Presbyterians, for example – in major sees. This would have been the same even had the latter agreed to join the church and been granted sees in 1661; in the secular equivalent where senior Presbyterians did work with the king as councillors, they still had less influence on him than impeccably royalist figures. Also, as far as local low-level nominations to parishes went, the influential royalist gentry – now providing most JPs – would have been naming Anglicans to the parishes they patronised whatever the number of senior posts given to their religious rivals. Would they have refused to cooperate with 'fanatic' ex-Presbyterian bishops or other men who had no respectable record of resistance to the Commonwealth?

The ecclesiastical conference took place on schedule, but the Presbyterians chose to be offended by the strength of its royally-named president Hyde's declaration in favour of episcopacy as divinely-sanctioned. Hyde was replaced by the Presbyterian peers Holles and Annesley, and the conference eventually agreed what became known as the 'Worcester House Declaration' (25 October). Sheldon, as Master of the Savoy Chapel, the host for the summit, remained in the background of the proceedings but was understood by contemporary observers (e.g. Burnet, Calamy, and Parker) to have a directing hand behind the scenes and to be keen to see that uniformity of ecclesiastical practice and belief be enforced.[47] The meeting required bishops to operate with the assistance of presbyters, and left it open to the clergy to use the various contents of the Prayer Book as their conscience dictated.[48] This was, however, pressed on the two parties, both but especially the Presbyterians reluctant, by the two peers plus Sheldon and thus could be expected to be denounced once the Presbyterians were operating freely and under pressure from their own irreconcilables; and unlike in the 1630s even the Anglican church lacked the disciplinary mechanism to intimidate objectors. Prynne and his faction attempted to secure a Commons vote to approve the measure when Parliament reconvened, but were defeated by 36 votes.[49] This represented the return to Westminster of reinvigorated hardline Anglicans, who had been encouraged to resist any compromise by their local constituents during the recess, and ominously petitions were now being laid before the House demanding a full return to the 1642 Church; there were seven county petitions in favour and the only place petitioning against full episcopacy was London.[50] Even if the vote had been won the successive panics over 'fanatic' involvement in assorted plots and risings from 1663 would have given a good excuse for the hardline Anglicans to bounce worried MPs into reversing this decision later. Nor were the Conference decisions always obeyed by hardline Anglicans who loathed presbyters as a seditious 1640s innovation, and who had some surviving 1630s Laudians like Bishop Cosin back in office to lead them. Gauden and Reynolds, both ex-Presbyterians, were the main bishops to use presbyters; most did not, and the grass-roots local parish or district

Presbyterian committees had obligingly dissolved themselves in summer 1660 in expectation of admission to the new church. Bishops Sanderson of Lincoln and Walton of Chester tried to insist that their junior clergy used the Elizabethan Anglican Prayer Book instead of the Calvinist Geneva one, though this was not yet required policy. The restoration of regional church disciplinary courts in the dioceses however anticipated legal sanction by Act of Parliament in some areas; they were legalised by the Cavalier Parliament in July 1661 but had already been in existence for over six months in Chichester, York and Chester and for a year in Canterbury. Grass roots action by parish Anglican zealots also led to the first presentation of legal cases against clergy for not using the correct Prayer Book, ahead of official legislation by Parliament to issue a revised version of the Elizabethan one in 1661–2.

Did what happened to the Scots Church serve as a 'trial run' for England – hardening the Anglican line once it was safe?

The initiative in Scotland lay with the pro-royalist wing of the Presbyterian church, the Resolutioners who had backed Charles II during his stay there in 1650. Charles had only taken the Covenant at all with distaste to show that he was a loyal ally of the militant Calvinists who had created this document as a rallying-point for the rising against his father's pro-Anglican church in 1637–8. The very notion of a Covenant implied that the Calvinist Scots rebels were the 'People of God' like those who had created the first Covenant, i.e. Moses' Israelites as detailed in the Old Testament – and that his father had been the oppressive and unholy equivalent of Pharoah in the Book of Exodus. Edinburgh had been worth a Covenant to Charles II in 1650 and he had signed up despite doubts by his adviser Hyde, but he had been alienated by the bullying attitude taken to him by the dominant Marquis of Argyll, the strongman head of the Campbell clan, and his hardline clerical allies. Argyll had indeed been the man who crowned Charles II at the final Scots coronation in 1651 – a role normally carried out by a bishop. Having regained secular power in Edinburgh in a coup after the moderate Covenanters had tried in vain to save Charles I by invading England in autumn 1648, he had then been driven from office again after the New Model Army overran the Lowlands in 1650–1 and imposed its own military government. The hardliners had been kept out of power by Monck in 1652–60 whereas most Resolutioners had collaborated with the occupation authorities, and were now in eclipse. Regicide republican activist Archibald Johnston of Warriston, who had acted as the Covenanters' representative on the English Parliament's 'Committee of Both Kingdoms' in London in the mid-1640s, was condemned *in absentia* for his acts in London against Charles I in 1648–9 – he was to be extradited from France and executed in 1662. Argyll himself was the most prominent of three unrepentant republicans to be condemned by the Scots Parliament and executed. Argyll's execution on 27 May 1661 was especially significant, given that his main crimes were political; apart from his judicial murder of the great royalist general Montrose in 1650 he had alienated the current king by ruthless coercion in 1650–1 but he had had no truck with republicanism or been involved in Charles I's trial. Arriving in London in July 1660 expecting pardon if not reward, he was treated by Charles with the same coldness he had used to his king in the early 1650s, being kept kicking his heels in the Presence Chamber at Whitehall expecting an audience and suddenly arrested by the guards. Technically the decision to try and condemn him was up to Parliament, but the king seems to have encouraged Argyll's execution (in revenge for the Marquis' treating him as a puppet and killing Montrose in 1650?). The other opponents of the Scots monarchy in the 1640s were spared, usually after grovelling repentance and sometimes after bribing the new Scots leadership. One of Argyll's most fanatical clerical allies, James Guthrie, was among the executed trio and their group was decimated by arrests; Charles was supposed to have wanted them driven out of Scotland. Given their loathing of monarchy in general and hostility to him in Scotland in 1650–1, this was probably wise. His refusal to return to that kingdom for the rest of his reign may well indicate his lingering resentment of the way he had been treated there.

The Covenant he had signed was ignored, as was the hopeful but unrealistic appeal of the Scots clergy to their restored king to ensure a Presbyterian church in England like he had promised in 1650. Indeed, the Convention in London had enthusiastically ordered the Covenant burnt in May 1660 to celebrate Charles' arrival, and the king could be expected to take a similar opinion given the way he had been harassed by Covenanting clerics in Scotland in 1650–1. Charles relied on the advice of James Sharp, a leading Resolutioner who headed the church delegation sent to England on his return, as well as his Scots royalist – Presbyterian – loyalists, the Earls of Middleton (leader of anti-

Cromwellian resistance in the mid-1650s) and Lauderdale (an Engager leader involved in the 1648 invasion of England, who had negotiated with Charles I in 1646–7). Middleton was now effectively viceroy in Scotland and was rumoured to have turned Anglican in exile. Charles duly confirmed the Kirk/ church in Scotland as established by law in a letter sent on his behalf by Lauderdale (10 August 1660), though this excluded all unofficial religious congregations outside the parish system. These could now be suppressed. But this was only an interim solution to keep those Presbyterians opposed to episcopacy quiet, and on New Year's Day 1661 Middleton opened a new Scots Parliament with a brief from the Council in London of regaining all past royal rights. The lords and gentry had chafed under theocratic domination since 1639, an unholy alliance of 'King Campbell' and the clerics which had led to military disaster and conquest in 1651, so the king's intentions had broad support from them in controlling the clergy. The work on bills by the Parliament was delegated to a committee of 'Lords of the Articles' named by Middleton as Royal Commissioner, and they duly restored all traditional powers (including appointments, foreign policy, and command of the army) to the king. Measures passed without royal approval, led by the Covenant, were outlawed and the oath of allegiance and supremacy (recognising royal control over the church) was extended to Scotland and required of all office-holders. Lacking the power of military coercion or aristocratic leadership, and faced by a firm and nearly united nobility and gentry, protesters were powerless. In March 1661 Middleton and his ally Glencairn advised Charles that it would be safe now to reimpose episcopacy, and while Lauderdale was still fighting a rearguard action against this in arguments at Whitehall the Scots Parliament acted as Middleton required.[51] The initial religious settlement and promises of 1660 that autumn had been overturned once it was safe to do so; would the same occur in England?

Grass-roots hostility to English Presbyterians and sectaries: a decisive block to implementing any comprehensive settlement?

Meanwhile, that autumn local English JPs – many more now full royalists than had been the case earlier – were prosecuting ministers for not using all the Anglican Prayer Book as ordained by old statutes, a sign that even if there had been more enthusiasm among Presbyterian clergy for taking up church posts they could have expected obstruction by the lay elite. This would not have affected bishops, but grass-roots opinion – in a country where feeling was strongly against central administrative control after the 1650s and thus royal orders to conform to toleration would be unpopular – was strongly in favour of Anglican hardliners. There were signs of that lay Anglican zealotry and desire for revenge against the 'fanatics' that was to lead to gleeful harassment of the Dissenters by JPs from the 1660s to the 1680s, even before the Presbyterians turned down the offer of bishoprics. One example of this was the arrest of the minor preacher John Bunyan, active in Bedfordshire, in December 1660; his harsh sentence of seven years in gaol for 'illegal' preaching and long imprisonment in Bedford Gaol gave the world a literary masterpiece but in political terms was a good illustration of local Anglican activism and law-bending.

As with old army personnel, there was also the option of harassment for alleged conspiracy in a country paranoid about attempted rebellion to overturn the Restoration, with only Anglicans seen as definitively loyal to the state and king. Charles to be fair, did his best to give a lead by example for a tolerant attitude to the non-political sectaries, even for the Quakers whose delegations he received personally in summer – autumn 1660. He was gracious and charming though as evasive as usual, and fooled their leaders into thinking him a man of 'sober countenance' while himself finding them amusing rather than dangerous as so many of the elite did.[52] This was another aspect of his tolerant streak towards the unconventional, which more usually operated in favour of assertive women, the raffish world of the theatre, and outrageous and libidinous rakes such as Sir Charles Sedley and John Wilmot, Earl of Rochester (son of his companion in the flight after the battle of Worcester). In practical terms he pressurised the local authorities into releasing around 700 Quakers that summer/autumn, set up a council committee in November to look into ways to release more, and promised a petitioner in front of the council that their meetings would not be prosecuted and they could retain their hats in appearances before authority – which he allowed them to do before himself in a breach of the usual protocol.[53] But winning over the majority of personnel in both the executive and legislature to tolerate most or all non-dangerous sectaries was probably hopeless in the current atmosphere. Securing acceptance of a fully integrated church containing both Anglican and peaceable sectary religious persuasions on the local level would have been difficult, whatever was agreed at Worcester House and even if the Presbyterian leadership had been more realistic about the potential danger from the next Parliament. Ultimately, a king determined on integration would have had to dismiss large numbers of obstructive JPs to prevent piecemeal denunciations and arrests of Presbyterian clergy and been at risk of criticism in Parliament for it. James II was to attempt this sort of adminstrative exclusion of obstructors from office in 1685–8, and met catastrophe – although his action was more controversial as undertaken on behalf of Catholics as well as Dissenters. At the time of the Anglican onslaught in the localities in the mid-1660s Charles was anxious to avoid such criticism by Parliament, which he had not acquired the means to manage. Ultimately he would have required a new election, run by loyal managers in the counties, to challenge the virulently anti-Disssenter mood of a majority of his MPs after 1661, though there was a coherent bloc of Presbyterian MPs in this new Parliament amounting to around a third of the total to rely on for moderation. There was no identifiable hardline Anglican leader in the House, with the King's effective 'business manager' in 1661–5, ex-royalist veteran Sir Hugh Pollard from Devon (Governor of Dartmouth in 1645–6 and now Governor of Guernsey), more of a disburser of hospitality and entertainment to win over MPs than an Anglican 'hard man'. However, the roles of committed Anglicans like the journalist Sir John Birkenhead, rabidly anti-republican editor of *Mercurius Publicus*, and Sir John Bramston were probably important in rallying MPs to vote for a hardline on the church – with Sheldon encouraging them behind the scenes. The mood of the younger MPs in particular was strongly pro-Anglican, with their age meaning that they could not remember the administrative and judicial harassment of local elites carried out by Laud which had turned so many against the bishops by 1641. Indeed, the church as well as the monarchy benefited from a mixture of nostalgic glamour and the idealistic aura of martyrdom. The executed Laud could be held up as a victim of sectary vengefulness, with his protégé Sheldon more than willing to take this uncompromising line and to adopt scare tactics in refusing to trust any of the 'fanatics' inside his church structure as they were all allegedly ex-rebels and potential future plotters.

As seen in Restoration pamphleteering, all sects who had benefited from the Civil War were traitorous fanatics and implicit rebels, with Presbyterians aligned with their real-life sectary enemies in pro-Anglican propaganda. The growing backlash, however, affected the separatist Independent sectary groups worst, as their secret meetings could be interpreted as plotting and their social levelling was an affront to conservatives. The issue of sectaries – particularly Quakers – refusing to doff their hats to social superiors assumed symbolic importance, though to do him credit Charles II was not so offended as were many of lower status. The alleged threat of sectaries participating in republican plots led to a large-scale round-up of their members in the second half of 1660, the most famous victim being John Bunyan, and revenge-seeking JPs left them to rot in prison. Charles did his best to have those arrested brought before magistrates and charges or released, but he was, however, without support among his senior advisers in endeavouring to combat the prevalent persecution. The disruptive tactics of the more zealous Quakers (women included) in interrupting and haranguing ministers, writing millenarian pamphlets promising divine retribution on the sinful, and carrying out public spectacles that offended the 'godly' public[54] did not exactly help their cause, and their refusal to take oaths enabled JPs to require them to swear the Oath of Allegiance to the King and arrest them as traitors if they refused.

The fears of a separatist plot to overthrow the Restoration seemed justified when a party of militant Fifth Monarchists attempted to take over the City of London on 6 January 1661. The shock caused by 'Venner's Rising' was out of proportion to its reality, as only thirty-odd extremists – a small cell of London millenarians which had escaped the notice of government spies – endeavoured to occupy St. Paul's Cathedral and were swiftly driven out by the trained bands. Retreating to Highgate, they launched a second attack and were defeated in a skirmish in the streets; the leading participants were executed. The reason for the revolt seems to have been an emotional reaction to the recent execution of captive regicides. The government was taken by surprise, and as is usual for such occasions there was panic with those who had been the most suspicious of a mass-conspiracy by wicked dissidents now seeming to have been justified. It was believed that the actual rising was the tip of an iceberg and massive preventive arrests were made – including thousands of

Quakers.⁵⁵ Those separatists under suspicion, like British Muslims after 5 July 2005, hastened to issue declarations of loyalty to the government and denounced the plotters. As usual, this had little perceived effect.⁵⁶ When no further revolts occurred the King made sure that most were quietly released, though in London the Council order of 25 January for this had to be rescinded after protests from the hardline Lord Mayor Sir Richard Browne (ironically, formerly a Parliamentarian general and possibly especially harsh in order to reassure his former antagonists of his conversion). The national release of arrested Quakers was ordered by the king on 4 March, excepting their leaders – who were presumably under more suspicion as they were determined organizers, not just 'believers', so they could co-ordinate anti-government action if so minded.⁵⁷ But in practice the forthcoming Easter Quarter Sessions saw more prosecutions of sectaries, this time for refusing the oath of allegiance⁵⁸ – all who did this were seen as subversives, not principled abstainers. The revolt aided Anglican extremists' perceptions that no 'fanatics' could be trusted and justified future repressive measures. It also played a part in deciding the king to retain a substantial force of Guards regiments for his security as the army was finally demobilised, and the Commons of 1661 in accepting this.

Chapter Five

The 'Cavalier Parliament': the Royalist and Anglican backlash gathers strength. Inevitable?

The recent revolt as well as the Quaker scare suggested that the new Parliament being elected in early spring 1661 would be strongly royalist and in favour of a hardline attitude on security and religion. Unlike in 1660 there was now a coherent government in place to influence elections in those boroughs where it had patronage, and naturally this was used to secure the election of firm royalists (old or, mostly, new). As usual the Presbyterians in London put up a strong showing and it returned four MPs opposed to bishops, amidst popular demonstrations where 'No bishops!' was shouted – feelings probably being exacerbated by the resolution Bishop Sheldon was showing in imposing Anglican clergy in the parishes. Lord Mayor Browne, as an uncompromising Anglican, was defeated but secured election from a courtier's borough instead. There was a similar effort to secure Presbyterian MPs by patrons in the provinces, though less successfully, and this infuriated the king. Where possible the government's borough patrons imposed their own candidates, e.g. Hyde as University Chancellor choosing his son and Solicitor-General Finch for Oxford, and clearly Charles I's mistakes of not 'borough-mongering' to produce a bloc of loyal MPs at the 1640 elections had been noted. Charles and his Council also tried to rig the concurrent elections for a new Parliament in Dublin in favour of loyal Protestants (mostly Anglicans) by specific instructions to the Council in Dublin to favour suitable candidates. The Irish Council, led by the Broghill and Coote factions – who had been part of the Cromwellian 'establishment' there in the 1650s and so were anti-Catholic by past actions – also banned all Catholic peers who had joined the 1640s rebellion from the Irish House of Lords, even if the king had restored their lands.[1] This was partly 'dog in the manger' tactics to keep a bloc of Catholic peers from voting for any change in the harshly pro-Protestant land settlements of the 1650s (as with controlling the MPs), but showed a determination to ignore the king's wishes for what would now be called a 'big tent' approach to support. The king had to restore lands to expropriated Catholic peers by individual grants, mostly to his most loyal followers in exile in the 1650s such as Lords Taaffe and Clancarty, not by a general order as the Irish Council strongly opposed the latter and it would not have been obeyed 'on the ground'. Similarly, the pre-1641 Protestant settlers who formed the bulk of the electoral roll and MPs for the next Irish Parliament (which opened in May 1661) were opposed to granting any significant amount of land or offices to Catholics in case it threatened their own position – and many of them had bought up land confiscated from Catholics in the 1650s. With government expenditure running at three times the amount of income in Ireland, it was no time to annoy the Irish House of Commons and cause a block on financial measures. The blocks on non-Anglicans political and religious power were thus a matter of grass-roots resistance' by the Anglican elites across the kingdoms rather than bad faith from London.

Although the government went ahead with the promised ecclesiastical conference in London it also ordered the arrests of people who had been accused of co-ordinating attempts to elect anti-episcopal MPs.[2] This amounted to bad faith and attempts to secure centralised control for the benefit of its own agenda. The English elections duly returned about 50 per cent Anglican, pro-episcopal MPs, most of them from families that had been royalist in the 1640s – and so likely to have a personal stake in demanding compensation for past sufferings in the king's cause, if not for themselves for friends or relatives. The government and leading royalists used influence where available, as for Hyde at Oxford where he was now the Chancellor, and some defeated candidates were later found seats in boroughs controlled by royalist peers; the Earl of Essex, leading Presbyterian patron in his native county (and younger son of the late earl who had led the Calvinist peers against Charles I), was certainly ordered to stay away from the poll by the king and other patrons may have been treated similarly, and many royalists were returned unopposed. The pro-royalist majority in the Commons duly enabled them to overturn some unsympathetic MPs' elections on petition from the defeated royalist candidates. Given the popular mood against 'fanatics' and the fear of rebellion in recent months, this and the control of local offices by royalists gave their candidates a built-in advantage in both 'open' and 'closed' seats; and even a pro-Presbyterian corporation could return its favoured MP yet see him evicted from the Commons on petition. No other result for the elections was practicable – and this duly gave the hardline Royalists in the Commons a chance to pass what measures they wished. However, an analysis of the membership's religious views indicates that the most determined and authoritarian Anglicans did not have a coherent 'majority' in strictly numerical terms – rather that they were more coherent and so were able to assert their views on the other MPs who lacked leadership. (Given the recent and continuing executions of leading republicans and sectaries for treason, the effect of this in intimidation of those of moderate views should not be forgotten.) As mentioned above, about a third of MPs were certainly or probably Presbyterian. As with the Tudor Parliaments, privy councillors and assorted 'borough-monger' peers could arrange strategy and plan bills behind the scenes and give leadership to the Commons – and the way that the latter had got out of hand in the 1620s and in 1640–2 was a warning to the executive of the need to take control. The government also had a skilled and aggressive journalist 'cheerleader' in the Commons in Sir John Birkenhead, whose *Mercurius Publicus* took the line that 'sectaries equals traitors' and arranged 'spin' to whip up fears of plotters – probably invaluable in scaring MPs to vote for hardline measures. The Lords was always royalist, and the only hope for amelioration of an aggressive Commons policy of amending the 1660 settlement was of the government reining them in, which arguably was not likely to happen at a time when the government still feared republican plots and the gentry feared 'fanatic preachers' (e.g. Quakers and Fifth Monarchists).

The mood had been set for the Cavalier Parliament's aggressive revision of the 1660 settlement by the Coronation on 23 April – a ceremony planned in detail by a committee set up by the Privy Council, so representing the court/council 'line' on monarchy. The latter was hardline reassertion of the grandiose and Divinely-appointed monarchy of the 1630s, with no concessions to the practical limitations placed on the Stuarts in 1641. The prime mover in the planning was the court's chief heraldic expert, Sir Edward Walker, who had been Charles I's personal secretary during the Civil War (as shown in a famous painting). The tone was aggressively triumphalist, with a full-scale procession through the

City for the first time since 1559 (James I's entry had been delayed by plague and Charles I had not had one). The City, centre of resistance to Charles I in 1640–5, was now used as the location for a series of grandiose tableaux flattering the new king as the modern equivalent of Aeneas, the wandering exiled Trojan hero who had founded the Roman nation in Italy in Vergil's *'Aeneid'*. The Vergilian propaganda theme of unstinting divine support for Aeneas could be equated with the way in which God had miraculously restored Charles to his throne, with the sub-text that defying the king was blasphemy as well as treason. The pageant was supplemented by the return of the medieval chivalric orders centred on the king, with a mass creation of Knights of the Bath as at medieval coronations. (These honours, along with the mass-grants of baronetcies in 1660–2, were flattering to the loyal royalist veterans who received them but were also cheap.) The King's Champion entered Westminster Hall during the coronation banquet to issue a challenge to any who denied the new monarch's right, another medieval revival which could easily have been dropped. The Laudian ceremonial of the coronation itself put out a similar message of timeless Divinely-backed monarchy, with the Popish anointing stressed and no attempt at limiting Catholic elements such as was to occur at the 1689 coronation. It is also significant that Charles revived the ancient practice of 'touching for the King's Evil' as early as 1660, a showpiece for the monarchy's 'magical' powers which he had kept up in exile and which served to stress his religious mystique to his humbler subjects. There was clearly a co-ordinated propaganda campaign to assert that the monarchy was immune from political constraints and owed its sanction to God, not Parliament or General Monck. This message was very much the centrepiece of the coronation festivities, and would have given encouragement to the new MPs to back it up with political action. But the current creation of a politically useful mythos of heroic veneration around the king and his office (implying the duty of obedience by all his subjects to God's chosen one) had its limits, as the attempt to create a new 'Order of the Royal Oak' celebrating Charles' sojourn in the famous oak tree at Boscobel in 1651 was abandoned despite its usefulness in providing honourable but cheap rewards for the royalist stalwarts of the Worcester campaign and its aftermath. A mythology and ritual of sacral kingship was being revived, with religious overtones of Charles I as martyr (plus traditional medieval punishment for those who impiously challenged it). Lacking the Commonwealth's huge army, the new King used ideology.

The new Commons now launched an assault on the symbolic victories of the Parliamentarian party in 1640–6, having the Covenant burned (though 103 MPs protested at this), Strafford's attainder of 1641 reversed (on the reasonable grounds that it had been obtained by violent demonstrations terrorising Parliament), bishops readmitted to the Lords, and the control of the militia vested in the king.[3] The latter was a pointed snub to the Parliamentarian attempts of 1641–2 and 1645–8 to seize military authority for the executive, but when it came to the cost of an actual army the Commons backed away from endorsing Charles' request in January 1662 for a paid standing army (to be headed by his brother the Duke of York) in favour of £70,000 per annum to pay for the militia continuing as at present (but only until 1665).[4] The Parliament also banned all petitions to change the laws unless licensed by a JP or a Grand Jury and limited the number of people allowed to present one to ten, thus preventing any repetitions of the rowdy mass-petitioning by which Pym's faction had intimidated Parliament in 1640–1. It was made illegal to call the king a Catholic, and the crucial licensing of all publications (which had lapsed in both 1641 and 1659 and so caused an explosion of popular literary agitation) was reintroduced. Printers would have to submit bonds for good behaviour, and all publications would be examined by a committee of senior ministers and bishops.[5] Already Charles had imposed the former mastermind of royalist propaganda in the 1640s-50s, Sir John Birkenhead, as the controller of the government pamphleteering organization, in place of the politially unreliable Nicholas Canne; he was now joined by the vituperative royalist Roger L'Estrange who took on the congenial task of hunting down seditious writings.[6] The government thus controlled spin as firmly as Charles I had done, using lessons learnt in the complex propaganda wars of the Civil War period. This was as much royalist triumphalism as had been the recent public executions and exhumations, but in practical terms many of the reforms of 1641 were allowed to stand. The Court of Wards, Star Chamber, the Council of the North, and the other paraphernalia of royal feudal jurisdiction (and money-raising), which even many royalist MPs had condemned, were not restored despite some discussion;[7] the only exception was the administratively useful and not locally unpopular Court of the Marches of Wales. Neither was the mechanism of church judicial abuse like the Court of High Commission restored. The controversial 1640 disciplinary canons were not reintroduced, and the Triennial Act requiring a new Parliament three years after the previous one closed remained in force though with no mechanism to ensure that it was enacted (Charles II was to ignore it in 1684). The government was able to secure a grant of £70,000 p.a. for three years to keep the militia in being, but not the money to pay for any standing army. Censorship was reintroduced, thus ending the free debate of the 1640s and 1650s and enabling action against secular or religious dissidents, although it could not always be enforced. In Ireland, the king had intended the new Parliament and Privy Council to compensate the landless Catholics dispossessed by the 1650s confiscations by finding ownerless land for them instead of trying to force the new owners to return any of it under his November 1660 declaration, but this was easier said than done. There were around sixty of the 'New English' landowners who had first come to Ireland and acquired land from the Cromwellian regime in the 1650s in the Irish House of Commons which met on 8 May 1661, a large enough bloc to obstruct any attempt to return seized land, and there was not nearly enough ownerless land left unoccupied to give to the dispossessed. The MPs obstructed royal orders to allow Catholics to reside in towns again, reversing a Cromwellian ban, and Charles gave way; but at least the Lords Justices (led by Broghill, now the Earl of Orrery) managed to have an inflammatory vote to restrict the Catholics to Connacht (repeating Cromwell's plans) reversed by warning of royal anger. The Irish government planned to confiscate more lands of potentially anti-Stuart 1650s republican settlers in Ireland to provide estates for the dispossessed, but Charles did not take it up lest such punitive action encourage English MPs to behave in a similar manner.[8] The continuing, if exaggerated, threat of an insurrection by dispossessed Catholic landowners played into the hands of constructive Protestant MPs and their backers on the Irish Privy Council, though the veteran 'moderate' Catholic organiser at the 'rebel' government in Kilkenny in the 1640s, Richard Belling, tried to reassure the governments in both realms by organising a petition of loyal Catholics in 1662 which denied the Pope's right to call for a revolt and assured that the signatories would not obey this. The King's old friends from exile, Taaffe and Clancarty (now in London so not closely connected to opinion in their home community), eagerly led the signatories but it had no effect.

Religion, corporations, and republicans: a search for revenge by the Commons. Bad faith on their part – but unanticipated by the more conciliatory king?

Lord Chancellor Hyde (now Earl of Clarendon in the Coronation honours) asked the new House to confirm the intentions of the Declaration of Breda – i.e. religious toleration – and to look after the interests of peaceful non-Anglicans in a stirring opening speech to the House on 8 May 1661.[9] The ecclesiastical conference which had been promised now opened at the Savoy, and Charles issued an order banning the imprisonment of Quakers for refusing to take oaths. This led to a brief respite as prisoners arrested on this charge were let out of gaol, but it did not stop arrests of more Quakers later across nineteen counties. This time the authorities usually targeted them for secret and thus seditious meetings, feeding off the public fear of conspiracy after the January 1661 revolt, and the commanders of provincial garrisons (mostly now ex-royalist officers) joined JPs in rounding up suspects. Some were arrested on flimsy grounds that showed the hatred of the new authorities for them, with Lord Mayor Browne in London arresting Quakers who would not doff their hats to him. Indeed, the defensive self-righteousness of Quakers when they met men in authority often made matters worse. When their leadership got together a petition to the Lords and Commons arguing for toleration they cited the correctness of their beliefs, not their loyalty, as the main argument, and the emergence of a penal bill against them in the Commons led to a Quaker deputation to the Lords which only enraged the latter. Having met the deputation and not been impressed, the Lords proceeded to create their own committee to form a penal bill of ther own; indeed, Hyde/Clarendon proceeded to lead the (successful) efforts to push this through the House himself and declared that leniency only encouraged their behaviour. Lord Treasurer Southampton backed him, as did Secretary of State Nicholas in the Commons, so the Privy Council were hardly eager to support Quaker toleration. Using the argument that refusing to swear oaths (especially of allegiance to the king) implied treasonable intent, not a principled stand against such measures, the hardliners won out and it was voted to increase fines for each refusal and to transport those guilty of a third offence.[10] The act was most strictly enforced in Cheshire, Lancashire, and Westmoreland (all strongholds of the northern Quakers) plus Wiltshire, Somerset, Oxfordshire, Devon, and Worcestershire, i.e. mostly royalist-dominated counties from the Civil War, plus London. In the latter Browne and his lieutenants vigorously enforced the act and imprisoned over 200 Quakers in a few months; an epidemic in the insanitary prisons carried off large numbers of the accused who were left to rot. The king issued a proclamation in August 1662 releasing all in the capital who were not leaders, but his efforts were only patchily obeyed and determined authorities could easily round up Quakers on a variety of charges connected to sedition by bending the rules. Around eighty leading Quakers were convicted on the medieval charge of premunire, though most were given a chance to announce their obedience to lawful royal authority in the required manner before imprisonment, most did not serve the full length of their sentences, and only three had their property confiscated. The anti-Catholic recusancy laws for not attending church were also used, e.g. on 203 Quakers in Cheshire in 1662–5, though fines were usually lower than on Catholics and it was the obstructive who refused to pay (often seeking 'martyrdom') who were imprisoned. The prosecutions were cheered on by the government press, which openly despised the Quakers and other sectaries as a mixture of lunatics, rebels, and fools.

On another aspect of religious toleration, the number of hardline, fiercely Anglican royalists in the new House (and in the Lords) and the part that English Catholics had played in the royal cause during the Civil Wars encouraged efforts to achieve relief for them from the new penal laws, which Charles promised would be amended. A petition for amending the penal laws was duly made to the Lords (which contained twenty-four Catholics) by Sir Samuel Tuke, but there was no co-ordinated or quick action and their bill to modify the punishments for secular priests was talked out. It is probable that the bishops allied to Clarendon to block Catholic relief, and that the latter was determined to stop it as a result of distaste for its principal Lords promoter, his old 1640s foe the Earl of Bristol (George Digby).[11] Indeed, back in 1644–6 Digby had been reaching out to both Irish and Continental Catholics as potential providers of military aid to rescue the King's crumbling cause, to Hyde's horror – his enthusiasm for Catholics thus revived the latter's old grudges. Wartime feuds thus trumped the possibility of a gracious gesture to the Catholic community for their support of the late King in the 1640s, though some hardline Anglican MPs could have been expected to cause trouble over any gesture to Papists so it would have been politically risky and might have led to MPs trying to block the king's funds to force him to give way. Charles, personally in favour of it, as usual did not take sides in a dispute among his feuding courtiers or risk any political credit by coming down firmly on one side. The Catholics had to be content with the de facto suspension of aggressive administration of the penal laws, which was due to greater laxity by sympathetic pro-royalist JPs impressed by their service to the king in the past decades; some JPs were not so much sympathetic to them as too busy arresting Quakers to bother with Catholics.

Restoring royalists to office in local corporations had been resisted in places with a strong and cohesive pro-Commonwealth group in control, or had led to new inter-factional and personal disputes. Once the spring 1661 elections were over the government used the legal excuse that many boroughs had received new charters since 1649 – now dubiously legal – to recall some under quo warranto writs. One of the most notable victims, Bristol corporation, had been refusing to restore royalist members, and managed to avoid a new charter by paying a large sum and agreeing to remove contentious members – evidently two of the main purposes in the action, apart from deliberate intimidation.[12] It was suggested that the king should have the right to name the first incumbents of each major corporate office when a new charter was issued, if not the entire corporation, and that the corporation alone should have the right to vote in Palriamentary elections in any new charters issued by him.[13] In June Palriament went further in proposing that they should provide a body of commissioners to carry out each corporate purge. Given the numerical advantages royalists possessed in the Commons, this would give their local figures – often landed gentry excluded from influence in the corporation by ex-Parliamentarian urban merchants – licence to take over the corporation. They could then nominate the boroughs' MPs as well. Prynne made a fruitless attempt to rally opposition in the Lords and in print, to be roundly rebuked by the Commons majority and effectively intimidated into silence for the future. The king endeavoured to resist the measure, which would limit his own ability to nominate to local office, but the Commons remained stubborn, rejected his compromise, and sat it out as he delayed agreement. The deadlock continued into the second session of Parliament but then, needing their goodwill over finance, he was forced to accept a compromise – they would get their commissioners but he would name them. The men he selected to remodel the corporations were the Anglican royalists who the Commons found acceptable; any others would have been vetoed.[14] The resultant purge varied from region to region, with only a few corporation members being removed in some cases and the majority in others; all members had to swear allegiance to the king and denounce the Covenant and the principle of resistance to the sovereign, but after this they could still be removed at the commissioners' discretion and often were. There is however no clear co-relation between the former pro-Parliamentarian towns or regions and the greatest number of removed members, and most boroughs who were now drastically purged had been as loudly welcoming towards Charles in 1660 as those who were not. The criteria for exclusion were not systematic, and local feuds or commissioners' greed to secure seats for their friends were probably as important as ideology or religion.[15] Once again, a degree of devolution to local elites was a noticeable feature of the Restoration settlement, in contrast to Cromwellian centralisation – probably a necessity given how unpopular intrusive central government committees and orders had been across many counties since Parliament set up its war-managing administration in 1642–3.

Making public examples of the king's enemies: legal chicanery, 'hits', and a manhunt.

Charles had reminded Parliament of the importance of the Act of Indemnity and Oblivion as it opened, but the Act had now to be confirmed to satisfy the legal objection that acts by a Convention – not called by a king – were not legal. The royalist 'hardliners' endeavoured to hold the confirmation up, and deadlock resulted for six weeks as they sought to add new categories to the list of people to be excluded from pardon. As with the Corporation Act, this went against the spirit and the word of the 1660 settlement. The king did his best to stand up for the principle of pardon and halt the bad faith, and the bill to confirm the earlier act received less amendment in the Lords. It was voted to exclude from pardon all regicide judges who had not signed the late King's death-warrant, the regicides who had surrendered in 1660 and been pardoned then, and the two most

The 'Cavalier Parliament' 189

dangerous republicans – Lambert and Vane. The latter cases were the most dubious in legal terms. They were blatant political prosecution of people who had not been involved in regicide, and in Vane's case who had opposed it and steered clear of working with Cromwell. But it was their actions in resisting the king's return in 1659–60 that mattered, though only Lambert had done so by armed force (twice). The regicide judges were stripped of their property and imprisoned for life, with an annual parade to remind the public of their crimes; the surrendered regicides were however saved from further punishment on Charles' personal appeal to Clarendon (who himself seems to have preferred more executions). The bill for their execution passed the Commons but Clarendon as Lord Chancellor saw that the Lords sat on it.[16] As Charles had promised the victims mercy in 1660, this was an example of him acting on principle for his enemies' benefit. Lambert, who was a potential military threat and a target for rescue by old army comrades, was sentenced to death but reprieved; he was then kept in prison well away from populated areas and the danger of rescue, first on the Channel Islands and later in the middle of Plymouth Sound. The use of isolated islands, where visitors could be monitored easily and the culprit could not receive messages or smuggle out information as in an English prison, had been pioneered by Cromwell for political nuisances such as Lilburne (and, ironically, Vane). Lambert was kept in custody even when his health declined, Charles ignoring all requests for clemency, and died at Plymouth in 1682. Also imprisoned for life in Plymouth Sound was Robert Lilburne, who had been both a regicide and a senior military commander who had tried to stop Monck invading England in December 1659 so he was doubly suspect.

Similar imprisonment in a remote area kept arch-republican Henry Marten away from the public eye after his condemnation in October 1660, at Chepstow Castle. The distance from London was also a useful hindrance to him should he have attempted to smuggle out anti-monarchical writings or contact other enemies of the Stuarts. Vane, who had refused to leave the country and been pardoned in 1660, had had the chance to slip away from his isolated mansion on the edge of Hampstead Heath and flee abroad since then but had not taken it. This might imply that he intended to become involved in plots – or so his enemies could tell the government. Like Marten, he was an ideological republican – and a sectary too. He was duly prosecuted for treason for his actions before the

Restoration on dubious grounds, as at that point Charles II had not been recognised as king by Parliament. He was supposed to be covered by a petition of both Lords and Commons to the king on 5 September 1660 to sentence him to death but not execute him, which Charles graciously granted. (The same petition and grant had applied to Lambert.) The new Commons in 1661, however, returned to the case and voted to try Vane. He was not tried for many months but was left imprisoned in legal limbo on the Scilly Isles – which may suggest that Charles initially hoped to avoid giving him a public platform to defend republicanism. He was then brought to London, and defended himself articulately without expressing contrition for his 'sins', unlike Lambert, although the prosecution ingeniously used the argument that he had waged war on the *de jure* King in 1659–60 as the latter's reign had commenced with his father's execution on 30 January 1649. He retorted that he had only been obeying the legal authority of Parliament, which had been the supreme body in the land until May 1660. Vane was technically in the right, but this act of principled devotion to the authority of Parliament only confirmed his dangerousness to the king whose lawyers had been praising 'Divine Right' at the regicide trials as if it was still the 1630s. Possibly if he had thrown himself on the King's mercy he would have had a better reception; Charles was especially harsh on principled defenders of the republican political system's legality. The cynical King probably preferred men who could be bought or blackmailed to those with inconvenient consciences who could be loose cannons. Vane was sentenced to death, on dubious legal grounds and at the king's personal request, after the jury had been deprived of food and drink so they would come to the correct verdict. Charles was said to have told Clarendon that Vane was too dangerous to let live.[17] He was executed on the anniversary of Naseby, probably as a pointed comment on the fate of rebels, and musicians were employed to drown out his speech at the scaffold to avoid him impressing the spectators as the equally unrepentant Harrison had done in 1660. The most that can be said is that he was beheaded not hung, as appropriate for the well-born son of a former secretary of state – and his 'harmless' younger brothers, one a former royalist officer, continued in Royal military service.

Vane's execution remains a blot on Charles' reputation and on those of his ex-colleagues (rivals as of 1659–60) who failed to impress on the king the need to show mercy – though in a sense this judicial murder was revenge for that of Strafford, as Argyll's was for the killing of Montrose. The government even went to the lengths of arranging for its ambassador in the United Provinces, George Downing (lately Cromwell's ambassador), to have three refugee regicides – most notably Colonel Okey, to whose regiment Downing had been chaplain in the 1640s – kidnapped and brought home for execution in March 1663. The Dutch chief executive, Grand Pensionary Jan De Witt, was persuaded to go along with the plan, and Downing lured the trio to Delft from Frankfurt and Amsterdam to examine a 'business opportunity' offered by merchant Abraham Kicke with promises that they need fear nothing from him. Kicke was in Downing's pay, and not only informed him when they arrived but when they came to his house for a meeting got them to put their guns and coats in a side-room which he then locked. A previous attempt to seize a fugitive regicide in the United Provinces, court clerk Edward Dendy, had seen a delay while the arrest party sought a warrant for his extradition, giving his Dutch friends time to apply successfully for his release and smuggle him away to safety. This time nothing was left to chance, and as soon as Kicke reported that the regicides had arrived at his house Downing acquired a warrant from De Witt and rushed it to Delft. An English ship, one of the new Dutch-designed 'yachts', moored secretly offshore, and the visitors were seized drinking in their room late at night by Downing and his men and incarcerated in the town prison. A sympathetic crowd gathered next day, but Downing arranged for one of his allies to be the local lawyer who the regicides asked for help from and the latter's appeal for release duly failed. They were handed over quickly to Downing's 'posse' to be rowed out to the ship and taken home where a court speedily sat to sentence them; on 17 April 1662 they were executed.[18] Another of this trio was the brutal and unpopular John Barkstead, the unscrupulous Cromwellian Lieutenant of the Tower of London; the third was Miles Corbet, aged civilian republican commissioner in Ireland (with John Jones) in the 1650s. Corbet was no conceivable threat to the new regime, unlike the other two, and had signed the late king's death-warrant last so he was not exactly keen to do it. Another civilian republican regicide exile, John Lisle (ex-Commissioner of the Great Seal and from a prominent Isle of Wight gentry family), was shot by a royalist assassin in Switzerland in 1664 in a 'hit' worthy of the Cold War KGB. He was one of the group of regicides and other exiles living at Vevey on Lake Geneva, across the lake from the Duchy of Savoy (a close ally of France), led by Edmund Ludlow, and earlier a group of Irish royalists headed by a former soldier in the Duke of York's regiment, Germain or John Riordane, had been spotted lurking in the town in an apparent bid to kill or kidnap Ludlow. The latter had been warned and stayed indoors and the attackers left, but ironically the nervous Lisle had decided to move to Lausanne to be safer and was tracked there. He was duly taken by surprise by a gunman on his way to church at Lausanne and shot down at the church door, and the escaping assassin shouted out his reasons so that the message would spread of what regicides could expect.[19] It is unclear if this was a local killing by an embittered royalist with a grudge against all regicides or ordered by the regime to remove a political threat; probably the murderer was one of Riordain's gang, possibly Miles o'Croli, and Riordain was certainly in touch with Secretary of State Bennet/Arlington reporting on the regicides' movements. Either Bennet or his chief of intelligence, Joseph Williamson, probably ordered the hit but made sure that there was no trail of written evidence.[20] The political point was that it was clear to all what would happen to regicides and how long the king's reach was, thus terrorising opposition. Among other feared exiles who in 1664–7 were potential allies for England's Dutch enemies, Ludlow had to keep a low profile and remained on his guard but survived, returning to England in 1689; the resourceful Goffe and Whalley were pursued to the 'godly' colony of New Haven in North America with the correct reckoning that the majority of residents would not assist their royalist pursuers. As royal commissioners landed and presented the authorities with their orders to assist a search, the pair went into hiding in the forests until their pursuers gave up. They duly entered legend, with Goffe as the aged 'Angel of Hadley' who appeared at an embattled colonial village in 1680 to successfully lead their defence against a Native American attack.[21]

The extent of the government's search for regicides may seem excessive in retrospect, but the atmosphere of plots in the 1660s shows that even scattered exiles could be plausibly suggested as potential conspirators. Most rumours of conspiracy were not fulfilled, but that does not mean they were invented by a Machiavellian government as an excuse for repression and spiteful targeting of old enemies. The government was, however, certainly aware of the importance of maintaining a tight grip on printed propaganda, using the former 1640s propagandist editor of

Mercurius Aulicus, John Birkenhead, to edit its official newsletter *Mercrius Publicus* and controlling all news books through Monck's clients Henry Muddiman and Giles Dury. The assorted panics that swept England were politically useful in that they stimulated loyalty to the king and fears of 'another '41' (ie the crises and near-anarchy of 1641), forcing moderate royalists who doubted current policies – and anyone nostalgic for Cromwell during the foreign policy humiliations of the Second Dutch War – to rally to the king. and silencing ex-Commonwealthsmen through guilt by association. The febrile atmosphere of frenzied rumour was nothing new, as it had been an important element of political crisis at the time of the Irish revolt in 1641; but now it applied to extreme Protestant/republican conspiracy as well as to the usual Catholic 'threat'. In practical terms Charles lacked a nationwide army ready to put down risings by disgruntled New Model veterans, making his government more vulnerable than the equally ruthless Cromwell and Thurloe had been in the 1650s. Giving an impression of strength and ruthlessness was important, as the king only had a small number of Guards regiments to call on against a revolt. 'Decentralization' to the localities and avoidance of high taxes, both demanded by Parliament, had their drawbacks.

There was an element of cynicism in the selection of victims in 1660–2, as all were currently marginalised and lacking political support; and Charles did succeed in limiting the execution of surrendered regicides. Thurloe had also kidnapped people and made examples – and had used the same man, Downing, as an instrument of harassment against exiles in Holland. The royalist exiles on the Continent had been murdering republicans who came within their grip as early as Isaac Dorislaus, already targeted for 'extra-judicial execution' for treason in 1649 for his part in regicide. They had also shot one Cromwellian double agent, Manning. But there were undoubted examples of legal harassment of 1650s civil offcials who were no threat, most notably ex-sequestration commissioners, who had to face local lawsuits which the government had not initiated but did not halt either. There was no concerted government attempt to see that amnesty was enforced, which was to set a bad precedent for the even more blatant actions of judicial hard men like Jeffreys in the 1680s. In harsh terms of morality, the ultimate failure to act lay with the cynical, pragmatic and amoral king – as in the example that he set of tolerating hooliganism by courtiers such as Thomas Thynne and Sir Charles Sedley.

Breach of faith on religious 'inclusion'? The so-called 'Clarendon Code'

The issue of the religious settlement in England was the most important area of contention in 1661, affecting the most people, and was the most hotly contested on both sides. As with political revenge and intimidation, the atmosphere in which events took place changed from 1660 into 1661–2, with evidence of official sanction for a harder line and breaches of faith encouraging Anglican triumphalism. However, Parliament, dominated by Royalists, could not be halted from burning the Covenant or reviewing the legality of pardons for its enemies, and Charles and Clarendon both opened the Cavalier Parliament with calls for moderation. The Quakers were possibly emboldened by Charles' orders to release prisoners and ban on prosecutions for refusing to swear oaths, as they made a public appeal to Parliament for justice which emphasised their moral righteousness rather than begging for generosity. The Commons formed a bill to punish all who refused to swear oaths, thus defying the king, and the Quakers' appeal to the Lords for help saw an unfortunately hostile encounter between the two parties in which the Quakers were mainly to blame. The Lords angrily considered their own legislation against Quakers after this, and were stiffened by an uncompromising approach by Clarendon.

Those who favoured moderation despite the seemingly haughty conduct of the 'fanatics', led by Bishop Gauden, were in the minority; the Baptists' more politic subservient appeal to the Commons failed too and the legislation that resulted punished all who refused the Oath of Allegiance and Supremacy or attended illegal meetings. Third offenders were to be transported, though this means of driving 'seditious' irreconcilables out of the country was only a religious equivalent of the Commonwealth's transportation of royalist prisoners (mostly Scots not Englishmen) to the Caribbean.[22] The implementation of it depended on the leniency of local JPs, though these were encouraged to be harsh by local anti-Quaker magnates like Clarendon in Oxford, and it was only one part of a widespread judicial harassment in which existing as well as new statutes were used (including the recusancy acts). Some juries and fellow-magistrates frustrated attempts to pass the harshest sentences, nobody was actually transported, and many accused were left in prison for a limited period and then released.[23] Crucially, the refusal of ministers and MPs alike to reconstitute the unpopular Court of High Commission meant that prosecution was a secular matter, not involving the church as in the 1630s. As in so much else, the Restoration was a triumph of local autonomy and the provincial elites and an end to the centralization of the 1640s and 1650s – which argues that no Royal initiatives for forced toleration and comprehension could have been implemented anyway.

In the church itself, the year or two after the Restoration saw local parishes resuming use of the pre-1642 Prayer Book without any official requirement to do so – indicating that grass-roots opinion among congregations was broadly orthodox Anglican. Presbyterian 'classes' mostly dissolved spontaneously, indicating local acceptance of the prospect of some Episcopal authority in any widened post-Savoy Conference Church. The Anglican hierarchy and its disciplinary mechanism (archdiaconal visitations and church courts) reconstituted itself in 1660–1 without waiting for Parliamentary sanction, which came in July 1661.[24] Some bishops ordained assisted by presbyters, led by ex-Cromwellian 'contact' John Gauden (chaplain to the king from summer 1660 and Bishop of Exeter from December) who had formerly been chaplain to and occupying a parish in the gift of the Calvinist/Parliamentarian leader Warwick in the 1640s, had preached before the Long Parliament and served briefly in the Presbyterian-led Westminster Assembly of Divines, and in 1656 had been engaged in the abortive Anglican/Presbyterian religious reconciliation talks arranged by Archbishop Ussher. Despite never abandoning bishops' rights in 1642–60 and leading a petition to Cromwell on behalf of impoverished Anglican ex-clergymen in 1655, Gauden had been readier than most of his faith to compromise in the interests of a united church, and was probably regarded by men like Sheldon with suspicion due to this; nor had his literary effusions condemning regicide been published until Cromwell was safely dead.[25] Hardliners did not admit presbyters to their church organizations, however, and it was not Gauden but Sheldon who had influence at court. The 1661 Parliament, more strongly Anglican than its precedessor, began with arranging for disciplinary measures against clergymen who failed to use the Prayer Book, while sympathetic Anglican clerical pamphleteers launched an effective smear campaign against the Presbyterians to counter-act their claims to have played a major role in the Restoration; leaders like Baxter had their past involvement with the New Model Army dragged up to portray them as rebels. The new licensing laws limited their ability to reply, as the JPs who would deal with such cases were likely to be Anglican royalists and not look favourably on complaints by real or imagined enemies. The king, far from backing or vainly opposing this propaganda campaign, did not bother to read official journals.[26]

Convocation met in May 1661, with Sheldon rigging the elections for it in the diocese of London to exclude Presbyterians; it resulted in a large hardline Anglican majority and added to Parliamentary belligerence. Charles gave them the job of revising the Prayer Book, which emerged largely unaltered from that of 1559 and then only to include some controversial ceremonies promoted by Laud in the 1630s; it was thus unacceptable to the Presbyterians. The Privy Council approved it (24 February 1662) and passed it on to the Lords, to be incorporated in the new Act of Uniformity based on the Commons' extant bill requiring full use of the Prayer Book on pain of expulsion from church office.[27] The result was not solely a question of a lack of leadership from the church hierarchy – under an elderly and ineffective Archbishop of Canterbury hardened by his sufferings and his grimly determined assistant Sheldon – or from a lackadaisical king. Even if a Laudian, Bishop Sanderson, had not been in charge of the Convocation revisions, due to careful arrangements made by Archbishop or King, plus a greater number of Presbyterian bishops, any moderate appointed by a more pro-Presbyterian Archbishop of Canterbury (most obviously Gauden?) would have been outvoted. The entire senior leadership of the Presbyterian churches would have had to enter the Church of England in 1660–1 (unlikely given its extant liturgy) to affect the voting, and even then Lords and Commons would have objected to any Prayer Book revisions that betrayed Anglicanism. As votes could not be won in Convocation or Parliament for toleration, the King – via Clarendon – now proposed that he be given the right to exempt individual clergy from the consequences of the Act of Uniformity. This would enable him to safeguard Presbyterian clerics from prosecution, and Clarendon lined up assorted Privy Councillors and moderate bishops to back a clause to this effect in the Lords. Sheldon and a majority of the bishops did not back this despite royal wishes.[28] The Commons refused to co-operate, and on 19 May passed the Act of Uniformity providing for the expulsion of all ministers who by 24 August (St. Bartholomew's Day, the anniversary of the notorious massacre of Protesatnts in 1572) did not swear to the Prayer Book and denounce the Covenant and the principle of resistance to the sovereign. As a result, at least 961 clergy out of around 9,000 in England were dismissed; the proportion was substantial in areas of high Puritan and 1640s Parliamentarian concentration such as London over a third), Sussex (a quarter), and Essex (a fifth).[29] The Act was duly followed by the first round of episcopal visitations since the Restoration, to ensure that local parishes were carrying out instructions and operating in an appropriate Anglican manner.

Charles promised in a royal declaration of December 1662 (sometimes referred to as the First Declaration of Indulence) that the Act would be amended later, or at least that extensive exceptions would be made for individuals who were not seen as dangerously seditious so that its effects would be limited. His main encouragers in this were apparently Sir Henry Bennet and two west country ex-Cromwellians, Sir Anthony Ashley Cooper (Dorset) and Lord Robartes (Cornwall). The main effort for this would presumably be done by government action in the next (spring 1663) session of Parliament, and if legislation could not secure a majority in the Commons individuals would be excepted from the current act by special royal licence – i.e. the king's 'dispensing' power. This was a sign of Charles' determination to mitigate the effects of the expulsions, but the threat of using royal prerogative power to do this was a gift to those MPs who feared the latter from the 1640s and so these were added to the hardline Anglicans in opposing this. The argument was duly used that the dispensing power was as bad as Ship-Money in 1637–40 as an affront to Parliament, and when Lord Robartes put forward a bill to back the power in spring 1663 it was blocked by a majority of MPs backed by Hyde (who had been opposed to Charles I's prerogative powers in Parliament in 1640–1 too, so his attitude was consistent). In any case, Sheldon led the bishops in the Lords in refusing to back the legislation or to support the royal dispensing power. The latter were thus to blame for sabotaging the royal plan, though in any case a large number of individual exemptions would no doubt have been reported to and denounced in the Commons; had the Presbyterians accepted bishoprics in 1660–1 Sheldon could have been stopped from initiating hardline legislation if the king had backed a faction of more moderate bishops led by Gauden but it would have led to trouble with the Commons. The attempt was likely to be blocked by a majority of the Commons even if the bishops had been neutralised, using fear of royal prerogative powers. (Usefully around 100 MPs had sat in the Long Parliament in the 1640s and so could remember the attack on Charles I's prerogative powers then, which even some royalists had supported.) But it is clear that Charles was only interested in relief for peaceable and loyal religious minorities who accepted the Restoration in full, not in tolerating a broad spectrum of beliefs. His instructions to the clergy of 14 October 1662 required them to avoid touching on such matters as royal powers and the contentious doctrines of grace and free will in their sermons, so as not to encourage controversy or dissension; the church was to breed obedience, not debate. In terms of religious plurality he was determined to 'put the genie back in the bottle' and suppress all challenges to royal authority, and significantly the new Licensing Act (where all printers were to be approved by the archbishop of Canterbury and the bishop of London) only licensed around twenty printers in 1661–2 instead of the previous sixty or so who had been active. Illegal printers were hunted down and put in prison or driven abroad, e.g. the 1650s activist Giles Calvert who had committed the sin of publishing an approving book on the Scottish Covenant of 1637 in 1661, and the same went for people who published the royal horoscope and so might be suspected of hoping for a new government (e.g. John Hydon).

1663–4: a propaganda coup for the enemies of the sects. Using the northern rebellion as an excuse for persecution.

The removal of the allegedly dangerous and pro-sectary part of the clergy was arguably an understandable reaction by the Commons to the perceived, if exaggerated, security threat from ex-Commonwealth enthusiasts. Such exaggerated fears of the subversive intentions of religious minorities were normal for the era and the unprecedented level of localised military garrisons and their financial demands between Parliament's victory in 1646 and the Restoration made all of England and Wales aware of what subversion by the king's enemies could lead to. This was shown by the provincial anti-army groundswell of opinion among the public as well as the gentry elite into which the king's allies had tapped in 1660–1. These leaders of militant royalism and the opponents of 'fanatic' clergy (including Anglicans removed from their position of privilege in local society and jobs by the 1646–60 Commons and Army plus those less ideologically committed but in fear of disorder) now dominated the Commons. The Lords, often forgotten in the narrative of these years, was full of a mixture of royalist peers ruined by 'compounding' (i.e. paying fines for their 'malignancy' to the Interregnum regimes) or their heirs, plus a bloc of Anglican bishops, so it could not act to veto the excesses of the Commons. Charles II had men who had risked their lives or gone in to exile for him to reward with peerages (cheaper than finding them non-existent or small in number offices), and these new peers would probably be Anglican too. By contrast, few of the pro-toleration occupants of the Cromwellian Upper House had managed to survive into the restored House of Lords – and in the crucial weeks of spring 1660 before Charles returned, the Restoration settlement had failed to 'write in' requirements to keep senior non-Anglicans who had backed Cromwell in the Second House. As shown by the nature of the 1659 constitutional debates, the idea of such a 'Senate' of senior regime allies had been active in that period. The lack of putting a bloc of non-Anglicans from the 1659–60 anti-army moderates group in the new Lords was arguably a serious failure of imagination by the Presbyterian leadership (e.g. Manchester, Annesley, and Coote) at a point when they still had the ability to bargain with the king. It would have involved reviving the idea of a royalist/Presbyterian settlement as seen in the abortive November 1648 talks with Charles I at Newport. But Monck had not bothered to back any stand, the king was against it and had suffered political humiliation at the hands of a Presbyterian oligarchy in Scotland in 1650–1, and even if the king had had to accept such details in 1660 the new Parliament of 1661 could well have cancelled it.

The Commons now returned to the attack against the 'fanatic threat' in 1663 with a bill to ban illegal meetings, 'conventicles', by Protestant ministers (ejected or not) who were not in the current church. Illegal meetings were already potentially bannable under an Elizabethan statute, and laws against riotous assembly could be interpreted in an elastic manner to indict such gatherings – but both were open to challenge by moderate JPs or by obstinate juries. The bill passed the Commons but was stopped in the Lords; unfortunately its defeat was followed by another Nonconformist plot scare involving sectaries which this time proved real. Already there was serious disillusionment with the government on the part of some ex-Parliamentarians and Presbyterians, notably Prynne, apart from the more inevitable harassed ex-army personnel and sectaries. If Prynne and his allies had hoped that their zeal for hunting down regicides would persuade the king and the majority of MPs that the Presbyterians were loyal to the new regime they were disappointed – though the question has to be raised of why Hyde and other privy councillors failed to exercise any control or leadership over the frequently hot-headed back-benchers by a judicious mixture of job-offers and threats. Now autumn 1663 saw a plan for armed revolt by groups of middle-ranking former 1650s military and civil office-holders across the North, and armed musters on a co-ordinated date in the north and West Ridings and Westmorland. No strongpoints were seized or blood shed, and the hapless rebels were soon dispersed by the militia; but the most implacable local royalist and Anglican JPs had the excuse they needed for draconian arrests, principally targeting Quakers who were made the scapegoats. Given the concentration of the latter in the affected area, e.g. George Fox and Margaret Fell's group in Furness in Cumbria, the revolt was obviously used by hostile local Anglican JPs as an excuse to destroy them. An example was made of those rebels captured by systematic terror – a smaller-scale anticipation of the Judge Jeffreys campaign in 1685? – with 26 out of 44 participants who were caught 'in flagrante' condemned and 24 of them executed.[30] But the wave of several hundreds of arrests of people suspected of rebel sympathies without any decisive proof was equally significant, and the government did not bother to intercede either for hundreds of gaoled Quakers (unlike in 1661) or for 'targeted' republican suspects. One pardoned regicide, Colonel Hutchinson, was left to die in an insanitary prison. Trials of sectaries took place over twenty-three counties, and the arrests of targeted Quaker suspects were particularly severe in the towns of Bristol, Reading and Colchester where their foes had recently been elected as mayors. Although the mass-arrests were as bad (and as exaggerated in their fears of supposed plots) as in 1660–1 the king did not respond to Quaker appeals this time;[31] nor did he bother to receive any Quaker delegations. His callous reaction foreshadowed that which he showed to similar local harassment in the 1680s and shows that his ruthlessness did not originate from the 'Exclusion Crisis'. Anyone perceived a political threat was excluded from his alleged generosity, even in 1663–4 – and the inclusion of the Quakers in his targets shows that it was not only serious potential threats like Vane and Lambert who were regarded as suitable for punishment. Due to the financial stringency enforced by the Commons in the 1660–1 settlements there was not a large army ready to put down revolt either, so a reign of terror had practical uses in scaring off potential rebels. In the wake of the revolt, the official press (led by the paranoid and conspiracy-seeking L'Estrange in the manner of a modern tabloid editor) resumed a vigorous campaign against the 'seditious' Nonconformists, lumping them all together as a traitorous menace, and in 1664 the Conventicle Bill passed both Houses on its second outing. This time the penalties – large fines for the first two convictions, imprisonment for those too poor to pay, and transportation for the third offence – were extended to JPs who failed to prosecute reported cases.[32] The fact that the Triennial Act requiring a new Parliament after every three years a rare relic of the legal restrictions on royal power in 1641, was now repealed at Charles' specific request (in his opening speech to the new session of Parliament) was a sign that it was seen as an opportune time to do this as any attempt to oppose this could be interpreted by Royal hardliners as sympathy for traitors.[33] In the manner of the US after 9/11, the government could use the opportunity to push through contentious legislation in a national mood of panicked patriotism.

Notably, only around an eighth of the ejected clergy became illegal preachers and around thirty-five became Nonconformist clergy; despite the latest rumours of immanent rebellion as immediate retaliation for the ejections in August 1662, nothing resulted. The victims showed little sign of determination to carry on their ministry or evade authority, let alone revolt; this shows that any conception of them by Parliament as a threat was inaccurate. Their ejection was a matter of principle (and Anglican triumphalism) rather than security, and on this occasion – as with the Quakers – Charles was in favour of more leniency than his MPs were, and did all possible to halt the evictions.

National politics after 1662 – a sense of drift and disappointment. Inevitable, or a sign of dangerous royal weakness of purpose?

As shown above, the Restoration government was constrained by its weak powers compared to those of the 1650s. The king, unlike his predecessors, could not enforce his wishes on matters like the religious settlement and went along with, rather than initiated, the unexpected revision of the 1660 indemnity by the new Parliament. He lacked the centralising control of the Protectorate, against which there had been an unstoppable provincial reaction in 1659–60, and had come to power as the candidate for stability of a nervous Parliament fearing above all else the army and instability. The army had been (mostly) neutered by Monck and was paid off in late 1660, and the government had now to rely on a local militia controlled by the provincial elites – with Parliament refusing to pay for or maintain it for more than a short period. A larger than intended central force, the royal Guards regiments, had been kept in London to ensure order and act as a nucleus for a national force in any emergency, following Venner's Rising. Apart from the commander-in-chief, Monck, most senior figures were ex-royalists – but in any case the army was too small and too badly funded to act as a deterrent to invasion by exiles and/or hostile states like the New Model had done. Even Monck's two private regiments which had been the nucleus of his army at Coldstream in January 1660 (the origin of the Coldstream Guards) were nearly disbanded in 1661. It was the Duke of York, not the king, who insisted on keeping them – as it was York who was to re-expand the army in the 1680s. Unlike Charles, he was active in what we would now call 'armed forces administration' (as a hands-on Lord Admiral commanding the Navy) and he had served as an officer in the royalist regiments fighting for Spain against France in the Spanish Netherlands campaign of 1658. In later years, he was to move towards admiration and emulation of the ruthless central government 'machine' plus large armed forces of his cousin Louis XIV's France – and towards militant Catholicism. The small size of the Army and its absence from the provinces helps to explain the government's aggressive policy towards potential sedition and extradition or murder of dangerous exiles, which made England seem stronger than it was in reality and deterred serious conspiracy or foreign aid to exiles.

Luckily, unlike in the 1650s there was no obvious foreign ally for potential rebels as the Franco-Spanish peace of 1659 had led to an end of the long-running rivalry of the two principal Western European powers for an English alliance. The two great Catholic powers were now in uneasy alliance with the ageing Philip IV's daughter Maria Theresa married off to her cousin Louis XIV – though this would lead to trouble in the long run when Philip's chronically sick son and successor Charles

II died leaving her and Louis' descendants as heirs to Spain (1700). Spain was now financially exhausted and in decline under Philip IV and still had not accepted the independence of Portugal (which had revolted in 1640), and France was the 'ally of choice' for the half-Bourbon Charles of England. His Bourbon mother Henrietta Maria still resided in France part-time and was to end up dying there in 1669, and she now proceeded to arrange the marriage of her youngest daughter Henriette Anne ('Minette'), born in Exeter during the Civil War in 1644, to Louis' bisexual brother Philippe to consolidate the alliance. The Dutch 'United Provinces', England's major commercial rival and a republic so more likely to be hostile, were less amenable to or approved by Charles, not least as now his eldest sister Mary, widow of their late 'Stadtholder' William II (d. 1650), had died in a smallpox epidemic late in 1660 and their son William was being kept from power by the mercantile oligarchy centred in Amsterdam. The head of the Dutch executive, Grand Pensionary Jan de Witt, had come to power as the enemy of William's Orange dynasty in 1652 and had stood aloof from any aid to the Stuarts pre-1660. Nor were the Amsterdam mercantile companies on good terms with their London equivalents due to commercial rivalry, the latter centred on the blatant Dutch elbowing all rivals (the English in particular) out of the East Indies since the 1620s. Cromwell and his City of London allies had suspected the Dutch of egging on Spain during its war with England in 1655–9, inciting the Danes against their ally Charles X of Sweden, and wanting to destroy the English ally Portugal (which the Dutch were fighting in Brazil).

Now Charles II's government had taken up the Commonwealth's alliance with Portugal – which negated the hopes of Philip IV, who had been Charles' host and military ally in exile from 1656 but had failed to provide adequate funds for his court or troops and ships for an invasion. This past reminder of Spain's poverty warned Charles off accepting Philip's ambassador's lavish promises of money in a treaty of alliance in 1660–2, despite the latter's hopes, and Spain miscalculated by initially trying to have Jamaica returned (which ex-Cromwellian naval commanders like Monck and Mountague would not like). Philip obsessively wanted 'rebel' Portugal reconquered and now sought English military help for this, which Charles would not give and to which anti-Papist English soldiers would object. Nor could Spain afford to pay Privy

Council members handsomely for voicing their support for the alliance, unlike the Portuguese ambassador De Mello – who was backed up by the French as a way to embarrass their Spanish rivals. De Mello initially miscalculated too by insisting that Charles pay for any troops sent to assist Portugal against Spanish attempts to reconquer it, but Louis XIV now offered to pay them – and his ex-'regent' Mazarin, who had abandoned Charles in favour of Cromwell in 1655 so royalists disliked him, usefully died in late 1661. Under the Anglo-Portuguese treaty that transpired, Charles was to marry King Afonso VI's sister Catherine of Braganza in 1662 and to acquire a dowry of around £300,000 plus the 'entrepot' of Bombay in India and extensive commercial opportunities there. As well as acquiring Tangier as a useful commercial and naval base from Portugal in the marriage-treaty, English merchants were now expanding into West African trade via the new Royal African Company to cross swords with the Dutch. (The Duke of York was the Company's patron.) The English now claimed the sovereignty of all the West African coast from Morocco south to the Cape of Good Hope, and as early as January 1661 Sir Robert Holmes as the Company's local admiral used a voyage to the Gambia River to seize and occupy a Dutch commercial fortress there (St. Andreas). Attacking the overseas commercial possessions of a supposed ally was nothing new for either country involved and the Dutch had done far worse in the 'Spice Islands' in the 1620s, as at the famous 'Amboyna Massacre'of local English merchants which the Stuarts had ignored but for which Cromwell insisted on compensation in 1654. The London East India merchants endeavoured to insist that the abortive Anglo-Dutch commercial talks of winter 1660–1 included guarantees of safety for their current personnel and posts in the Far East plus reparations for past misdeeds (as Cromwell had secured in the 1654 Anglo-Dutch treaty), but the Dutch refused. This provided a useful excuse for them to rouse anti-Dutch feeling, and the Council did not countermand their 'narrative' of Dutch hostility – which could be interpreted as a defeat for those ministers (mostly ex-Cromwellians) who regarded Protestant solidarity as important. The London merchants investing in trade in Africa were clearly keen to establish a local monopoly in an area known for Dutch commercial penetration and nonchalant about its escalation, and in January 1664 Holmes returned to the attack on his next expedition and evicted the major Dutch trading-post at Goree by force. He also played up the malevolence of intruding Dutch trading-captains on the River Gambia, one of whom had exchanged cannonfire with an English fort and was accused of offering money to local chiefs to kill Englishmen. His exact instructions from his superiors in London were somewhat (deliberately?) evasive so the government could disown him if necessary, but Sir William Coventry among the Admiralty leadership appears to have backed him and so been prepared for the risk of war following from such continued provocations. The king was notoriously uninterested in the minutiae of Council business and may well not have known what exactly the Company was up to. But given his later enthusiasm for toppling the (republican) Dutch government in 1670–2 it should not be ruled out that he was not averse to a war rallying English patriotic feeling and removing the Amsterdam oligarchy – to his nephew William's benefit? The Dutch government was, however, cautious about initiating open war as commercial provocations in the form of clashes at sea escalated through 1663–4.

The English navy had been kept up, substantially smaller than in the 1650s (until re-expansion to face the Dutch in 1664–5) and divided between mutually hostile ex-Cromwellians, like admiral Sir William Penn and adminstrator Sir William Batten, and ex-royalists like Treasurer Sir George Carteret, Navy Commissioner Sir William Coventry, and naval commander Sir Robert Holmes. Indeed, while Penn had been leading Cromwell's unsuccessful 'godly' colonial attack on the 'evil empire' of Spain in Hispaniola in the Caribbean in 1655, ending up with Jamaica instead, Holmes had been an officer in Prince Rupert's anti-Commonwealth pirate squadron. Having sailed with Rupert in African waters in the early 1650s, Holmes now used his experiences there to command on behalf of the Royal Africa Company. The Lord Admiral was the Duke of York, an experienced and enthusiastic sailor, with 1660 supreme commander Edward Mountague, Earl of Sandwich (Pepys' cousin and patron), as his deputy. There is supposed to have been an influx of more politically reliable ex-Royalist captains, at least as complained of by their foes; only around thirty-eight of ninety-one new appointments at officer-level in 1661–4 had Cromwellian experience. Some senior commanders such as Admiral Goodson were not kept on, and a group of experienced Interregnum officers (including the 'turncoat' adventurer Whetstone) resorted to privateering careers in the West Indies based on Cromwell's conquest, Jamaica. This may have helped to kick-start the local 'Golden Age of Piracy' as more and more adventurers flocked to the area. The threat of mutiny by undetected or supposedly loyal ex-Cromwellians in the navy's officer corps and in the ranks was constant in the early 1660s, though only a few serious plots took place (e.g. Tonge's in 1662)[34] and none succeeded in attracting demonstrable naval support. As illustrated in Pepys' diaries, there were feuds between ex-royalists and ex-rebels and between the professional seamen promoted for merit, the 'tarpaulins', and civilian Court appointees. The Duke of York was supposed to rely mainly on Coventry, a veteran of his father's government, but also trusted Lawson. The Navy was led and administered by a body of highly competent and experienced officials, though despite this the long-running problems of inefficient and corrupt practices in the dockyards continued: the Pett dynasty kept their hereditary 'fiefdom' in Chatham as they had done since Charles I's time. Only its small size (affected by fears of revolt as much as by lack of money) weakened the Navy in 1661–5; more ships and men had to be commissioned as tension with the Dutch rose in 1664–5. It was not as formidable a weapon as Cromwell's Navy, but had a larger degree of continuity and striking ability than the minimal and heavily purged army.

Finance: an 'Achilles Heel' for an under-funded government? Badly-handled by a lax administration, or par for the era?

Quite apart from the collapse of central control and eclipse of the army, the Restoration exacerbated financial difficulties for the government in carrying out its duties. This was partly inevitable in a provincial reaction against the high and arbitrary taxation of the 1640s and 1650s, which the men now dominating Parliament did not wish to see continue. Keeping the government on a tight leash would ensure compliance with Parliament's wishes, not least with the religious settlement in mind (as seen in 1661–2) and over the prevention of a potentially dangerous and unpopular standing army. As with the succession of James I to Elizabeth in 1603, there was also the prospect of a monarch with a family and a large new court to sustain, though in the event one of Charles' two brothers (the Duke of Gloucester) soon died of smallpox in September 1660 and Queen Mother Henrietta Maria chose to spend most of her time at home in France. Her second post-Restoration visit to England, in summer 1662, also brought along the king's illegitimate son by the late Lucy Walter, James 'Crofts' – later to challenge his uncle James of York for the throne by armed rebellion in 1685. There were rumours later in Charles' reign that the king had been married secretly to Lucy, possibly in Holland in 1649, and his late sister Mary had referred to her in letters as Charles' wife (a joke?); the impoverished South Wales gentry member Lucy had not been a suitable marital partner for any royal by seventeenth-century social stndards but was dead so even if they had 'married' it did not affect the king's 1662 Portuguese marriage. The king's apparent attempts to find a legal precedent in Scots (not English) law for legitimizing a royal bastard suggests that the king was considering making his son his heir – at least if the Duke of York, who had no living children by his wife Anne Hyde yet, died. The boy, aged thirteen, was now engaged to the heiress of the (Scots) Duchy of Buccleuch and in 1663 became the (English) Duke of Monmouth. Restoring a monarchy also entailed financial outlay on suitable residences, though the Stuarts did not have the vast expense of all Henry VIII's and Elizabeth's residences and the Commonwealth had failed in its initial bold plan to sell off all the palaces. The two largest and most prestigious Stuart residences pre-1642, Whitehall Palace in Westminster and Hampton Court up the Thames (which had been kept up for Cromwell and been used by his court), had to be repaired and refurbished, and a new set of Crown Jewels had to be ordered for the coronation on 23 April 1661 (St. George's Day, a symbolic choice). Initial financial outlay on the jumbled warren of mainly Tudor buildings at Whitehall, the central London base for the regime so an obvious site for impressive building, was notably restrained. Only individual royal apartments, not entire blocks, were remodelled. Charles I's abortive plan to rebuild the palace around 1647, drawn up by John Webb (Inigo Jones' assistant as Surveyor of Works), was not revived; quite apart from the cost of demolition, clearing out a multitude of minor private owners would have led to lengthy lawsuits and pay-offs. Charles kept up the old Tudor Privy Lodgings behind the Banqueting House, inadequate though these were, and only gradually moved his personal residence to the new 'Volary Buildings' facing onto the Thames; major work had to wait until the 1680s. Some former royal residences, such as Prince Henry's birthplace Oatlands, had to be abandoned; the building-work undertaken at Greenwich by Surveyor Sir John Denham was the sole major project of the 1660s and was so slow the result was never inhabited. (Patronage for past services outweighed architectural merit in the choice of surveyor; Denham, a sequestrated Royalist poet, had carried Charles I's last letter to his successor in 1649 and was Hyde's protégé.) Other residences, like Richmond, were 'down-sized' to become what would nowadays be called 'grace-and-favour' residences for Royal relations and dependants or sold off to courtiers and royal mistresses. (Not all of these recipients took good care of their gifts; Barbara Villiers notoriously 'asset-stripped' and wrecked Nonsuch Palace in Surrey.) There were grants of nominal offices, pensions, and lands to a host of needy royalists and to those whose goodwill was needed for political reasons, headed by the Privy Council, Monck, and Mountague. The king's personal Bedchamber attendants' offices became a centre for the employment of promising young men from 'old' royalist families as a reward for their loyalty. The head of the Bedchamber, the 'Groom of the Stool', was the Earl of Bath (John Grenville).

Unfortunately for political purposes, there was no massive body of land handed over to the regicides – mostly men of modest means and ambitions – to be confiscated and used to pay off ruined royalists. Indeed, the political block on forcing the return of all royalist lands sold off in England and the lack of Parliamentary compensation given to 'deserving cases' crowding Whitehall in 1660 led the king to reimbursing some claimants out of his own lands. But when all this is considered, it is still true that post-1660 royal extravagance added to the dwindling financial prospects for the new government. A new tone of munificence and generosity at court was essential and a necessary prop of monarchy, but the sums the king spent on gambling was another matter. The amount of assets granted away to royal mistresses was another practical problem arising from Charles' generosity and fondness for buying off potential complainers, with Barbara Villiers the most notably demanding and acquisitive recipient. In future years, an additional problem was to be caused by the need to find appropriate landed endowments for the peerages created for the fecund king's collection of illegitimate sons – in which his generosity was more in keeping with the actions of his French grandfather Henri IV, another notorious roué, than with those of previous English kings. However praiseworthy his devotion to his 'family' was, it is notable that the rapacious and insistent

Barbara secured quicker rewards for her sons than the less financially adept Nell Gwyn did. Barbara's sons became Dukes of Grafton and Northumberland, and her daughters Countesses of Sussex and Lichfield. Nell was supposed to have threatened to drop her unprovided-for son out of a window unless Charles gave him a peerage, which may express a psychological truth about Charles needing prompting to provide as well for other children as for Barbara's brood. Standing outside the court with a more impartial approach to the king's generosity, the cynical and hard-headed adminstrator Pepys confirmed that the Navy was short of money even in 1661 due to the King wasting it on Court extravagance. But Pepys had grown up during the Civil War and Commonwealth and was not used to the norms of seventeenth-century Court life and the level of spending that was entailed by projecting a façade of invincible success by conspicuous consumption.

The financial needs of the Restoration were centred on paying off most of the army and twenty-five of its warships in summer-autumn 1660, and were met by a 'one-off' poll tax. Dismissed officers and all soldiers who took the oath of allegiance were granted full arrears of pay,[35] and the king added some money of his own. A graded poll tax was voted for by the Commons on 12 June 1660, with the amount to be paid differing according to social status as assessed by commissioners; this turned out to be more difficult to work out in London than in the counties. The City of London was prodded into granting the king an emergency loan ahead of the local poll-tax due to the time it would take to assess the latter, once it became clear that money was needed quickly to pay the still-employed soldiers of the army at their pre-Restoration rates.[36] The customs were revised in July 1660 to increase the duties on imported manufactures, and before the first Convention recess they set the government's annual revenues at £120,000 p.a. (the average revenue of Charles I's government plus an 8 per cent allowance for inflation). A lump sum was granted to tide the government over until the sources of permanent revenue were decided upon, and when the latter was considered after the recess landowners led opposition to continuing direct taxation (hugely unpopular since 1642/6). An excise on alcohol was preferred, not least for discouraging vice. This was duly approved in November (by two votes), and Hyde thought that it would be adequate;[37] however in the event the extra state outlay on paying off both Charles I and Charles II's debts in 1660–1 proved that this was not so. The Commons only proceeded slowly to resolve this during winter 1660–1 despite repeated official reminders, led within the House by the senior official Sir Philip Warwick, and debated a voluntary subscription – arranged through local commissioners appointed by them, not by royal officials – and the collection of past arrears of taxes. Neither achieved much revenue, and in November Charles made a personal appeal for more money; £126,000 was granted in an assessment, but no means provided for putting it into effect. The issue was still outstanding in March 1661, and a second Royal reminder led to the hasty expedient of a tax on the hearths in each house.[38] The Hearth Tax was meant to serve as a form of universal poll tax, with more tax paid by wealthier people, but as it was to be collected by self-assessment of the number of hearths involved there was massive latitude for cheating. This diminished the resistance in the House and it was agreed, but it was only a temporary expedient. It was however an improvement on past confrontations between crown and Parliament and represented a belated agreement by MPs to make an effort to meet royal requirements – without giving the king much leeway for extra spending in emergencies. This added to his restricted military and naval power in reducing his options for a successful international profile, which had been diminished by the failure of his marriage-treaty with Portugal to produce all the £300,000 dowry plus trade-opportunities worth over £1 million which he was supposed to receive.[39] The cession of Tangier and Bombay was no practical compensation for a serious financial shortfall in the money which he had expected to gain from his marriage. Portugal had been selected to provide a royal bride over its rival Spain – the king's former host and ally in exile in 1656–9 – as it was supposedly a more remunerative ally and Spain had a poor record for fulfilling financial pledges. Clarendon and other court enemies of Spain's principal promoter in the debates over alliance in 1660–1, Bristol, had their own reasons for backing Portugal to discomfit him, though this does not make their arguments about financially declining Spain being a poor ally less valid. Indirectly, the choice of the Portuguese princess Catherine of Braganza as a wife was also a major political disaster as she turned out to be infertile and so the religion of Charles' next brother and heir, James, became a major issue as he turned Catholic in the early 1670s.

The financial failings of the over-generous and spendthrift king were an issue as early as 1663, with disgruntled MPs able to cite evidence of waste and corruption at court and in the administration. Certainly Charles II lacked the carefulness of his father, who had drawn up all sorts of rules to run the Court and enforce seemly behaviour as soon as he became king in 1625 – but his grandfather James VI and I, used to the constraints of the Scots court, had been equally lax and open-handed in England from 1603. James had frustrated his careful chief minister Sir Robert Cecil's attempts to rein in expenditure as Lord Treasurer in 1608–12 and Sir Lionel Cranfield's in the early 1620s. Where Charles II failed was in avoiding the opportunity to appoint a more vigorous and 'book-balancing' Lord Treasurer of proven administrative experience in 1660, as he handed the job to the loyal and trustworthy but not exactly pro-active ageing Earl of Southampton, a veteran moderate royalist landowner descended from 1540s minister Sir Thomas Wriothesley. A self-made career man of proven adminstrative rigour like Lord Chancellor Hyde/Clarendon from the royalist secretariat in exile would have been better at reining in expenditure, though the latter was clearly not seen as a priority and this key job could not be given to an experienced but Cromwellian administrator from the previous government (e.g. Cromwell's household organiser Philip Jones) for political reasons. Generosity and doling out sinecures to aspiring courtiers was more politically useful to a new regime in need of friends, and the king understood the advantages of providing a honeypot at court for ambitious nobles and gentry. Notably, when Southampton died in May 1667 aged sixty, Charles did not appoint a 'new broom' despite the financial demands of wartime but handed the post to the equally unqualified but politically key General Monck, now Duke of Albemarle.

A Commons bill in spring 1663 sought to set up an enquiry into selling offices across the government, and nearly extended to cover the sale of honours. Already disgruntled Sir Philip Warwick was presenting (and under-estimating) the amount of annual royal expenditure at £1,085,000 – allegedly after stringent economies – and stating the amount of annual income at £978,000; unofficially he reckoned that Charles was spending twice his revenue.[40] The Hearth Tax was a disappointment, as could have been expected due to the number of hearths being assessed by the taxpayers not government officials – though the Commons would not have accepted the latter anyway. They belatedly did do in 1664, with money needed for the Dutch crisis. Some useful measures had been undertaken by the Commons (who had bothered to try to work out how to improve collection and so help the king), such as a plan of autumn 1662 to 'farm out' the collection of the excise taxes to commissioners (who thus had motivation to stop evasion and scams to recoup what they had paid the government). The farmers' investigations caused an outcry and attempts to create muddle and evade paying, a sign that the plan was working.[41] The Hearth Tax was also hugely unpopular – a sign that it could not be evaded easily. But the endemic lack of money caused by Parliament's inadequate estimation of the king's needs in grants of 1660–1 was undoubtably made worse by Charles' improvidence and public extravagance, of which Pepys – who had his ear to the ground as a well-placed middle-ranking official – was the most famous complainant of whom we have evidence at this point.[42] The work of modern analysts such as Chandman confirm continuing royal expenditure on projects or persons that were not strictly essential and which amounted to self-indulgence by the king and a weakness for listening to appeals from importunate courtiers – and mistresses. The worst offender among the latter was probably the greedy and acquisitive Barbara Villiers/Palmer, Countess of Castlemaine, an impoverished junior member of the huge Villiers dynasty who was producing a string of his bastards (and demanding lands and titles for them). The king even gave Barbara a major but decaying former Tudor country palace, Nonsuch in Surrey – which she proceeded to 'asset-strip' for its materials which she apparently sold off. The amount spent at royal gambling evenings at court did not give a good impression either, and grumbles at royal improvidence and greedy mistresses could spill over into Parliament and influence MPs in their willingness to cause trouble in other areas apart from finance. If Charles was causing his own semi-bankruptcy – the Treasury was reliably said to be nearly empty by December 1662 – why should MPs indulge his wishes on other policy-matters?

Discontent over the level of royal expenditure was nothing new and James VI and I's court had also been full of gambling and well-lubricated social events about which backbench rural MPs could enjoy feeling scandalised. But this fed into antagonism to doing the king's business in other matters, and affected government measures' chances of passing into law. This included Anglican hardline MPs' concern over religion, where the king was still attempting to secure greater toleration.

The February 1663 session of Parliament saw a hostile reaction to the king's personal request for them to approve his right to dispense (i.e. give individual exemptions from the laws for) peaceable and non-dangerous Protestant sectaries and non-rebel Catholics. Charles was prepared to allow measures to tighten up the penal laws against Catholics in general in return, though if he could dispense individuals from these and did so for substantial numbers MPs could and did ask what was the point of passing them. The king got his brother the Duke of York to introduce his dispensing proposals, for Protestants only (so far), in the more amenable Lords, but the Commons turned even the idea of debating it down and the king's side could only muster thirty votes for it.[43] Evidently Charles' request to Clarendon and Secretary of State Bennet to gather together their Commons allies and dependants to vote for it had backfired. On 6 March the militant Anglican MPs prepared a bill which was proposed to tighten up on implementation of the anti-Catholic laws (by punishing JPs who did not enforce them and enrolling churchwardens to hunt down recusants) and to banish all priests from the realm.[44] The Lords sub-committee working on the 'dispensation bill' now voted to exclude Catholics from its provisions,[45] a snub to all Bristol's efforts to rally pro-Catholic feeling there, and Charles had to abandon his planned legislation for toleration and issue an anti-Catholic proclamation as advised by his MPs. Clarendon's belated speech in favour of tolerating loyal Catholics in the Lords, after an absence caused by illness, only succeeded in losing him remaining Anglican trust in both Houses and the annoyed King blamed him for not being able to control (or wanting to control?) either body.[46] The overall picture is one of Clarendon losing influence in both Houses and having to surrender to the hardliners, though he lacked the votes in either anyway – but the humiliation was hardly just due to his own inadequacy as even with Bennet and Bristol both working with him (for once) the Lords as well as the Commons stood firm against the king. The Commons also used the plans for financial reform put forward by Warwick to set up a committee in March into who Charles had granted estates since his return, evidently expecting to find evidence of improvidence or grants to rebels and Catholics.[47] In May, the MPs extended their investigations to all recent grants of office amidst lurid claims about the habit by junior officials of selling their offices to their successors – hardly a new problem. The irritated king accused them of jeopardising his governance by their slowness in coming up with hard cash, and only won a vote to supply the latter by forty-eight votes in a fullish House of over 300.[48] In the event, the immediate financial crisis was averted and the government was not forced to go 'cap in hand' to the Commons in return for cash, though the latter continued obliviously with their own priorities centring on purging non-loyalists from local office and harassing religious dissidents. The Commons even accepted in June 1663 that collection of the Hearth Tax had produced a lower yield than expected so this was as much to blame as corruption at Court, though the extra grant that they made to the King was to be raised by the outdated 'subsidy' arrangements not the efficient 1640s method of 'assessment' (presumably so as not to annoy their voters). Revenues from customs and excise improved as the extending post-crisis domestic and international security brought more trade in 1663–4, coupled with good harvests and improved methods of tax-collection by officials who were becoming used to their new work, and the tax-farmers were able to meet their promised targets for money to hand over to the government. The overall deficit remained around £500,000 p.a., which would have restricted the government from reviving the armed forces and denied it the ability to wage an aggressive foreign policy – but these were not yet contemplated as of the early 1660s anyway. Only when the Commons were applauding the hardline being taken against the Dutch and accepting the need for a larger navy in autumn 1664 did they agree to a massive royal request for £2,500,000 over three years.[49]

These problems also had an impact on the monarchy's ability to wage an assertive foreign policy. The latter might be advisable to warn off potential overseas threats from aiding the king's enemies, but unlike with Cromwell's well-armed and militant regime post-1660, Britain was not a major target for its neighbours as it was not seen as a major threat. The new government avoided the cost and danger of major involvement in Europe, quite apart from the Commons and the nation not wanting to pay for the large armed forces that would be necessary for this. The return of peace between France and Spain in 1659 meant that there was no need to choose between them as an ally, and Charles sold England's costly new (1658) possession of Dunkirk back to Louis XIV in 1662. This led to nationalistic complaints that Cromwell's hard-won conquest had been sold off cheaply by unpatriotic – and bribed – royal ministers. Anglo-Dutch relations were no more tense over commercial rivalries than they had been in the mid-1650s, and were managed by the same man – Downing – as ambassador in Holland until 1665. After the close involvement of the embattled Protectorate in international conflict, Charles – his ministers divided over their choice of ally anyway – could afford to stand back from international involvement, returning to his father's caution and balancing of rival factions in the 1630s and his grandfather's in the 1610s. Unlike in both cases, there was no major European confrontation between rival Habsburg-Bourbon power blocs where England had to choose one side or the other. The death of the warlike Charles X of Sweden also brought peace to the Baltic, with the major military power of the region neutralised during a long minority. The affordable cost of English neutrality was another reason for nostalgic discontent at the comparison with England's international position in the 1650s; one lampoon complained of the results of the King's foreign policy in the early 1660s as: 'Three things to be seen/ Tangier, Dunkirk, and a barren Queen'.[50] With typical cynicism, the public presumed that Clarendon had been bribed by the French to hand Dunkirk back and called his large new mansion in Piccadilly, supposedly paid for by this, 'Dunkirk House'. The public attitude to Clarendon would be reflected among angry patriotic backbench MPs, but as long as the Lord Chancellor retained the king's confidence it would not be of much political import. Unfortunately, Clarendon – never known for his emollience, and in a weak position at court as a 'gentry careerist' without a bloc of useful aristocratic friends and relations – was to be under greater pressure at Court too from the second half of 1661 as his old rival from exile politics in the 1650s, the Earl of Bristol, returned to Court from an embassy to Parma and took against him. As usual for a Stuart court, small matters of disputed patronage in the share-out of perks could lead to major feuds, and Clarendon foolishly chose to 'insult' Bristol by (as its Chancellor) removing him from the Stewardship of Oxford University. This then added a personal element to Bristol's taking up the unsuccessful cause of promoting formal legal relief for Catholics from the penal laws in the Lords, in which Clarendon spoke against this. In fact Clarendon was not anti-Catholic as such and had been in favour of the exiled King allying with European Catholic states in the 1650s, from which time he had a coterie of individual Catholic friends (especially the Irish intriguer Richard Belling, former middleman between the rebel Catholic regime at Kilkenny and the Papacy). Nor was legislative relief for the Catholics an urgent issue in 1661–2, as most JPs were following royal wishes and not enforcing the penal laws. But now the twenty-five Catholic peers in the Lords were added to Clarendon's foes, to whom the (Catholic) Queen Mother gravitated along with Barbara Villiers, who was sulking over him obstructing royal grants to her.

Lack of coherence, and a divided Court and administration. Nothing new for a Stuart regime, and inevitable given the context? How much can be blamed on Charles II?

It is thus unfair to put all the blame for the political drift, religious repression, financial problems, and diminished international position of post-1660 Britain on an inadequately focussed monarch and his squabbling ministers. The government's political and financial position in the early 1660s was bound to produce major problems given the priorities and constraints of the Restoration settlements. Nor were the quarrels over domestic and foreign policy and personal feuds at Court anything new, as intrigue and factionalism was endemic at any Court and the difficult situation of the 1660s partly arose from the legacies of over two decades of conflict. Royalist and Parliamentarian courtiers and ministers surviving from the Civil Wars were bound to distrust each other, with a legacy of bitterness from the sufferings of the defeated party and the disappointment of royalist hopes of compensation in 1660–1. As with resentful Royalists who had regained office in the localities pursuing vendettas against their 1650s supplanters once they had the power to do so – and taking out their feelings on 'fanatics' in general – courtiers who had been in exile or financially ruined in the 1650s would dislike men who had served Cromwell, such as Anthony Ashley Cooper (whose case was made worse by being a former Royalist who had changed sides in 1644). Monck had initially been royalist as well, though he was not a civilian minister involved in formulating domestic policits as Cooper was. Even some aristocratic ministers like the Earl of Southampton had been moderate Parliamentarians, and in the early 1660s ex-Parliamentarian commander Manchester and his fellow Presbyterian leader Holles (the latter one of the 'Five Members' of January 1642 were still politically powerful and were sporadically consulted over policy. In the event, the only one of the 1640s Parliamentarians and 1650s Cromwellians at court who was reckoned to be trusted by the King was Monck; the Earl of Annesley (a Presbyterian and Cromwellian but not as divisive for his 1640s role as Cooper) and Cooper, prominent in government, were not personally close to the King who seems to have found them not amenable enough to his suggestions. In Ireland, it is notable that late in 1661 Charles chose to use the fortuitous death of (ex-Cromwellian) Coote, now Earl of Mountrath, to replace him in his provincial appointments in Connacht by a hardline 1640s Royalist with no local appointments, Lord Berkeley, and that November the 1640s royalist commander-in-chief, Ormonde, was restored as Lord Lieutenant to supersede the 1660–1 Lords Justices. This was a parallel to the simultaneous eclipse of moderate Cromwellians from the 1650s by old royalists from the 1640s and their kin in England.

Charles seems to have resented being lectured by advisers, a drawback for the prosy and managing Clarendon, and it is notable that in his personal relationships too he would rarely put up with bullying. The only person who could get away with an overbearing approach was Barbara Villiers, who had the advantage of her sexual allure and even so lost her lustre during the 1660s due to her frequent tantrums. When the new queen attempted to sulk her way into making Charles abandon his proposal that he make Barbara her lady-in-waiting he ignored her and took his mistress' side instead. Managing the king was of great importance for ministers and courtiers in promoting their causes, personal or political, and this is one reason apart from personal distaste for their religion why the (usually older) senior Presbyterian peers lacked success with him. The best wits and flatterers were almost exclusively ardent Anglicans (or Catholics) and 'ultra' monarchists, and often of a younger generation than the Civil War veterans. Those of the king's closest non-royal advisers as of 1660–4 who had been active in the 1640s were all dependable royalists who had served his father loyally, led by Hyde/Clarendon and Ormonde; as was the non-governmental senior court figure Bristol, who as George Digby had been Hyde's militaristic 'ultra' critic as well as personal foe then.

In Scotland, a mixture of political misjudgement as Commissioners and diverging from the King's interests cost the senior minister of 1660–3, ex-1650s Royalist commander Middleton, his post and Royal trust in 1663. Middleton had made the classic mistake of using Charles' sporadic laziness and willingness to devolve major and minor business to trusted ministers to presume on his goodwill on a matter of personal one-upmanship in politics in September 1662 over the Scottish Act of Indemnity, namely who was to be on the list banned from future office. Charles had left the matter to Middleton, who proposed a seemingly moderate solution of banning only twelve men – but then he arranged for the twelve to be selected by secret ballot in the Scots Parliamant and for his old foe Lauderdale, a Covenanter leader and Commissioner to the Parliamentary regime in England in the mid-1640s, to be included. Middleton gave the 'royal assent' to it in his role as Commissioner, and the list was then taken quietly to London for royal approval by Middleton's agent Sir George Mackenzie of Tarbert. However, it appears that someone, probably Archbishop Sharp's brother William, who was Lauderdale's agent in Edinburgh, sent an urgent report of what had happened in invisible ink in a letter to Lauderdale in London, and the latter duly alerted the king and had himself taken off the list. Mackenzie was sent back to Edinburgh in disgrace, and Charles sent Lauderdale there too to keep an eye on Middleton.[51] Nor was Charles pleased that Middleton had arranged for the Scots Parliament to ban the sons of attainted 'rebel' peers from petitioning the king to have their lands restored, as this trespassed on his prerogative of mercy. Middleton was received with notable coolness on his next visit to London, and on 5 February 1663 Lauderdale attacked his usurpation of royal prerogatives to his face in the Privy Council. Foolishly, Middleton then added to his sins by trying to oppose Charles' orders to halt the collection of fines from those condemned to pay up for their political 'crimes' under the Covenanter regime and told the Scots Privy Council to resume collecting the money – which Lauderdale was only too keen to inform the king about. Middleton clung onto office in name for a few months, but was replaced later that spring – according to Bishop Burnet after the King called an (English) Council meeting for this purpose.[52] His partner and fellow-ex-general, Chancellor Glencairn, died in 1664. Their successors were the Earl of Rothes, a younger 'new man' who was personally congenial to the king (and another heavy drinker) and more effective, and Lauderdale who had to overcome the disadvantage of taking the wrong side in the 1640s but proved himself by a mixture of rakish geniality, political suppleness, and ruthless effectiveness as a royal servant.

Clashes of personality and policies were inevitable at any court, and the interest in specific policies (e.g. religion and foreign affairs) of senior non-governmental courtiers like Bristol (or the Duke of Buckingham later) would lead to this spilling over into matters of government. In that sense, the political result of the problems over Anglican MPs' block on religious toleration bills and penny-pinching MPs' refusal to grant Charles all the money he needed in May-June 1663, see above – Bristol 'going rogue' and trying to impeach Clarendon – was a return to normal Elizabethan or Jacobean politics, not a sign of chaos in government or royal weakness. Charles, as seen above, was angry with Clarendon over his religious measures being thwarted, and the Commons was seen to be 'out of control'. An ambitious backbench MP from a royalist family who was short of cash and in need of Court office to earn some, Sir Richard Temple, offered to help Bristol 'manage' the Commons in return for office. Bristol apparently agreed, keen to show the king that he could succeed where Clarendon could not, but he and Temple soon quarrelled and Temple joined the faction of MPs blocking the king's financial supplies, acting as a teller for the Noes in a crucial vote. The angry king informed the Commons that Temple had previously been offering to control them in order to damage his credit with the opposition, and when pressed by MPs to name Temple's middleman in the plan did so, fingering Bristol on 26 June. Temple cleared himself to MPs by insisting that it had all been a misunderstanding, and the vengeful Bristol sought to cover his position by launching an impeachment in the Lords against Clarendon – the charges including the supposedly corrupt sale of Dunkirk to Louis XIV plus arranging for Charles to marry a barren Queen so his daughter's children by the Duke of York would sit on the throne. This was all unproveable, and even peers irritated at Clarendon's failure over toleration rallied to the minister as the charges were debated on 10–14 July. The impeachment was thrown out for lack of evidence or votes, and Bristol was barred from court and had to go into hiding as the king ingeniously reversed his usual policy of toleration and had the earl arraigned as a Catholic recusant.[53] The fiasco said nothing for unity at court and played up inter-courtier feuding, but that was not new for Stuart politics – indeed, back in 1621 the present Duke of Buckingham's father had inspired the impeachment of his court rival Sir Francis Bacon and in 1624 he and the late king had done the same to Lord Treasurer

Cranfield. Nor was Bristol accusing Clarendon of being a French puppet, using popular rumours and libels, unique. Powerful courtiers and/or family groupings had also been associated with particular 'lines' in foreign policy before, such as the aggressively pro-Protestant and anti-Spanish Dudley/Sidney connection at Elizabeth I's court, who lobbied for war with Spain in the pre-1585 period, and the pro-Spanish Howards (either Catholic or crypto-Catholic) under James I who sought to keep him from a European Protestant alliance. Both groupings had been willing to proceed further with their chosen alliances with overseas ideological allies than their more even-handed sovereigns would go, with the Dudley/ Sidney faction favouring early intervention to aid the Protestant rebels in Holland and the Howards favouring a marital alliance with Spain via James I's son Charles marrying the Infanta on easy terms. The latter had also been backed – temporarily – by Buckingham's father, then James I's 'favourite', who had induced Charles to go to Spain and woo the Infanta in person and accompanied him there – and after their failure a miffed Buckingham senior lobbied for war with Spain instead. The French birth and proselytizing Catholic sympathies of Henrietta Maria had led to her Court allies favouring her homeland and the international interests of her religion under Charles I. In contrast, Lord Treasurer Weston and later Secretary of State Windebank, plus some Catholic courtiers such as Endymion Porter, had been associated (fairly or not) with the interests of France's enemy Spain. As yet, unlike with the nubile young Breton and alleged French spy Louise de Keroualle in the 1680s, none of Charles' mistresses was considered to have an impact on major policy matters; though Barbara, as a Villiers distantly related to Buckingham, duly promoted her large clan and secured a title for herself as Countess of Castlemaine. She was as much of a political actor as male courtiers, and was valued by potential allies accordingly; Bristol formed an alliance with her against Clarendon. Her rival from 1663, Frances Stuart, was less active in court intrigue and was indeed reluctant to take on the role of a royal mistress – though she was used by the Villiers' enemies to undermine Barbara. The way that Barbara's enemies hopefully dangled attractive young women under the king's nose to undermine the relationship was reminiscent of the use made of attractive young men like George Brett (and initially George Villiers) by ambitious courtiers under James I.

For the first time in the Stuart dynasty's rule in England, there were adult royal male relatives with a major input in policy, at least in naval affairs and associated diplomacy – the king's brother James, Duke of York and Lord Admiral, whose capacity as a hands-on head of the navy is evidenced by Pepys, and their cousin Rupert, former royalist general and 1649–52 Royalist naval supremo. The relationship between James and Clarendon was complicated by the fact that the Duke had secretly married Clarendon's pregnant daughter Anne Hyde late in 1660, and their daughters Mary (born April 1662) and Anne (born February 1665) remained the king's next heirs after James; several brothers died as infants. Clarendon's enemies alleged that he had pimped his daughter to James in order to put his grandchildren on the throne, and had landed the King with a barren bride too to improve their chances. In fact, the secret James/Anne Hyde relationship seems to have embarrassed Clarendon, who had no idea of what was going on until after the marriage; indeed, some courtiers encouraged James to break off the relationship and offered to pretend that they were the baby's father instead. The 'official' story, by the editor of James' (augmented) 'Memoirs' decades later, was that the king sought to dissuade them from marriage but James loyally persisted and had his way. In fact, it appears that a shabby proposal was made to marry Anne off to courtier Charles Berkeley, who falsely claimed that Anne had slept with him too and he was the father, and it was the king who insisted on the marriage to James taking place. Hyde then secured an earldom to raise himself to a more appropriate rank for a royal connection.[54]

James had had his own circle of political allies at the exiled Stuart court at St Germain in the 1650s, such as Berkeley, and was used to operating independently of his older brother; Rupert had been the leader of the Royalist hardliners then and had favoured foreign Catholic help more than the circle of civilian advisers (e.g. Hyde) close to the king. Rupert now concentrated on his role as Governor of Windsor Castle and his scientific and colonial interests rather than politics. James and Rupert were major shareholders in the Royal African Company and promoters of its aggressive colonial ventures, which brought about much of the escalating tension with the Dutch, leading to war. As head of the navy, James had the personnel and funds to arrange such ventures. The seizure of Dutch ships and outposts in Africa in 1663–4 by their Company's expedition was led by Rupert's former 1650s naval subordinate and continuing ally

Sir Robert Holmes, and it acted independently and in contrast to 'official' peace with the Dutch government. It did not, however, mark new duplicity by the restored monarchy. Similar colonial clashes with a supposed ally had occurred in the 1630s against Spain in the West Indies, organised by powerful ultra-Protestant nobles at arm's length from the government (the Warwick/Saye faction's Providence Islands Company). It had also occurred in the 1650s against the Dutch in the East Indies – and a similar strong line had been taken to the authorities in The Hague then, indeed by the same person as English ambassador (George Downing). Colonial warfare with a domestic ally in pursuit of trade had taken a particularly vicious turn by the Dutch East Indies Company in the 1620s, as they sought to drive English merchants out of the Spice Islands (Indonesia), Their resultant atrocities, as at Ambon/Amboyna, had been defended by the Dutch government despite its concurrent need of English aid against Spain. The private war carried out by the Royal African Company was evidently designed to put pressure on the Dutch and risked the threat of European war, and a substantial group of royal advisors – including ex-Cromwellians Monck and Mountague, the latter involved in similar Cromwellian naval intimidation of Spain and Portugal – then backed this official hardline. So did some ministers, notably Bennet, in defiance of Clarendon's cautious approach, and by 1664 the Commons was being stirred up with petitions by merchants affected by Dutch harassment.[55] The committee on trading problems that heard this was stuffed with clients of James and of Bennet, so they were sure of a favourable hearing.

Warning signs for future stability that could have been avoided. Tilting foreign policy towards the autocratic Louis XIV of France: was Clarendon rightly blamed?

The sense of drift – or a deliberate move – away from the initial compromises of 1660–1 to a hardline royalist action was also visible in foreign policy, as Cromwellian allies were treated with more hostility and the increasingly autocratic French regime became a closer ally. The Dutch republic and its shipping were treated with increasingly bold hostility, with the high command of the navy led by the king's competent but autocratic younger brother James, Duke of York (not yet a Catholic). The determination of overall policy and the general tone of orders sent to naval commanders was in the hands of the Privy Council and the ministers who implemented its orders. But a lot depended on the actions of individual naval officers 'on the spot' in determining whether English shipping would take a high hand with its rivals and spark an incident that could lead to war – and James was actively promoting former royalists like Captain Robert Holmes, often in the service of France or Spain as exiles pre-1660 and hostile to the king's then foes the Dutch. But the escalation of the potential for conflict in sending a fleet to the Mediterranean in 1664 to attack Dutch shipping and hopefully seize their wealthy Smyrna fleet as it brought goods back from the Ottoman Sultanate – in time of peace – was not that unusual or unprecedented. It was a repeat of Cromwell's orders to his admirals (including Mountague) to seize Spanish shipping and treasure-fleets in European waters in time of peace (1655) and do likewise to Portugal over a diplomatic dispute (1656). The Dutch had harassed the English in the East Indies quite blatantly since the 1620s, irrespective of needing English support in their struggle against their ex-occupier Spain.

The major war of Clarendon's ministry was thus begun against his wishes at the instigation of his rivals at court, and with the king standing back from backing either side in the argument but tacitly encouraging a hardline approach. But the hardline taken towards the Dutch by Downing, at least in the talks preceding their 1662 commercial treaty, was not so much due to a willingness to risk war as a hope that England's old rivals could be successfully persuaded to back down over points at issue for fear of war. The Amsterdam merchants had too much to lose from war, and would therefore pressurise the De Witt government to give way. Those of the seven Dutch United Provinces which had a strong party in favour of Grand Pensionary De Witt's eclipsed rivals, the Orange dynasty, would not want war either. Downing was correct in his analysis as the Dutch did back down in 1662; although his hopes for an unwanted Anglo-Dutch crisis enabling the Orangists to overthrow De Witt in favour of Charles' nephew William III were premature, a major foreign crisis (with France) was to see De Witt lynched in 1672. The unhelpful attitude of France towards England in the early 1660s despite their kings' close kinship also meant that the Dutch regime was in no immanent danger of an Anglo-French alliance threatening them and so could afford to respond aggressively to English naval attacks. This played a part in the resulting Dutch resilience and failure to hurry to negotiate a commercial settlement of outstanding issues as the English government and navy piled the pressure on the Dutch in 1664–5, though in any case the Amsterdam merchants would not have stood for any obvious diplomatic climb-down that affected their commercial profits – and they had been equally obdurate towards Cromwell in 1654–8 despite needing his goodwill against the Spanish and Swedes.

The corresponding hardline mood in London was partly driven by the same City interests linked to councillors in Whitehall as under Cromwell (but now with an added stake in the game due to the development of the Royal Africa Company that was challenging the Dutch commercial interest in West Africa), and partly the new factors of hostile figures among the English leadership and navy commanders alike. Both the Duke of York and Prince Rupert had major commercial interests in the Royal Africa Company and other commercial ventures that tangled with the Dutch e.g. the 1664 Corporations of the Royal Fishery (which sought to dominate the North Sea fisheries) – and so did the ex-Cromwellian commanders who were to join them in command of the navy in 1665–7, Monck/Albemarle and Mountague/Sandwich. York was indeed identified by the French ambassador as the principal architect of the Dutch war.[56] This group of anti-Dutch elite figures was in turn backed up by hardline captains (often ex-royalists used to independent command in the 1640s and 1650s) like Robert Holmes, the swashbuckling captain and former post-1649 naval officer under Rupert who was chosen to tackle local Dutch predominance in West Africa in 1663 with maximum discretion to do as he thought fit in the Gulf of Guinea. This duly led to him taking a Dutch fort and assorted Dutch ships which was bound to lead to anger, and instead of reining the navy in Charles chose in summer 1664 to send a second expedition there under the equally incautious Rupert. At the same time a separate expedition retaliated against Dutch piracy and smuggling based at New Amsterdam in North America by invading and overrunning it – since which the defunct Dutch colony has been known as 'New York' after James' ducal title. (This colonial incaution about causing war to spread to Europe did however follow Cromwell's policy, as he had had French colonies in Acadia attacked in time of peace by the Leverett-Sedgewick expedition.) To add to the danger of war following, Charles' (and before him Cromwell's) hardline ambassador to the Dutch,

Downing, encouraged those London merchants who had grievances against the Dutch to present their claims to the Commons in 1664, with the intention of stoking up anger in the latter so a diplomatic compromise was implausible. In any case, the special post-1660 factor of a host of bored and belligerent young gentry and nobles at Court clamouring for a war so they could earn glory was pressurising Charles towards launching one, and Clarendon and other cautious veterans of the miseries and costs of war in the 1640s were left isolated. All of this duly made a Dutch war more likely, and in November 1664 the Commons duly voted for the sums of money in taxation which Charles told them were needed – though the Privy Council later lost their nerve when the Dutch proved readier for a clash than expected and tried to ask for French mediation. (The primacy of aggressive English commercial interests in Commons thinking was a major factor in other contemporary matters too – the mid-1660s saw this lobby blocking efforts for an Anglo-Scottish customs union except on extortionate terms and banning the import of Irish cattle to protect the English agricultural sector.)

Backed by the belligerent Commons and public, war was declared in March 1665 – though in practical terms it is surprising that experienced officers like Albemarle and Mountague as well as the king and his brother expected the well-armed and resilient Dutch navy and its experienced admirals to be easier to crack than they had been in 1652–4. In retrospect, the drawn naval battles of 1665–6 could have been expected from two such well-matched fleets. English over-confidence was duly to lead to the lack of planning and security-measures that enabled the Dutch to conduct their humiliating raid on the English naval bases in the Medway in 1667, when several major ships were sunk at their moorings and Charles' flagship was towed away to Holland. Other major disasters that had a serious psychological impact were more a matter of bad luck than clumsy governmental leadership, such as the serious outbreak of the plague in London in 1665 and the Great Fire of September 1666 – but they left many of the capital's population dead or in flight and two-thirds of the capital in ruins and led to a general mood that the hopes of 1660 had gone horribly wrong and God was punishing the sinful English. This could easily turn against the government as the scared public sought scapegoats, and the physical effects on the capital (where the gunfire from successive naval battles could be heard during the war) made the danger to the regime more dangerous. The only good side-effect of the succession of crises was that the provincial hunt by Anglican JPs and their allies for 'fanatic' Nonconformist violators of the new penal laws was petering out by 1665–6, and prosecutions for violating the Conventicle Act in particular dropped off. The new bogeymen were the Catholics (again), who were blamed for the Great Fire of London which was supposed to have been started by 'Papist agents'.

Scotland also faced more turbulence in the mid-1660s, though the restored bishops did not regain much political influence and although centralised mechanisms of ecclesiastical discipline were restored there were no more doctrinal experiments with Anglicanising the liturgy. The two archbishops again sat on the Privy Council, but other clerical councillors were rare. Even Archbishop Sharp of St Andrews lacked the political influence of his pre-1637 predecessors, and the nobility jealously watched the senior clergy for any signs of a return to their old pretensions. When the inevitable purge of those clerics who refused to recognise the legality of the restored Episcopal Church led to ousted ministers holding illegal services for their ex-congregations in 1663 government police action followed, with heavy fines on those who boycotted their local churches – collected by the army, who billeted themselves on the delinquents until they paid up. This led to an armed rising in Galloway in September 1666, on a small scale and hampered by bad weather and local indifference as the protesters attempted to march on Edinburgh. They were defeated by Sir Thomas Dalzell of the Binns, Linlithgowshire (a royalist veteran of Worcester in 1651 who had fought for the Czar of Russia during exile in the 1650s) at Mullion Green and a long train of prisoners were hauled off to Edinburgh and locked up in the Greyfriars Kirkyard. Around thirty men were hanged and hundreds more sent as indentured servants to Barbados. Most of the others were amnestied in 1667 provided that they swore allegiance to the King (i.e. rejected the supremacy of ecclesiastical over royal authority). Among other casualties of the episode was a senior royal minister, the duke of Rothes, who had been in London assuring Charles that Scotland was quiescent as the revolt broke out so his reputation suffered and who his ambitious colleague Lauderdale now undermined at Court to prevent him gaining credit for the victory. Some individual pardons and reinstatements of those ex-clergy who would swear to recognise the king's authority –

without accepting bishops – followed under a generous Church policy of comprehension in the early 1670s, and hardline anti-Presbyterian leader Archbishop Alexander Burnet of Glasgow was replaced in 1671 after he had organised a clerical petition to the king against toleration. Lauderdale persuaded Charles that the petition was an attempt to coerce him, and Burnet was sacked and replaced by the more moderate Robert Leighton, Bishop of Dunblane since 1661. Leighton believed in 'comprehension' of as many Presbyterians as possible within the Episcopal church, and in banning bishops from exercising a veto over diocesan synods, and allowing the junior clergy to salve their consciences by recognising bishops as administratively necessary to uphold order as head of the local presbyteries rather than being theologically correct. But there was no formal acceptance of a parallel church structure for those unable to accept governance by bishops, and those ex-Covenanters who accepted readmission into the national church on these individual royal indulgences were treated as collaborators and anathematised by the hardliners.

Physically, both Court and government affairs in the 1660s played out in close proximity at Whitehall – and the king's lack of control of his feuding intimates (or of one dominant faction) meant that the court was an unrestrained hotbed of seething jealousies and back-stabbing. This all mattered in terms of the perceived drift of policy in the early-mid 1660s, though even at the orderly and hierarchical court of the unapproachable Charles I there had been rival factions and a noticeable lack of decisiveness over choosing a foreign policy between the rivals' suggestions in the mid-1630s. Crucially, it undermined the potential for dominance by the most powerful minister, Clarendon, whose impressive capacity for work and devotion to duty helped to cement the new government together and made up for Charles' only sporadic interest in matters of governance. The king was more prepared to attend to state business and more conscientious in his duties than has sometimes been suggested, and it is too simplistic to suggest that he had to be called to attend to council business reluctantly by a schoolmasterly Clarendon who he came to resent. The effect of a bored king chafing at having to attend council meetings and Clarendon – a figure from another generation who did not approve of his licentious lifestyle – chiding him for his inattentiveness can be exaggerated. It represented a clash of values, but a monarch bored with business and leaving the minutiae of official paperwork to a workaholic chief minister had been seen before – Henry VIII with Wolsey and James I with Robert Cecil, Earl of Salisbury. Complaints had been legion that James left business unattended and spent his time hunting. Neither was less able or willing to take initiatives in policy when they were interested. Conscientious administrator Charles I was the exception rather than the norm for recent adult male monarchs.

Clarendon, hampered by sporadic ill-health, was alienated from and disliked by many at court even without the king encouraging this. Logically, this alienation from the active (and often louche) young aristocrats around his sovereign dated back to Clarendon's experiences as a harassed and not always royally-valued civilian minister during the Civil Wars, when he had first clashed with Bristol. His role as head of the future Charles II's administrative Council in the south-west had been under fire from impatient and more bellicose young nobles as early as 1645–6, when he had feuded with aristocratic generals such as George Goring (the Earl of Norwich's son) and Sir Richard Grenville. His lower social rank and lack of close aristocratic relatives to promote his reputation at court or in the King's bed did not help either. Charles II had ignored his advice over major policy matters before, notably, in taking the gamble of signing up to the Covenant in order to be invited to Scotland in 1650. There had been tension between him and other senior advisors at the exiled court through the 1650s, with Hyde (as he then was) as the king's chief civilian advisor at odds with some of the more daring or hopeless schemes for plots thought up by his companions in exile. He had also been at odds with the queen mother and her circle of Catholic or pro-Catholic advisers, such as the ever-intriguing Henry Jermyn, who had leaned towards the European Catholic monarchies as invaluable allies for the exiled king. The ultimate aim of this faction's reliance on either France or Spain as the best means of restoring the Stuarts had been to persuade them to invade England and put Charles on his throne by force, even if Charles had to convert to Catholicism to achieve this – and Hyde had seen the political folly of this and tried to downplay Charles' reliance on Spain in 1656–60. Such matters had not been forgotten by those courtiers who he had frustrated, though he had been vindicated by unexpectedly managing to have Charles restored by negotiations in 1660 and as of that summer had been the king's unchallenged chief minister. Maximum mischief was however created by his detractors as early as autumn 1660 – with noticeable impact and success – over the much-publicised allegation that he had sought to pander his daughter Anne Hyde to the Duke of York so that he could secure his grandchild as the next monarch-but-one rather than being unaware of and embarrassed by her becoming pregnant. He was said to have threatened to throw Anne out of his house as a harlot, not take advantage of the social benefit a royal son-in-law would bring him. The relationship between James and Anne dated back to her time as Princess Mary's lady-in-waiting at The Hague in 1659, when they appear to have gone through some private form of marriage ceremony (as Charles and his mistress Lucy Walter were also said to have done). After the Restoration it led to Anne becoming pregnant, and she and James married secretly at her father's London house on 3 September 1660 (six weeks before her child's birth).

Clarendon's efforts to counter royal leniency towards the Quakers were not successful until the scare caused by the northern rising in autumn 1663, and his control of government policies was limited even at the height of his influence. There was no coherent 'Clarendon government' of England in 1660–7, and once his equally competent rival Sir Henry Bennet was Secretary of State (and spymaster) in 1663, his influence was further reduced though expectations of his dismissal proved premature. Bennet – allied to the Earl of Bristol, who was seeking to alleviate the legal position of his fellow-Catholics, and probably to Cooper and Annesley over relief for Presbyterians – was able to plan measures to extend the royal ability to dispense with the laws against non-Anglicans in Parliament in 1663, in defiance of Clarendon's stance though without effect. As seen above he stirred up a harsher line against the Dutch in the Commons too, in defiance of Clarendon's distaste for conflict. In foreign policy in general the king relied on a group of advisers, including James, Monck, Lord Treasurer Southampton (against conflict with the Dutch on account of the cost), and Cooper, not just Clarendon and the Secretaries of State. Clarendon's lack of languages (e.g. Dutch) compared to the linguist Bennet was a problem, though he had a translator ready to tackle foreign documents in Richard Belling. The lack of enthusiasm that Clarendon had for the Dutch war did not prevent him being the obvious political scapegoat for it when England failed to win any glorious naval victories, with the possible partial exception of the 'St James' Day' fight in 1666, and the costs began to mount – and his personal isolation at court and perceived haughty arrogance made him an easy target for ambitious courtiers with the King's ear like Buckingham. His enemies co-ordinated their efforts with Buckingham having useful allies in the Lords ready to ask embarrassing questions about his past supposed financial indiscretions, and his indictment by Parliament and flight abroad were to follow in 1667.

The lack of leadership that Charles II took in matters of policy like the escalation of the Dutch dispute in 1663–4 was notable compared to Cromwell's approach, when whatever the disputes of rival factions over the desired course of policy the government had taken a clear agreed line once it was decided. Charles, probably for reasons of personal insecurity, hung back from giving his full confidence to any one person or faction – and went against Clarendon's and Sheldon's initiatives on confronting Quakers, at least until the rebellion of autumn 1663 hardened his approach. Determining what approach would appeal to the King was sometimes difficult for the ambitious and/or the sycophantic minister or courtier, though Bennet had success in his approach to formulating a pleasing foreign policy in the early-mid-1660s. Clarendon, by contrast, lost out by proceeding from principle rather than from a desire to please the king. Indeed, the impression received is that Charles – in genteel revenge for his minister's priggish tone? – took to enjoying going behind his back. Charles was more attracted to the wild and the risk-taking at Court than to the sedate and prosy, little though this affected policy; personal friendship for a politically ambitious 'rake' only seems to have had some importance in explaining the rise in importance of his long-excluded crony Buckingham in the mid-late 1660s. The latter played a major role in undermining Clarendon during the Second Dutch War and was reckoned to be one of the dominant group of advisers around the king in 1667–72, the supposed 'Cabal' – though he never achieved a major post and his influence has probably been exaggerated. Charles was supposed to have reckoned this mercurial intriguer safer within the royal circle, causing trouble for those outside it, than outside causing mischief for his ministers. But by proxy Buckingham did provide Charles with an invaluable asset for the 1670s, his Yorkshire client Sir Thomas Osborne (Lord Danby) who was the king's Lord Treasurer and agent in controlling the Commons after 1673. The *'secret du roi'*, a notion of a private royal foreign policy conducted via the backstairs not the Council meeting, was to be as important for (the half-Bourbon) Charles as it was for his French relatives in the later seventeenth and eighteenth century. As ambitious Spanish diplomats had sought the backing of the current royal 'toy-boy' Robert Carr to influence James I, so Louis XIV was to seek to place a French 'agent' in Charles' heterosexual bed in the form of Louise de Keroualle, the Breton beauty despatched to Whitehall. An additional close connection with the French court arose through the early 1660s diplomatic meddling of Henrietta Maria, as ever politically disastrous to the reputation of her husband's family in England. Having failed to convert Charles II or one of his brothers to Catholicism in exile during the 1650s, she secured the marriage of her only surviving, youngest daughter Henriette-Anne ('Minette') to Louis' homosexual younger brother, 'Monsieur', the Duc d'Orleans, in 1661. This had long-term consequences, given that Charles had already lost one brother (the Duke of Gloucester) and one sister (Princess Mary, still only twenty-nine so able to have children) in autumn 1660. Had 'Minette' been given a Protestant husband her children would have been the logical heirs to James' daughter Anne in the Act of Settlement in 1701, not the more distant descendants of Charles' aunt Elizabeth of Bohemia. The House of Hanover would have been unlikely to inherit the throne had 'Minette' left Protestant descendants; instead her daughters by 'Monsieur' had Catholic husbands arranged by their French uncle, Louis XIV.

The frequent correspondence between Charles and 'Minette' duly provided the culturally Francophile king with his own access to the French court, with his sister acting as his unofficial ambassador to Louis and receiving Bourbon advances in return. (She was not just a 'French agent', as sometimes crudely supposed; her suggestions for helping Louis to dismember the United Provinces in 1669 were presented as beneficial to England too, and as not excluding a later breach with Louis.) The interests of a sovereign, with personal connections in the European dynastic network, and their ministers in foreign policy were still divergent in the period 1714–60 over the Hanoverians' involvement with their German Electorate's interests. Ultimately, this divergence between the king's 'personal' foreign policy and that of the government was to lead to the secret diplomatic initiatives for an Anglo-French alliance of 1668–70, which went against the diplomatic tenor of the 'official' endeavours to contain the growing threat of French expansionism in Europe. The

Triple Alliance of Britain, the Dutch, and Sweden in 1668, arranged by Bennet/Arlington after the humiliating end of the expensive Dutch War, was designed to offset Louis' aggressive Catholic militarism as well as to break up his alliance with the Dutch. In 1667 his massive army had wrenched substantial parts of the Spanish Netherlands from Spain, but the prospect of all his neighbours combining forced him to a quick peace. The Triple Alliance was a seeming guarantee of England's commitment to its Protestant allies and thus a conciliatory gesture to the Protestant and not too Francophile MPs who held the national purse-strings in Parliament. But it was shaky even without Charles yet considering abandoning it. His secret backing of 'Minette's' idea of a concurrent French alliance had the advantage of preventing Louis from accepting Dutch offers and wrecking the Triple Alliance – it thus supported rather than undermined Arlington's policy. But the French King would now try to lure him into a rather more dangerous course of action.

A wrong choice by 'Francophile' Charles?

Thanks to a mixture of English court rivalries, Charles' dislike of the De Witt regime, and the efforts of 'Minette', Charles' willingness to confront Louis in 1667–8 was short-lived despite the way his cousin had refused to help him against the Dutch earlier. This duly frustrated the Whitehall proponents of a sensible alliance with England's fellow-Protestant powers, the Dutch and Sweden, most notably the level-headed and highly capable diplomat Sir William Temple. Nor were the pro-Dutch and anti-French, anti-Catholic ministers in the so-called 'Cabal' ministry that succeeded Clarendon's in 1667–72, led by the veteran ex-Cromwellian earl of Shaftesbury (Sir Anthony Ashley Cooper), secure in Charles' backing against their rivals in an ever-shifting and disunited nexus of power. But restricting English policy to an open promotion of the Triple Alliance and ignoring French offers would have run the risk of Louis and the Dutch combining against Charles, as they had officially done in 1667 (though Louis had not been actively at war with England despite the terms of his then Dutch alliance). Charles was won back by Louis to a French alliance in 1669–70, aimed at crushing the Dutch republic's commerce and replacing De Witt's republican regime with the Orange dynasty. Charles' brother James, not yet Catholic but already sympathetic to them and long hostile to the Dutch, claimed in his later memoirs that the original initiative for the French alliance was Charles' early in 1669 and that the king also envisaged converting to Catholicism in return for French military aid – but James had his own reasons by then for asserting that and his veracity has been doubted. More to the point, both De Witt and Louis had been trying to lure each other into a division of the Spanish Netherlands between them (leaving England out) – so the Triple Alliance was not secure, thanks to Dutch not English 'treachery'. Charles went further than just securing a safer French anti-Dutch alliance in the mysterious and highly risky 'Secret Treaty of Dover', signed behind many of his ministers' backs with the French ambassador in May 1670 during his sister Minette's final visit to England. He secured promises of French money and if needed troops as part of the alliance, even though his promised conversion to Catholicism did not occur until he was dying and was probably a political lure more than a sincere offer. Also, the treaty was only known to pro-Catholic ministers like Bennet/Arlington and treasurer Lord Clifford, plus minor adviser Lord Arundell, which could cause a political explosion once it leaked out to opponents like Shaftesbury.

Charles' reliance on the maverick and arrogant Louis was problematic, not least as Louis had deserted his cousin to sign up to a Dutch alliance before and was clearly not to be trusted – unless Charles assumed that his own offers to Louis would now prove irresistible in the long term. The key to this, if it was Charles' reasoning, was religion, given Louis' aggressive Catholicism and disdain for the French Protestants; the 'devot' clerics at the French court constantly worked on Louis to deal with the latter by forcible reconversion and they were to have their way in 1685. Thus Charles' seeming eagerness to turn Catholic could bring this influential body of advisers to back allying with him, and thwart the mercantilist efforts of those of Louis' advisers (e.g. Colbert) who preferred Louis to choose allies on more pragmatic and commercial/strategic grounds. With 'Minette' to give him the inside news on how policy was decided in Louis' personal circle and who the French King listened to most, Charles had pragmatic as well as allegedly religious reasons to play up his keenness on Catholicism after the shock of a Franco-Dutch alliance in 1667. How much Charles' promises to declare himself Catholic and then reconvert England to that religion in return for French troops and money were sincere remains, open to heated speculation. But it was the ultimate triumph of personal court intrigue or the king's own personal gamble over official ministerial policy-making by his advisers, and was a sign of what had changed since the monarchy returned. The change was, however, a return to the inner workings of the court (especially the Royal Bedchamber personnel) as a centre of policy-making in the time of James VI and I, when Buckingham (senior) and the Howards had possessed great influence by means of personal access to the king rather than through office. Its international context was new, in that for a century it had been Spain that had been associated in the mind of English Protestants with the causes of imperialistic Catholic oppression and a 'Papist master-plan' for world domination.

The 'Black Legend' of Spain had been a potent factor since the Armada, and had been linked in the popular imagination with hordes of priests despatched by Rome to reconvert England to Catholicism. Indeed, the 150-year-old rivalry of Bourbon/Valois and Habsburg dynasties for supremacy in Europe had led to France allying itself with north European Protestant powers against the Holy Roman Emperor and the King of Spain. An English alliance with Henri IV and the north German Protestants around 1610, or with Richelieu's ministry and the Swedes against Spain around 1635–7, would have entailed England joining a combined Protestant-Catholic alliance. Anti-Catholic feeling in the Commons and nation was centred on the fear of a Spanish alliance. But that traditional era of inter-dynastic European conflict, with the Habsburgs as the leading Catholic threat, had ended with the 'Peace of the Pyrenees' in 1659. Now, however, the steadily expanding French state and its aggressively Catholic proselytism was making Louis XIV's government seem a larger threat to both Protestantism and European peace. Louis had not yet launched the military intimidation by his *dragonnades* on French Protestants to achieve a one-religion state, but his religious zeal was an increasing factor in attitudes to France – and already under Cromwell there had been official English concerns about French Protestants' security. Then, the argument had won out that the Protestants could be best aided by a policy of friendship with and polite pressure on France. Now, Charles II showed no interest in his co-religionists' fate in France and envied the autocracy of the French government. The King of England's partiality for his French cousin, and close personal and cultural ties between Charles' Court and Louis', were to play a leading role in the alienation of 'Country' from 'Court' in England in the 1670s. The growing fear of France and its agents was to link up with the continuing fear of Catholicism, and bring about the next major crisis of Charles' reign in the 'Popish Plot' and the 'Exclusion Crisis' in 1678. The failure of the intended alliance of England with the European Protestant cause in 1668–70 was due to the Dutch as much as to Charles, but once the United Provinces were under a more congenial government – that of his nephew William III – his alliance with them against Louis after 1674 was brief and reluctant. Undertaken to win support in and money from Parliament, it never had Charles' enthusiasm and was abandoned with relief. The perception that the court and ministry were riddled with Catholics and their fellow-travellers and being bribed by France was to bring the restored monarchy to the brink of catastrophe in 1678–9. Indeed, the spectre of Court intrigue and Stuart royals working for Catholic interests was a negation of all the hopes of those former Parliamentarians who Monck led to accept Charles II in 1660. Their gamble had failed, though they had had little alternative in securing (temporary) stability.

Conclusion

In the late 1630s one major reason for discontent against Charles I by those of a Puritan (or more accurately a hardline and pro-Calvinist Protestant) world-view in England and Scotland had been his perceived enthusiasm for Continental-style monarchy and Catholic-influenced court culture. This 'Popish threat' from the centre of government was combined with his Laudian allies' reintroduction of excessive and Catholic-influenced ceremonial to the church in England and Scotland, which seemingly went back on the 'godly' purges of Catholicism in both countries in 1559 and necessitated a radical purification of religion. Revolt followed against Charles' reformed – though actually still theologically Calvinist – church in Scotland in 1637–9, egged on by Protestant radicals in England, and the defeat of the king's attempt at military coercion in 1639–40 led to the return of Parliament in England, a radical campaign of secular and religious reform that was deeply controversial and split the nation's political classes, and eventually led to civil war. By 1670 the supposed compromise between the royalist and Parliamentarian groupings to restore Charles II and stability in the 'three kingdoms' in 1660 seemed to have led to the same sort of situation as in the late 1630s, with a court stuffed full of Catholics, a Catholic queen, a Catholicised and 'alien' court culture (now with added moral laxity), and a king in thrall to autocratic European Catholic monarchic governance (now as in France, not Spain). An anti-Papist explosion eventually followed in 1678–9 over the so-called Popish Plot, stirred up by the 'opposition media' as a threat to English liberty and religion and aimed at coercing the monarch. The comparison to the 1640–2 crises and the result – civil war – was indeed made by pro-royal propagandists, as they cautioned the public to 'remember Forty and One' when 'the rabble got up, the nobles pulled down'. To a certain extent the wheel had come full circle, though in the event Charles II was a more subtle and ruthless – and realistic – politician than his father and he managed to survive with his powers intact and to enhance them afterwards.

The mistakes made in and after the settlement in 1660, as laid out earlier, can be seen to have made the situation in the 1670s more dangerous, though in any case Charles had been influenced by French court culture and concepts of royal power in exile in the 1650s and was bound to want the greater security that relatively untrammelled power and an aggressively loyalist Anglican church gave him. Co-opting more of the Cromwellian elite – had they been willing to serve him and not in fear of revanchist royalist prosecution for 1650s 'crimes' if they had had greater political prominence – and the less anti-episcopal Presbyterians and sects to join his Church was arguably not pursued vigorously enough in 1660–1, though the king did make appropriate and probably sincere noises about reconciliation. It was the choice of the moderate Presbyterians not to enter office in his Church at and after the Worcester House Conference, arguably a serious miscalculation, though in any case anti-reconciliation hardliners among the Anglicans (led by Gilbert Sheldon) and their royalist Anglican gentry allies in the Commons were lying in wait for such a move and would have caused major trouble over it. As with secular reconciliation and limiting the list of 1640s-50s Parliamentarians to be prosecuted or driven from public life, the king did initially support a less vindictive policy but was constrained in his actions by the fact that from the 1661 elections the hardliners dominated the Commons and held the 'power of the purse' over him. They were after all his reliably loyal allies, so why should he risk his good relations with them on behalf of men who had driven his family into exile and financially ruined his father's loyal supporters?

As show, above, it was the Commons majority – not a 'lying and treacherous' Clarendon – who was responsible for the vindictive 'Clarendon Code' that marginalised the Dissenter sects, and this action also followed evidence – albeit exaggerated – of hardline republicans plotting rebellion in 1661–3 which necessitated coercion and 'police action' as much as the plots of the mid-1650s had necessitated Cromwellian repression. The nature of the second settlement in the early 1660s, which modified the more generous one of 1660, was due to grass-roots royalist pressure on a monarchy that was still uneasy on its throne and was considerably weakened from its position in 1640 – so the political wheel had not entirely come full circle and there was no 'return to Stuart autocracy'. This was arguably to follow the crises of the 'Popish Plot' and 'Exclusion' in 1679–81, and even then be limited. Criticism can be made of Charles for his lack of concentrated action or devotion to business in the crucial 1660s, and his allowing himself to be buffeted by rival Court factions (and some of his mistresses?) and waste money on a sumptuous court (though this had a political logic in propagandist displays of power) rather than exerting leadership. It is partly a cliché, but though the king was an intelligent and shrewd operator who had to bind factions together to avoid a return of civil war (like his equally louche grandfather Henri IV of France) he lacked direction at first and arguably betrayed – politically dangerous? – opponents who had expected more mercy and 'forgive and forget', led by Sir Henry Vane. The regicides and their allies were also cynically thrown to the wolves, though some degree of revenge for the execution of Charles' father was logical, and a disturbing degree of revanchist royalist propaganda about the divinity of monarchy re-emerged that betrayed the more logical and practical political thinking of the 1650s. Tellingly there was no 'constitutional settlement' with a chief executive/monarch restored and limited by specific and untouchable Parliamentary fiat in spring 1660, and symbolically Charles was allowed to claim that he had been king since his father's death in 1649 (i.e. by hereditary right), not been created, such by the Commons in 1660. The settlement of 1689 was to be more careful and specific, and arguably Monck and his allies missed a major chance to rein in royal power by law in April 1660 – though a later Parliament with a royalist majority could have tried to overturn any such laws. The reason was probably a mix of haste to secure a stable new government (with Monck a 'plain soldier', not a constitutional enthusiast like Lambert or Ireton) and the distaste of the king and his allies for any such move. But the lop-sided nature of the Restoration settlement was a major mistake, as seen in retrospect, and was to aid the continuation of faction and instability through Charles II's reign.

Notes

Prologue
 1. Clarke Papers vol iii pp. 9–10; 'A Second Narrative of the Late Parliament' in *Harleian Miscellanry*, vol iii, pp. 489–93, 501; Edmund Ludlow, *Memoirs*, vol I p. 366. Thurloe State Papers vol I pp. 630, 637.
 2. Austin Woolrych, *Commonwealth to Protectorate* (Clarendon Press 1982), especially pp. 236–343.
 3. Ludlow, vol I p. 369.
 4. Thurloe I pp. 589–610, 628; National Archives: S.P. 31/3/92, ff. 36, 48, 83–4. Calendar of State Papers Venetian 1653–4, p. 155; Bodleian Library: Clarendon Mss. 47, f. 113.
 5. C. Abbott, *Writings and Speeches of Oliver Cromwell*, vol iii p. 455.
 6. Abbott vol iv p. 418.
 7. N. A: S.P. 18, vol 42, f. 9; Woolrych, p. 355; S. R. Gardiner, *History of the Commonwealth and Protectorate* vol 2 pp. 270–2.
 8. N.A: Thomason Tracts: The Protector (So-Called) In Part Unveiled, 24 October 1655, p. 12.
 9. Abbott vol iii pp. 136–8; N.A. Thomason Tracts: Severall Proceedings of State Affairs, no. 221 (15–22 December 1653) pp. 34, 98–500; The Protector Unveiled, p. 13; Ludlow vol I p. 373.
 10. T.A. Armstrong, 'The inauguration ceremonies of the Yorkist kings, and their title to the throne', in *Transactions of the Royal Historical Society*, 4th series, vol 30 (1948) pp. 51–73.
 11. Thurloe vol I p. 641; N.A.: Thomason Tracts: *Mercurius Politicus*, 16–22 December 1653, p. 3054.
 12. Calendar of State Papers Domestic 1653–4 pp. 304–8.
 13. Ibid pp. 286–7; Thurloe vol I pp. 641, 650.
 14. Gardiner, *History of the Commonwealth and Protectorate* iii p. 182.
 15. Ibid pp. 184–5.
 16. N.A: S.P. 31/3/94, French ambassador Antoine de Bordeaux to Count de Brienne, 14/24 September 1654.
 17. *Commons Journal* vol vii p. 368; Thomas Burton, *Diary*, vol I pp. xxxiii – xxxv.
 18. Burton vol I p. lx.
 19. Ibid p. li; British Library Additional Mss. 17677 U, f. 433.
 20. Worcester College Oxford: Clarke Papers vol iii p. 15.
 21. Gardiner, vol iii pp. 211–13.
 22. Ibid, pp. 236–9; *Commons Journal* vol vii p. 413; Burton vol I p. cxx; Bodleian Library: Carte Mss. lxxiv, ff. 64, 113.

Chapter One

1. See Christopher Durston, *Cromwell's Major-Generals: Godly Government During the English Revolution* (Manchester UP 2001).
2. C. H. Firth, *Last Years of the Protectorate*, vol 1 (1909) p. 63.
3. J. S. Morrill, 'Rewriting Cromwell: A case of deafening silences' in *Canadian Journal of History*, vol 38 (2003) pp. 553–78; Jonathan Fitzgibbons, 'Hereditary Succession in the Cromwellian Protectorate: the offer of the crown reconsidered' in *E. H. R.* 2013, pp. 1095–1128.
4. Peter Gaunt, ed, Correspondence of Henry Cromwell 1655–1659 (Camden Society, 5th series, vol 21, 2007) pp. 188–9.
5. Giavarina to Senate, 28 Nov/8 December 1656, CSP Venetian, pp. 287–9.
6. Burton's Diary. Vol I, p. 321.
7. Patrick Little, *Oliver Cromwell: New Perspectives* (Palgrave 2009) pp. 231–2.
8. Whitelocke, *Memorials*, pp. 548–53.
9. Michael Roberts, ed, Swedish Diplomats at Cromwell's Court, 1655–1656, Camden Society 4th series (Royal Historical Society, London, 1988), pp. 317–18.
10. Ibid p. 326; *The Poems of Edmund Waller*, ed George Thorn-Dury, London 1905, vol ii p. 27.
11. National Archives: S.P. 31/3/101, ff. 43–4.
12. Historical Manuscripts Commission 15th Report, appendix part vii: Ailesbury Mss. p. 160; G. R. Elton, ed, *The Tudor Constitution: Documents and Commentary* (Cambridge 1960) pp. 2–5.
13. Clarke Papers vol 3, pp. 89–90.
14. Thurloe State Papers vol vi p. 15; Ludlow, *Memoirs*, vol I p. 353.
15. Bamfylde to Thurloe, Sept 1657, quoted in Abbott, *Letters and Speeches*, vol iv p. 436.
16. N.A. S.P. 31/3–100: Bordeaux to Brienne, 9/19 October 1657.
17. Burton, Diary, vol I pp. 362–3.
18. Thurloe State Papers vol vi, pp. 37–8; Gaunt, ibid, pp. 194–5.
19. N.A. S.P. 31/3/101, f. 43.
20. *Commons Journal* vol vii p. 496; Clarke Papers vol iii pp. 91, 94.
21. *Commons Journal* vol vii p. 511.
22. N.A. Thomason Tracts: *Mercurius Politicus*, 26 March – 2 April 1657; Thomas Carlyle, *Letters and Speeches of Oliver Cromwell*, vol iii pp. 27–9.
23. C. F. Egloff, 'Robert Beake: a letter concerning the Humble Petition and Advice, 28 March 1657' in *Bulletin of the Institute of Historical Research*, vol 68, no. 166 (June 1995) pp. 233–9.
24. Ibid p. 233; Carlyle, vol iii pp. 487–8.
25. George Fox, *Journal*, ed Norman Penny (London 1924), p. 71.
26. Carlyle, vol iii pp. 29–33; Burton, Diary, vol I p. 411.
27. Carlyle, vol iii pp. 22–38.
28. Bulstrode Whitelocke (attrib.): 'Monarchy Asserted to be the Best, most Ancient and legal form of Government, in a conference held at Whitehall with Oliver, late Lord Protector, and a Committee of Parliament (London 1660) pp. 1–3, 9.
29. Monarchy Asserted, pp. 19–21, 23; Thurloe, vol ii p. 614.
30. Monarchy Asserted, pp. 16–35, 39–44.
31. British Library: Lansdowne Mss. 822, f. 57.
32. Monarchy Asserted, pp. 53–4.

33. N.A. S.P. 31/3/101, ff. 160–1.
34. Thurloe vol vi, pp. 261, 281.
35. Ibid, pp. 219, 261.
36. Ludlow, *Memoirs*, vol ii p. 24.
37. H. M. C. 4th Report: Appendix: Sutherland Mss. 163; NA: TT: *Mercurius Politicus*, 7–14 May 1657; Monarchy Asserted pp. 111–12.
38. A Collection of the State Letters of the Rt Hon. Roger Boyle, the first Earl of Orrery… together with the life of the earl of Orrery, by the Reverend Mr Thomas Morrice (London 1742) pp. 21–2; Gilbert Burnet, *History of My Own Time* (Dublin 1724) vol I p. 40.
39. British Library: Additional Mss. 32093, ff. 348–9.
40. *Commons Journal* vol vii pp. 535, 537, 539; Acts and Ordinances of the Interregnum, ed C. H. Firth and R. S. Rait (HMSO, 1911), vol ii pp. 1184–5.
41. C. H. Firth, *The House of Lords during the Civil War* (London 1910) p. 251.
42. H. Henfrey, *Numismata Cromwelliana* (London 1877), p. 103.
43. Roy Sherwood, *Oliver Cromwell: King In All But Name 1653–1658* (Sutton 1997), pp. 99, 103; Sir Philip Warwick, *Memoirs of the Reign of King Charles the First with a Continuaiton to the Happy Restauration of Charles the Second* (London 1701) p. 248.
44. C. H. Firth, *The Last Years of the Protectorate*, vol ii p. 3; N.A.: S.P. 31/3/101, Bordeaux to Brienne, 30 July/ 9 August 1657.
45. Ibid; Thurloe vol vi pp. 219, 261.
46. Thurloe vol v p. 146; H. M. C. Frankland-Russell-Astley Mss. (HMSO 1900), p. 22.
47. British Library: Harleian Mss. 991, p. 223.
48. CSPV 1657-9, pp. 38, 70.
49. Calendar of State Papers Domestic 1656–7, p. 349; Calendar of State Papers Venetian 1657–9, pp. 38, 70; Thurloe vol vi pp. 600, 628; N.A.: Thomason Tracts: *Mercurius Politicus*, 19–26 September 1657; *The Conway Letters*, ed. Marjorie Hope Nicholson (Oxford 1992) p. 142.
50. Thurloe vol vi pp. 426, 495–6.
51. Francois Guizot, *History of Oliver Cromwell and the English Commonwealth* (London 1854), vol ii p. 583; N.A.: S.P. 31/3/101, Bordeaux to Brienne, 5/15 November 1657.
52. Thurloe vol vi p. 579.
53. Ibid pp. 614–15.
54. Calendar of State Papers Clarendon vol iii p. 381.
55. British Library: Rawlinson Mss. 63, f. 210.
56. British Library: Additional Mss. 6125, f. 82.
57. National Archives: S.P. 108/55: Anglo-French treaty, 1658.
58. Thurloe vol vii, p. 197–8, 206.
59. Thurloe vol i, pp. 759–63.
60. British Library: Somers Tracts, vol vi p. 331.
61. Clarke Papers, vol iii pp. 207–8.
62. Harleian Miscellany, vol 1 pp. 287–9.
63. B. L. Additional Mss. 6125, f. 82.
64. Thurloe vol vii p. 63.
65. Ibid pp. 215 and (1659 Dunkirk revenue report) 715–19.
66. Ibid vol vii, p. 215.
67. H. M. C. 6th Report: Appendix: ffarington Mss., p. 442.

68. H. M. C. Egmont Mss. vol I part 2, p. 593; Calendar of State Papers Domestic 1657–8, pp. 255, 258.
69. Antonia Fraser, *Cromwell Our Chief Of Men*, p. 457.

Chapter Two
1. H. M. C. 5th Report: Appendix: Sutherland Mss. p. 180.
2. Clarke Papers vol iii, pp. 141–2.
3. H. M. C. 6th Report: Appendix: ffarington Mss., p. 442.
4. William Woolrych, *Lives of Eminent Sergeants-at-Law of the English Bar* (London 1869) vol I, pp. 33–1; Bulstrode Whitelocke, *Memorials of the English Affairs* (London 1682) p. 674.
5. Samuel Carrington, *The History of the Life and Death of His Most Serene Highness Oliver, Late Lord Protector* (London 1659) pp. 218–19; H. M. C. 5th Report: Appendix: Sutherland Mss., p. 146; National Archives: T.T.: *Mercurius Politicus*, 5–12 August 1658; Robert Ramsey, *Studies in Cromwell's Family Circle* (London 1930) p. 17; Andrew Marvell, Poems and Letters, pp. 129–37.
6. George Fox, *Journal*, p. 173; Thurloe vol vii p. 320.
7. For the official version of events: Thurloe vii p. 320, Some Further Intelligence of the Affairs of England (1659) p. 2; for the poisoning claim, see George Bate, *Elenchus Motuum Nuperorum in Anglia: or a Short Historical Account of the Rise and Progress of the late Troubles in England* (London 1685) part 2 pp. 236–7.
8. Alleged orchestrated official nature of the addresses at Richard's accession: Ludlow, p. 614. Reaction to Cromwell's death: Clarendon State Papers vol iii p. 421. Provincial reaction: A True Catalogue or an account of the Several Places and most Eminent Persons where and by whom Richard Cromwell was proclaimed Protector (London September 1659).
9. Some Further Intelligence of the Affairs of England, p. 2; Stuart Royal Proclamations, vol ii p. 2.
10. The private funeral: Clarke Papers vol iii pp. 167–8; Calendar of State Papers Venetian 1657–9, p. 268; Arthur Stanley, *Historical Memorials of Westminster Abbey* (7th edition, 1890) p. 160; Frances and Margaret Verney, eds, *Verney Family Memoirs During the Seventeenth Century*, vol ii p. 129. Official ceremony: J. Burrough, 'A Testimony Against a Great Idolatry', in Memorable Works, p. 457; National Archives: T.T.: *Mercurius Politicus*, 18–25 November 1658; Sir John Prestwich, *Respublica* (London 1787), pp. 175–6.
11. On the crown used at the lying-in-state: Prestwich, pp. 174, 188. See also National Archives: TT: *Mercurius Politicus*, 14–21 October 1658; Roy Sherwood, *Oliver Cromwell: King In All But Name*, pp. 147–8.
12. Ludlow, p. 242.
13. Firth and Rait, eds, *Acts and Ordinances of the Interregnum*, vol ii, pp. 1184–5.
14. Antonia Fraser, *Cromwell Our Chief of Men*, p. 117.
15. Guizot, *Richard Cromwell*, vol I p. 367.
16. Ibid; see also an unsupported royalist claim that Richard negotiated with royalist agents and agreed to flee London to Montague's fleet and then declare for the king in return for a £20,000 pension, but then lost his nerve. Clarendon State Papers, vol iii pp. 469, 477.
17. As chapter 1, note 31.
18. Thurloe vol vii, pp. 436, 447–9 (draft of Richard's speech), 500; Clarke Papers vol iii, pp. 165–6; Calendar of State Papers Venetian 1657–9, pp. 254–8.

19. D. Masserella, 'The Politics of the Army and the Quest for Settlement' in Ivan Roots, ed, *Into Another Mould*, p. 60.
20. N.A.: TT: *Public Intelligencer*, 18–25 October 1658; C. H. Firth, ed, 'A Speech by Richard Cromwell', in *English Historical Review*, vol xxiii (1908) pp. 734–6.
21. N.A: S.P. 18/182, ff. 136–9; S.P. 183, ff. 15–139.
22. Thurloe vol vii pp. 436, 500; Clarke Papers vol iii, pp. 168–70; Guizot, vol I pp. 262–4; Worcester College Oxford: Clarke Mss. 30, ff. 190v – 192.
23. F. Guizot, *History of Richard Cromwell and the Restoration of Charles II* (trans. F Scoble, London 1856) vol I p. 238.
24. N.A: TT: *Public Intelligencer*, 15–22 November 1658.
25. H. M. C. Leybourne-Popham Mss. pp. 114–15; BL: Lansdowne Mss. 823, ff. 245v, 278; Ludlow, pp. 634–5.
26. F. Guizot, vol I pp. 271–3.
27. NA: S.P. 31/3/105, f. 230 (Bordeaux on the change in electoral system). *Commons Journal* vol vii pp. 594–603; Burton, *Diary*, ed John Towill Rutt (1828 edition), vol iii pp. 17–287. On the 7 April report by the Committee of Public Accounts: *Commons Journal* vii pp. 627–31.
28. Burton *Diary*, vol iii pp. 288–96; *Commons Journal* p. 604.
29. Ibid pp. 605–21; Burton, vol iii pp. 307–574; vol iv pp. 7–298. British Library: Lansdowne Mss. 523, ff. 229, 251, 259, 639–42.
30. *Commons Journal*, pp. 627–31; Burton, Diary, vol iv pp. 361–448.
31. Register of the Consultations of the Ministers of Edinburgh, vol ii, ed Rev. W. Stephen (*Scottish Historical Society* 1930) pp. 158, 163–8.
32. Clarke Papers vol iii pp. 187–8; Old Parliamentary History, vol xxi pp. 340–1; *Commons Journal* p. 632.
33. National Archives: TT: To His Excellency the Lord Fleetwood... the Humble Address of the late Lord Pride's Regiment, 8 April 1659.
34. Ludlow, *Memoirs* (1698 edition) pp. 633–6.
35. Ronald Hutton, *Restoration*, pp. 35–6.
36. Clarke Papers, vol iii p. 189; British Library: Lansdowne Mss. 823, ff. 291, 299.
37. *Commons Journal* p. 641; Burton, vol iv pp. 448–63; British Library: Lansdowne Mss. 823, f. 299.
38. Clarke Papers vol iii pp. 190–4; Guizot, vol I pp. 363–8, 372–5; Thurloe vol vii pp. 659–62; British Library: Lansdowne Mss. 823, ff. 299, 301; Ludlow, pp. 639–42.
39. Guizot, vol I pp. 372–5, 379; Clarke Papers, vol iii pp. 194–6, vol iv pp. 1–2; Thurloe vol vii, pp. 666–7; H. M. C. 3rd Report, p. 88; British Library: Lansdowne Mss. 823, f. 308; British Library: Additional Mss. 22919.
40. Clarendon State Papers vol iii p. 469; *Commons Journal* pp. 655, 664–5, 705, 720; Thurloe vol vii pp. 683–4; Richard Baker, *A Chronicle of the Kings of England* (1670) pp. 662–4.
41. National Archives: TT: Forty-Four Queries To The Life of King Dick, 15 July 1659; Nicholas Papers, vol iv p. 148.
42. *Commons Journal*, pp. 646, 648, 659, 662: Nicholas Papers vol iv pp. 155–7. National Archives: TT: The Petition and Address of the Officers of the Army, 12 May 1659.
43. NA: TT: A Vindication of Sir Henry Vane, 7 June 1659; T. Collier, The Decision and Clearing of the Great point Now In Controversy, 1659; The Humble Petition of Many Inhabitants In And About the City of London, 12 May 1659; William Cole, Several Proposals Humbly Tendered. B. Reay, 'The Quakers, 1659 and the Restoration of the Monarchy', in *History*, vol 63 (1978), p. 93.

44. *Commons Journal*, pp. 644–59, 664; Firth and Rait, eds, Acts and Ordinances of the Interregnum, vol ii, pp. 1270–9; Whitelocke, *Memorials* (1854 edition), vol iv p. 349; Bodleian Library: Rawlinson Mss: C 179 (Council of State proceedings, May – August 1659) and National Archives: S.P. 25/179 (ditto August – October 1659).
45. *Commons Journal*, pp. 678, 707.
46. *Commons Journal*, pp. 655, 660, 669, 675, 684, 689, 703, 707–8.
47. J. F. MacLear, 'Quakerism and the end of the Interregnum' in *Church History*, vol 19 (1950) pp. 240–60; National Archives: TT: Roger Cruip and others, A Voyce From Zion, 1659.
48. *Commons Journal* p. 671; Corporation of London Record Office: Journal 41, f. 204.
49. *Commons Journal*, pp. 721–6; Bodleian Library: Rawlinson Mss. C 179, p. 37; NA: TT: *Mercurius Politicus*, 7–14, 14–21 and 21–28 July 1659: Bloodie News From Enfield: A Relation of the Cruelties and Barbarous Murders…, 1659.
50. Clarendon State Papers, vol iii pp. 459–60; Bodleian Library: Rawlinson Mss. A259, pp. 1–20; C 179, pp. 5–11, 160, 224–57; National Archives: S.P. 25/98, pp. 48–92.
51. David Underdown, *Royalist Conspiracy in England 1649–1660*, pp. 276–81; N.A: TT: *Mercurius Politicus*, 25 August – 1 September and 8–15 September 1659; Bodleian Library: Clarendon mss. 63, ff. 193, 243.
52. Firth and Rait, *Acts and Ordinances of the Interrgnum*, vol ii pp. 1277–82.
53. *Commons Journal*, p. 666; Clarke Papers, vol iii pp. 279–80, 296–8; N.A: S.P. 78/114/ 273 and 25/79 pp. 25–79. Bodleian Library: Carte Mss. 73, f. 284, 464–6; Clarendon Mss. 61, f. 303; Tanner Mss. 51, f. 98.
54. Bodleian Library: Wood Mss. C13, f. 6.
55. *Commons Journal* pp. 775, 790–1; Guizot vol I pp. 474–5.
56. Ibid p. 467; Bernard Capp, *The Fifth Monarchy Men*, p. 126. Friends' House mss: L. Barclay Mss. 73 and Howard Mss. 8.
57. N.A: TT: The Army's Proposals to The Parliament, September 1659; Ludlow p. 698; Clarke Papers vol iv pp. 57–8.
58. *Commons Journal* pp. 784–6; Ludlow p. 765; Whitelocke, Memorials (1854 edition) vol iv p. 361; Baker, Chronicle, pp. 676–8; Guizot, vol I pp. 482–4; Clarke Papers, vol iv pp. 56–7.
59. *Commons Journal* pp. 789–90; Bodleian Library: Carte Mss. 213, f. 365.
60. NA: TT: The Humble Representation and Petition of the Officers… the 5th of October, 1659; Guizot, vol I pp. 496–8; Baker, *Chronicle*, pp. 681–2.
61. T. Gumble, *The Life of General Monck* (London 1671) pp. 103–9; J. Price, *The Mystery and Method of His Majesty's Happy Restauration* (London 1680) pp. 12–31.

Chapter Three
1. John Evelyn, *Diary and Letters*, ed. W. Bray, 4 vols (London 1850), vol I p. 337.
2. Ronald Hutton, *Restoration*, p. 101.
3. Calendar of State Papers Venetian 1657–9, p. 86.
4. Ludlow, p. 714; Calendar of State Papers Domestic 1659, pp. 255–7; NA: TT: *Mercurius Politicus*, 20–27 October 1657.
5. Hutton, p. 69.
6. Clarke Papers vol iv, pp. 151–4, 227–8.
7. Barry Reay, 'The Quakers in 1659', p. 210. Also see Reay, 'Early Quaker Activity and the Reaction To It', Oxford D Phil thesis 1980.

8. NA: TT: *Mercurius Politicus*, 20–27 October and 27 October – 3 November 1659; A Declaration of the General Council of the Army, 27 October 1659; Bodleian Library: Clarendon Mss. 66, ff. 80–1, 143.
9. Bodleian Library: Clarendon Mss. 66, ff. 74–5, 78–9, 84–6; Clarendon State Papers no. 591.
10. Guizot, vol I p. 284; Barclay, ed, Letters, pp. 71–3.
11. Clarke Papers vol iv pp. 91–5, 103–4, 105–7, 109–10.
12. Ibid pp. 108–9; Baker, *Chronicle*, p. 69; Worcester College Library, Oxford: A Conference Between Two Soldiers (November 1659) and Information from some soldiers (November? 1659).
13. NA: TT: *Mercurius Politicus*, 10–17 November 1659.
14. Ibid: *Public Intelligencer*, 22–28 November 1659 (Newcastle bulletins); Clarke Papers vol iv, pp. 113–15, 116–17, 117–18, 120–1, 124–5, 155.
15. H. M. C. 9th Report, part ii, pp. 493–4.
16. Bernard Capp, *The Fifth Monarchy Men*, pp. 127–8; NA: TT: The Acts and Monuments of our Late Parliament, 19 October 1659 and Complaints and Querries upon England's Miserie, 20 October 1659 (by John Canne, pro-Monck).
17. Guizot, vol ii pp. 285, 290; NA: TT: *Mercurius Politicus*, 10–17 November 1659; Bodleian Library: Clarendon Mss. 66, ff. 103–4; *Old Parliamentary History*, vol xxii, pp. 10–17 on the 8 November speeches at the Guildhall.
18. Bodleian Library: Clarendon Mss. 67, f. 42.
19. Ibid, ff. 34–5; NA: TT: A Letter from Sir Arthur Hesilrige in Portsmouth..., 1659; W. D. Christie, *The Life of Sir Anthony Ashley Cooper* (1871) vol I p. 196.
20. Clarke Papers vol iv pp. 164–7; Rugge, *Diurnal*, pp. 13–15; Corporation of London Record Office: *Journal* 41, f. 212; Bodleian Library: Clarendon Mss. 67, f. 119; Baker, *Chronicle*, p. 697.
21. Whitelocke, *Memorials* vol iv pp. 378–9; Clarke Papers, vol iv pp. 186–7, 189; Corporation of London Record Office: Repertory 66, ff. 22–3; Worcester College Oxford: Clarke Mss. 32, f. 175v.
22. Calendar of State Papers Domestic 1659, p. 268; Clarendon State Papers, vol iii pp. 629–30; Guizot, vol ii pp. 315–16; Clarke Papers pp. 210, 215–17; NA: TT: Two Letters from Vice-Admiral John Lawson, 1659.
23. Guizot, vol ii pp. 315–16.
24. NA: TT: *Public Intelligencer*, 19–26 December 1659; *Weekly Post*, 21–27 December 1659. Clarendon State Papers vol iii pp. 634–5, 637; Guizot vol ii pp. 318–19; Whitelocke, vol iv p. 383; Clarke Papers vol iv pp. 219–20.
25. Guizot, vol ii pp. 318–19, 327; Clarke Papers vol iv pp. 182–231; Worcester College Oxford: Clarke Mss. 32, ff. 20v, 210, 218–227v; *Commons Journal* vol viii p. 804; NA: SP 18/219/ 2 and 5.
26. *Commons Journal*, pp. 804, 805, 812, 826–33; Clarke Papers vol iv pp. 240–1, 247–8; Guizot, pp. 329, 331; *Memoirs* of Colonel Hutchinson, pp. 312–14.
27. Corporation of London Record Office: *Journal* 41, f. 218; Clarendon State Papers, vol iii pp. 639, 644–6; Rugge, *Diurnal*, pp. 25–9; Bodleian Library: Clarendon Mss. 68, ff. 100–01.
28. NA: TT: *Mercurius Politicus*, 5–12 and 12–19 January 1660; H. M. C. Buccleuch Mss. vol I pp. 311–12; Bodleian Library: Clarendon Mss. 69, ff. 20–1, 33–4; G. Davies, 'The Political Career of Sir Richard Temple' in *Historical Library Quarterly*, vol iv (1940–1) p. 50.

29. Bodleian Library: Clarendon Mss. 68, ff. 204–5; 69, ff. 33–4; NA: TT: *Mercurius Publicus*, 29 January – 2 February 1660.
30. NA: TT: William Prynne, *A Brief Narrative*, 26 December 1659; *Six Important Queries*, 30 December 1659; *Seven Additional Queries*, 4 January 1660; *A Full Declaration*, 30 January 1660. Guizot ii pp. 320, 323–4.
31. Corporation of London Record Office: *Journal* 41, f. 218; Bodleian Library: Clarendon Mss. 68, ff. 100–101; *Commons Journal* p. 802.
32. Bodleian Library; Clarendon Mss. 68, ff. 204–5; 69, ff. 33–4; Clarke Papers vol iv, pp. 249–50.
33. Baker, *Chronicle*, pp. 704–6; Whitelocke, *Memorials*, vol iv pp. 393–4.
34. Leybourne-Popham Mss. f. 145; Whitelocke vol iv p. 394; NA: TT: *Mercurius Publicus*, 2–9 February 1660.
35. Bodleian Library: Clarendon mss. 69, ff. 117–18, 126–8; Clarendon State Papers vol iii pp. 674–5; Corporation of London Record Office: *Repertory* 67, ff. 42v-43. *Commons Journal* p. 841; Ludlow pp. 824–30; Guizot, pp. 345–50; Rugge, *Diurnal*, p. 39.
36. Hutton, *The Restoration*, p. 95.
37. Ibid, pp. 95–6.
38. Guizot, pp. 354–61; *Commons Journal*, p. 842; Ludlow, pp. 832–47; Baker, *Chronicle.*, pp. 709–12; Calendar of State Papers Domestic pp. 358–72.
39. *Commons Journal* p. 849.
40. Leybourne-Popham Mss. ff. 157–69; NA: TT: *Public Intelligencer*, 27 February – 5 March 1660; Baker, *Chronicle*, pp. 713–14.
41. Ludlow, A Voice From the Watchtower (Camden Society, 4th series, vol 21, 1978) pp. 88–92; *Commons Journal*, pp. 852–5; *Memoirs* of Colonel Hutchinson, pp. 314–15.
42. Bodleian Library: Clarendon Mss. 70, ff. 112–13, 122–3; *Commons Journal*, pp. 859–67; NA: TT: *Mercurius Publicus*, 8–15 March 1660; Guizot, pp. 376–9; Baker, *Chronicle*, p. 716; Rugge, *Diurnal*, p. 53; Nicholas Papers, vol iv pp. 200–03.
43. Firth and Rait, *Acts and Ordinances of the Interregnum*, vol ii nos. 1425, 1459–63, 1465–9.
44. *Commons Journal* pp. 871–80; Guizot, pp. 782–3; Thurloe vol vii, p. 861; Calendar of State Papers Domestic pp. 39304; H. M. C. Portland Mss. vol iii pp. 218–19; Firth and Rait, vol ii nos. 1425–55.
45. *Commons Journal*, pp. 868–80; Firth and Rait, vol ii, nos. 1469–72; Guizot pp. 380–1; Bodleian Library: Carte Mss. 213, f. 667.
46. Clarendon State Papers vol iii pp. 703, 705, 711–12, 721–2; Mordaunt's Letter Book, pp. 82, 95–6.
47. Hutton, *Restoration*, p. 111 and note.
48. NA: TT: *Mercurius Politicus*, 16–17 July 1656.
49. Baker, *Chronicle*, pp. 673, 675, 717–18; Clarendon State Papers, vol iii p. 697.
50. Ibid, pp. 710, 726–7; Guizot p. 393.
51. G. Davies, 'The General Election of 1660' in *History Library Quarterly*, vol xv (1951-2) pp. 211–35; L. F. Brown, 'Religious Factions in the Convention Parliament' in *English Historical Review*, vol xxii (1907) pp. 52–5; Alan Everitt, *The Community of Kent and the Great Rebellion* (1966), pp. 312–13; Anthony Fletcher, *A County Community in Peace and War: Sussex 1600–1660* (1975) pp. 321–2; John Morrill, *Cheshire in the Civil War*, p. 326; David Underdown, *Somerset in the Civil*

Notes 247

War and Interregnum (Newton Abbot 1973) p. 192; Clive Holmes, *Seventeeth Century Lincolnshire* (Lincoln 1980) p. 218; Mary Coate, *Cornwall in the Great Civil War and Interregnum* (1933) p. 313; Latimer, *Annals of Bristol*, p. 293; Leybourne-Popham Mss. f. 173; H. M. C. Portland Mss. vol iii p. 220; *Victoria County History of Huntingdonshire* vol ii pp. 29030; Nottinghamshire Record Office: DO/ SR/ 221/ 96/ 14–15.
52. Hutton, pp. 112–13.
53. Baker, *Chronicle*, p. 719; Clarendon State Papers vol iii pp. 710–11; Bodleian Library: Clarendon Mss. 71, ff. 80, 100; NA: TT: *Mercurius Publicus*, 5–12 April 1660.
54. Clarke Papers vol iii pp. 708, 715; vol iv, pp. 266–7. NA: TT: *Mercurius Publicus*, 22–29 March, 29 March – 5 April, and 5–12 April 1660.
55. Ibid, 19–26 April 1660; Rugge, *Diurnal*, p. 69; Leybourne-Popham Mss. f. 175; Clarke Papers vol iv p. 267; H. M. C. 13th Report, part vi, pp. 3–4; H. M. C. 5th report, p. 361; Guizot, vol ii pp. 408–12; NA: TT: An Exact Accompt, 13–27 April 1660 and London's *Diurnal*, 18 April – 2 May 1660.
56. *The Diaries and Papers of Sir Edward Dering* (1976): Diary, pp. 36–7; Clarendon State Papers vol iii p. 727 and 729–32; *Commons Journal*, vol viii 1–7; *Lords Journal*, pp. 6–9; Bodleian Library: Carte Mss. 214, ff. 71–2; Clarendon Mss. 72, ff. 19–20.
57. Baker, *Chronicle*, p. 718; Bodleian Library: Clarendon mss. 71, ff. 127–8 and British Library, Egerton Mss. 2542, ff. 328–9 (drafts of Declaration of Breda).
58. *Commons Journal*, vol viii pp. 14–49; E. Hyde, *The Life of Edward Hyde, Earl of Clarendon* (Oxford 1836) vol I pp. 326–7; Baker, pp. 730–4; Rugge, *Diurnal*, pp. 79–80; Staffordshire Record Office: D 868/4/45a.
59. Clarke Papers vol iv, pp. 247–8.
60. Clarendon State Papers, vol iii pp. 744–5, 747–9.
61. *Lords Journal*, pp. 27–50.

Chapter Four
1. Sir A. Bryant, ed, *Letters of Charles II* (2nd edition, New York 1969) pp. 90–1.
2. National Archives: P/C2/54, f. 91 and S.P. 29/23/ 93–104; Baker, p. 734; *Calendar of State Papers Domestic 1660–1*, pp. 59–604; Hyde, *Life of Clarendon*, vol I p. 370.
3. For Heneage Finch: *New Dictionary of National Biography*, vol 19, pp. 563–6 (article by D E C Yale)
4. British Library: Egerton Mss. 2537, f. 231; N.A: s.P. 2918/4.
5. Thurloe: *New DNB* vol 54, pp. 711–15 (article by T M Venning).
6. Ronald Hutton, *Charles II*, pp. 143–5.
7. Philip Jones: *New DNB*, vol 30, pp. 604–6 (article by Stephen Roberts); Thomas Birch: vol 5, pp. 801–2 (article by David Whitehead).
8. Bodleian Library: Dep. F.9, ff. 22–4; F. Varley, ed, The *Restoration* Visitation of the University of Oxford (*Camden Miscellany*, vol xviii, 1948); H. M. C. Leybourne-Popham Mss. pp. 183–4; A. S. Clark, Lincoln College (1898) pp. 132–3; Brasenose Quartercentenary Monographs (*Oxford Historical Society*, 1909) vol ii, pp. 5–7; F. G. Hardy, Jesus College (1899) pp. 128–31; T. Fowler, *History of Corpus Christi*, (Oxford Historical Society 1897) pp. 230–2; Sidney Hamilton, *Hertford College* (Oxford 1903) p.33; John Magrath, *The Queens' College* (Oxford 1921) vol ii pp. 4–32; Herbert Blakiston, *Trinity College* (Oxford 1898) p. 149.
9. See J. Price, *The Mystery and the Method of His Majesty's Happy Restauration*.

10. D. Jordan and M. Walsh, *The King's Revenge: Charles II and the Greatest Manhunt in British History* (Abacus 2012) pp. 146–7, quoting Price as above.
11. *Commons Journal*, vol viii, entries for 4 and 8 June 1660.
12. Jordan and Walsh, pp. 184–5.
13. *Lords Journal*, entry for 8 September 1660.
14. *Lords Journal*, pp. 95–148; *Commons Journal*, pp. 19–140; British Library: Egerton Mss. 2537, f. 60.
15. *Memoirs of Colonel Hutchinson*, pp. 321–7.
16. Ruth Spalding, *The Improbable Puritan: The Life of Bulstrode Whitelocke*, pp. 225–9.
17. Hutton, *Restoration*, p. 133.
18. Jordan and West, p. 192.
19. Ibid pp. 203–5, 210, 215, 228–31, 239–40.
20. Ibid pp. 205, 207.
21. Ibid pp. 167–8, 202–4, 255–61.
22. Hutton, p. 133.
23. NA: Thomason Tracts: A Most Exact and Impartial Account of the Indictment Arraignment Trial and Judgement of Nine and Twenty Regicides; Thomas Howell, State Trials (1816) vol v, pp. 973–1256. .
24. Pepys, *Diary*, vol I pp. 263–9; NA: TT: Speeches and Prayers of the Regicides.
25. *Commons Journal* p. 117–202; *Lords Journal* pp. 205–26; Pepys, Diary, vol ii p. 26; John Dart, *Westmonasterium*, vol 2 p. 144.
26. See Jonathan Fitzgibbon, *Cromwell's Head* (Bloomsbury 2008).
27. Staffordshire Record Office: D 868/9/10.
28. Ibid; also The Autobiography of Sir John Bramston (*Camden Society*, 1845) p. 117.
29. Calendar of State Papers Domestic 1660–1, pp. 72 ff, 123–5; NA: CRES 6/21 and L/R2/266, f. 58; *Calendar of Treasury Books*, ed W Shaw (HMSO 1905), p. 181–452.
30. Hyde, *Life of Clarendon*, vol I p. 354.
31. *New DNB: Henry Cromwell*: vol 14, pp. 313–20 (article by Peter Gaunt); *Richard Cromwell*, ibid pp. 356–66 (Peter Gaunt). Also see J. A. Butler, *A Biography of Richard Cromwell, the Second Protector* (1994).
32. NA: P/C/ 2/54.
33. Jeffrey Brotton, *The Sale of the Late King's Goods: Charles I and His Art Collection* (Pan Macmillan 2006) pp. 333–42.
34. Ibid.
35. Brotton, p. 344.
36. H. J. Habbakuk, 'The Parliamentary Army and Crown Lands', in *Welsh History Review*, vol 3 (1966) pp. 403–26; Habbakuk, 'The Land Settlement and the *Restoration* of Charles II' in *Transactions of the Royal Historical Society*, 5th series, vol 28 (1978) p. 201–2; Ian Gentles, 'The Sale of Crown Lands' in *Historical Review*, vol 26 (1973) pp. 614–75; Gentles, 'The Sale of Bishops' Lands' in *English Historical Review*, vol cxv (1980) pp. 573–90; Joan Thirsk, 'The *Restoration* Land Settlment' in *Journal of Modern History*, vol xxv (1954) pp. 315–28; W. J. Shiels, 'The *Restoration* and the Temporalities' in *Borthwick Historical Institute Bulletin*, vol 1 (1975) pp. 17–30.
37. Thirsk, ibid, pp. 317–18; Habbakuk, 'The Land Settlement...', pp. 209–10, 213–14; *Commons Journal* pp. 72–3, 86, 113; *Lords Journal* p. 93; Bodleian Library Mss: Dep. F9, ff 19, 69–73, 121–8, 139, 146.

38. Rugge, *Diurnal*, p. 12.
39. NA: CRES 6/1–3; S.P. 29/16/35; TT: Parliamentary Intelligencer, 26 November – 3 December 1660; British Library: Egerton Mss. 2542, f. 578; Calendar of Treasury Books, pp. 65, 70, 359.
40. Thirsk, pp. 320–8; Thirsk, 'The sales of Royalist Lands' in *Economic History Review*, 2nd series, vol 5 (1952) pp. 188–207; Habbakuk, 'Landowners and the Civil War' in *Economic History Review*, 2nd series, vol 18 (1965) pp. 130–8; P. Holiday, 'Land Sales and Repurchases in Yorkshire' in *Northern History*, vol v (1970) pp. 67–92; Blackwood, Lancashire Gentry, pp. 120–47.
41. Bodleian Library: Carte Mss. 49, ff. 4, 48; Mss. 66, ff. 493–512; Mss.70, f. 28; NA: S.P. 63/304/ 71, 131; P/C/2/54, f. 126, 55, ff. 28–47; S.P. 63/307/4.
42. W. Pope, *The Life of Seth Ward, Bishop of Salisbury* (1697) p. 55.
43. *Reliquiae Baxterianae*, pp. 229–30; Bodleian Library: Tanner Mss. 49, ff. 7–10; H. M. C. Mss.: Le Fleming Mss. no. 26; John Pruett, *The Parish Clergy under the Later Stuarts* (1978) pp. 10–19; Rev. G. Ormesby, The Correspondence of John Cosin (*Surtees Society* 1872) pp. 4–6; H. M. C. 13th Report: Part 4, pp. 343–4; National Library of Wales: Bettisford Mss. ff. 108–9.
44. *New DNB*: Edward Reynolds, vol 46 pp. 529–31 (article by Ian Atherton); Richard Baxter, vol 3 pp. 418–33 (article by N H Keeble).
45. R Beddard, 'Sheldon and Anglican Recovery' in *Historical Journal*, vol 19 (1976) pp. 1005–17.
46. *New DNB*: Brian Duppa, vol 17 pp. 374–5 (article by Ian Green); William Juxon, vol 30 p. 848–52 (article by Brian Quintrell); Accepted Frewen, vol 21 pp. 16–17 (article by William Shiels).
47. As note 45.
48. *Reliquiae Baxterianae*, pp. 242–79; Bodleian Library: Clarendon Mss. 73, ff. 182–3, 196.
49. *Commons Journal* pp. 175–9; *Lords Journal* pp. 193–211.
50. R. Beddard, '*The Restoration Church*' pp. 161–2.
51. Bodleian Library: Clarendon Mss. 74, ff. 222, 224, 290–2; Mss. 75, f. 400; Acts of the Privy Council of Scotland, vol vii pp. 86–8; Gilbert Burnet, *History Of My Own Times*, vol I pp. 196–8, 215–16.
52. Friends House Library: Spence Mss. 3/56; Hyde, *Life of Clarendon*, vol I pp. 362–3; *Fox's Journal*, p. 393.
53. Ibid, p. 383–8; Boase, *Sufferings of the Quakers*, vol I p. 366.
54. For Quaker disruption: NA: S.P. 29/21/ 107; Dorset Record Office: P 155/130; Kent Record Office: U 350/C2/110.
55. C. Burrage, 'The Fifth Monarchy Insurrections' in *English Historical Review*, vool xxv (1910) pp. 722–45; Hyde, *Life of Clarendon*, vol I pp. 474–7; Rugge, *Diurnal*, pp. 139–40: NA: TT: *Mercurius Publicus*, 3–24 January 1661 and 10 January – 14 February 1661; *The Kingdom's Intelligencer*, 14–21 January 1661; also H. M. C. 8th Report, p. 439; H. M. C.: Hastings Mss. vol ii p. 141; British Library Additional Mss. 34306, pp. 8–9 and 34222, pp. 16–18; Thomas Crosby, *History of the English Baptists* (1736) vol 2 p. 91; for arrests, see Surrey Quarter Sessions Records, vol xxxv, p. 147 .
56. For Quaker protests of innocence: NA: TT: A Declaration from the Harmless and Innocent People of God (1660–1); The Humble Apologies of some commonly

called Anabaptists (1660–1); A Renunciation and Denunciation of the Ministers of Congregational Churches (1660–1).
57. NA: P.C. 2/55, pp. 108, 113, 1523, 174, 194.
58. Wiltshire Record Office, Q/5, Great Rolls, Easter 1661; Kent RO: Q/5 Mc/1, Easter 1661; Staffordshire RO: D3159/2/18, ff. 1–8; Norfolk RO: C/ 51/8, Easter 1661; Kendal/Cumbria RO: Kendal Indictment Book, f. 54 .

Chapter Five
1. Hutton, Charles II, p. 174.
2. Ibid, p. 163–4.
3. *Commons Journal*, pp. 247–368; *Lords Journal*, pp. 252–472; House of Lords Record Office: Committee Book Minutes 1661-4, pp. 8–9; BL: Egerton Mss. 2043, ff. 8–12; BL Additional Mss. 1116, ff. 202–3; H. M. C. 5th Report, p. 159; Staffordshire RO: D868/8/17.
4. *Commons Journal*, p. 395; *Lords Journal*, pp. 293–314, 369–70; H. M. C. 7th Report, p. 159.
5. *Commons Journal*, pp. 247–472; H. M. C.: Gawdy Mss. 19203; Statutes of the Realm, vol v pp. 304–6, 308, 428–33.
6. P.W. Thomas, Sir John Berkenhead (Oxford 1969) pp. 212–13, 223–4; Muddiman, *The King's Journalist*, pp. 126–30.
7. *Commons Journal*, p. 395; *Lords Journal*, pp. 293–314, 369–70, 382; H. M. C. 7th Report, p. 159.
8. Hutton, Charles II, p. 174.
9. *Lords Journal*, pp. 240–4.
10. Hutton, p. 180.
11. Hutton, *Restoration*, pp. 166–7.
12. Latimer, Bristol, pp. 308–10.
13. NA: S.P. 29/ 30/ 28 and 35/18.
14. William Lamont, Prynne, pp. 224–8; NA: S.P. 44/3, p. 2; P/C 2/55; *Commons Journal*, pp. 275–388; *Lords Journal*, pp. 308–58.
15. J Sacret, 'The Restoration Government and Municipal Corporations' in English Historical Review, vol xlv (1930) pp. 247–54; R Austin, 'The City of Gloucester and the Regulation of Corporations' in Transactions of the Bristol and Gloucester Archaeological Society, vol 58 (1936) pp. 257–74; N Palmer, 'The Reformation of the Corporation of Cambridge' in Proceedings of the Cambridge Antiquarian Society, vol xlvii (1912–13) pp. 76–105; T Pope, The Corporation of Newcastle-under-Lyme (Manchester 1938) pp. 14–30; T Greaves, The Corporation of Leicester (Oxford 1939) p. 8; J S Davies, A History of Southampton (1883) pp. 494–5; P Styles, 'The Corporation of Bewdley' in *Studies in Seventeenth Century West Midlands History* (Kineton 1978) pp. 46–8. NA: S.P. 29/ 61/ 105 and 81/78, 44; P/C/ 2/ 56, pp. 151–182; TT: *The Kingdom's Intelligencer*, 18 August – 1 September 1662.
16. *Commons Journal*, pp. 247–306, 317–52, 353–6; *Lords Journal*, pp. 316–30, 373–81; Bodleian Library: tanner Mss. 239, f. 19; B.L. Egerton Mss. 2043, f., 21; Lister, *Life of Clarendon* vol iii pp. 234–8.
17. Dawson, *Cromwell's Understudy*, pp. 404–5; Violet Rowe, *Sir Henry Vane the Younger*, pp. 234–41; BL: Lansdowne Mss. 1236, f. 132 (Charles says he wants Vane executed).

18. H. Tibbutt, Colonel John Okey, in *Bedfordshire Historical Society*, vol xxxv (19540 pp. 130–71.
19. Dawson and Walsh, pp. 303–6.
20. Ibid.
21. *New DNB*: William Goffe, vol 22 pp. 636–8 (article by Christopher Durston).
22. *Commons Journal*, pp. 263–353; *Lords Journal*, pp. 316–43; Bodleian Library: Tanner Mss. 338, f. 135; Calendar of Treasury Books, p. 282; Statutes of the Realm, vol v pp. 350–1; H. M. C. 7th Report, p. 148.
23. NA: S.P. 19/ 63/ 70.
24. Peterborough: Cathedral Library Mss. 20, ff. 68–80; Kent RO: U 2134/ B3/ 234; West Sussex RO: Ep. 1/ 10/ 46; Essex R.O.: D/ACA 55; Cambridge University Library: EDR: D/ 2/ 52; Cheshire R.O.: EDC 1/59/ 64–83; Wiltshire RO: Salisbury Court Instance Book, 1661–4 and Episcopal Court Office Book D; Norwich R.O.: Act/ 70; Cumbria R.O.: DRC 5/2.
25. *New DNB*: John Gauden, vol 25 pp. 646–8 (article by B Spink).
26. Thomas, *Sir John Berkenhead*, p. 219.
27. *Reliquiae Baxterianae*, p. 333; Edward Cardwell, ed, Synodalia (Oxford 1842) pp. 621–33; C. A. Swainson, *The Parliamentary History of the Act of Uniformity* (1875) pp. 15–16; Bodleian Library: Tanner Mss. 282, ff. 52–3; NA: P/ C/ 2/ 55, pp. 549–54.
28. *Commons Journal*, pp. 402–24; *Lords Journal*, pp. 393–450; Statutes of the Realm, vol v pp. 364–70; Swainson, pp. 22–46; Clarendon State Papers, vol iii: Appendix xcviii-xcvix; Spalding, *The Improbable Puritan*, pp. 235–6; Bodleian Library: Tanner Mss. 239, ff. 453–6 and 282, ff. 44–7; Carte Mss. 81, ff. 100–05.
29. Lister, *Life of Clarendon*, vol iii, pp. 532–4; Burnet, *History Of My Own Time*, p. 341; Bodleian Library: Carte Mss.3, f. 47; Mss. 31, f. 602; Mss. 47, f. 359; Clarendon Mss. 77, ff. 319–20, 339–40.
30. John Walker, 'The Yorkshire Plot, 1663' in *Yorkshire Archaeology Journal*, vol 31 (1932–4) pp. 348–59; C. Whiting, 'The Great Plot of 1663' in *Durham University Journal*, vol xxii (1920) pp. 151–62; S. Chadwick, 'The Farnley Wood Plot' in *Thoresby Society*, vol xv (1903) pp. 122–6; NA: A 551/ 42/1, ff. 126–7.
31. Besse, *Sufferings of the Quakers*, vol I pp. 92, 139, 175, 216, 293–4, 3923, 532, 569, 714; vol ii, pp. 11–13; State Trials, vol v, pp. 629–48; Friends House Library: Abraham Mss. no. 7; H. M. C.: Le Fleming Mss. nos. 32–3; Durham RO: Q/ 5/ 08/ 5, ff. 1182–1203; B. Quintrell, ed, 'Proceedings of the Lancashire Justices of the Peace' in *Lancashire and Cheshire Record Society*, vol 121 (1981) p. 114.
32. Statutes of the Relam, vol v pp. 516–20; *Commons Journal*, pp. 539–66; *Lords Journal*, pp. 604–21; Bodleian Library: Tanner Mss. 47, f. 143; Rawlinson Mss. A130.
33. *Lords Journal* p. 582–3.
34. Hutton, *Restoration*, pp. 178–9.
35. Rugge, *Diurnal*, pp. 111, 128; NA: P/C/54, pp. 163–4; TT: *Parliamentary Intelligencer*, 1 October – 3 December 1660 and *Mercurius Publicus*, 1–22 November 1660.
36. *Commons Journal*, pp. 7–171; *Lords Journal*, p. 97; Statutes of the Realm, vol v pp. 207–26; H. M. C. Kenyon Mss. 67.
37. C. D. Chandaman, *The English Public Revenue 1660–1688* (1975) pp. 11–15, 36–40, 196–202; *Commons Journal*, pp. 11, 40, 48, 68–103, 136–228; *Lords Journal* pp. 110, 148, 164, 214–36; Statutes of the Realm, vol v pp. 181–207, 252–66, 282–7.

38. Chanaman, pp. 77, 203–4; *Commons Journal*, pp. 257–314, 317–25, 376–85; *Lords Journal*, pp. 279–330, 352–8, 408–11, 474–5; Statutes of the Realm vol v pp. 306–8, 325–48, 390–3.
39. See Hutton, *Charles II*, pp. 156–60 on the Anglo-Portuguese negotiations.
40. *Commons Journal*, pp. 451–6; BL: Harleian Mss. 1223, ff. 200–46 and 1243, ff. 1726–30.
41. Calendar of Treasury Books, pp. 367–558; Warwickshire Sessions Order Book, no. 225; Essex R.O.: Q/ SR 395/72.
42. Pepys, *Diary*, vol ii p. 189.
43. *Lords Journal*, p. 478–9, 482–90; NA: S.P. 31/3/110, f. 557.
44. *Commons Journal*, pp. 436–52; Bodleian Library: Tanner Mss. 239, ff. 708–71.
45. Pepys, *Diary*, vol iv p. 44.
46. NA: S.P. 31/3/ 111, ff. 55, 106; Calendar of State Papers Venetian, p. 238; *Commons Journal*, pp. 452–63; *Lords Journal* pp. 495–500.
47. British Library: Harleian Mss. 1223, ff. 200–46 and 1243, ff. 1726–30; *Commons Journal*, pp. 451–6.
48. Ibid, pp. 471–553; *Lords Journal*, pp. 561–79.
49. Ibid, pp. 624–7; *Commons Journal*, pp. 567–89; British Library: Additional Mss. 36988, f. 88 and 32092, ff. 26–7.
50. Hutton, *Charles II* pp. 184–5.
51. Acts of the Privy Council of Scotland, vol vii pp. 415–29; Sir George Mackenzie, *Memoirs*, pp. 64–77; Bodleian Library: Carte Mss. 32, ff. 68, 69.
52. Acts of the Privy Council of Scotland, vol vii pp. 448–51 and 459–61; Burnet, *History Of My Own Time*, vol I, pp. 363–4.
53. Hutton, *Charles II*, pp. 203–4.
54. J. S. Clark, ed, *The Life of James II* (1816), vol I pp. 387–8; Hyde, *Life of Clarendon*, vol I pp. 371–403; NA: S.P. 94/44; 31/ 3/ 108, ff. 1–138 and 31/3/109, f. 12; Bodleian Library: Clarendon Mss. 74, ff. 126–35.
55. Paul Seaward, 'The House of Commons Committee of Trade and the Origins of the Second Anglo-Dutch War', in *Historical Journal* vol 30, 1987, pp. 437–52.
56. N.A. 31/3/114, f. 126.

Bibliography

Part 1: The End of the Protectorate
W. C. Abbott, *Letters and Speeches of Oliver Cromwell*, 4 vols (Cambridge UP 1937–47)
The Army's Proposals to the Parliament (September 1659).
Maurice Ashley, *Cromwell's Generals* (Jonathan Cape 1954).
Philip Aubrey, *Mr Secretary Thurloe: Cromwell's Secretary of State 1652–1660* (Athlone Press 1990).
G. E. Aylmer, *The State's Servants: The Civil Service of the English Republic 1649–60* (Routledge and Kegan Paul 1961).
——, ed, *The Interregnum: The Quest For Settlement 1648–1660* (1972).
Sir Richard Baker, *A Chronicle of the Kings of England* (1670).
Richard Baxter, *Reliquiae Baxterianae* (London 1696).
Maurice Bond, ed, *The Papers and Letters of Sir Edward Dering* (1973).
Robert Bosher, *The Making of the Restoration Settlement* (1951).
A Collection of the State Letters of the Rt Hon. Roger Boyle, the first Earl of Orrery... together with the life of the Earl of Orrery, by the Reverend Mr Thomas Morrice (London 1742)
William Braithwaite, *The Beginnings of Quakerism* (London 1912).
Gilbert Burnet, *History Of My Own Times*, ed Osmund Airy (London 1897).
Thomas Burton, *Diary*, with introduction by Ivan Roots (1974 reprint).
Calendar of the Clarendon State Papers preserved in the Bodleian Library, ed. W. D. Macray and C. H. Firth (Oxford 1882).
Calendar of State Papers Domestic Prserved in the State Paper Department of Her Majesty's Public Record Office (CSP Domestic), ed. Mary Everett Green: 1656–7 (1883), 1657–8 (1884), and 1658–9 (1885).
Calendar of State Papers Relating to English Affairs preserved in the Archives of Venice (CSP Venetian), ed Allen B Hindes: 1655–6 (HMSO 1930) and 1657–9 (1931).
Bernard Capp, *The Fifth Monarchy Men* (London 1972).
——, *Cromwell's Navy: The Fleet and the English Revolution 1648–1660* (Clarendon Press 1989).
Thomas Carlyle, *Letters and Speeches of Oliver Cromwell*, ed. T. C. Lomas, 3 vols (London 1904).
Samuel Carrington, *The History of the Life and Death of His Most Serene Highness Oliver, Late Lord Protector* (London 1659).
Thomas Carte, ed, *A Collection of Original Letters and Papers Concerning the Affairs of England from the Year 1641 to 1660*, 2 vols (London 1739).
The Case of Colonel Matthew Alured (London 1659).
Janet Clare, ed, *From Republic to Restoration: Legacies and Departures* (Manchester UP 2018).

Mary Coate, *Cornwall in the Great Civil War and Interrgenum* (Clarendon Press 1933).
T. Collier, The Decision and Clearing of the Great Point Now In Controversy, 1659; The Humble Petition of Many Inhabitants In And About the City of London, 12 May 1659 (London 1659).
Commons Journal, vols vi and vii.
The Conway Letters, ed. Marjorie Hope Nicholson (Oxford UP 1992).
G. Davies, 'The Army and the Downfall of Richard Cromwell' in *History Library Bulletin*, vol 7 (1935) pp. 135–67.
———, 'The Election of Richard Cromwell's Parliament' in *E. H. R.* vol. LXIII (1948) pp. 489–501.
———, *The Restoration of Charles II* (1955).
W. H. Dawson, *Cromwell's Understudy: The Life and Times of General John Lambert* (William Hodge 1938).
F. D. Dow, *Cromwellian Scotland* (Edinburgh 1979).
Christopher Durston, *Cromwell's Major-Generals: Godly Government During the English Revolution* (Manchester U.P. 2001).
C. S. Egloff, 'Robert Beake: a Letter concerning the Humble Petition and Advice, 28 March 1657' in *Bulletin of the Institute of Historical Research*, vol 68 (June 1995) pp. 233–9
John Evelyn, *Diary*, ed E de Beer (Oxford UP 1959).
Anthony Everitt, *The Community of Kent and the Great Rebellion* (Leicester U.P. 1966).
C. H. Firth, 'Cromwell and the Insurrection of 1655' in *E. H. R.* vol III (1898), pp. 313–50.
———, 'Cromwell and the Crown' in *E. H. R.*, vols XVII and XVIII (1902 and 1903).
———, *Last Years of the Protectorate*, 2 vols (Longmans 1909).
———, *The House of Lords during the Civil War* (London 1910).
C. H. Firth and F Rait, *Acts and Ordinances of the Interregnum 1642–60*, 3 vols (London 1911).
Jonathan Fitzgibbons, 'Hereditary Succession in the Cromwellian Protectorate: the offer of the crown reconsidered' in *E. H. R.* 2013, pp. 1095–1138.
Anthony Fletcher, *A County Community in Peace and War: Sussex 1600–1660* (1975).
George Fox, *Journal*, ed Norman Penny (London 1924).
Antonia Fraser, *Cromwell Our Chief Of Men* (Weidenfeld and Nicolson 1973).
S. R. Gardiner, *History of the Commonwealth and Proectorate*, 4 vols (Windrush Press edition 1987).
Peter Gaunt, 'The Single Person's Confidants and Dependants: Oliver Cromwell and his Protectoral Councillors' in *Historical Journal*, vol XXXII (1989) pp. 537–60.
———, ed, The Correspondence of Henry Cromwell, 1655–1659' in Camden Society, 5th series vol 21 (2007).
M. Guizot, *History of Oliver Cromwell and the English Civil Wars*, trans A. Scoble (London 1854).
———, *The History of Richard Cromwell and the Restoration of Charles II*, trans A. Scoble (London 1856).
K. H. D. Haley, *The First Earl of Shaftesbury* (Clarendon Press 1968).
Harleian Miscellany, vol 3 (London 1745).
Earl Hause, 'The Nomination of Richard Cromwell' in *The Historian*, vol 27 (1965) pp. 185–209.
———, *Tumble-Down Dick* (New York 1972).

Clive Holmes, *Sevententh Century Lincolnshire* (Lincoln 1980).
The Humble Petition of Many Thousand Citizens to the Parliament (15 February 1659).
The Humble Petition to the Parliament against Tithes (14 June 1659).
Lucy Hutchinson, *Memoirs of Colonel Hutchinson*.
Ronald Hutton, *Restoration: A political and religious history of England and Wales 1658–1667* (Oxford UP 1985) .
Edward Hyde, Earl of Clarendon, *History of the Rebellion and Civil Wars in England begun in 1641*, ed. W. Dunn Macray, 6 vols (Clarendon Press 1888).
M. James, 'The Political Importance of the Tithes Controversy in the English Revolution' in *History*, new series, vol 26 (1941–2) pp. 1–18.
J. Jones, 'Booth's Rising of 1659' in *Bulletin of the John Rylands Library*, vol xxxix (1956–7).
The Diary of The Reverend Ralph Josselyn, ed. E. Hockcliffe (Camden Society, 3rd series vol XV, 1908).
William Lamont, *Marginal Prynne* (1963).
——, *Godly Rule: Politics and Religion 1603–1660* (Macmillan 1969).
Memoirs of Edmund Ludlow, ed. C. H. Firth, 2 vols (Clarendon Press 1894).
Kathleen Lynch, *Roger Boyle, First Earl of Orrery* (Knoxville, 1965).
J. F. MacLear, 'Quakerism and the end of the Interregnum' in *Church History*, vol 19 (1950) pp. 240–60.
Norman McClure, ed, The Letters of John Chamberlain (*American Philosophical Society*, Philadelphia, 1939), vol 2.
William Maltby, *The Black Legend in England: The Development of Anti-Spanish Sentiment 1558–1660* (Duke University Press, N. Carolina 1978).
Philip Meadowe, *A Short Narrative of the principal actions in the Wars between England and Denmark*.
Monarchy Asserted to be the best, most Ancient and legal form of Government, in a conference had at Whitehall with Oliver, the Lord Protector and a Committee of Parliament (London 1660).
John Morrill, *Cheshire 1630–1660: County Government and Society during the English Revolution* (Oxford 1974).
——, ed, *Oliver Cromwell and the English Revolution* (London 1990).
——, 'Rewriting Cromwell: a case of deafening silences' in *Canadian Journal of History*, vol 38 (2003) pp. 153–78.
New Dictionary of National Biography (Oxford UP 2004): articles on: Matthew Alured (vol 1, pp. 908–9 by David Scott), John Desborough (vol 16 pp. 260–4 by Stephen Roberts), Nathaniel Fiennes (vol 19 pp. 524–6 by Marc Schwarz), Charles Fleetwood (vol 20, pp. 19–22 by Toby Barnard), Thomas Harrison (vol 25 pp. 539–33 by Ian Gentles), Sir Arthur Haselrig/Heselrig (vol 20, pp. 873–6 by Christopher Durston), Denzel Holles (vol 27 pp. 708–14 by John Morrill), Philip Jones (vol 30 pp. 604–6 by Stephen Roberts), John Lambert (vol 32, pp. 655–70 by D. N. Farr), John Lawson (vol 32 pp. 895–7 by Jack Binns), George Monck (vol 38, pp. 579–92 by Ronald Hutton), Edward Montague/Mountagu (vol 38 pp. 708–13 by J. Davies), Gilbert Pickering (vol 44 pp. 207–8 by Timothy Venning, Thomas Scot/Scott (vol pp. 479–80 by C. H. Firth and Sean Kelsey), John Thurloe (vol 54 pp. 711–15 by Timothy Venning), Sir Henry Vane jr (vol 55, pp. 108–20 by Ruth Mayers), Bulstrode Whitelocke (vol 54 pp. 694–6 by Ruth Spalding), Sir Charles Wolseley (vol 60 pp. 3–4 by Timothy Venning).

John Nickolls, Original Letters and Papers of State addressed to Oliver Cromwell, found among the Political Collections of Mr John Milton (London 1743).
G. Nourse, 'Richard Cromwell's House of Commons' in *Bulletin of the John Rylands Library*, vol 60 (1977–8) pp. 95–113.
Richard Ollard, *Cromwell's Earl: A Life of Edward Mountagu, First Earl of Sandwich* (Harper Collins 1994).
John Packer, *The Transformation of Anglicanism 1643–1660* (Manchester UP 1969).
R. Petty, 'The Rebellion of Sir George Booth' in *Journal of the Cheshire and North-West Archaeological Society*, new series, vol xxiii (1939) pp. 119–37.
J. G. A. Pocock, ed, *The Political Works of James Harrington* (Cambridge 1977).
Sir John Prestwich, *Respublica* (London 1787).
Proclamation of Richard Cromwell as Lord Protector (London 1658).
William Prynne, A True and Perfect Narrative of what was spoken of by and between Mr Prynne... (London 7 May 1659).
———, The True Good Old Cause rightly stated, and the False un-cased... (13 May 1659).
Robert Ramsey, *Studies in Cromwell's Family Circle* (London 1930).
———, *Richard Cromwell* (London 1935).
Henry Reece, *The Army in Cromwellian England* (OUP 2016).
Michael Roberts, *Essays in Swedish History* (Weidenfeld and Nicolson 1953).
Ivan Roots, 'The Tactics of the Commonwealthsmen in Richard Cromwell's Parliament' in Pennington and Thomas, eds, *Puritans and Revolutionaries*.
Violet Rowe, *Sir Henry Vane the Younger* (1970).
A Second Narrative of the Late Parliament (20 April 1659).
Roy Sherwood, *The Court of Oliver Cromwell* (Croom Helm 1977).
———, *Oliver Cromwell: King In All But Name* (Sutton 1997).
Ruth Spalding, *The Improbable Puritan: The Life of Bulstrode Whitelocke*.
Arthur Stanley, *Historical Memorials of Westminster Abbey* (7th edition, 1890).
Register of the Consultations of the Ministers of Edinburgh, vol ii, ed. Rev. W Stephen (*Scottish Historical Society* 1930).
Henry Stubbe, *A Light Shining Out Of Darknesse* (17 June 1659).
Steven Taylor and Kenneth Fincham 'The Restoration of the Church of England 1660–1662: ordination, re-ordination and conformity' in *Essays in Honour of John Morrill*, eds S. Taylor and G. Tapsell (Boydell 2013) pp. 197–232.
Thurloe State Papers, 7 vols (London 1742).
N. Tucker, 'Richard Wynn and the Booth rebellion' in *Transactions of the Caernarfonshire Historical Society*, vol 20 (1959) pp. 46–64.;
David Underdown, *Royalist Conspiracy in England 1649–1660* (Yale UP 1960).
Sir Henry Vane, A Healing Question Propounded and Resolved (1656).
T. Venning, *Cromwellian Foreign Policy* (Palgrave 1995).
Frances and Margaret Verney, eds, *Verney Family Memoirs During the Seventeenth Century*, vol 2.
The Poems of Edmund Waller, ed. George Thorn-Dury (London 1905).
Sir G. F. Warner, ed, The Nicholas Papers, vol 4 (*Camden Society*, 3rd series, vol 27, 1920).
Sir Philip Warwick, *Memoirs of the Reign of King Charles I with a Continuation in the Happy Restoration of King Charles II* (London 1701).
Bulstrode Whitelocke, *Memorials of English Affairs*, 4 vols (1853 edition).

Bulstrode Whitelocke (attrib.): 'Monarchy Asserted to be the Best, most Ancient and legal form of Government, in a conference held at Whitehall with Oliver, late Lord Protector, and a Committee of Parliament (London 1660)

Austin Woolrych, 'The Good Old Cause and the Fall of the Protectorate' in *Cambridge History Journal*, vol 13, no. 2 ((1957) pp. 138–44.

——, *Commonwealth to Protectorate 1649–1653* (Clarendon Press 1982).

——, 'The Cromwellian Protectorate: A Military Dictatorship?' in History, vol LXXV (1990) pp. 207–31.

William Woolrych, *Lives of Emminent Sergeants-at-Law of the English Bar* (London 1869) vol I.

Primary Sources

'A Second Narrative of the Late Parliament' in Harleian Miscellany, vol iii, pp. 489–93, 501.

A True Catalogue or an account of the Several Places and most Eminent Persons where and by whom Richard Cromwell was proclaimed Protector (London September 1659).

Bodleian Library Oxford: Carte Mss. 74.

—— Clarendon Mss.

—— Rawlinson Mss: A29–48, 62, A 261.

—— C179 (Council of State Order Book May-August 1659).

—— Tanner Mss. 52.

British Library: Additional Mss. 2884, 4156, 6125, 11411.

—— Lansdowne Mss. 523, 745, 822, 823.

—— Historical Mss Commission, 4th Report: Appendix: Sutherland Mss. 163.

National Archives: *Mercurius Politicus*, August 1658, September 1658, May 1659, June 1659.

—— S.P. 18/ 153–7 (SP Domestic 1657).

—— 179–83 (ibid 1658).

—— S.P. 25/ 77: Council of State Order Book March 1656–September 1657.

—— 78a: ibid, July 1657 to September 1658.

—— 79: ibid, August – October 1659.

—— S.P. 31/3/101, transcriptions of the French ambassador

—— Bordeaux's letters.

Worcester College Oxford: Clarke Papers.

Part 2: The Restoration and After

Secondary sources as earlier; and: George Abernathy jr, 'Clarendon and the Declaration of Indulgence' in *Journal of Ecclesiastical History*, vol 11 (1962) pp. 64–72.

The English Presbyterians and the Stuart Restoration (Transactions of the American Philosophical Society, new series pt 2, 1965).

Patrick Adair, *A True Narrative of the Rise and Progress of the Presbyterian church in Northern Ireland*, ed. D Kilen

Osmund Airy, ed, The Lauderdale Papers (*Camden Society*, 1885), vol 1.

T.A. Armstrong, 'The inauguration ceremonies of the Yorkist Kings, and their title to the throne', in *Transactions of the Royal Historical Society*, 4th series, vol 30 (1948) pp. 51–73.

Maurice Ashley, *John Wildman* (1947).

―――, *General Monck* (1977).
Thomas Baker, *History of St John's College* (Cambridge 1869).
R. Beddard, 'Sheldon and Anglican Recovery' in *Historical Journal*, vol 19 (1976) pp. 1005–17.
John Beresford, *Sir George Downing: The Godfather of Downing Street* (London 1930).
B. G. Blackwood, The Lancashire Gentry and the Great Rebellion (*Chetham Society*, 3rd series, 1975).
Maurice Bond, ed, *The Diaries and Papers of Sir Edward Dering* (1976).
Jerry Brotton, *The Sale of the Late King's Goods*. Pan Macmillan (2006).
L. F. Brown, 'Religious Factors in the Convention Parliament' In *E. H. R.* vol XXII (1907) pp. 52–5.
Julia Buckroyd, *Church and State in Scotland 1660–1681* (Edinburgh 1980).
C. Burrage, 'The Fifth Monarchy Insurrections' in *E. H. R.* vol XV (1910) pp. 722–45.
William Carr, *University College* (Oxford 1902).
S. Chadwick, 'The Farnley Wood Plot' in *Thoresby Society*, vol 15 (1909) pp.122–6.
A. Clark, *Lincoln College* (Oxford, 1898)
Charles Cooper, *Annals of Cambridge* (1845).
Barry Coward, *The Stanleys* (Chetham Society, 1983).
Thomas Crosby, *History of the English Baptists*, vol 2 (1736).
G. Davies, 'The General Election of 1660' in *HLQ*, vol 15 (1951) pp. 211–35.
C. Edie, 'The Popular Idea of Monarchy on the Eve of the Stuart Restoration' in *Historical and Literary Queries*, vol 39 (1975–6) pp. 344–63.
Sir Keith Feiling, *British Foreign Policy 1660–1672* (Oxford 1930).
T. Fowler, *History of Corpus Christi* (Oxford Historical Society 1893).
Ian Gentles, 'The Sale of Crown Lands' in *Economic History Review*, vol 26 (1973) pp. 614–35.
―――, 'The Sale of Bishops' Lands' in *E. H. R.* vol XCV (1980) pp. 573–96.
Rev. G. Gould, ed, *Documents Relating to the Settlement of England by the Act of Uniformity* (1862).
Arthur Gray and Frederick Brittain, *A History of Jesus College* (1960).
Ian Green, *The Restoration of the Church of England 1660–1663* (Oxford 1978).
C. Grose, 'The Dunkirk Money, 1662' in *Journal of Modern History*, vol 5 (1933) pp. 1–18.
Thomas Gumble, *The Life of General Monck* (1671).
H. J. Habbakuk, 'The Parliamentary Army and Crown lands' in *Welsh Historical Review*, vol 3 (1966–7) pp. 403–26.
―――, 'The Land Settlement and the Restoration of Charles II' in *Transactions of the Royal Historical Society*, 5th series, vol 28 (1978) ppl 201–2.
Sidney Hamilton, *Hertford College* (Oxford 1903).
G. B. Harrison, ed, *The Church Book of Bunyan's Meeting* (1928).
P. Holiday, 'Land Sales and Repurchases in Yorkshire' in *Northern History*, vol 5 (1970) pp. 67–92.
Thomas Howell, *State Trials* (1816).
Ronald Hutton, *Charles II: King of England, Scotland and Ireland* (Clarendon Press 1989).
J. R. Jones, *Britain and Europe in the Seventeenth Century* (1966).
――― ed, *The Restored Monarchy* (1979).
D. Jordan and M. Walsh, *The King's Revenge* (Abacus 2012).

Reverend James Kirkton, *The Secret and True History of the Church of Scotland* (Edinburgh 1817).
George Kitchin, *Sir Roger L'Estrange* (1913).
T. H. Lister, *The Life and Administration of Edward Hyde, First Earl of Clarendon* (1837) vol 3.
Lords Journal.
D. Macleane, *History of Pembroke College* (Oxford Historical Society, 1897).
J F Maclear, 'Quakerism and the end of the Interregnum' in *Church History*, vol 19 (1950) pp. 240–60.
Montgomeryshire Collections, vol 20 (1886), pp. 43–4: transcript of Herbert letter to Carbery in collction of 'Old Herbert Papers'.
Mordaunt's Letter-Book.
J. R. Muddiman, *The King's Journalist* (1923).
Donald Nicholas, *Mr Secretary Nicholas* (1955).
John Nicholl, *A Diary of Public Transactions* (Edinburgh 1836).
F. Nicholson, 'The Kaber Rigg Plot' in *Transactions of the Cumberland and Westmoreland Antiquarian and Archaeological Society*, new series, vol 11 (1911) pp. 212–32.
Old Parliamentary History (London 1760), vol 22.
David Ogg, *England in the Reign of Charles II* (1934), vol 1.
John Price, *The Mystery and Method of His Majesties Happy Restauration* (London 1680).
B. Reay, 'The Authorities and Early Restoration Quakerism' in *Journal of Ecclesiastical History*, vol 34 (1983).
Michael Roberts, ed, Swedish Diplomats at Cromwell's Court, 1655–1656, Camden Society 4th series (*Royal Historical Society*, London, 1988), pp. 317–18.
W. L. Sachse, ed, *The Diurnal of Thomas Rugge* (Camden Society 3rd series vol XCI, 1961).
J. Sacret, 'The Restoration Government and Municipal Corporations' in *E. H. R.* vol XLV (1930) pp. 247–54.
W. G. Searle, *History of the Queens' College* (Cambridge 1967).
Victor Sutch, *Gilbert Sheldon* (The Hague, 1973).
P. W. Thomas, *Sir John Berkenhead* (London 1969).
Joan Thirsk, 'The Restoration Land Settlement' in *Journal of Modern History*, vol 26 (1954) pp. 315–28.
———, 'The Sales of Royalist Land' in *Economic History Review*, 2nd series vol 5 (1952) pp. 188–207.
H. G. Tibbutt, *Colonel John Okey* (Befordshire Historical Society, 1954).
Murray Tolmie, *The Triumph of the Saints* (Cambridge 1977).
David Underdown, *Somerset in the Civil War and Interregnum* (Newton Abbot 1973).
F. Varley, ed, The Restoration Visitation of the University of Oxford (*Camden Miscellany*, vol XVIII, 1948).
E. A. O. Whiteman, 'The Restoration of the Church of England' in *Transactions of the Royal Historical Society*, 5th series, vol 5 (1995) pp. 120–35.
C. Whiting, 'The Great Plot of 1663' in *Durham University Journal* vol 22 (1920) pp. 155–67.
Robert Woodrow, *History of the Sufferings of the Church of Scotland* (Edinburgh 1721).
Blair Worden, ed, *A Voyce from the Watchtower* (by Edmund Ludlow)(Camden Society, 4th series, vol 21, 1978).

Primary sources
Bodleian Library: Carte Mss. 66, 70.
—— Clarendon Mss. 68, 71.
—— Rawlinson Mss. A 259.
—— Tanner Mss. 239.
British Library: Additional Mss.: 3071, 3476, 32324, 34222, 34306,. 17677 U.
—— Lansdowne Mss. 236.
—— Sloane Mss. 813.
Corporation of London Record Office: Journal 41 .
H. M. C.: Buccleuch Mss. Vol 1.
—— Egerton Ms. 2043, 2542.
—— Leybourne-Popham Mss.
—— Portland Mss. Vol 3.
National Archives: *Mercurius Publicus, Mercurius Britannicus.*
—— CRES 6/1–3, L/R 1/61; L/R 2/56, 134, 266.
—— PC 2/54, 2/55.
—— S.P. 18/ 219.
—— S.P. 25/99.
—— S.P. 29/ 16/35.
—— S.P. 29/19/75.
—— S.P. 29/21.
—— S.P. 63/ 304.
—— S.P. 71/131.
Thomason Tracts, in chronological order:
  Mercurius Publicus, weekly newsletters.
  Severall Proceedings of State Affairs, no. 221 (15–22 December 1653).
  The Protector (So-Called) In Part Unveiled, 24 October 1655.
  A Narrative of the Proceedings of the Fleet (London, late 1659).
  Newsletter: The Weekly Post, 21–27 December 1659.
  (William Prynne) A Brief Narrative (26 December).
  Six Important Quaeries (30 December)
  Seven Additional Quaewries (4 January 1660).
  Anti-Quakerism (5 January 1660)
  (William Brownsword) The Quaker-Jesuite (5 January)
  (Thomas Danson) The Quakers Folly (January)
  The Case of the Old. Secured and Now Exalted Members (13 January)
  A Declaration of some of those people in or near London, called Anabaptists (14 January).
  The Speech and Declaration of His Excellency Lord General Monck (21 February).
  A Letter from General Monck and the Officers here... (21 February)
  Newsletter: London Apprentice's Grand Politic Informer, 27 February–5 March.
  The Readie and Easie Way to establish a Free Commonwealth (3 March).
  Newsletters: An Exact Accompt (4 issues, 16 March to 4 April); also issues of 15–27 April and 27 April–4 May.
  Newsletters: Parliamentary Intelligencer, 16–30 April, 14–21 May, 18 June–30 August, 1 October – 3 December.
  Newsletter: Mercurius Civicus, 18–24 April
  A Character Of Charles II (30 April).
Worcester College Oxford: Clarke Mss. 52.

Index

Aeneas, legendary hero 182
Afonso VI, king of Portugal 204
Alured, Colonel Matthew vi, lvii, 72, 100, 107
Annesley, Arthur, earl of Anglesey vii, 59, 69, 108, 115, 117, 119, 126, 137, 155, 198, 217
Arundell, Lord 233
Ashburnham, John, aide to Charles I 148
Ashe, John, MP 13
Ashfield, Colonel 55, 64

Bacon, Sir Francis 219
Bamfylde, Colonel James, secret agent 11
Barbon, Praise-God clv, 47
Barkstead, Colonel John, regicide 4, 148, 152, 191
Bate, Dr George, physician to Cromwell 43–4
Batten, admiral Sir William 205
Baxter, Richard, Presbyterian divine 165, 167–8, 195
Belling, Richard, Irish Catholic activist 184, 215
Bennet, Henry, earl of Arlington vii, viii, xxxiv, 31, 141–2, 192, 197, 213, 222, 229, 233–4
Berkeley, Sir John, 142, 148, 217
Berry, Colonel James 4, 7, 25, 29, 95, 103
Bethel, Slingsby, republican 33, 128
Birch, Colonel John lviii
Birch, Thomas 146
Berkenhead/Birkenhead, Sir John, journalist viii, 181, 183, 193
Blackwell, alderman 45
Blair, Tony 92
Blake, Admiral Robert 10, 45
Bonde, Count, Swedish ambassador 7
Booth, George, lord Delamere, royalist general ix, 50, 75–8, 81, 91, 95, 107, 119, 125, 127, 142
Bordeaux, Antoine de, French ambassador liii, 8, 13, 19, 56, 84
Boyle, Robert, scientist ix

Boyle, Roger, lord Broghill and Orrery ix, 8, 14–16, 20–1, 35, 47, 52, 66, 119, 125, 133, 143, 162, 184
Bradshaw, John, regicide lvii, 157
Breda, Declaration of 133–4
Bridgeman, Sir Orlando, courtier/ minister x, 139–40, 153
Broughton, Andrew, regicide collaborator 9
Browne, Sir Richard, lord mayor of London 178–9
Bunyan, John xxxv, 54, 175, 177
Burnet, Alexander, archbishop 227
Burnet, Gilbert, Presbyterian divine and historian 21–2, 30, 172
Burton, Thomas, MP and diarist 7
Butler, James, marquis of Ormonde xl, 137–8, 141, 163, 217

Calamy, Edmund, Presbyterian divine 167–8, 172
Campbell, Archibald, earl/ marquis of Argyll xi, 172–3
Carew, John 156
Carr/ Kerr, Robert, earl of Somerset 231
Carteret, Sir George, Channel Islands royalist leader 137, 205
Cecil, Robert, earl of Salisbury 228
Charles I, king of England/ Scots x–xxii, xxiv, xxvi–xxx, xxxviii–ix, xl–xliii, xlv, xlvii, 3, 8, 9, 11, 14, 26, 35, 39, 43, 46–7, 64, 69, 75–7, 85, 91, 110, 114, 118, 134, 138, 143–5, 147–9, 152–3, 160, 164, 166, 169, 172–3, 179–83, 197, 199, 206, 208–9, 211, 220, 227
Charles II, king of England/ Scots ix–xiii, xvi–xvii, xxi–xxxiv, xxxviii, xli, l, liv, 5, 7–8, 11–12, 16, 20–2, 27–8, 30–4, 41, 45, 45–6, 49, 51, 75–8, 82, 85, 91–2, 96, 114, 118–235
Charles II, king of Spain 202–3
Charles X, king of Sweden 32–4, 58, 78–9, 215
Churchill, Sir Winston 136

Chute, Chaloner, speaker of Parliament 57–8
Claypole, Elizabeth, daughter of Oliver Cromwell xxii, 40, 42, 45
Clifford, Sir Thomas/ lord C, treasurer xii–xiii, 233
Clobery, John 125
Colbert, Jean-Baptiste 293
Conde, prince de, French royal and rebel 12
Cony's Case, famous Protectorate lawsuit 38
Cooper, Sir Anthony Ashley, lord Shaftesbury xiv, xxv, 1, 70, 100, 114, 116, 126, 129, 137, 141–2, 151, 158, 197, 216–17, 229, 232
Coote, Charles, lord Mountrath 143–4, 162–3, 198
Corbet, Miles, republican officer 70, 163, 191
Cosin, John, bishop 169
Coventry, Sir William, courtier/ minister 205
Crew, John, MP 119, 133
Cromwell, Elizabeth, mother of Oliver C. 40
Cromwell, Frances, daughter of Oliver C 21–2, 26, 28–9
Cromwell, Sir Oliver, grandfather of Oliver C 40
Cromwell, Henry, third son of Oliver C xiv, lvii–lix, 14–15, 19, 25, 35–7, 41, 51–2, 65, 70, 95–6, 162
Cromwell, Mary, daughter of Oliver C 28–9, 157
Cromwell, Oliver, Lord Protector vi–x, xiii–xx, xxii–xxxi, xxxiii–xl, xliv–51, 53–4, 57–62, 67, 71–2, 79, 83, 85, 92–3, 97, 107, 112, 120, 123, 125, 131, 133, `36–7, 140, 145–6, 151–3, 157, 160, 162, 164, 189, 193, 195, 199, 204, 211, 214, 223
Cromwell, Oliver, eldest son of Oliver C 51
Cromwell, Richard, Lord Protector, second son of Oliver C xv, xx, xxv, xxvii, xl, 15, 19, 27, 35, 37, 40–67, 70, 75–6, 80, 83, 85, 91–3, 95, 98, 116, 122, 124, 127, 133, 147, 159
Cromwell, Thomas, earl of Essex 39
Cunningham, William, earl of Glencairn 143, 174, 218

Dalzell, Sir Thomas of the Binns, general 226

Dendy, Edward, regicide collaborator 9, 191
Denham, Sir John, architect 208
Desborough, John, republican general xv–xvi, xlix, lviii, 7, 20, 35, 55–6, 59, 61–2, 64–8, 70, 75, 83–4, 93, 100, 104, 150, 159
De Vic, Henry, royalist ambassador 142
Digby, George, earl of Bristol xvi, 186, 213, 215, 217, 219–20, 228–9
Dorislaus, Isaac, ambassador 193
Dover, Treaty of 233–5
Downing, Sir George, spy/ ambassador/ speculator xvi–xvii, 134, 142, 191, 193, 222, 225
Drake, Sir Francis 12
Dryden, John, playwright xiii
Dudley, John, earl of Warwick/ duke of Northumberland, regent 97
Durston, Christopher, historian 4
Dury/ Durie, John, ambassador 53
Dutton, William, Cromwellian family connection 28

Earle, Sir Walter, MP 135
Edward III, king of England 15
Edward IV, ditto lviii, 26
Edward V, ditto liii
Elizabeth I, queen of England 9, 12, 26, 32, 44–6, 206, 220
Elizabeth, 'Winter Queen' of Bohemia/ Electress Palatine xxxviii, 231
Evelyn, John, diarist 81, 92, 142

Fauconberg, Viscount, son-in-law of Oliver Cromwell 28, 52, 55, 59, 66, 75, 157
Fairfax, Mary, daughter of Sir Thomas F 26
Fairfax, Sir Thomas, Parliamentarian general xiv, xvii, xx, xliv, 103, 105, 108, 113, 153
Feake, Christopher, militant preacher lv
Fell, Margaret, patron of Quakers xix, 200
Fell, Thomas, patron of Quakers xix
Fiennes, Celia, traveller/ author, daughter of Nathaniel F 138
Fiennes, Nathaniel, Cromwellian councillor xviii, 16, 36–7, 138
Fiennes, William, lord Saye and Sele, father of Nathaniel F 25, 36, 137–8
Firth, Sir Charles, historian 6
Finch, Sir John, lord chancellor/ speaker of Parliament 139
Finch, Sir Heneage, solicitor-general 130, 139, 150, 159, 179

Fitzjames, Colonel 7
Fleetwood, Charles, general/ Cromwellian councillor xviii–xix, xxxix, lviii, 26, 35, 37, 52, 55, 61–2, 64–88, 93–104, 106, 115, 120, 131, 150–1, 159
Fleetwood, George, general in Swedish service and brother of Charles F 151
Fleming, Sir Oliver, cousin of Oliver Cromwell 13
Fox, George, Quaker leader xix, 16, 43, 200
Franco, Francisco, Spanish dictator 40
Frederick III, king of Denmark 79

Gauden, John, bishop xix–xx, 169, 194–7
George V, king of UK 136
Goffe, Colonel William, Cromwellian stalwart xx, 25, 69, 72, 76, 99, 127, 154, 192–3
Gondomar, count, Spanish ambassador 33
'Good Old Cause', the 53, 73, 96, 120
Goodson, Sir William, admiral 31, 58, 205
Goring, George, lord G/ earl of Norwich, Royalist general 137, 228
Goring, George, son of previous, Royalist general 137, 228
Graham, James, marquis of Montrose, Royalist general xi, xxxi, 173
Great Fire of London 225–6
Great Plague, the 225
Grenville, Sir Bevil, Royalist general xxi, 141
Grenville, Sir John, earl of Bath xxi, 141, 145, 208
Grenville, Sir John, Monck/ Charles II go-between 124, 135, 138
Grenville, Sir Richard, Royalist general 14, 229
Grey, Lady Jan 67, 97
Grimston, Sir Harbottle, speaker of Parliament xxi, 130, 118
Guthrie, James, Scots Presbyterian leader 173
Gwyn, Nell, actress/ royal mistress 209

Hacker, Francis, colonel, republican 84, 149–50
Hamilton, James, earl/ marquis of H 58
Hampden, John, Parliamentarian leader xxv, xxxix
Harington, James, constitutional theorist xxi–xxii, 72–3, 81, 92
Harrison, Thomas, republican general/ Fifth Monarchist leader xxii, xlvii, xlix, l, lv, lix, 38, 65, 148, 153, 155–6, 190

Haselrig/ Heselrig, Sir Arthur, republican leader xxiii, xxxv, lvi–lvii, 47, 55, 57–8, 62, 68, 70–1, 81–4, 92–4, 100–03, 108–9, 111–12, 116, 122, 125, 128, 152, 155–7
Henri IV, king of France 208, 234
Henrietta Maria, queen of England/ Scots xxii–xxiii, xxvi, xxxv, xxxvii, liv, 11, 39, 110, 144, 153, 203, 206–7, 216, 220, 228
Henriette Anne, aka 'Minette', daughter of previous, duchess of Orleans xxiii, 203, 231–3
Henry VII, king of England 8, 39, 134
Henry VIII, ditto 228
Henry, duke of Gloucester, brother of Charles II xlii, 7, 11, 85, 151, 206
Heveningham, William, regicide 153
Holland, Cornelius, MP 148
Holles, Denzel, Parliamentarian leader 92, 118, 131, 133, 137, 139, 155, 216
Holmes, Sir Robert, Royalist/ Restoration naval commander xxiii–xxiv, 140, 204–5, 222–4.
Honeywood, Sir Robert 79
Howard, Charles, earl of Carlisle, Cromwellian/ Restoration courtier xvi, 4, 65, 125–6, 133, 137, 145, 158–9
'Humble Petition and Advice', Cromwellian monarchic plan 15–21, 37–8, 42, 5, 68
Huncks, Hercules, Colonel, regicide participant 147, 153
Hutchinson, Ann, author xl–l
Hutchinson, Colonel John, husband of previous, Parliamentarian general/ regicide 150–1, 200
Hyde, Anne, duchess of York 207, 221, 229
Hyde, Sir Edward, father of previous, earl of Clarendon, Royalist adviser/ lord chancellor xvi, xx, xxiv, xxvi, 26, 35, 49, 76, 107, 135, 137, 139, 146, 150–1, 165, 167, 179–80, 185, 190, 194, 197, 210–11, 213–17, 219–20, 223, 227, 229–30.

Ingoldsby, Sir Richard, cousin and aide of Cromwell xxv, 22, 25, 66, 76, 115, 125–7, 147
Ireton, Henry, general xxx, 62, 157
Ireton, Robert 150

James VI and I, king of Scots/ England 39, 44, 46, 168, 182, 206, 212, 220, 231, 234
James VII and II, king of Scots/ England, earlier entries as Duke of York xi–xii,

Index 263

xxii, xxiv–xxv, 11, 122, 138, 140, 176, 183, 202, 204–6, 219, 221, 222–4, 229, 232–3
James, duke of Monmouth, son of Charles II 22, 123, 207, 229
Jeffreys, judge 155, 193, 200
Jephson, William, Cromwellian aide and ambassador 15
Jermyn, Sir Henry, courtier and speculator xxv–xxvi, 144, 228
Johnston, Archibald of Warriston, Scots Presbyterian leader xxvi, 95–7, 173
Jones, Inigo, architect 207
Jones, Colonel John, republican 29, 95, 148, 156, 191
Jones, Colonel Philip, Cromwellian aide/councillor 15, 35, 49, 52, 146, 211
Juan Carlos, king of Spain 40–1
Juxon, William, archbishop xxvii, 169–70

Kerouaille, Louise de, duchess of Portsmouth/ royal mistress 220, 231

Lambert, John, Cromwellian general and republican leader xx, xxiii, xxvi–xxvii, xxxii, xxxix, xlv, li–liii, lvi–lvii, 4, 9, 22, 27, 35, 37–8, 47, 50, 61, 66–7, 69–88, 91, 93–115, 120–1, 125–31, 135, 147, 155, 160, 189–90, 201
Laud, William, archbishop xxiii, xxvii, xxxviii, 9, 146, 151–3, 164–5, 176, 196
Lawson, John, republican admiral xxviii, 80, 91, 102–3, 107–8, 113, 115–16, 140, 206
Leighton, Robert, Scots bishop 227
Leopold I, Holy Roman emperor 34
Lenthall, William, speaker of Parliament xxviii–xxix, 1, 70, 84, 104, 110, 119, 150
Leslie, Alexander, Scots general xxxi
Leslie, David (no relation), Scots general 144
L'Estrange, Roger 158
Lilburne, John, Leveller leader xxxiii, lv–lvi, 100, 189
Lilburne, Robert, general, brother of previous 97–8, 100, 189
Lionne, Hugues de, French diplomat 11
Lisle, Alice, victim of Judge Jeffreys xxix
Lisle, John, republican administrator and regicide, husband of previous xxix, 148, 153, 191–2
Lockhart, William, Cromwellian officer/ aide-ambassador 28–32
Louis XIV, king of France xxiii, xxix, xxxi, xxxvi, liv, 202–4, 2014, 219, 222–3, 231–5

Ludlow, Edmund, Colonel, republican activist xxx, li, lviii–lix, 56–7, 70, 82, 95, 97, 112–13, 125–9, 131, 144, 148, 153, 156, 163, 192

Maitland, Elizabeth (nee Murray), Restoration hostess 143
Maitland, John, earl of Lauderdale, Scots Presbyterian leader/ Restoration administrator, husband of previous xxx–xxxi, 143–4, 174, 218
Major, Dorothy, wife of Richard Cromwell 35
Major, Richard, father of above 51
Major-General, constitutional experiment by Cromwell 4–5, 41
Maria Theresa of Spain, queen of France 202
Marten, Henry, MP, republican xxx, 68, 189
Marvell, Andrew, poet and MP xviii, 145
Mary I, queen of England 97
Mary II, queen of England and Scots xxiv
Mary (Stuart), princess of Orange, sister of Charles II 203, 229
Massey, Edward, Parliamentarian general 37, 119, 125
Mather, Increase, New England leader xx
Maurice, Prince, brother of Prince Rupert xxiii
Maynard, John, MP and lawyer 42
Mazarin, Cardinal Jules/ Giulio, chief minister of France 9, 11–12, 31, 34, 78
Middleton, John, earl of M, Scots Royalist leader xxxi–xxxii, 143, 173–4, 217–18
Middleton/ Myddleton, Sir Thomas, North Welsh commander 75–8, 125
Mildmay, Sir Henry, administrator 149
Milton, John, republican poet/ publicist/ administrator xxxii, 100, 117–18, 141, 145, 152
Monck, Anne (nee Clarges), duchess of Albemarle, wife of George Monck 96, 120
Monck, George, duke of Albemarle, general, governor of Scotland and mastermind of the Restoration vi, xv, xix, xxi, xxiii–xxv, xxxii–xxxiv, xxxvii, 9, 22, 29, 49, 65–7, 84–135, 137, 140–5, 147, 151, 155–8, 161–3, 172, 182, 189, 193, 202–3, 208, 217, 222, 224–5, 229, 235
Monck, Nicholas, brother of above 95
Montague, Edward, earl of Manchester, Parliamentarian general/ Presbyterian

leader 36, 118, 130, 134–5, 138, 146, 155, 158, 168, 199
Montague/ Mountagu, Edward, earl of Sandwich, admiral/ Cromwellian and Restoration councillor xxviii, xxxiii–xxxiv, xxxvi, l, 35, 49, 52, 58–9, 67–8, 79–80, 85, 115–16, 119, 122, 125, 133, 136–8, 140, 158, 160, 203–5, 208, 222, 224–5
Montfort, Simon de, baronial leader xliii
Mordaunt, John, viscount M, Royalist leader xxxiv, 75–7, 107, 118, 122–3, 130, 133, 143–5
Morgan, Sir Henry, Cromwellian commander 30
Morice, William, Restoration secretary of state 124, 141, 145
Morland, Samuel, Cromwellian administrator/ ambassador/ hydraulicist 79, 85
Morley, Colonel Herbert MP, Sussex Parliamentarian leader 84, 101, 107, 110–12, 114
Moyer, Samuel, MP 73
Muddiman, Henry, Restoration journalist and publicist viii, 193
Murray, William, aide to Charles I 143

Napoleon I, emperor of France 84
Nayler, James, Interregnum religious millenarian 24
Nedham, Marchamont, Cromwellian journalist/ publicist 37, 122, 16
Neville, Henry, MP 72
Nicholas, Sir Edward, Royalist administrator/ secretary of state xxxv, 137, 141, 185
Norton, Colonel Richard, friend of Cromwell 115

Okey, Colonel John, republican and regicide xvi, xxxv, lvii, 51, 83–4, 100–01, 104, 107, 115, 117–18, 121, 127, 191
Oswald, Lee Harvey 13
Overton, Richard, republican 61, 72, 106
Osborne, Sir Thomas, earl of Danby/ marquess of Carmarthen/ duke of Leeds, Restoration minister 230
Owen, John, republican divine 146, 164

Pack, Sir Christopher, Cromwellian adviser and City merchant 13–15, 25, 47
Palmer, Geoffrey, attorney-general 139
Peake, Robert, MP 14

Penruddock Rising, the (Royalist) 4, 29, 48, 77
Pepys, Samuel, diarist/ administrator 116, 122, 137, 140, 209, 212, 221
Percy/ Hay, Lucy, countess of Carlisle, conspirator and hostess 138
Percy, Thomas, earl of Northumberland, Parliamentarian grandee, brother of previous 138
Peter(s), Hugh, republican divine 149, 156, 164
Pett family, shipbuilders 206
Philip IV, king of Spain xxxv–xxxvi, 49, 159, 202
Philippe, Duke of Orleans, brother of Louis XIV xxiii, 203, 231
Pickering, Sir Gilbert, Cromwellian councillor xxxi, xxxvi, 49, 159
Pierrepont, William, Cromwellian adviser 14–15, 133, 152
Pollard, Sir Hugh MP, Parliamentary manager 176
Porter, Endymion, adviser to Charles I 220
Powell, Vavasour, Interregnum divine lv
Pride, Colonel Thomas, republican and purge-leader xviii, 3, 20, 24–5, 29, 62, 69, 73, 77, 91, 108–9, 131
Putney Debates, the (Army) 61
Pym, John, Parliamentarian leader 183

Rainsborough, Colonel Thomas, democratic activist 61
Retz, cardinal de (Jean de Gondi), foe of Mazarin (France) 34
Reynolds, Edward, Restoration divine 165–7
Reynolds, Sir Henry, Cromwellian general 30
Rich, Colonel Nathaniel, republican 72, 115
Rich, Robert, earl of Warwick, Parliamentarian leader/ admiral xx, xxxviii, 8, 25–6, 28–9, 36
Rich, Robert, grandson of above 26–8, 42
Richard III, king of England liii, 8, 16, 26, 38–9
Robartes, John, lord Radnor, Presbyterian leader xxxvii–xxxviii, 138, 141–2, 197
Robinson, Luke, MP 111
Rous, Francis, Pym's stepbrother, Cromwellian councillor xlviii, l
Rupert, Prince, Royalist commander/ admiral xviii, xxxviii, 140, 221, 224
Russell, Francis, earl of Bedford 8

Russell, Sir Francis of Chippenham, Cambs 19, 25

St. John, Oliver, Parliamentarian leader and cousin of Cromwell xiv, xxxix, xl, 14, 66, 111, 115–16, 122, 152–3
Scot, Thomas, republican and spymaster xxxviii, 56, 70, 76, 95, 100, 102, 111, 119, 125–6, 156
Salwey, Richard, MP and Cromwellian ally 80, 95
Savoy Conference 168
'Sealed Knot', the, Royalist secret society 28, 75–8
Sedley, Sir Charles, Restoration rake 172, 193
Seymour, Edward, duke of Somerset/regent liii, 38
Sexby, Colonel Edward, republican plotter 13
Shakespeare, William xlii
Sharp, James, Scots archbishop 173–4, 218, 226
Sharp, William, brother of previous 218
Sheldon, Gilbert, archbishop xxvii, xxxviii–xxxix, 169–70, 172, 176, 179, 195–6, 230
Sidney, Algernon, republican officer and activist 56, 79
Sidney, Philip, lord Lisle, brother of previous, Cromwellian councillor 79
Sidney, Robert, earl of Leicester, father of previous two, Parliamentarian administrator 56, 137
Sindercombe, Miles, anti-Cromwellian plotter 6–7, 12, 157
Stayner, Captain, Cromwellian naval officer 12
Stuart, lady Arbella, cousin to James VI and I 22
Stuart, Frances, duchess of Richmond, mistress of Charles II 230
Sydenham, Colonel William, Dorset Parliamentarian and Cromwellian councillor xxxix–xl, 26, 94

Temple, William, Restoration diplomat 219, 232
Thurloe, John, Cromwellian secretary of state and spymaster xl, 4, 7, 9–11, 13, 15, 19, 20, 22–3, 27, 29–35, 37, 44, 48–50, 52, 56, 58, 76–9, 83, 116, 122, 129, 142, 156, 193
Thynne, Thomas, MP and Restoration rake 126, 193

Tomlinson, Colonel Matthew, republican 70, 147
Triennial Act 184, 201
Tudor, Jasper, earl of Pembroke/ duke of Bedford 39
Tuke, Sir Samuel 123, 186

Vane, Sir Henry, Parliamentarian leader and republican xxxix, xl–xli, l, lix, 10, 55, 57, 68, 70–3, 79, 80–4, 92–4, 97–8, 102, 108, 110, 125, 152, 154–6, 189–90, 200
Venner, Thomas, Fifth Monarchist rebellion leader 160, 177–8
Villiers, Barbara, countess of Castlemaine, mistress of Charles II xi, 209, 212, 216–17
Villiers, George, first duke of Buckingham 219–20, 234
Villiers, George, second duke of Buckingham, son of previous, courtier and rake xli, 28–9, 219, 230

Waller, Edmund, poet 7, 12, 145
Waller, Sir Hardress, republican officer 149, 153
Waller, William, Parliamentarian general viii, 77
Walker, Sir Edward, courtier 181
Walter, Lucy, mistress (and rumoured wife) of Charles II 22, 123, 207, 229
Warbeck, Perkin, anti-Tudor pretender 39
Warwick, Sir Philip, Restoration administrator 210, 213
Webb, John, architect 207
Wentworth, Sir Thomas, earl of Strafford, minister to Charles I 9, 183
Whalley, Colonel Edmund Whalley, republican xx, xli, 55, 62, 69, 72, 76, 99, 127, 154, 192–3
Wharton, Philip, lord W, Cromwellian ally 36, 134
Whetstone, Captain Thomas, naval officer 79, 156
Whitelocke, Bulstrode, Cromwellian administrator and memorialist xli–xlii, 7, 9, 19, 39, 47, 49, 70, 84, 95, 100, 123, 151
Widdrington, Sir Thomas, speaker of Parliament 14–15, 26, 57
Wildman, John, Leveller leader vi
William II, Dutch Stadtholder xxxi, 203
William III, Dutch Stadtholder and king of England/Scots xxi, xxx–xxxi, 13, 122, 156, 203, 205, 223, 235

Williams, Robert, New England religious leader xl
Williamson, Sir Joseph, Restoration administrator 141, 192
Willis, Sir Richard, Royalist agent 78, 145
Wilkins, John, bishop 146
Wilmot, John, earl of Rochester, poet and rake 175
Winthrop, Stephen, Massachusetts settler and Parliamentarian adviser 65
Witt, Jan de, Grand Pensionary of Holland and Dutch chief minister 191, 203, 223, 232–3

Wolseley, Sir Charles, Cromwellian protégé and adviser xlii, xlviii–xlix, 7, 16, 35, 44, 152
Woolrych, Austin, historian 96
Worcester House Declaration 172, 176
Wren, Sir Christopher, architect/mathematician 165
Wren, Matthew, bishop 165
Wriothesley, Thomas, earl of Southampton, treasurer xlii, 158, 185, 211, 216, 229